Intelligent Systems for Machine Olfaction:
Tools and Methodologies

Evor L. Hines, University of Warwick, UK

Mark S. Leeson, University of Warwick, UK

Senior Editorial Director:	Kristin Klinger
Director of Book Publications:	Julia Mosemann
Editorial Director:	Lindsay Johnston
Acquisitions Editor:	Erika Carter
Development Editor:	Joel Gamon
Production Coordinator:	Jamie Snavely
Typesetters:	Keith Glazewski & Natalie Pronio
Cover Design:	Nick Newcomer

Published in the United States of America by
Medical Information Science Reference (an imprint of IGI Global)
701 E. Chocolate Avenue
Hershey PA 17033
Tel: 717-533-8845
Fax: 717-533-8661
E-mail: cust@igi-global.com
Web site: http://www.igi-global.com

Library of Congress Cataloging-in-Publication Data

Intelligent systems for machine olfaction : tools and methodologies / Evor L.
Hines and Mark S. Leeson, editors.
    p. cm.
  Includes bibliographical references and index.
  ISBN 978-1-61520-915-6 (hardcover) -- ISBN 978-1-61520-916-3 (ebook) 1.
Chemical detectors--Automatic control. 2. Gas detectors--Automatic control.
3. Odors. 4. Olfactometry. 5. Artificial intelligence. I. Hines, Evor,
1957- II. Leeson, Mark S., 1963- III. Title.

  TP159.C46I48 2011
  681'.754--dc22

2011004016

British Cataloguing in Publication Data
A Cataloguing in Publication record for this book is available from the British Library.

All work contributed to this book is new, previously-unpublished material. The views expressed in this book are those of the authors, but not necessarily of the publisher.

Table of Contents

Foreword...xiii

Preface xv

Acknowledgment.. xix

Section 1
Methods

Chapter 1
Feature Selection and Sensor Array Optimization in Machine Olfaction.........1
Alexander Vergara, University of California, USA
Eduard Llobet, University Rovira i Virgili, Spain

Chapter 2
Evolutionary Algorithms for Multisensor Data Fusion................................. 62
Jianhua Yang, University of Warwick, UK
Evor L. Hines, University of Warwick, UK
John E. Sloper, University of Warwick, UK
D. Daciana Iliescu, University of Warwick, UK
Mark S. Leeson, University of Warwick, UK

Chapter 3

**Making an Electronic Nose Versatile: The Role of Incremental Learning
Algorithms** 78

*Nabarun Bhattacharyya, Centre for the Development of Advanced Computing
  (C-DAC), India*
Bipan Tudu, Jadavpur University, India
Rajib Bandyopadhyay, Jadavpur University, India

Chapter 4

Noise and Repeatability of Odorant Gas Sensors in an E-Nose 102

Fengchun Tian, Chongqing University, P.R. China
Simon X. Yang, University of Guelph, Canada
Xuntao Xu, Mianyang Vocational and Technical College, P. R. China
Tao Liu, Chongqing University, P. R. China

**Section 2
Applications**

Chapter 5

Odor Reproduction with Movie and its Application to Teleolfaction 126

Takamichi Nakamoto, Tokyo Institute of Technology, Japan
Takao Yamanaka, Sophia University, Japan

Chapter 6

Statistical Gas Distribution Modeling Using Kernel Methods 153

Sahar Asadi, Örebro University, Sweden
Matteo Reggente, Örebro University, Sweden
Cyrill Stachniss, University of Freiburg, Germany
Christian Plagemann, Stanford University, USA
Achim J. Lilienthal, Örebro University, Sweden

Chapter 7

**Characterization of Complex Patterns: Application to Colorimetric
Arrays and Vertical Structures** 180

Yannick Caulier, Fraunhofer Institute IIS, Germany

Chapter 8
**Detection of Diseases and Volatile Discrimination of Plants: An
Electronic Nose and Self-Organizing Maps Approach** 214
Reza Ghaffari, University of Warwick, UK
Fu Zhang, University of Warwick, UK
D. Daciana Iliescu, University of Warwick, UK
Evor L. Hines, University of Warwick, UK
Mark S. Leeson, University of Warwick, UK
Richard Napier, University of Warwick, UK

Chapter 9
Tomato Plant Health Monitoring: An Electronic Nose Approach 231
Fu Zhang, University of Warwick, UK
D. Daciana Iliescu, University of Warwick, UK
Evor L. Hines, University of Warwick, UK
Mark S. Leeson, University of Warwick, UK

Chapter 10
**Improved Gas Source Localization with a Mobile Robot by
Learning Analytical Gas Dispersal Models from Statistical Gas
Distribution Maps Using Evolutionary Algorithms** 249
Achim J. Lilienthal, Örebro University, Sweden

Chapter 11
**Enhancing the Classification of Eye Bacteria Using Bagging to
Multilayer Perceptron and Decision Tree** 277
Xu-Qin Li, University of Warwick, UK
Evor L. Hines, University of Warwick, UK
Mark S. Leeson, University of Warwick, UK
D. Daciana Iliescu, University of Warwick, UK

Compilation of References 294

About the Contributors 323

Index 329

Detailed Table of Contents

Foreword... xiii

Preface xv

Acknowledgment.. xix

Section 1
Methods

Chapter 1
Feature Selection and Sensor Array Optimization in Machine Olfaction.........1
Alexander Vergara, University of California San Diego, USA
Eduard Llobet, University Rovira i Virgili, Spain

In recent years, growing attention has been paid to strategies for feature and sensor selection in multi-sensor systems for machine olfaction. The two main approaches are the use of features selected from the sensor response to build a multivariate model and the selection of an optimal subset of factors. Selecting from the full set of features is challenging because they overlap considerably and are affected by noise. A range of variable selection methods has been reported as useful, both deterministic and stochastic. In the majority of machine olfaction applications, it is usually infeasible to undertake an exhaustive search given the large number of variables to be considered for selection. The chapter thus provides a thorough review of feature or sensor selection for machine olfaction. It covers the needs for variable selection, examples from the literature, and a vision of how the field may evolve in the future.

Chapter 2
Evolutionary Algorithms for Multisensor Data Fusion.................................. 62
Jianhua Yang, University of Warwick, UK
Evor L. Hines, University of Warwick, UK
John E. Sloper, University of Warwick, UK
D. Daciana Iliescu, University of Warwick, UK
Mark S. Leeson, University of Warwick, UK

Multisensor Data Fusion (MDF) is a technique by which data from a number of sensors are combined through a centralized data processor to provide comprehensive and accurate information. MDF technology has undergone rapid growth since the late 1980s as a result of the emergence of new sensors, advanced processing techniques, and improved processing hardware. MDF aims to eliminate redundant, noisy, or irrelevant information, and thus find an optimal subset from an array of high dimensionality. The signals in MDF are constantly evolving rather than static, and this provides an opportunity for Evolutionary Computation (EC) algorithms to be developed to solve MDF tasks. This chapter describes the application of three EC algorithms to widely used datasets, showing that utilizing ECs at the feature selection stage greatly reduces the dataset dimensionality and dramatically increase rules when input data are not clustered.

Chapter 3
Making an Electronic Nose Versatile: The Role of Incremental Learning
Algorithms 78
Nabarun Bhattacharyya, Centre for the Development of Advanced Computing
    (C-DAC), India
Bipan Tudu, Jadavpur University, India
Rajib Bandyopadhyay, Jadavpur University, India

Pattern recognition systems for machine olfaction are complex and challenging to develop for several reasons. First, it is extremely difficult in practice to obtain adequate computation model training data compared to other applications of pattern recognition such as image processing. Second, the samples often arrive in batches or are available over multiple seasons, or even over multiple years. Third, industrial users are generally reluctant when approached for samples but desire immediate result. Finally, the availability of data in batches makes the training process difficult and requires storage of data for all the samples. These factors mean that pattern recognition systems must be flexible in such a way as to update an existing, stable, and plastic classifier without affecting the classification performance on old data. Incremental learning algorithms offer the required features, making electronic nose systems versatile. The chapter describes a range of incremental learning algorithms for machine olfaction.

Chapter 4
Noise and Repeatability of Odorant Gas Sensors in an E-Nose 102
Fengchun Tian, Chongqing University, P.R. China
Simon X. Yang, University of Guelph, Canada
Xuntao Xu, Mianyang Vocational and Technical College, P. R. China
Tao Liu, Chongqing University, P. R. China

The effect that the characteristics of the sensors used for electronic nose (e-nose) systems on the repeatability of the measurements is considered. Given that e-noses are composed of gas sensor arrays and corresponding signal processing and pattern recognition algorithms, they are susceptible to sensor interference and noise in addition to their artificial olfactory purpose. E-noses have found wide application in environmental monitoring, food production, and medicine, so it is more important than ever to fully understand the imperfections that they display so as to compensate for them. In this chapter, the noise performance of the different types of sensors available for e-nose utilization is first examined. Following the theoretical background, the probability density functions and power spectra of noise from real sensors are presented and the impact of sensor imperfections on repeatability investigated.

Section 2
Applications

Chapter 5
Odor Reproduction with Movie and its Application to Teleolfaction 126
Takamichi Nakamoto, Tokyo Institute of Technology, Japan
Takao Yamanaka, Sophia University, Japan

Humans perceive sensory information through their senses whilst various equipment types have widely been used for recording and reproducing the visual and auditory information in daily living. Electronic-noses have found widespread application in detecting odors within closed chambers, but odor recording in the atmosphere is challenging because of the turbulent airflows. A solution is offered by the recording and reproduction of both olfactory and visual information. This enhances the sense of presence by combining video images and olfactory stimuli. Moreover, it facilitates a teleolfaction system where users can sniff objects far away from themselves whilst watching video images of the objects in real time via the Internet. Thus, users can perceive much of the sensation of reality of the object, even at the remote site. Although there have been several reports on the fusion of vision and olfaction in virtual environments, the system described is unique in being able to record and reproduce olfactory information synchronized with visual information.

Chapter 6

Statistical Gas Distribution Modeling Using Kernel Methods 153
Sahar Asadi, Örebro University, Sweden
Matteo Reggente, Örebro University, Sweden
Cyrill Stachniss, University of Freiburg, Germany
Christian Plagemann, Stanford University, USA
Achim J. Lilienthal, Örebro University, Sweden

Comprehensive information about many gas concentration measurements may be provided by gas distribution models but current physical modeling methods are computationally expensive. This chapter reviews kernel methods that statistically model gas distribution by treating gas measurements as random variables enabling the prediction of gas distribution in unseen locations via kernel density estimation or kernel regression. The resulting statistical models make no strong assumptions about the functional form of the gas distribution. The chapter concentrates mainly on two-dimensional models that provide estimates for the means and predictive variances of the distribution. Furthermore, it extends the kernel density estimation algorithm to three dimensions, and also to incorporate both wind information and time time-dependent changes of the random process that generates the gas distri-bution measurements. All methods are discussed based on experimental validation using real sensor data.

Chapter 7

Characterization of Complex Patterns: Application to Colorimetric Arrays and Vertical Structures 180
Yannick Caulier, Fraunhofer Institute IIS, Germany

Here, the focus is on the problem of a colorimetric sensor array description method within the machine olfaction field for the visual enhancement of volatile organic components (VOCs). The method described is based on the enhancement of a qual-ity control machine vision system that utilizes structured light patterns. The chapter demonstrates the similarity between the colorimetric and the structured pattern interpretation. Investigations are based on a linear spatial transformation between both types of patterns based on the main features characterizing the patterns, which enables the employment of existing structured pattern description methods. Feature-based investigations utilizing a reference annotated structured pattern dataset lead to an optimized feature combination, selection, and classification principle. Different methodologies for retrieving, combining and selecting the most appropriate structured feature sets are presented, demonstrating increased classification rates.

Chapter 8
Detection of Diseases and Volatile Discrimination of Plants: An Electronic Nose and Self-Organizing Maps Approach 214
Reza Ghaffari, University of Warwick, UK
Fu Zhang, University of Warwick, UK
D. Daciana Iliescu, University of Warwick, UK
Evor L. Hines, University of Warwick, UK
Mark S. Leeson, University of Warwick, UK
Richard Napier, University of Warwick, UK

Plant disease diagnosis is a very important part of the production of crops in commercial greenhouses and can also facilitate continuous disease and pest control. Plants that are subject to infection typically release exclusive volatile organic compounds (VOCs) which may be detected by appropriate sensors. In this chapter, an Electronic Nose (EN) is employed as an alternative to Gas Chromatography - Mass Spectrometry (GC-MS) to sample the VOCs emitted by control and artificially infected tomato plants. The particular case of powdery mildew and spider mites present on the tomatoes is considered. Data from the EN were analyzed and visualized by using Fuzzy C-Mean Clustering (FCM) and Self-Organizing Maps (SOM) to successfully distinguish VOC samples in healthy plants from infected ones. These results indicate that employing an EN with clustering is a promising method for enhancing the automated detection of crop pests and diseases in horticultural settings.

Chapter 9
Tomato Plant Health Monitoring: An Electronic Nose Approach 231
Fu Zhang, University of Warwick, UK
D. Daciana Iliescu, University of Warwick, UK
Evor L. Hines, University of Warwick, UK
Mark S. Leeson, University of Warwick, UK

The use of an electronic nose to monitor the health of greenhouse tomatoes is considered, with the focus on two common problems, namely powdery mildew and spider mites. An experimental arrangement is described based on a commercial 13-sensor e-nose, where tomato plants are grown in an isolated, controlled environment inside a greenhouse. The data collected are first analyzed using Principal

Component Analysis, which shows change in the components as the plants develop disease or infestation. Using Grey System Theory, it is possible to identify groupings in the sensor responses and thereby stronger trend differences in the Principal Component between healthy and unhealthy plants. The initial results show that the e-nose with appropriate data post-processing is a promising approach to greenhouse tomato plant health monitoring.

Chapter 10
Improved Gas Source Localization with a Mobile Robot by
Learning Analytical Gas Dispersal Models from Statistical Gas
Distribution Maps Using Evolutionary Algorithms... 249
Achim J. Lilienthal, Örebro University, Sweden

A method is presented to compute an estimate of the location of a single gas source from a set of localized gas sensor measurements. The estimation process first computes an estimated two dimensional gas distribution grid map using the Kernel DM algorithm. After this, the parameters of an analytical model of the average gas distribution are learned by nonlinear least squares fitting of the analytical model to the statistical gas distribution map using Evolution Strategies (ES), a special type of Evolutionary Algorithm (EA). Finally, an improved estimate of the gas source position is derived by examining the maximum in the statistical gas distribution map, considering the best fit as well as the corresponding fitness value. Different methods to select the most truthful estimate are introduced, and a comparison of their accuracy is presented based on gas distribution mapping experiments with a mobile robot.

Chapter 11
Enhancing the Classification of Eye Bacteria Using Bagging to
Multilayer Perceptron and Decision Tree... 277
Xu-Qin Li, University of Warwick, UK
Evor L. Hines, University of Warwick, UK
Mark S. Leeson, University of Warwick, UK
D. Daciana Iliescu, University of Warwick, UK

The human eye is continuously exposed to a harsh outside environment teeming with pathogenic airborne organisms. Although few of these are responsible for eye infection, they can proliferate rapidly, causing serious and irreversible damage. Thus, fast and accurate classification of eye bacteria is vital to the diagnosis of eye disease. It may be performed by utilizing the distinctive and specific characteristic odors arising in different diseases, smelling these by means on an electronic nose.

Here, following multi-layer perceptron (MLP) and decision tree (DT) classification, the bagging technique is introduced to both algorithms, and the accuracy of the MLP is significantly improved. Furthermore, in the case of DT, bagging reduces the misclassification rate and selection of the most important features. This reduces the dimension of the data, facilitating an enhanced training and testing process.

Compilation of References 294

About the Contributors 323

Index 329

Foreword

Olfaction is one of the main five senses that convey perception of the external world to the brain. The Chemical Senses (Olfaction and Taste) have often been considered as second class senses when compared to vision or hearing. However, advances in olfaction research in the last two decades have greatly increased our level of scientific understanding. In particular, the discovery of the olfactory receptors and the description of the organization of the olfactory system by Buck and Axel (Nobel Laureates in Medicine and Physiology in 2004), was a breakthrough and opened new research paths. In this new light, olfaction appears as a very intriguing and sophisticated chemical information processing system. The presence of hundreds of different receptors with overlapped specificities but also diverse molecular receptive fields, together with a high degree of redundancy provides an information rich set of neural signals that are very efficiently processed by the neural circuitry, both in vertebrates and insects.

Machine Olfaction tries to mimic the sense of smell in electronic instrumentation, and uses biology as a model system. Commencing with the pioneering work of Moncrieff in the early sixties (*Journal of Applied Physiology, 16,* 742-749, 1961), this has been a dream of many scientists and engineers. Persaud and Dodd's seminal 1982 paper (*Nature, 299,* 352–355) established the basis of what today is considered the field of *Artificial Olfaction* or *Machine Olfaction*. Since those early works, the field of Machine Olfaction has generated much interest for its ability to approach a diverse set of problems in areas as food production, environmental monitoring, and lately medical diagnosis. Today, a consolidated research community supports advances in this field, and a number of companies offer the technology in a commercial basis.

In this book, a number of papers survey the latest advances in Machine Olfaction, with emphasis in the signal and data processing component of the systems. Individual chapters have been written by recognized researchers in the field. They cover not only fundamental methodological issues such as optimum feature selection, data fusion using evolutionary algorithms, incremental learning and noise in chemical sensors but also applications such as odor reproduction for movies, modeling gas distributions for odor robot navigation, application of colorimetric arrays, disease identification in plants and the detection of bacteria.

Researchers in the Machine Olfaction community, as well as users wishing to know more about the underpinning technologies, will find this book to provide a useful update in the latest state of the art.

Santiago Marco
Universitat de Barcelona and Institute for Bioengineering of Catalonia, Spain

Santiago Marco *completed his university degree in Applied Physics in 1988 and received a PhD in Microsystem Technology from the University of Barcelona in 1993. He held a Human Capital Mobility grant for a postdoctoral position in 1994 at the Department of Electronic Engineering at the University of Rome "Tor Vergata". Since 1995, he has been an Associate Professor in the Department of Electronics at the University of Barcelona. In 2004 he spent a period of sabbatical leave at EADS-Corporate Research, Munich, working on Ion Mobility Spectrometry. He has recently been appointed leader of the Artificial Olfaction Lab at the Institute of Bioengineering of Catalonia (http://www.ibecbarcelona. eu/artificial_olfaction). His research concerns the development of signal and data processing algorithmic solutions for smart chemical sensing based in sensor arrays or microspectrometers typically integrated using Microsystem Technologies.*

Preface

The subject of Intelligent Systems (IS) has expanded considerably since its beginnings in the 1940s, and this volume considers the application of IS to machine olfaction, an area that has itself undergone substantial growth in recent years. IS includes a broad range of complementary techniques that provide attractive solutions to many hard and nonlinear problems. Modern work in IS includes methods such as Artificial Neural Networks, fuzzy systems, evolutionary algorithms, support vector machines, particle swarm optimization, memetic algorithms, and ant colony optimization. In addition, hybrid combinations also play a significant role with *inter alia*, neuro-fuzzy, neuro-genetic, and fuzzy-genetic systems firmly established in the literature. IS methods offer particular advantages in the robust handling of the large datasets containing uncertainties which have become more common with the growth of modern data storage capacity. The ability of IS solutions to learn from the data, extracting patterns, and to explore very large, multi-modal solution spaces taking into account multiple, often conflicting objectives, has further consolidated their place in the modern optimization toolbox.

The first section of the book presents some of the fundamental and more generic issues that underpin the application if IS to machine olfaction. The second section presents a series of specific applications to a range of olfaction tasks across industrial, medical, and horticultural topics.

Chapter one provides the reader with a thorough review of feature or sensor selection for machine olfaction. It covers the need for variable selection followed by a critical review of the different techniques employed for reducing dimensionality. Further, examples from the literature are used to illustrate the application of the various techniques machine olfaction followed by coverage of sensor selection and array optimization. In addition to conclusions, the chapter ends with a visionary look toward the future in terms of how the field may evolve.

In the second chapter, the combination of data from a number of sensors, known as Multisensor Data Fusion (MDF), is considered. The requirement is to provide comprehensive and reliable information, and MDF has expanded rapidly in tandem with improvements in computing power and the emergence of new sensors over the last 30 years. One of the key aims in MDF is the elimination of redundant, noisy, or irrelevant information to discover an optimal subset from an array of high dimensionality. Since the signals in MDF are constantly evolving, an opportunity is provided for Evolutionary Computation (EC) algorithms to assist in this aim. Here, the application of three EC algorithms to widely used datasets is described, demonstrating that ECs are of great utility in the MDF task. This leads nicely into the role of incremental learning considered in the next chapter.

Machine olfaction presents a significant challenge for pattern recognition systems because it is relatively difficult to obtain quality training data, and the samples arrive in batches widely spaced in time. Furthermore, industrial users are generally reluctant to supply samples but would like instant results. These characteristics mean that suitable pattern recognition algorithms need to be flexible in that they must update an existing, stable, and plastic classifier without affecting the classification performance on old data. Incremental learning algorithms offer the required features, and in chapter three, a range of such algorithms for machine olfaction are reviewed.

The final chapter of this part (chapter four) is concerned with the causes of the errors and inconsistencies that contribute to the problems of MDF. Given the wide application of electronic noses (e-noses) in environmental monitoring, food production, and medicine, understanding the imperfections they display is crucial so that they may be compensated for. Thus, in this chapter, the impact of sensor interference and noise on measurement repeatability is considered. Probability density functions and power spectra of noise from real sensors are presented to deliver a pragmatic view of sensor imperfection effects on repeatability.

The use of electronic noses for odor recording in the atmosphere is challenging because of the turbulent airflows present. Chapter 5 addresses this challenge by utilizing visual information to enhance the sensitivity of an electronic nose by combining senses. The system also offers the prospect of teleolfaction, where users can sniff distant objects whilst watching video images of the objects in real time via the Internet. Thus, users can perceive much of the sensation of reality of the object even at the remote site. Although there have been several reports on the fusion of vision and olfaction in virtual environments, the system described is unique because it is able to record and reproduce olfactory information synchronized with visual information.

In the sixth chapter, the determination of the distribution gas is considered and an alternative sought to current computationally expensive physical models. In the chapter, kernel models are introduced that treat gas measurements as random variables, enabling the gas distribution predictions, but making no strong assumptions about the gas distribution's functional form. In addition to two-dimensional models, the kernel density estimation algorithm is extended to three dimensions, with additional incorporation of wind information and time-dependent changes of the random process. The methods covered are discussed based on experimental validation using real sensor data.

Chapter 7 tackles the problem of a machine olfaction colorimetric sensor array description method for the visual enhancement of volatile organic components (VOCs). The solution presented utilizes structured light patterns, demonstrating the similarity between the colorimetric and the structured pattern interpretation. Once the calorimetric data has been transformed into a structured form, existing structured pattern description methods may be employed. Different methodologies for retrieving, combining, and selecting the most appropriate structured feature sets are presented, demonstrating increased classification rates.

The important topic of plant disease diagnosis, using the specific example of tomato plants, forms the basis of chapter 8. Since plants that are subject to infection typically release exclusive volatile organic compounds (VOCs), these may be detected by appropriate sensors. In this contribution, an electronic nose (EN) is used to sample the VOCs emitted by control plants and plants artificially infected with powdery mildew and spider mites. The EN data were analyzed using Fuzzy C-Mean Clustering and Self-Organizing Maps with results that indicate that this is a promising automated crop pests and disease detection method.

The ninth chapter continues the theme of the previous one by again examining powdery mildew and spider mites on tomatoes using and electronic nose (e-nose), but this time in a greenhouse setting. A commercial e-nose was used to collect data from tomato plants grown in an isolated controlled greenhouse environment. Principal Component Analysis and Grey System Theory are utilized to analyze the data, producing noticeable groupings in the sensor responses between healthy and infected plants. The results show that the approach is potentially a highly effective in greenhouse tomato plant health monitoring.

Chapter 10 returns to the area of gas sources, in this case, the location of a single gas source from a set of localized gas sensor measurements. Nonlinear least squares fitting is applied to a two dimensional gas distribution grid map and the parameters learned using Evolution Strategies (ES), a special type of Evolutionary Algorithm (EA). By considering the best fit to the statistical gas distribution map, an improved estimate of the gas source position is derived. A comparison of methods to ascertain the true source position in made based on gas distribution mapping experiments with a mobile robot.

The final chapter addresses a topic from medicine, namely the classification of eye bacteria. Human eyes are constantly exposed to airborne organisms, with those that cause eye infection able to proliferate rapidly. There is thus a requirement for fast and accurate classification of eye bacteria that may be achieved by smelling the distinctive and specific characteristic odors arising in different diseases using an e-nose. The focus of the work in this contribution is the enhancement of classification by introducing the bagging technique to both multi-layer perceptron (MLP) and decision tree (DT) classification. In the case of the former, the accuracy significantly improved, and in the latter, the misclassification rate is reduced. Using bagging, the dimension of the data is reduced to enhance training and testing.

These chapters give an indication of wide ranging areas of machine olfaction, in which IS methods have found application, and they present a representative selection of the available approaches. The IS field continues to evolve rapidly with more data constantly available, coupled with new hardware and software. This collection will be particularly useful as a reference for graduate students and researchers in engineering, computer science, system sciences, and Information Technology, as well as or practitioners in a range of industries. It collects together some of the major techniques that are available to make sense of the wealth of data that may be obtained with modern machine olfaction technology.

Evor L. Hines
University of Warwick, UK

Mark S. Leeson
University of Warwick, UK

Acknowledgment

We would like to thank all of the contributors to this volume. First, the chapter authors, without whom there would be no book at all. Second, the referees, who provided detailed and constructive feedback to ensure that the chapters were of the high standard that has resulted. Finally, our heartfelt gratitude goes to the members of staff at IGI Global, particularly Joel Gamon, without whom the project would have stalled at various phases; your faith in us is greatly appreciated.

Evor L. Hines
University of Warwick, UK

Mark S. Leeson
University of Warwick, UK

Section 1
Methods

Chapter 1
Feature Selection and Sensor Array Optimization in Machine Olfaction

Alexander Vergara
BioCircuits Institute (BCI), University of California, USA

Eduard Llobet
University Rovira i Virgili, Spain

ABSTRACT

In the last few years, growing attention has been given to strategies for feature and sensor selection in multi-sensor systems for machine olfaction. The two main approaches consist of selecting the features extracted from the sensor response to be used to build a multivariate model, or selecting an optimal subset of factors; for example, principal components or latent variables. Selecting from the full set of features is challenging because there is considerable overlapping among them. Furthermore, features are affected by noise. However, methods based on selected features are interesting because the variables chosen carry direct and relevant chemical information; i.e., response time is connected to chemical kinetics. Therefore, these methods are expected to be robust toward the experimental conditions of each specific application. Unlike feature selection, factor selection uses the full set of variables, including noisy variables, to compute the factors before selecting from among them. The selection of an optimal subset of factors is not necessarily straightforward because the magnitude of an eigenvalue is not always a measure of its significance for the calibration.

DOI: 10.4018/978-1-61520-915-6.ch001

Several variable selection methods have been reported as useful (Blum & Langely 1997, Guyon et al. 2006, Naes & Martens 1998, Sun 1995). These include deterministic methods such as forward or backward selection methods, correlated principal component regression analysis of weights resulting from multiple linear regression, branch and bound regression, and stochastic methods such as generalized simulated annealing or genetic algorithms. In most machine olfaction applications, it is usually out of the question to make an exhaustive search because it is a very time-consuming process, given the large number of variables to be considered for selection. Deterministic methods are, most of the times, greedy methods in which, once a choice has been made, e.g. the selection or elimination of a variable, this decision is never reconsidered. Such techniques can make a good selection with relatively few operations but can get easily trapped in a local optimum of the search space. Unlike deterministic methods, stochastic methods such as simulated annealing or genetic algorithms are more likely to find a global optimum in reasonable computational time. In the case of stochastic methods, the next point to be explored in a solution space is chosen by stochastic rather than deterministic rules, and no assumptions about the characteristics of the problem to be solved are needed. Therefore, they are normally more generally applicable. Although stochastic methods are useful for selecting features, it has been shown (Jouan-Rimbaud, Massart, & Noord 1996, Llobet et al. 2004) that the solution found should be investigated carefully because these algorithms do not prevent meaningless features, such as random non-relevant variables, from being selected.

In this context, the main objective of this chapter is to provide the reader with a thorough review of feature or sensor selection for machine olfaction. The organization of the chapter is as follows. First the 'curse of dimensionality' and the need for variable selection in gas sensor and direct mass spectrometry based artificial olfaction is discussed. A critical review of the different techniques employed for reducing dimensionality follows. Then, examples taken from the literature showing how these techniques have actually been employed in machine olfaction applications are reviewed and discussed. This is followed by a section devoted to sensor selection and array optimization. The chapter ends with some conclusions drawn from the results presented and a visionary look toward the future in terms of how the field may evolve.

INTRODUCTION

Machine olfaction applications would greatly benefit from gas sensors with high sensitivity and specificity or selectivity to target analytes, low cross-sensitivity to interfering species, fast response and full reversibility of the detection mechanism and, finally, no long term drift (Göpel, Hesse, & Zemel 1991, Gardner & Bartlett 1999, Nanto & Stetter 2003). However, such ideal gas sensors are largely unrealizable today. Real sensors show a trade-off between sensitivity, selectivity, response time and reversibility. While highly sensitive and selective sensors showing fast responses are typically associated with strong analyte to sensing material interactions, full reversibility is only achieved if the interaction between analytes and sensing material is weak. A weak enough interaction allows the total desorption of analytes or reaction by-products from the sensor surface, i.e. re-establishment of the clean surface conditions, during a recovery phase. Since reversibility is an essential aspect for any machine olfaction application, it is necessary to compromise, and hence it is normally necessary to use sensors which show only partial specificity for some of the target species. Gas sensors experience long term response drift often due to changes in the sensitive material; e.g. mechanisms that cause poisoning or changes in the material micro/nano structure after long operation at temperatures well above room temperature; or to degradation of the transducer element which is needed to support the gas sensitive material.

The response of an individual sensor to a given gaseous environment or odor generally consists of a current measured at a fixed voltage, a resistance of the active material or a resonant frequency. When this response is measured in a steady-state situation, which is often the case, a stand-alone feature per sensor is obtained at a time. To improve the poor selectivity performance of individual sensors, arrays of several sensors are commonly used, from which response vectors; i.e. a response feature per sensor within the array; are obtained and treated by employing pattern recognition engines (Brereton 1992). Increasing the dimensionality of response vectors; i.e. increasing the number of response features per measurement; seems logically to be a useful way to significantly improve the analytical capabilities of a machine olfaction instrument (Lorber & Kowalski 1988), provided that the new features response carry additional information.

Exploiting sensor dynamics is a useful way to obtain additional features, and this can be implemented through the modulation of either internal (e.g. operating temperature, bias voltage) or external (e.g. gas flow, pre-concentration or separation columns, etc.) parameters. Features extracted from out–of–equilibrium sensor responses carry information about the interaction between odorant molecules and the gas-sensitive materials (e.g. kinetics of adsorption, desorption, diffusion, and, eventually, reaction); therefore, such features can help with the identification or quantification of specific analytes or complex odors (Llobet 2006, El Barbri et al. 2008).

However, exploiting sensor dynamics is not the only existing strategy for making use of an extended set of features. This can be further combined with other possibilities that include the use of hybrid sensor arrays consisting of a number of different gas sensitive materials together with suitable transducer architectures (e.g. optical fiber, surface acoustic wave devices, microbalances, chemo-resistors) and geometries (electrode configuration, micro-hotplate, etc.), which employ different properties to convey information from the chemical domain into the electrical or optical domains. Göpel (1988) estimated that the full exploitation of all these combinations would lead to 10^{21} chemical sensor features. Although this figure is highly hypothetical since the number of useful parameters and realizable variations is for sure significantly lower, this shows that the number of potential features available to solve a given odor analysis problem can be extremely large.

The number of features available is also very large in mass-spectrometry based machine olfaction (MS-e-nose). In MS-e-nose applications a sample of a complex odor is injected directly into the ionization chamber of the mass spectrometer, and a corresponding complex mass-to-charge (m/z) spectrum is obtained. Each m/z component of the spectrum can be considered as an individual sensor (Vinaixa et al. 2004). In direct injection mass spectrometry, the simultaneous fragmentation from all components within odors results in extremely complex mixtures of mass fragments, which impairs odor identification or classification. On the other hand, in the case where there is coupling of gas chromatography to mass spectrometry, it is almost the case that each odor constituent is time-resolved prior to undergoing fragmentation and thus, the classification is made easier at the cost of significantly increasing the processing time. The use of short chromatographic columns makes it possible to keep sample throughput high, while making use of the advantages brought by partially time-resolved spectra (Burian et al. 2010). In the latter approach, the number of features available can also be very high. As an example, if in a short GC-MS e-nose, 400 m/z ratios were scanned at 1 scan/s for say 5 minutes, there would be $400 \times 300 = 1.2 \times 10^5$ features available for processing. This presents its own set of challenges because the search has to be conducted in a high-dimensional feature space where many of these features are likely to be highly correlated and many others surely affected by noise.

In the previous paragraphs, we have suggested that increasing the data dimensionality (i.e. increasing the number of sensors and the number of features per sensor) could significantly improve performance in machine olfaction. So an obvious question would be: Is it true that the more sensors or features we use, the better? In fact, it is generally accepted that increasing the dimensionality of the feature space (each measurement can be thought of as a data point in multi-dimensional feature space) is at the risk of experiencing the curse of dimensionality.

The concept of the curse of dimensionality was introduced by Bellman (1961) after his studies in adaptive control theory, and refers to the problem caused by the exponential increase in volume associated with adding extra dimensions to a mathematical space. In other words, it generally refers to the difficulties involved in fitting models, estimating parameters, or optimizing a function in many dimensions. As the dimensionality of the feature space increases, it becomes exponentially more difficult to find global optima for the parameter space, i.e., to fit models. Many classifiers can be assumed to be mappings from the feature space to an output space, for example the space of odor classes in a machine olfaction application. A classifier needs to cover or represent every part of its feature space in order for it to be able to determine how the space should be mapped; the number of resources needed is proportional to the volume of the input space. The classifier is likely to employ most of its resources to map irrelevant portions of the feature space and even if the algorithm is able to focus on important portions of space, the higher the dimensionality, the more data (i.e. measurements) that may be needed to identify what is important and what is irrelevant. The only practical way to best account for the curse is either to apply prior knowledge to the data collected (Jain, Duin, & Mao 2000) or to carefully select a subset of features or sensors that are of likely to be able to be sufficiently capable of representing the problem (Bishop 1995). This chapter is devoted to the second approach.

FEATURE SELECTION TECHNIQUES

In the context of machine olfaction, feature selection is the process of identifying the most representative subset of the original features which are to be used in the construction of a classifier that leads to the highest classification success rate. According to Blum et al. (1997) there are three basic approaches for classifying feature selection techniques, namely filters, wrappers and embedded methods. These three approaches differ in terms of the criteria used to select the features, in terms of how the search is performed, and finally in terms of how the results of the features that are selected impact on what is subsequently being assessed (e.g. the performance of a classifier model). In the case of filters (see Figure 1 (a)), the selection criterion is based on feature (or feature subset) relevance. Relevance is a measure of the information content provided by a feature or a given combination of features. To give a few examples, relevance can be associated with variance (eigenvalues of a principal component analysis or a partial least squares discriminant analysis) or interclass discrimination (eigenvalues of a linear discriminant analysis). The search is usually performed by ranking individual features or nested feature subsets and the assessment consists of using statistical tests. Since filters employ selection criteria that are independent of the classification model being built, they usually find a feature subset that works well on a very wide range of classifiers (relatively robust against overfitting). Additionally, filters are not computationally intensive when compared to other approaches (Guyon et al. 2006). However, it is difficult to design filters

Figure 1. Filters (a) select features based on relevance, they work independently of the classifier model chosen. Wrappers (b) select features based on usefulness estimated by training the classifier model on any particular feature subset. In embedded methods (c), the process of feature selection is conducted in the process of training the classifier model.

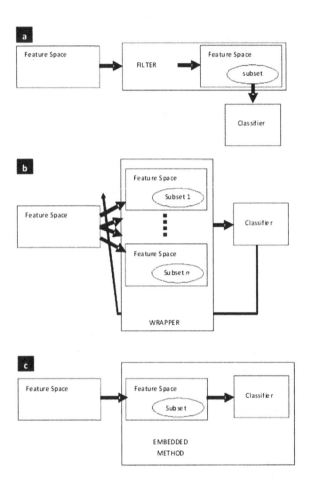

that correlate well with the final accuracy of the classifier. In that sense, filters may fail to select the most useful features to solve a given odor classification problem (Hierlemann & Gutierrez-Osuna 2008).

In wrappers (see Figure 1 (b)), the selection criterion is based on feature usefulness. The search is performed in the space of all feature subsets and the assessment consists of using re-sampling techniques on training data. In other words, wrappers evaluate each combination of features by the classification performance of a chosen classifier model trained on that particular feature subset. Performance is estimated by employing re-sampling techniques on a training dataset. Wrappers can in principle find the subset of most useful features and reach a higher predictive ability, since the selection is tuned with respect to the particular bias of the classifier model employed. However, they are more prone to being overfitted than filters (Hierlemann et al. 2008).

In a similar way to wrappers, embedded methods (see Figure 1 (c)) also use a selection criterion based on feature usefulness. Once more the search is performed in feature space, and the assessment consists of using re-sampling techniques on training data. Unlike wrappers that use a learning machine as a 'black box' to score subsets of features according to their predictive power, embedded methods perform feature selection in the process of training and are usually specific to given learning machines. In other words, in embedded methods the search for an optimal subset of features is built into the classifier construction. They yield similar results to wrappers, but are less computationally intensive and also less prone to overfitting. Table 1 further discusses the particularities of these different approaches and compares their main advantages and drawbacks.

The reader is referred to the book edited by Guyon et al. (2006) and to the useful review by (Saeys, Inza, & Larrañaga 2007) for an in-depth description of these three different approaches for feature selection.

An Introduction to Factor Selection

Because samples which are measured in typical machine olfaction applications are usually described by hundreds or even thousands of features that are not mutually independent (i.e. usually there is a high degree of colinearity among features), their multivariate modeling is very often performed using principal component analysis (PCA), linear discriminant analysis (LDA) or partial least squares discriminant analysis (PLS-DA). The main advantage of PCA, LDA and PLS is their ability to compress the relevant information into fewer orthogonal factors (i.e., principal components in the case of PCA, discriminant factors in the case of LDA or latent variables in the case of PLS-DA). Their orthogonality makes it possible for irrelevant factors to be removed. Relevance/Irrelevance is judged in terms of the data variance (or co-variance) explained by each factor (e.g., via the magnitude of associated eigenvalues) (Naes et al. 1998). Factor selection uses the full set of features (e.g. including noisy features) to compute the factors, before selecting from among them. The selection of an optimal subset of factors is not necessarily straightforward because the relative magnitude of an eigenvalue is not always a measure of its significance for the correct classification (Sun 1995). In comparison to factor selection, selecting from the full set of features is challenging because there is typically considerable

Table 1. Different types of feature selection strategies. Their main advantages and disadvantages are highlighted.

Model	Type	Advantages	Disadvantages	References
Filter	Univariate	Fast	Ignores synergies between features	Guyon et al. 2003, 2006, Sun 1995, Bhattacharyya 1943, Brezmes et al. 2002, Arturs-son et al 2002, Gualdron et al. 2006.
	Multivariate	Exploits feature synergies	Slower than univari-ate approach	Llobet et al. 2007, Gualdron et al. 2007.
	Both univariate or multivariate	Independent of the classifier. Lower computa-tional load than wrappers	Ignores interaction with the classifier	
Wrapper	Deterministic	Simple Less computation-ally intensive than stochastic	Risk of overfitting Prone to get stuck in local optima of search space	Vinaixa et al. 2004, Narendra et al. 1977, Guyon et al. 2003, Bro 1997.
	Stochastic	Less prone to get stuck in local optima. Exploits feature synergies	Computationally intensive Higher risk of over-fitting than in deter-ministic approach	Llobet et al. 2004, 2007, Gardner et al. 2005.
	Both deterministic and stochastic	Interacts with the classifier	Selection depends on the classifier model	
Embedded		Lower computa-tional load than wrappers Interaction with the classifier Exploits feature synergies	Selection depends on the classifier model	Guyon et al. 2006, Gualdron et al. 2007.

overlapping among them and, furthermore, features may be affected by noise. How-ever, methods based on selected features are interesting because, unlike factors, the variables chosen carry direct and relevant chemical information. In other words, the relationship between features and chemical information is easier to identify than in the case of factors. Therefore, feature selection methods are expected to be robust toward the experimental conditions of each specific application.

Exhaustive vs. More Efficient Feature Selection Approaches

Performing an exhaustive evaluation of all possible combinations of features guarantees that the optimal subset of features will eventually be found. However, it is usually out of the question to make an exhaustive search because it is a very time consuming process, given the relatively large number of features to be considered for selection in most machine olfaction applications. Therefore, different selection methods have been devised, which explore the space of feature combinations in a more efficient way. These include deterministic and stochastic or random methods (Devijver & Kittler 1982). Within deterministic methods (Guyon et al. 2006) two different search strategies can be found, namely exponential or sequential search. In exponential search, complexity grows exponentially with the number of features and, similarly to exhaustive evaluation, it may become impractical for even a moderate number of features. Sequential methods significantly reduce the number of trials to be performed during the search by applying local search; however, at the risk of getting trapped in local minima of the search space. Unlike deterministic methods, stochastic methods (Guyon et al. 2006) are an attempt to alleviate the computational costs of exponential methods and avoid the risks of getting trapped in local minima often experienced with sequential methods. A short review of the different approaches is given in the next two sub-sections.

Deterministic Feature Selection Techniques

Branch and Bound Algorithm for Feature Selection

Feature selection employing the branch and bound (Narendra & Fukunaga 1977) algorithm is very efficient because it avoids exhaustive enumeration by rejecting suboptimal subsets without direct evaluation and guarantees that the selected subset yields the globally best value of any criterion that satisfies monotonicity. Monotonicity merely assumes that a subset of features should not be better than any larger set that contains the subset. The basics of the branch and bound method can be illustrated as follows. Let's consider a feature set of four features labeled $\{1, 2, 3, 4\}$. If we envisage the selection of the optimal subset of two features, the solution tree is shown in Figure 2. Each node of the solution tree is identified by the discarded feature. If we consider now that B is the lower bound on the optimum (maximum) value of the criterion and monotonicity is satisfied, this means that whenever the criterion evaluated for any node is less than the bound B, all nodes that are successors of that node also have criterion values less than B, and therefore cannot be the optimum solution. The branch and bound algorithm successively generates portions of the solution tree and computes the criterion. Whenever a partial sequence or

Figure 2. Solution tree for the selection of up to two features from the four available. Node labels indicate the discarded feature. Following the leftmost path, features 1 and 2 are discarded (i.e., features 3 and 4 are selected).

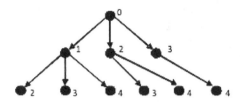

node is found to be sub-optimal (i.e. the criterion value is below the bound B), the sub-tree under the node is implicitly rejected, and enumeration begins on partial sequences which have not yet been explored. For example, if node 1 in Figure 2 was found to be sub-optimal, 3 sequences would be immediately discarded without further calculations.

Although some feature selection criteria such as discriminant functions and distance measures (e.g. the Battacharyya distance (Bhattacharyya 1943)) satisfy monotonicity, this assumption is often violated in practical problems since the addition of noisy features does increase the risk of overfitting.

Sequential Feature Selection Methods

Sequential methods are simpler and faster than the branch and bound approach, and they do not require that the selection criterion satisfies any particular condition (e.g., monotonicity). However, they are prone to being trapped in local minima of the search space. There are three different approaches in sequential feature selection, namely sequential forward selection (SFS) sequential backward selection (SBS) and stepwise selection.

SFS starts from an empty set of selected features. It considers every feature individually and selects $z1$, i.e. the one that obtains the best value for the selection criterion (e.g. the lowest prediction error of a classifier). The second step consists of considering again the value of the selection criterion for any combination of two features including $z1$. The new variable chosen is the one that, taken together with $z1$, most improves the value of the selection criterion. The process of adding new features continues until either a pre-set number of selected features have been reached or the value of the selection criterion is no further improved by the inclusion of new features or all features have been selected.

SBS, which is also known as sequential backward elimination, starts with the full set of features available. In any particular iteration of the algorithm, the method identifies a feature, the removal of which does not degrade (or most improves) the value of the selection criterion. The process of removing new features continues until either a pre-set number of the remaining features has been reached or the value of the selection criterion degrades by the removal of new features or only one feature remains selected.

The main problem experienced with SFS or SBS is that once one feature has been added to, or removed from the set of selected features, there is no possibility for reconsidering the decision and this explains why these two methods show an inherent risk of getting trapped in local minima of the search space. In an attempt to lower such a risk, stepwise selection (Guyon et al. 2006, Guyon & Elisseeff 2003) is able to backtrack the selection or remove a feature and reconsider the decision.

Stepwise selection consists of consecutively employing SFS followed by SBS. If the strategy of performing SFS and SBS is implemented several times on a given feature set, the algorithm is likely to obtain an optimal or a good sub-optimal set of selected features within a fraction of the computation needed by the branch and bound approach (Guyon et al. 2003).

Stochastic Feature Selection Techniques

The two main feature selection techniques that fall within this category are genetic algorithms (GAs) and simulated annealing (SA). Let us consider each in turn:

Genetic Algorithms

GAs have been shown to be able to solve optimization problems by exploring all regions of the potential solution space and exponentially searching promising areas through mutation, crossover and selection operations applied to individuals (i.e. chromosomes) in a population. The population (i.e. set of possible solutions) is maintained and manipulated by implementing a 'survival of the fittest' strategy in the search for the optimal solution. Because the next explored point in a solution space is chosen by stochastic rather than deterministic rules, GAs do not need to make assumptions about the characteristics of the problem to be solved and, there-fore, can apply generally (Davis 1991). When employed for feature selection in a classification problem, the GAs works as follows. Possible solutions to the problem are encoded as binary strings called chromosomes, where the code *1* means that the feature (or gene) has been chosen to build a classifier model and *0* means that the variable has not been chosen. The initial population (initial set of possible solutions) consists of a given number of chromosomes encoded at random. Depending on the algorithm used the size of the population can either be kept constant or may diminish from generation to generation. At each generation, each member (chromosome) is ranked according to its fitness, which may be evaluated as the prediction error rate (PER) of the cross-validation of the classifier model built using only those variables set to *1* in the chromosome. A lower PER value indicates better fitness. At each generation, half of the chromosomes with the better fitness are allowed to live and breed. Pairs of these chromosomes are randomly selected for breeding. Also, some of the genes in the chromosomes may be randomly flipped (mutation rate is set to a low value) after each generation. This helps in exploring all regions of the solution space. The chromosomes with better fitness are kept unchanged in the next generation (elitism). Iterations are performed until either the population converges or the maximum number of iterations is reached. The population converges when the percentage of duplicate chromosomes in the population is high (when population size is kept constant) or when the number of surviving chromosomes has reached a lower bound (when population size decreases as the algorithm progresses) (Davis 1991).

Although GAs are useful for selecting variables, Jouan-Rimbaud et al. (1996) have shown that the solution found by a GAs should be investigated carefully, because the algorithm does not prevent meaningless features (e.g. random non-relevant features) from being selected.

Simulated Annealing

Simulated annealing (SA) is a stochastic technique derived from statistical thermodynamics for finding near globally optimum solutions to complex optimization problems (i.e. problems which have a high number of degrees of freedom) (Kirkpatrick, Gelatt, & Vecchi 1983). The algorithm proceeds stepwise through a search space defined by all possible solutions to the optimization problem. After each iteration (e.g. after a feature has been removed), the value of the cost function for the new step is compared to that of the previous step. If the new solution is better than the old one, the removal of the feature is confirmed. If the new solution is worse than the old one, there is still a probability, p, for the removal of the feature to be accepted. This offers the algorithm the possibility to jump out of a local optimum. Otherwise, the removal of the feature will be discarded and the previous step will be the starting point for the next attempt to eliminate a variable. The probability p for accepting a worse solution depends on the difference between the new and the previous solution as follows:

$$p = \exp\left(-\frac{\Delta E}{T_i}\right) \tag{1}$$

where ΔE = fitness (new) – fitness (old) and T_i is the annealing temperature during the i-th iteration. Since the cost function (or fitness) being optimized by the SA is usually the prediction error of a classifier model, ΔE is positive when the new solution is worse than the old one. The initial temperature is set by the user, and the whole process of feature selection is repeated a fixed number of times for monotonically decreasing annealing temperatures (as the annealing temperature is reduced, the probability for accepting a worse solution decreases significantly since T_i appears in the denominator of the exponential factor in Equation 1). After every change in the annealing temperature, the algorithm starts selecting from the complete set of features. Therefore, the role of temperature in the SA algorithm is to set the tolerance of the algorithm to accept a worse solution. For example, a high initial value would imply a high tolerance during the first few iterations. In order to correctly explore the solution space it is necessary to apply the SA algorithm over a wide range of temperatures with small enough temperature leaps (Kirkpatrick et al. 1983).

Both GAs and SA are well suited for finding a global optimum of the feature selection problem but at the cost of lengthy computation. This is especially true when a wrapper approach is employed and the cost function is the fully cross-validated prediction error of a classifier model on a training set of measurements devised for conducting the feature selection process.

FEATURE SELECTION IN MACHINE OLFACTION

This section reviews how feature selection has been employed in machine olfaction applications. Since artificial olfaction systems that use gas sensor arrays have very different characteristics to those employing mass spectrometry, feature selection is reviewed separately for these two machine olfaction approaches.

Feature Selection for Direct Mass Spectrometry Based Machine Olfaction

In the last few years, with the use of mass spectrometry (MS), a new branch within machine olfaction research has developed and gained importance. Unlike in classical gas chromatography/mass spectrometry systems (GC/MS), in MS based machine olfaction the sample delivery unit directly injects complex volatile mixtures (such as the ones generated in the headspace of foodstuffs or beverages) into an ionization chamber, without a previous separation step (provided by GC). This results in very complex ionization patterns that are recorded at the detector side. These ionization patterns are then processed by a pattern recognition engine to perform the tasks associated to machine olfaction systems such as classification, recognition and, to a limited extent, quantification (Marsili 1999, Fallik et al. 2001, Peres et al. 2003, Vinaixa et al. 2004, Martí et al. 2003, Martí et al. 2005). In accordance with the machine olfaction philosophy, *a priori* knowledge of the components present in the headspace being analyzed should not been required. This is why most applications developed using this approach consider spectra consisting of a wide range of m/z ratios fully covering the fragmentation of volatile molecules. This implies that over two hundred features are going to be available for the pattern recognition analysis. Therefore, it is not uncommon that the number of features exceeds the number of measurements available to train the pattern recognition methods and this is not an acceptable situation to be in because there is a high risk of overfitting (Dittmann & Nitz 2000). Actually, a significant number of sensors (i.e., m/z ratios) can be irrelevant (i.e., noisy) for the application being considered, while other sensors can show highly correlated responses. A feature step leading to a reduction in dimensionality seems, therefore, imperative prior to any attempt to build appropriate pattern recognition methods.

By far, the most employed dimensionality reduction strategy in MS machine olfaction has been to select among factors computed via a PCA, a linear discriminant analysis or discriminant partial least squares (Cozzolino et al. 2005). In this sense, the application of multivariate statistical techniques provides the possibility to understand the data generated by MS e-noses based on the overall properties of the sample and to be able to perform data compression and classification without the need of additional information about its chemical composition. There are a number of examples of this approach, especially in the agro-food field. For example, Marsili and co-workers (1999) applied PCA as a dimensionality reduction technique to analyze off-odors from milk employing an MS e-nose. Similarly, Mallik and co-workers (2001) employed this strategy to characterize melons. Vinaixa and co-workers employed either PCA, LDA or PLS coupled to different neural network architectures to determine the fungal spoilage of bakery products (Vinaixa et al. 2004, Marín et al. 2007) or rancidity in crisps (Vinaixa et al. 2005a, Vinaixa et al. 2005b) with a solid-phase microextraction MS e-nose. Guasch et al. (2005) employed a similar experimental set-up to study the effect of aging in oak barrels in spirits. Finally, Cozzolino et al. (2005) applied these methods to sort white Australian wines according to their varietal origin.

Very recently the use of short chromatographic columns within the MS e-nose set up has enabled the study of the advantages brought by partially time-resolved spectra (Burian et al. 2010). This resulted in adding a third dimension to the data usually obtained with the standard MS e-nose set up and thus, the number of features available was highly increased. Twenty mixtures of nine isomers of dimethylphenol and ethylphenol (2,3-Dimethylphenol; 2,4-Dimethylphenol; 2,5- Dimethylphenol;

2,6-Dimethylphenol; 3,4-Dimethylphenol; 3,5-Dimethylphenol; 2-Ethylphenol; 3-Ethylphenol and 4- Ethylphenol) were measured and analyzed by means of gas chromatography coupled to mass spectrometry. The nine isomers were chosen based on their theoretically similar mass spectra and retention times to challenge the short chromatographic column MS e-nose. By analyzing these solutions with two-way (PCA, PLS-DA) and three-way (Geladi 1989, Bro 1997) (PARAFAC, n-PLS-DA) methods, it was shown that the addition of the extra information in the form of short chromatographic separation improved the results obtained compared to the two-way analysis of the mass spectra or total ion chromatogram (TIC) alone (i.e., the usual information available in MS e-nose without any GC separation). It was found that when short chromatographic separation was used (i.e., getting a somewhat coeluted chromatogram with a short measurement time) three-way methods performed better than classic two-way approaches.

However, the techniques described above cannot be properly considered as feature selection approaches. Factors (i.e., principal components, discriminant factors or latent variables) are included in the classification model in sequence based on the variances explained by the factors (i.e. factors with high associated eigenvalues are chosen). Therefore, factors with small variances are rarely used. As pointed out by some authors (Jouan-Rimbaud et al.1996, Guyon et al. 2003), a low variance for a component does not necessarily imply that the corresponding component is unimportant, especially when prediction is of primary interest. In an attempt to solve this problem, correlation principal component regression (CPCR) has been introduced (Bellman 1961). In CPCR the importance of principal components, in terms of predicting the response variable is used as a basis for the inclusion of principal components in the regression model. In comparison to standard PCR or PLS, CPCR shows similar optimal prediction ability, but CPCR performs better than standard PCR and PLS in terms of the number of components or factors needed to achieve the optimal prediction ability. This technique has been demonstrated with near infrared spectroscopy but, to the best of our knowledge, it has never been applied in the context of MS based machine olfaction.

Instead of selecting factors, selecting from the full spectrum of mass to charge ratios is challenging because there is a considerable overlapping among the spectra and distinctive features can be almost imperceptible. Furthermore, spectra are affected by noise. There are different sources of background noise in MS systems. For example, spectral background noise is associated with contaminants present in the ionization chamber (such as ambient air and contaminants present in the carrier gas). To a higher extent, spectral background noise is mainly due to the inherent noise associated with the ion multiplier. Additionally, a baseline drift may appear due to coeluting compounds, septa and temperature induced column bleed. However, methods based on the selection of m/z ratios are interesting because the variables chosen carry directly relevant chemical information. Therefore, these methods are expected to be robust toward the experimental conditions of each specific application.

Llobet and co-workers introduced a three-step method for variable selection in MS machine olfaction (Llobet et al. 2007). The first two steps help in detecting and removing non-informative, noisy or highly correlated features. Finally, in the third step, a greedy search method (e.g. a stochastic one) is applied to the reduced feature set, which results from applying the first two steps. With this approach, the whole variable selection process is time efficient since the first two steps are able to dramatically reduce the number of features at a very low computational cost. In the first step of feature selection, a Fisher's linear discriminant analysis, was used to rate the discrimination ability of each feature (i.e. m/z ratio). The higher the discrimination ability for a given m/z ratio is, the more important is this m/z ratio to correctly discriminate between the categories. Therefore, a set of m/z ratios, which comprises those that have the higher figure of merit, are selected for further analysis. This process is univariate and there is a risk of eliminating those synergetic variables that have low discrimination ability when considered individually. To minimize this problem the process was repeated considering all the possible combinations between two m/z ratios. As a result, a new list of figures of merit, $DA_{i,j}$, i.e., the discrimination ability when m/z ratios i and j are used simultaneously, is obtained. This allows for the re-selecting variables that had been removed previously, if a synergistic effect is revealed. The threshold value for the discrimination ability was heuristically set to a value that made it possible to retain about 30% of the originally available m/z ratios. This step does not prevent redundant features (i.e., highly collinear) from being selected, therefore, in the second step an unsupervised collinearity check is performed so that highly redundant features can be identified and removed. The value of the collinearity threshold was heuristically set to a value that allowed for about 20% of the originally available m/z ratios (i.e., the ratios available prior to perform any variable selection) to be retained. In the first two steps, feature ranking and selection were conducted independently of the classifier model; therefore, a filter approach was employed. Finally, in the third step a simulated annealing algorithm was implemented to further select among the 20% of features that remained. The cost function to be optimized was the prediction error associated to a fuzzy ARTMAP classifier model (i.e. a wrapper approach was envisaged in this last step). Applying the method to the discrimination of Iberian hams resulted in the number of features being reduced from 209 down to 14. Using the surviving features, a fuzzy ARTMAP classifier was able to discriminate ham samples according to producer and quality (11-category classification) with a 97% success rate. In contrast, success rate degraded down to 80% when all features were employed.

Gualdrón and co-workers introduced a new feature selection strategy inspired in sequential forward selection and specifically designed to work with support vector machines both for classification and regression problems (Gualdrón et al. 2007). The feature selection procedure was conducted as follows: in the first step, the squared norm of the optimal weight vector of the separation (or regression) hyperplane (Meyer, Leisch, & Hornik 2003), $\|\omega_{s0}\|^2$, was computed using all the variables available. Then, the effect of removing the i-th variable in the decision hyperplane is studied by computing:

$$\delta_i = \|\omega_{s0}\|^2 - \|\omega_{si}\|^2, \text{ for } i = 1,..., n \tag{2}$$

$\|\omega_{si}\|^2$ is the squared norm of the optimal weight vector of the separation (or regression) hyperplane when all features but the i-th one are used. If variable i is important for classification (or regression), its removal will result in a significant change in the resulting separation (or regression) hyperplane (Maldonado-Bascon, Khalifa, & Lopez-Ferreras 2003) and, consequently, in $\|\omega_{si}\|^2$. Therefore, the higher the value of δ_i is, the stronger is the effect of removing variable i in the decision (or regression) hyperplane. Those variables with higher associated δ are the most important for classification (or regression). Finally, variables are added to the classification (or regression) SVM model starting from the one with the highest δ. A new variable is included if this improves classification (or regression) results. The process ends when adding a new variable does not improve results. This can be considered as an embedded strategy for feature selection. When applied to the same Iberian ham database discussed above, the variable selection procedure led to a dramatic reduction (by a factor of 10) in the number of input features used by the SVM models and to a significant increase in classification performance. For example, from 80% (using all variables) to 90% (using a reduced set of variables) in the 11-category classification of Iberian hams, or reaching a 100% correct classification of hams from pigs fed on acorn or fodder. Additionally, the variable selection method helped to improve the performance of SVM models for regression. A good accuracy in the prediction of humidity, water activity and salt in ham samples was obtained. These results are summarized in Table 2.

The comparison of the two feature selection strategies applied to the same database reveals that the SVM-based approach selects twice as many features as the 3-step selection approach. The former results in a slightly lower classification success rate (90% instead of 97%) but at a fraction of the computational cost of the latter. Both the different number of features selected and the classifier model used (SVM vs. fuzzy ARTMAP) have an impact on the classification success rate.

Table 2. Validation results of the SVM-based regression models built to estimate humidity (model 1), water activity (model 2) and salt (model 3) in Iberian ham samples. The correlation coefficients of the linear regression between actual and predicted values are shown for models with and without variable selection. The last row shows, for each model, the average value of the correlation coefficients (computed over 6 folds). Adapted from Gualdron et al. (2007), with permission.

	Without variable selection			With variable selection		
Fold #	1	2	3	1	2	3
1	0.855	0.858	0.780	0.947	0.964	0.955
2	0.964	0.938	0.908	0.974	0.985	0.983
3	0.955	0.915	0.884	0.975	0.979	0.976
4	0.963	0.950	0.942	0.988	0.969	0.945
5	0.951	0.962	0.933	0.987	0.960	0.860
6	0.933	0.919	0.920	0.976	0.972	0.933
Average	0.937	0.924	0.894	0.975	0.972	0.943

Feature Selection for Gas Sensor Based Artificial Olfaction

The use of both static and dynamic features from the response of each sensor within the array has resulted in an explosion of the features that can be input to the pattern recognition (PARC) engine of a multi-sensor system. However, as stated in the Introduction of this chapter, the use of a high number of variables at the input of a PARC system does not necessarily guarantee better performance. In fact, using noisy or irrelevant variables can jeopardize the training phase and result in lower performance during the recognition phase. Therefore, the idea behind feature selection is to get rid of those response features that are redundant, noisy or irrelevant for the classification/quantification tasks envisaged, in such a way that the dimensionality of data can be reduced without loss of useful information.

Paulsson, Larson and Winquist (2000) used a multilayer perceptron (MLP) neural network based machine olfaction system to estimate ethanol concentration in breath samples. The sensor array consisted of 12 MOSFET, 4 metal oxide gas sensors and an infrared light absorption sensor. A sequential forward selection procedure was implemented to select important features from the sensor signals. The feature selection procedure is shown to improve accuracy by reducing the standard error of predicted ethanol concentration down to 15.3 ppm (prediction error decreases ~40%). Eklöv, Mårtensson and Lundström (1999) examined methods to select relevant variables from a large set of features from gas sensor signals. They used a sequential forward selection procedure coupled to a multilinear regression model to obtain good prediction accuracy from a MLP network in the monitoring of E. coli batch cultivation processes. For example, prediction error for biomass concentration was reduced from 0.089 g/l down to 0.070 g/l when feature selection was performed. They showed that this variable selection strategy outperformed the more classical dimensionality reduction achieved using score vectors of a principal component analysis or partial least squares as descriptors. Since the MLP network requires lengthy computation during training, the fitness function (i.e., a function that enables comparisons between different solutions to the variable selection problem) was not based on the MLP but on linear calibration models, which can be trained quickly. Brezmes and co-workers (2002) applied a straightforward feature selection procedure for the classification of olive oil samples using a metal oxide gas sensors based machine olfaction system. A figure of merit, which was based on a variance criterion, was computed. This figure of merit estimated the discrimination power of each feature by comparing the external variance (variance of a feature for measurements of different types of olive oils) to the internal variance (variance of a feature for replicate measurements of a given olive oil). Only the first five features with higher figure of merit, those with high external variance and low internal variance, were input to a fuzzy ARTMAP classifier and this improved oil discrimination performance to 80%. For example, performance in oil discrimination was 54% when all variables were used. Using the same variance criterion, Artursson and Holmberg (2002) showed that it was possible to effectively perform data compression from a pulsed-voltammetry based electronic tongue (e-tongue), since they could reduce by a factor of 18 in the number of features employed to build a classifier model aimed at predicting water quality. The reason for using the e-tongue was to use it to monitor water quality at different stages of the process undergone by water in a drinking water production plant. However, the use of a discrimination parameter based on the variance criterion did not prevent from informative but redundant features being selected. Therefore, an additional step for detecting the occurrence of redundancy or co-linearity among features would help further reducing the number of features.

Llobet et al. (2004) showed that it is possible to enhance the performance of fuzzy ARTMAP classifiers by performing a variable selection procedure based on cascaded GAs. In this approach a GAs feature selection is performed several times, where the i-th GAs selects among the features that have been selected by the $(i\text{-}1)$-th GAs. The procedure was shown to perform well in the classification of 3 volatile organic compounds using an array of 12 TGS sensors because it allowed for removing non-informative features that had been selected by the initial GAs. The method made it possible to reduce the number of variables used to build the classifiers from 120 down to 9, which significantly increased the generalization ability of the fuzzy ARTMAP classifier. The same group benchmarked different deterministic and stochastic feature selection approaches coupled to fuzzy ART-MAP and probabilistic neural network classifiers (Gualdrón et al. 2006). Selection algorithms such as forward, backward and stepwise selection were used with some success, but were easily trapped in a local minimum of the optimization process. GAs found the best solutions for the application envisaged but they required lengthy computation. While sequential selection algorithms converged in minutes, GAs for selection took several hours to convergence when a Pentium IV PC platform was used. A possible solution was introduced by defining a two-step procedure in which, initially, a Fisher's discriminant filter was implemented to eliminate non informative features. This resulted in a highly effective variable selection method and computing time was significantly shortened from several hours down to a few minutes. Gardner, Boilot and Hines (2005) compared the use of different variable selection techniques such as SFS, SBS and GAs to find a good subset of sensors within an array of 32 carbon-black polymer resistors. The methods were tested using a dataset consisting of samples from 6 bacteria species causing ocular infections. A modified GAs, where the number of sensors or features selected is set in advance, was shown to be accurate and fast at determining the sensors that should be used to discriminate bacteria.

Buratti et al. (2007) employed a conventional GAs to select features from a combination of metal oxide and amperometric machine olfaction system. The selected features were employed to build models able to predict red wine sensorial descriptors.

Perera and co-workers (2006) proposed a technique inspired by receptor convergence in the olfactory system. The algorithm is split in two stages. First two quality measures are computed, which describe the discrimination power and the confidence in the discrimination power of each feature. The second stage selects features according to these two measures. The grouping of features was performed in class-space constructed with information that takes into account the relationship between the mean and variance for each feature. The algorithm was shown to be efficient even when a high number of features, i.e. 3000 features, and a small sample set, i.e. 27 measurements, were available. More recently, Pardo and Sberveglieri (2007) employed exhaustive search to evaluate the classification performance of coffee aroma using a 6-element metal oxide gas sensor array. They systematically studied different 5-feature subsets derived from 30 features (i.e. 127,260 combinations) using 3-nearest neighbor clustering as classifier model. This exhaustive study was feasible in this particular case because the total number of features available was moderate, i.e. 30.

SENSOR SELECTION AND SENSOR ARRAY OPTIMIZATION TECHNIQUES

Odorant chemo-sensors interact with various types of analytes and show a large variety of response patterns (Persaud & Dodd 1982). These devices can serve not only as simplified distributed olfactory systems, but also as non-invasive detectors in a wide range of applications, such as process control, medical diagnosis and the detection of explosives (Persaud et al 1982, Gardner & Bartlett, 1999, Freund & Lewis 1995, Dickinson et al. 1996). The capabilities of odor sensors are broad and include many challenging tasks such as discriminating organic compounds with chain lengths that differ by a single carbon atom (White et al. 1996, Persaud & Travers 1997). However, their limitations in characterizing odor-stimuli including the poor sensitivity to analytes and the lack of reproducibility in their responses in repeated trials are still very serious (Moseley & Tofield 1987). Among the different strategies implemented to overcome these apparent limitations, the interaction with the conditioning parameters at the sensor level (e.g., working temperature for metal-oxide gas sensors) has been remarkably successful in many critical applications (Moseley et al. 1987).

In principle, almost every odorant sensing technology offers the advantage of being tunable through the selection of parameter values. Interacting with such parameters influences many critical qualities of the measurement, including sensitivity to analytes and reproducibility. For example, the temperature modulation technique, for metal-oxide gas sensors, takes advantage of such a relationship to enrich the information content of the sensor, since it directly alters the reaction kinetics at the sensor surface in the presence of an odorant (Sears et al. 1990, Sears et al. 1989b, Nakata, Kaneda, Yoshikawa 1992, Nakata et al. 1996, Nakata, Ozaki, & Ojima 1998, Semancik & Cavicchi 1999). A thorough understanding of how such interactions take place in the chemo-sensory system requires quantitative characterizations of the response of individual sensors, both within and among chemical stimuli. This approach will enable us to generalize the relationship between the control variable and the target quality.

Once the odorant-sensing/parameter interaction is known (or can be inferred from previous observations), a natural avenue to follow is the optimization of the chemo-sensory system with respect to a solid criterion that properly expresses the observed goal. A number of approaches under the notion of optimization have been implemented in the literature, but only a handful of authors have approached the problem in a systematic fashion. Such a criterion will be taken into account as we proceed further here.

Before embarking upon the subject of optimization, we would like to make a final point in the context of terminology. The label 'optimization' has been very popular for many years when used to describe the terms of 'sensor optimization' and 'sensor-array optimization' indistinctly. We believe, however, that this terminology can be very misleading, since the former mostly refers to finding the 'optimal operational condition' of the sensor device, while the latter usually means selecting an 'optimal' combination of sensors between a potentially large pool of different sensors that are best suited to the identification task; i.e. very much like feature selection. Therefore, although these two groups of procedures are fully complementary and valuable tools of analytical chemistry, they deserve to be treated as two separate topics. In this section we review both. Moreover, an overview of the operating temperature dependence for the response of semiconductor gas sensors has also been included as an appendix. In order to gain a better understanding of how the optimization processes are occurring at the sensor level, or even to discuss whether the processes are or are not working, we strongly recommend that the reader reviews the appendix to this chapter.

Initial Methods

Corcoran, Lowery, & Anglesea (1998) applied a triangular waveform (4.16 mHz) to modulate the operating temperature of 8 commercially available gas sensors (from Figaro Engineering Inc., Japan, http://www.figaro.co.jp) between 250 and 500°C. They extracted features from the sensor transients using two approaches. The first one consisted of sub-sampling the response transients obtaining a 26-point vector (equivalent to 10°C steps) per transient. The second approach consisted of calculating 8 secondary features from each response transient, such as the time to maximum value, time to minimum value, maximum positive slope, etc. An optimization procedure was then implemented to determine which sensors and features should be used to better classify the aromas from three loose leaf teas using a neural network classifier. The optimization process consisted of applying a GAs for variable selection (Davis 1991). Applying this technique, the authors showed that it was possible to reach a high success rate in tea classification (93%) using only 21 dynamic features out of the 208 features available. However, the optimization of the temperature-modulating signal (frequency, temperature range and waveform type) is not considered by the authors. Had this optimization been envisaged, further improvements in classification performance would have been obtained.

More recently, Fort, et al. (2002) and (2003) used temperature modulated metal oxide gas sensors (using a pure sinusoidal signal) to show that the selection of the signal frequency was of paramount importance for gas identification. If the temperature of the sensors is varied relatively quickly in comparison with the chemical response time, the sensor resistance varies as a function of temperature with an exponential law (characteristic of metal oxides). In such a case the response shape has only a slight dependence on the chemical environment. On the other hand, when the operating temperature varies slowly compared to the chemical response time, the response profile is given by a series of quasi-stationary chemical responses. The best discrimination among the species studied (vapors from water solutions containing ethanol and other volatile organic compounds) was obtained by selecting a temperature profile with a period close to that for the chemical response time of the sensor. These results suggested that the effectiveness of the temperature modulation analysis depends on the period of the sine wave that must be chosen in agreement to the chemical reaction rate of each sensor. Similar results were found by other authors using different temperature modulation signals such as pulse, trapezoid, triangular and saw-tooth (Choi et al. 2002, Huang et al. 2003). By experimenting with different modulation frequencies (50, 30, 40 and 20 mHz), Huang et al. (2003) showed that as the modulating frequency was lowered down to 20 mHz, specific response patterns developed. This suggests that a low-frequency temperature modulation alters the kinetics of adsorption, diffusion and reaction phenomena occurring at the sensor surface, i.e. alters the interaction of odorous compounds and the gas-sensitive surface.

Sensor-Array Optimization

A wide variety of sensors and feature extraction methods that are available to the experimenter, when considering a new sensing problem, have been described in previous sections of this chapter. However, when one is working with an array of non-specific sensors, the biggest concern to the experimenter is the number of sensors that need to be considered when a chemo-sensory array is to be formed. One approach might be to augment an existing array by adding sensors appropriate to the new task. However, this is a computationally expensive and potentially wasteful solution because using more sensors does not guarantee improved performance. A conceivable way to address this issue is to design an optimal array of sensors (even comprising completely different sensing technologies) that promote the maximum accuracy with which the sensory system can estimate the stimulus; or optimally discriminate between neighboring stimuli. A number of theoretical studies, concerned with the notion of 'array optimization', have been performed and described in the literature and can be explored when one is approaching to a new odor identification scenario. One of the pioneering investigations in this context is the one presented by Zaromb and Stetter (1984). They proposed, over 20 years ago, a theoretical model to estimate the minimum number of parameters $P = (S$ sensors $\times M$ operating modes) that would be required to discriminate a mixture of up to A analytes from a pool of n different odorants. By assuming that the response of each sensor is noiseless and binary related to each odor stimulus (i.e., response/no response), they argued that a combinatorial measure of the number of sensors required to detect a given number of chemical species as

$$2^p - 1 \geq \sum_{i=1}^{A} \frac{n!}{(n-i)!\,i!} \tag{3}$$

A 'rule of thumb' is proposed in their work, according to which sensors and operating modes should be selected so that each of the P parameters does not respond to more than P/A individual compounds. Similar to this assumption are the simulation results further obtained by Alkasab, White, and Kauer (2002). In a seminal paper, Niebling and Müller (1995) proposed to use an inverse feature space to design sensor arrays. In this inverse feature space, each of the n analytes is represented as a separate dimension, and each of the s sensors is represented as a point in this n-dimensional space. The authors show that this visual representation enables the experimenter to detect potential discrimination problems and to design new sensors to address these problems. Gardner and Bartlett (1996) proposed a computational model for cross-selective sensors that also considers the effects of noise and errors. An upper limit of the number of analytes that can be discriminated by a given array was estimated by using the ratio between the total volume of the sensor space and the volume made up by the sensor errors. A measure of performance was proposed, which was essentially equivalent to the classical Fisher's linear discriminant analysis ratio; i.e., the ratio of between-class distance to within-class variance.

It was not until the early 2000s that Pearce and Sanchez-Montañes (2003) implemented for the first time an information-theoretic based approach for the optimization of chemo-sensory array systems. In particular, they demonstrated how the 'tunings' of individual sensors may affect the overall performance. In order to demonstrate the effects of noise and tuning on array performance, they have incorporated the concept of 'hyper-volume of accessible sensor space', (V_S), which is defined as the volume in sensor space that contains the sensor-array response to a specific set of analytes. For a three-odor by two-sensor problem, collinearity limits the number of possible sensor responses, as Figure 3 (a) suggests. Therefore, the maximum number of analyte mixtures that can be discriminated by the array is limited by the ratio between V_S and V_N, the hyper-volume defined by the accuracy of the sensor array, as is illustrated in Figure 3 (b).

Assuming that errors/noise do not exhibit any correlation with the analyte stimulus, the authors showed that the geometric interpretation in Figure 3 can be expressed by means of the Fisher information matrix (*FI*), defined as

Figure 3. (a) Visualization of a three-odor-to-two-sensor transformation. (b) The maximum number of feature vectors that can be discriminated is the ratio between the hyper-volume of the accessible sensor space (V_s) and the accuracy of the sensor array response. Figure reproduced with permission from Pearce et al. (2003) Copyright 2003 Wiley-VCH, Weinheim.

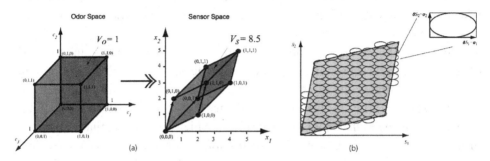

$$J_{i,j}(c) = \int p(x \mid c)\left(\frac{\partial}{\partial c_i} \ln p(x \mid c)\right)\left(\frac{\partial}{\partial c_j} \ln p(x \mid c)\right) dx, \qquad (4)$$

where c is a vector containing the concentration of the analytes, x is the response of the sensor array to the stimulus c, and $p(x|c)$ is the conditional probability of observing the sensor response x upon a given stimulus c. *FI* is important in this context, because it provides a lower bound (i.e., best-case case) on the accuracy with which the stimulus, c, can be predicted from the sensor response, x. This lower limit has been determined as

$$\operatorname{var}(\hat{c} \mid c) = \sum_{i=1}^{S}\left(J^{-1}(c)\right)_{ii} \qquad (5)$$

where '*var*' means variance, and $\hat{c}$ is the estimation/prediction of the component i of c, $i = 1,..., N$. This result is called the 'Cramér-Rao Bound' and limits the performance of the best unbiased estimator that can be built.

In order to use these theoretical constructs in practice, the first stage one should perform is the formal description of the sensory context C and a clear specification of the task. The context C quantitatively describes the likelihood of occurrence of each odor stimulus, whereas the chemosensory task is an interpretation of the sensory response (i.e., either a quantification or identification task). Then, one would assume a parametric density $p(x|c)$ for each individual sensor, estimate the parameters from experimental data (i.e., by measuring the sensor array responses to a number of analyte mixtures), compute *FI* using Equation (4), and finally compute the expected accuracy of the array using Equation (5). This accuracy estimate would then be used as a 'figure of merit' to select an optimal array configuration from a pool of cross-selective sensors. Once this 'optimal' array has been found, a catalog of parameters for each sensor used within practical systems today may be envisaged, which would make the optimization of sensory array systems to particular detection tasks a simple and routine operation.

More recently, in the same domain of information theory, Muezzinoglu et al. (2010) introduced a sensor array optimization scheme for odor identification. The authors demonstrated the effects of tuning the sensor's operating parameter in a chemo-sensory array by incorporating a measure-index widely used in signal theory, namely the Mahalanobis distance (*MD*), which gives a quantitative measure of the separability among probability distributions. Since chemo-sensory records associated to a given odor-class have certain variability regardless of the features selected, they can be assumed to be probability distributions that log the history of each sensor in response to a specific odor-class over a feature space. Therefore, optimizing this index over a controllable operating parameter (e.g. the operating temperature in metal-oxide gas sensors) of the sensory array, results in improving the classificatory capabilities of the sensor, i.e., maximizing the spread of the class prototypes (the class centers) in the feature space while the response variability within each class is minimized.

To demonstrate their scheme, the authors first assumed a two-odor class formulation, where all possible measurements may belong to one of the two disjoint classes C_1 and C_2 in a specific feature space. Then, given a sample x^s, their goal was to determine accurately which one of the two-class-conditional distributions $f(x|C_1)$, $f(x|C_2)$ is more likely to have produced x^s. The squared *MD* between two-class-conditional distributions is given by

$$D^2\left(C_1, C_2\right) = \left(\mu_1 - \mu_2\right)^T S_{1,2}^{-1} \left(\mu_1 - \mu_2\right) \tag{6}$$

where $\mu_i = \langle x|C_i \rangle$, $i = 1, 2$, are the class centers and $S_{1,2}$ is the weighted average of the two covariance matrices S_1 and S_2 associated to the two-class-conditional distributions. The *MD* is proportional to the distance between-class centers (the between-class scatter) and inversely proportional to the individual co-variances (the within-class scatters). For normally distributed classes, *MD* constitutes the best possible quantification of the overlap. In this case, the index also becomes the most accurate indicator of the classification performance for any unbiased classifier in the sense that the probability of misclassification is in inverse proportion with the *MD* value.

In a more generic case, i.e., when the number of classes is greater than two, the between-class scatter component of *MD* that promotes the dispersion of class centers can be generalized by the sum of their pair-wise distances, thus,

$$MD^2 = \sum_{i,j=1}^{|C|} D^2\left(C_i, C_j\right) \tag{7}$$

where $|C|$ denotes the number of classes in the problem.

Since the class-conditional distributions are unknown to the designer, it is important to be able to estimate the *MD* value from previous observations; i.e., previous measurements. Being dependent on the mean and variance, the sample *MD* is obtained by substituting these two moments by their sample estimates:

$$MD^2 = \sum_{i,j=1}^{|C|} \left(\hat{\mu}_i - \hat{\mu}_j\right)^T \hat{S}_{i,j}^{-1}\left(\hat{\mu}_i - \hat{\mu}_j\right) \tag{8}$$

here $C=\{1,\ldots,|C|\}$ denote the class labels, where class $i \in C$ is represented by n_i pre-recorded samples. Each class centre $\hat{\mu}_i$ is approximated by the sample average of all samples in class i. The joint covariance $S_{i,j}$ is given by

$$\hat{S}_{i,j} = \frac{n_i \hat{S}_i + n_j \hat{S}_j}{n_i + n_j - 2} \tag{9}$$

being $\hat{S}_i$ the sample covariance matrix, i.e., the average of the outer products of the observations in class i.

Intuitively, *MD* quantifies the difficulty of the classification problem. When this quantity is large, an arbitrary classifier is expected to perform with higher accuracy, since, relative to a small *MD*, the distributions within each class is shrunk (the within-class scatter is small) and/or the two classes are located away from each other in the feature space (i.e., the between-class scatter is large).

With θ being a parameter of a sensor array that alters the response characteristics, the problem configuration is then expected to be sensitive to this operating parameter; making, therefore, *MD* dependent on θ. Hence, the value

$$\theta^* = \arg\max_{\theta} MD^2\left(\theta\right) \tag{10}$$

Figure 4. (a) Feature maps obtained for three operating temperatures as indicated by θ on each figure. The two features (i.e., axes) used in this representation are the transient features extracted from the response x_1 of TGS2600 and x_2 of TGS2610. Each of the analyte classes contain 10 samples, which are labeled with a different colour/shape on the maps. (b) $MD^2(\theta)$ evaluations estimated from the dataset for 11 heater voltages. Figure reprinted from Muezzinoglu et al (2010), Copyright (2010), with permission from Elsevier Science.

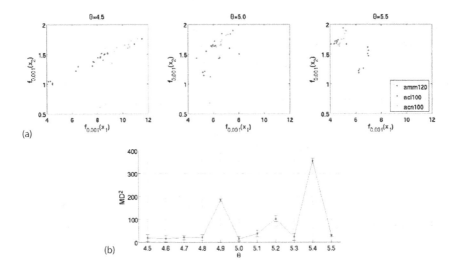

defines an optimum operating condition for the classification problem at hand, see Figure 4.

Moreover, the form of dependence of *MD* on θ is initially unknown, yet to be inferred from a provided training set containing labeled measurements from the same sensor array at representative θ values. Therefore, any change in the problem setup, e.g., addition or removal of an analyte class, necessitates a re-calculation of θ* with the updated dataset. A consequence of this is that the sensor array must be re-conditioned for each class configuration, meaning that the solution is customized to the set of analytes being analyzed.

Although this optimization criterion is applicable to any number and complexity of probability distributions, hence, to any type and number of odorants, as well as any sensor technology with a conditioning parameter, the authors have shown the applicability of their approach to a particular three-class classification problem, i.e., ethanol, acetaldehyde and ammonia. Figure 4 (a) shows the maps of 30 samples, grouped with respect to their class labels, to the selected feature space for heater voltage values applied to the sensor array. As this example shows, the three classes move and change their relative positions with the temperature, making the classes easier or more difficult to separate along the sweep. Note also that the two sensor responses can be highly correlated at certain temperatures and uncorrelated at others. As a measure of separability, the evaluation of the *MD* estimate, given in Equation (10), for the triple of classes at each operating temperature, labeled as the parameter θ, yields the profile shown in Figure 4 (b). Based on this evaluation, the best operating condition to distinguish among the triple of classes is determined by the maximum of this curve, which occurs at θ=5.4 V, i.e., the best voltage applied to the sensor heater that yields the optimal sensor's operating temperature.

Finally, the sole reason for such an example was its non-triviality found when performing the classification task within the range of the selected parameters i.e., operating temperature. Nevertheless, the method could be extended to an arbitrary classification instance as needed, including complex odors at different concentrations or mixtures of gases, provided that a sufficiently representative database of relevant measurements is available.

Using a similar statistical argument, Raman et al. (2009) developed an optimization method to design micro-sensing arrays for complex chemical sensing tasks. The method consisted of using statistical methods to systematically assess the analytical information obtained from the conductometric responses of chemo-resistive elements at different operating temperatures, i.e., the similarity/orthogonality of responses; test their reproducibility; determine an optimal set of material compositions to be incorporated within an array of sensors for the recognition of individual species. They presented qualitative and quantitative approaches to determine both the sufficiency of the chosen materials for sensing targets in the test matrix and an optimal array configuration for the desired application.

In order to optimize the array configuration, the authors presented a modular approach, which includes a sophisticated temperature pattern, see Figure 5 (a), and micro-hotplate platforms with different metal oxide chemo-resistors, see Figure 5 (b), to examine a target matrix with five high-priority chemical hazards; that is ammonia, hydrogen cyanide, chlorine, ethylene oxide, and cyanogen chloride. The temperature program used to operate the sensing elements toggles the temperature between (*a*) 32 ramp values that sample most of the temperature range of the device and (*b*) four different baseline temperature values to allow relaxation toward some initial state prior to each ramp temperature. Moreover, different baselines allow different film-analyte interactions; adsorption/desorption, decomposition, and reaction at the sensing surface prior to the ramp measurements. Then, they defined the following objective function with three components:

$$O = \gamma_1 J - \gamma_2 N_1 - \gamma_3 N_2 \qquad (11)$$

Figure 5. (a) Temperature program used for the detection of high-priority chemical hazards. A conductance measurement was made at each base and ramp temperature, but only the ramp values were used for further analysis in this study. (b) Microsensor array platform. A layered schematic showing the three primary components of the microsensor elements: polycrystalline silicon heater, interdigitated platinum electrodes, and metal oxide sensing film. Figure reprinted from Raman et al (2009), Copyright (2009), with permission from Elsevier Science.

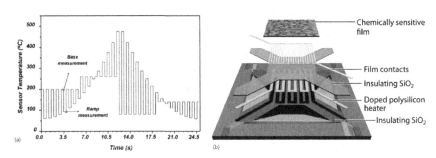

where J is the maximization term that takes into account the sufficiency of solution; i.e., separability of the five chemical analyte clusters from different background conditions and from each other, N_1 and N_2 are two penalty terms that symbolize the number of different materials used and the array size respectively, and γ_1, γ_2, and γ_3, are component weights. The two penalty terms allow comparison between solutions with different numbers of materials and array sizes. In order to be able to increase the objective function, each new material or array element must increase the analyte's cluster separability sufficiently to compensate for its 'cost'. This cluster separability is derived from Fisher's LDA as follows:

$$J = \frac{trace(S_B)}{trace(S_B) + trace(S_W)} \tag{12}$$

where S_W and S_B are the within-cluster and between-cluster scatter matrices, respectively. Being the ratio of the spread between classes relative to the spread within each class, the measure J increases monotonically as classes become increasingly more separable.

With this, the authors were able to demonstrate that cycling each sensing film through the 32 temperatures shown in Figure 5 (a) did not necessarily create information that spanned 32 different dimensions. The responses were highly correlated and information seemed to be grouped based on temperature ranges; all lower temperature responses of a film type provide similar information that differs from that available from high temperature signals. On the other hand, cross-correlations computed across materials were comparatively lower than self-correlations. Therefore, taken together with the results from the dimensionality reduction analysis, this suggests that different materials provide orthogonal information about the target analytes.

To summarize, the statistical methods presented in this section provided a generalizable methodology for designing and evaluating such array-based solutions for a wide variety of specific detection problems. These advances are critical to the production of pre-programmed micro-sensors for non-invasive, real-time, multi-species recognition relevant to homeland security and other applications involving trace analyte detection in complex chemical cocktails.

On The Optimization of Chemical Sensors

Much less attention has been paid to the optimization of metal-oxide sensors as a single device. As stated at the beginning of Section 4, and more specifically in subsection 4.1, there are a large number of articles reporting empirical studies dealing with dynamic features obtained from transient responses: e.g., different temperature waveforms patterns and stimulus frequencies implemented as a countermeasure to the effects of selectivity and reproducibility encountered in gas sensors. There is no doubt that a high variance in response is detrimental in most chemo-transduction applications that must be tackled. This general treatment, though, constitutes only one facet of the sensor optimization problem that does not necessarily yield better performance in the odor identification task. The reason for this is that a reduction in the response variance does not ensure a non-overlapping class configuration in the feature space. Therefore, to maximize classification performance, one needs a more comprehensive formulation that quantifies the separation of specific odor classes in the sensor response. Both of these aspects have been covered in literature under the notion of optimization. The thematic issues relevant to the previous work will be reviewed here.

Optimization of Excitation Profiles

Chemical sensing can benefit from a variable-temperature signal generation. In most of the cases, the temperature variation (a.k.a. temperature modulation) has been approached empirically by implementing various temperatures waveforms and stimulus frequencies (Sears et al. 1990, Sears et al. 1989a, Sears et al. 1989b, Nakata et al. 1992, Nakata et al. 1996, Nakata et al. 1998, Semancik et al. 1999). Although the results achieved by such a technique are very promising, in most of the reported works the selection of waveforms and the frequencies used to modulate sensor temperature has been conducted in a non-systematic way (Cocoran et al. 1998, Davis 1991, Fort et al. 2002, Fort et al. 2003, Choi et al. 2002, Huang et al. 2003). Even the selection of features from the sensor transients is a somewhat obscure process. Therefore, since these selections are based on a trial and error procedure, there is no way to ensure that the modulation frequencies, modulation depth or features chosen are the optimal for a given application. Very few authors, though, have systematically addressed this problem by suggesting different optimization strategies.

The first approach to reviewed, in this context, is the one implemented by Kunt, et al. (1998) and Cavicchi et al. (1996), who developed an optimization method for micro-hotplate devices. In temperature programmed sensing, a sequence of pulses of increasing amplitudes are input to the heating element of the micro-hotplate and the sensor resistance is acquired at room temperature; i.e., between two consecutive pulses. The objective was to optimize the sequence by adapting the pulse amplitude, pulse duration, delay between two consecutive pulses and number of pulses in a cycle to better discriminate between ethanol and methanol vapors. In a first step, black-box dynamic models based on input-output data were developed in order to predict the sensor responses in the presence of ethanol and methanol for a given temperature profile. Among the different dynamic modeling methods studied, the wavelet network (WNET) method was the most accurate. The WNET combines the multi-resolution feature of the wavelet transform with artificial neural networks with one hidden layer. Such a neural network was able to approximate any function to an arbitrary accuracy. In this particular case, the Mexican hat wavelet was used as analyzing wavelet, and coefficients from the first four scales were selected by stepwise selection to form the initial model structure.

This initial model was further trained to set the parameter values of the neural network. The predictive models for ethanol and methanol were used in an off-line optimization scheme, where an optimal temperature profile for vapor discrimination was computed and validated. Given a temperature profile u, yMeOH and yEtOH are the conductance responses predicted by the WNET models for methanol and ethanol, respectively. Since the predicted responses for each gas are functional mappings that depend on the temperature profile u, the optimization can be formulated as finding u that maximizes the distance between yMeOH and yEtOH. The metric used to quantify this distance is the normalized sum of squared differences (NSSD) between two response curves:

$$\text{NSSD} = \sum_{i=1}^{n} \left(y_i^{\text{MeOH}} - y_i^{\text{EtOH}} \right)^2 \Big/ n \qquad (13)$$

where n is the number of temperature pulses in a cycle.

The search space for the optimal temperature profile is over a limited subset of realizable temperature pulses; e.g., lower and upper limits are chosen based on the sensor structure; and under the constraint that two consecutive pulses cannot differ in more than 40°C in order to avoid drastic changes in the surface. Figure 6 shows the optimal temperature profile to discriminate ethanol and methanol that was computed and validated through experimental measurements. This temperature profile; see the temperature profile shown in parts (c) and (d) of Figure 6; produces methanol and ethanol responses that are out of phase; i.e., easy to discriminate. On the other hand, when applying a simple linear ramp (see parts (a) and (b) of Figure 6), the sensor responses to ethanol and methanol are highly overlapping; i.e., becoming a non-trivial case of discrimination.

Although this methodology is systematic and should be applicable to other analytes, its application to the qualitative and quantitative analysis of multi-component mixtures is not straightforward. The fact that the method relies on the construction of good predictive response models complicates the optimization process for multi-gas, concentration variant environments.

More recently, Vergara et al. (2005a, 2005b, 2007, 2008) introduced a system-identification method for optimizing the temperature-modulation frequencies in order to solve a given gas analysis problem. The optimization method consisted of using one of the most useful types of periodic signal for process identification, the pseudo-

Figure 6. (a) Normalized conductance response to methanol (solid) and ethanol (dashed) upon applying a linear temperature ramp as shown in (b). (c) Actual experiments with methanol (solid line) and ethanol (dashed line) gases, model predictions are shown by circles for methanol and plus for ethanol models; (d) the optimum temperature profile derived from the off-line optimization process. Note the dramatic improvement in discrimination between (a) and (c). Figure reprinted from Kunt et al (1998), Copyright (1998), with permission Elsevier Science.

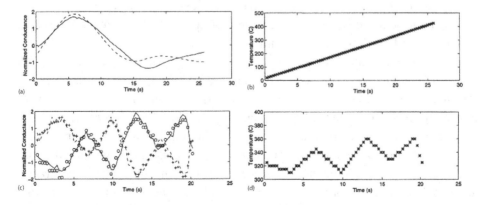

random sequences of maximum length (PRS-ML), either binary or multi-level, to determine the most suitable temperature-modulation frequencies for discriminating and quantifying a number of specific target compounds at different concentrations.

Pseudo-random sequence signals have been used as test signals in system identification for many years. The most common application is the identification of linear systems using pseudo-random binary sequences (PRBS), which have excellent correlation properties for this purpose (Vergara et al. 2005a). In a similar fashion to PRBS, multi-level pseudo-random sequences (MLPRS) are also periodic, deterministic signals, having a flat power spectrum over a large frequency range, which makes them very suitable for system identification. These properties imply that a PRS-ML shares some properties with white noise, but have the advantage of being repeatable. One of the main reasons for considering signals with more than 2 levels is that they can provide a better estimate than is the case with binary sequences of the linear dynamics of a process with non-linearity and they can also be of use in the identification of the non-linear characteristics themselves (Vergara et al. 2005b, Vergara et al. 2007).

The pseudo-random signal sequences considered by the authors are based on maximum-length q-sequences, the generation and properties of which were described by Zierler (1959). The relevant theory behind PRS-ML is based on the algebra of finite fields. When q (the number of levels) is a prime, the digits of the sequence are the integers $0, 1, \ldots, (q-1)$ and the sequence can be generated by a q-level, n-stage shift register with feedback to the first stage consisting of the modulo q sum of the outputs of the other stages multiplied by coefficients $a_1, \ldots, a_n$ which are also the integers $0, 1, \ldots, (q-1)$. The length (or period) of a maximum-length sequence is $q^n - 1$. In other words, after $q^n - 1$ logic values, the sequence repeats itself. The generator of such a sequence and an example of a 5-level sequence (fragment) are shown in Figure 7 (a) and (b), respectively. The initial state of the shift register can be any combination of length n of the values $0, 1, \ldots, (q-1)$, exception made of n = zeros. Each combination of these values (except n zeros) appears as the state of the register exactly once during a period of the PRS-ML (Godfrey 1993).

The impulse response, $h(t)$, is the main descriptor of a linear invariant system. Among the different strategies to estimate the impulse response, noise based methods allow to excite the system under study for enough time to supply it with the necessary energy to obtain a good estimate of $h(t)$. Using white noise as the excitation signals ensures that there is a homogeneous distribution of the energy over a large frequency range. Since PRS-ML signals have a low crest factor (i.e. low peak-to-average factor) they minimize the risk of saturating the system under study. In practice, this means that the signals contain energy enough to obtain a good signal-to-noise ratio in a wide frequency range (i.e., measurement with high dynamic range) and avoid possible sensor non-linearity caused by signals with high crest factors;

Figure 7. (a) A q-level pseudo-random maximum length sequence generator. (b) Fragment of a 5-level pseudo random sequence. (c) Discrete power spectrum of a PRS-ML signal. Spectral resolution is f_c/L, where f_c is the frequency of the clock signal applied to the shift register and L is the length of the sequence. Figure reprinted from Vergara et al. (2007), Copyright (2007), with permission Elsevier Science.

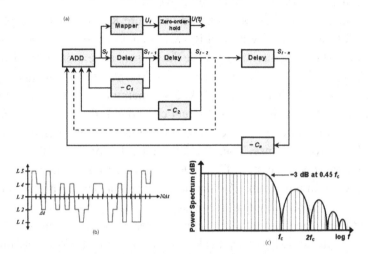

e.g., impulsive signals. Furthermore, because the noise signal is deterministic, reproducible results would be obtained, provided that the conditions of the system under analysis remain unchanged.

The power spectrum envelope of a PRS-ML is almost flat up to a frequency equal to $0.45 \times f_c$, where f_c is the frequency of the clock signal applied to the shift register used to generate the signal. The power spectrum is discrete and the separation between spectral lines (i.e., the spectral resolution) is f_c/L, where L is the length of the PRS-ML. The power spectrum envelope is similar to the power spectrum of white noise up to the −3 dB cut-off frequency, which is equal to $0.45 \times f_c$. Figure 7 (c) shows the power spectrum of a PRS-ML signal.

When the pseudo random sequence is a maximum length signal, the impulse response estimate, $\hat{h}(n)$, can be obtained by computing the circular cross-correlation between the excitatory signal, $x(n)$, and the response signal, $y(n)$. The circular cross-correlation of two sequences x and y in $\mathbb{R}^L$ may be defined as:

$$\hat{h}(n) = \frac{1}{L}\sum_{l=0}^{L-1} y(l+n)x(l), \qquad n = 0, 1, 2, \cdots, L-1, \tag{14}$$

The cross-correlation is circular since *l+n* is interpreted as modulo L, where L is the length of the sequence. In Equation (14), L is a normalization factor that is optional. The circular cross-correlation between input and output sequences can readily be interpreted in terms of $\hat{h}(n)$ because the autocorrelation function of the PRS-ML signal is of approximately impulsive form.

The optimization method is illustrated in Figure 8, and in a practical instance it works as follows. First, a voltage PRS-ML signal is applied to the heating element of a micro-hotplate gas sensor while the sensors are exposed to various target compounds (e.g., nitrogen dioxide, ammonia, ethylene, ethanol, acetaldehyde, and their binary mixtures); therefore its working temperature is modulated over a wide frequency range. For each individual target compound, the impulse response $h(t)$ is computed as the circular cross-correlation between the excitation signal (PRS-ML) and the sensor response. Then the absolute value of the FFT of the impulse response estimates is calculated. This is done in order to determine which spectral components contain important information for the identification and quantification of gases. Second, each individual frequency is ranked on the basis of its information content (between-class to within-class scatter ratio), and a subset of the most informative frequencies is selected. The authors show that this procedure can be used to discriminate and quantify various gases and their mixtures using even a single sensor with its optimized set of modulating frequencies.

The authors further demonstrated the consistency and robustness of the optimization method by performing a completely independent validation procedure. The

Figure 8. Study of the sensor/gas system using MLPRS signals. The MLPRS voltage signal, x(n), is input to the heating element of a micro-hotplate gas sensor. The transient of the sensor conductance (i.e. the response in the presence of gases), y(n), is recorded. An estimate of the impulse response, $\hat{h}(n)$, can be computed via the circular cross-correlation of x(n) and y(n). Finally, by performing the FFT of $\hat{h}(n)$, the spectral components of the impulse response estimate are found. Figure reprinted from Vergara et al. (2007), Copyright (2007), with permission Elsevier Science.

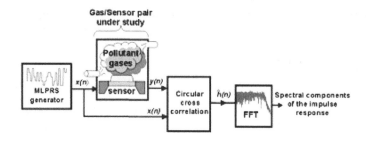

optimization process was conducted using a micro-sensor array and the validation process employed the use of a different sensor array (of the same type) and a new set of measurements. This new set of measurements was based on a temperature-modulating multi-sinusoidal signal showed in Figure 9 (a), the frequencies of which were a reduced set of the optimal ones. Figure 9 (b) and (c) show the FFT spectra of the transient response of a sensor in the presence of two different analytes (acetaldehyde (50 ppm) and ethylene (50 ppm)). The peaks in these plots correspond to the 'optimal' temperature-modulating frequencies selected. As the figure suggests (see variation of peaks' height (i.e. the pattern) in panels (b) and (c)), their results showed significant improvements in the classification and quantification capability of a single gas sensor operated under the temperature modulation scheme.

Figure 9. (a) Setup used to generate a multi-sinusoidal signal, which consists of the sum of 6 sinusoids of identical amplitudes and different frequencies. The signal is applied to the heating element of the micro-sensors studied. FFT (absolute value) of the transient response of a temperature-modulated WO₃ micro-hotplate sensor in the presence of (b) 50 ppm acetaldehyde and (c) 50 ppm ethylene. Figure reprinted from Vergara et al. (2007, 2008), Copyright (2007) and 87, Copyright (2008), with permission Elsevier Science.

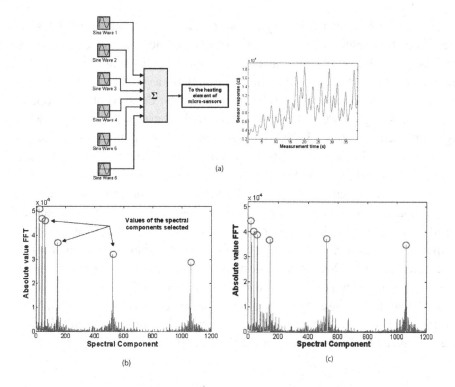

Particularly their results revealed a classification performance of up to 98.2% even when a single sensor is used, and a shift of the odor concentration prediction of down to 0.92 ppm for single species and 2.81 ppm for binary mixtures. These illustrated performance improvements were expected, though, in the sense that, as the panels (b) and (c) of Figure 9 show, a different pattern develops when different odorant species are measured, whereas the resulting pattern is preserved to a large extent when the vapors concentrations change, meaning that the illustrated evaluation is a reliable indicator of the improvement of the classification capability of the sensors when their operating temperature is modulated at the frequencies selected.

Finally, it was demonstrated that for each gas-sensor pair, the modulating frequencies selected are related to the characterization of the interaction between the metal oxide layer and the gas, e.g. film microstructure; surface diffusion; and reaction kinetics. Even though the method was implemented for the analysis of the specific qualitative and quantitative task earlier described, this optimization procedure is generic and it could be applied to many qualitative and quantitative gas analysis applications.

Optimization of the Operating Temperature: Internally Tuning the Chemical Sensors

It has long been known that varying or setting different values of the sensors' operating temperature influences many critical qualities and aspects of the sensor response, including its selectivity and sensitivity to different volatile compounds (i.e., the sensor's ability to encode the odor information), as well as its reproducibility. For example, carbon monoxide (CO) is usually best detected at lower operation temperatures (e.g., 250°C) when using a tin dioxide based sensitive layer, whereas higher temperatures (e.g., 350°C) are typically used for monitoring hydrocarbons such as methane. In view of this, different strategies, such as the idea of periodically changing the sensor working temperature, have been implemented to maximize the performance of the sensors. However, despite the promising results obtained in all this previously cited attempts, one question remains unanswered: given a metal-oxide based chemical sensor, how does one select the best (i.e., the optimal) operating temperature (or temperatures) for fast and reliable discrimination or quantification of chemical species? One conceivable manner to address this issue is to empirically vary the operating temperature through all the possible values available in the sensor such that its response to each gas is maximized (Cavicchi et al. 1996, Maziarz and Pisarkiewicz 2008). However, this is an expensive and inefficient solution that does not guarantee the improvement of the performance of the sensors.

Undoubtedly, heightened sensitivity to a spectrum of chemical hazards is necessary for the detection of analytes at relevant concentrations. However, this general treatment constitutes only one facet of the problem, a substantial selectivity is also necessary to rapidly and accurately perform the odor identity representation task. The reason for this is that, an increase in the response does not ensure a non-overlapping class configuration in the feature space. Therefore, to maximize the classification performance, one needs a more comprehensive formulation that quantifies the separation of specific odor classes in the sensor response.

With this motivation, Vergara et al. (2009, 2010) formulated an optimization method to select, for a single sensor, the best operating temperature to discriminate a given set of odorants. The authors presented a rigorous way of selecting the best operating temperature for a chemo-sensor. The method hinges on an information measure widely used in information theory, namely the relative entropy or Kullback-Leibler divergence (*KL*-divergence) (Kullback & Leibler 1951), which gives a measure of the difference between two distributions. These probability distributions may belong to one of the disjoint classes of interest in a particular odor universe. Thus, a quantitative measure of how odors are encoded in every odorant chemo-receptor and how distinguishable they are from each other at different parameter values was given. Tuning a control parameter, such as the sensor's operating temperature, will maximize such a difference, yielding thus a substantial improvement in the classification performance (separation of classes) and reproducibility. In particular, using a metal oxide gas sensor in an odor-discrimination instance, the authors demonstrated the proposed criterion by studying the impact of adjusting the sensing parameter on the odor-sensor pair interaction and on the confidence of the information yielded by the sensor individually.

The *KL*-divergence is a very well-known index for class separation that is a non-commutative measure (a 'distance' in a heuristic sense) of the difference between two distributions: a conceptual reality (probability distribution $g(\cdot)$) and an approximate model (probability distribution $h(\cdot)$). For two continuous functions qualifying as probability distributions, the *KL*-divergence is defined by the integral:

$$KL(g \,||\, h) = \int_{-\infty}^{\infty} g(x) \log \frac{g(x)}{h(x)}\, dx, \tag{15}$$

where *KL* is the measure of 'information' lost when a model $h(\cdot)$ is used to approximate reality (i.e., model $g(\cdot)$) (Kullback et al. 1951).

The utility of the *KL*-divergence is based on a certain number of properties that make it unique in measuring the difference between two probability distributions. For example, this approach can account for a number of key characteristics of a response. These include for example, higher order moments (e.g., skewness) or multi-modality, that may be involved in the response distribution (at least in odor representation), causing loss of information. However, the measure is still not commutative, i.e., $KL(g(x)\|h(x))$ is in general different from $KL(h(x)\|g(x))$; therefore, the *KL*-divergence is not a legitimate metric by itself. As a consequence, a symmetrized version, namely the *KL*-distance, can be readily composed after a straightforward manipulation:

$$KL(g,h) = \frac{1}{2} KL(g \parallel h) + \frac{1}{2} KL(h \parallel g), \tag{16}$$

which the authors adopted as a measure of the class-conditional distributions' separation for the specific purpose.

In a fixed problem context C (i.e., the likelihood of occurrence of each odor stimulus from a finite list of analytes whose classes are known), in which the discrimination problem is complicated by the similarities/overlaps among the class-conditional distributions, the *KL*-distance index, given in Equation (16), constitutes an accurate measure of discrimination, and hence is a good indicator of the classification performance for any unbiased classifier. Therefore, given the simplest two-dimension discrimination problem (i.e., two-class discrimination task), when the class-conditional distributions depend on a measurement parameter (e.g., operating temperature in metal oxide gas sensors), maximizing the *KL*-distance is a valid objective in tuning that parameter; see Figure 10.

Using a binary classification instance as a case of study may be very convenient from many perspectives; in odor representation, however, this assumption may be very unrealistic. When the number of classes (i.e., the possible outcomes of the identification problem) is more than two, the *KL*-distance should be generalized to promote the dispersion of the whole classes. The authors have addressed this issue by replacing (16) with the sum of pair-wise distances, thus:

$$CKL = \sum_{i,j=1}^{|C|} KL(g_i, h_j), \tag{17}$$

where $|C|$ denotes the number of classes in the problem and $g_i(\cdot)$ and $h(\cdot)$, $i \in C, j \in C$, are the class-conditional distributions, each potentially depending on the operating parameter (e. g., the sensor's operating temperature).

The *CKL* quantifies the difficulty of the classification problem. When this quantity is large, an arbitrary classifier is expected to perform with higher accuracy, since,

Figure 10. Class-conditional probability distributions in a 2-class discrimination instance. Each class response models the histograms by a normalized fifth-order polynomial (plain and dashed lines). These models accurately approximate the sensor's response to an odor class while accounting for the asymmetry (i.e., skewness) in the distribution. The KL-distance index then captures the influence of the operating parameter on the separability of such distributions. Maximizing this index for a pair of distributions results in a better discrimination between the corresponding two classes (top vs. bottom figures). Figure reprinted from Vergara et al. (2010), Copyright (2010), with permission Elsevier Science.

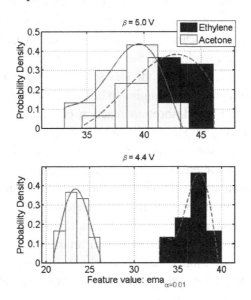

relative to a small *CKL*, the distribution within each class is shrunk and/or the two classes are located away from each other in the feature space.

Assuming that β denotes an intrinsic parameter of a sensor device that alters the response characteristics (see Figure 10), then the problem configuration *CKL* is expected to be sensitive to β. Hence, the value

$$\beta^* = \arg\max_{\beta} CKL(\beta), \tag{18}$$

defines an optimum operating condition for the classification problem at hand.

In demonstrating their optimization scheme, the authors have applied the criterion (18) to optimize the operating conditions of metal-oxide gas sensors. In particular, they have examined the performance of each commercially available metal oxide gas sensor offered in a sensing array (sensors provided by Figaro Engineering Inc.,

Japan, http://www.figaro.co.jp), in a six-class classification problem, comprised by six different analytes dosed at different concentrations, i.e., ethylene, ethanol, and toluene dosed at 10 ppm; acetone and acetaldehyde at 100 ppm; and ammonia at 120 ppm. In doing so, they studied the impact of adjusting its sensing parameter β on the odor-sensor pair interaction and on the confidence of the information yielded by the sensor individually.

In principle, any controllable variable that alter or modify the operating characteristics of the sensor (such as the environment temperature, flow rate or even construction methodologies) can be used as a parameter of the response profile, thus requiring to be tuned to improve a certain data processing performance. However, in this popular odor sensing technology, it is very well-known, and proved in many empirical works (see e.g., works from Sears et al. 1989a, 1989b and Nakata et al. 1996, 1998), that there is a strict dependence of the sensor response on its operating temperature (temperature normally ranging in high orders of magnitude, e.g. 400°C, responsible of the adsorption/desorption reaction occurring at the micro-porous surface of the sensor in response to an analyte). Therefore, having such an easy way of interacting with the sensor, the most natural way to optimize the sensor device is with respect to this parameter (i.e., the sensor's operating temperature), while assuming that all other parameters remain constant. Moreover, since the sensor packaging does not permit direct access to this temperature, its tuning can be achieved via a resistive heater element with controllable voltage, which has a deterministic one-to-one mapping with the actual active layer temperature; a look-up table has been provided in by Figaro Engineering. Accordingly, the authors have considered this heater voltage and the operating temperature interchangeably as the sensing conditioning parameter β to be optimized.

In practice, the form of the dependence of CKL on β is initially unknown, yet to be inferred from a provided training set (containing labeled measurements) from the same sensor at representative β values. Thus, to demonstrate the optimization scheme in a practical instance, the authors compiled for each sensor model a comprehensive dataset containing the analytes described above. Each set of time series contained 30 independent measurements taken from each class at each of the 13 sensor operating temperatures corresponding to the heater voltages $\beta \in \{3.8, 4.0, ..., 6.2 \text{ V}\}$. These temperature values were utilized to perform the dataset with a resolution (i.e., separation between temperatures evaluated) of 20°C. Then, regardless of the feature selected, the authors represented each of the chemo-sensory records, associated with each odor-class and operating temperature, as independent and identically distributed (i.i.d.) samples, from which the class-conditional distribution is derived. Then, they modeled each odorant class by a polynomial fit to the histogram of previously collected samples from that odorant type. In particular, they consider a fifth-order polynomial to represent the odorant-class/histogram relation. By plugging these functions into Equation (18), the *CKL* criterion was implemented, and the maximum β value obtained, yielding thus the optimal operating temperature values for the particular discrimination task. As a measure of separability, the evaluation of the *CKL* for the six classes at each temperature β yielded the profile shown in Figure 11 (dashed lines). Based on this evaluation, the best operating condition for each sensor to distinguish between the set of classes is determined by the maximum value of their respective curves.

To demonstrate the consistency and robustness of the optimization method, the authors conducted a validation process that consisted of measuring the correlation between the information given by the optimization criterion (18) and the performance given by an arbitrary classifier. For simplicity, they used a linear support-vector classifier to verify this. As expected, the results yielded by the SVM classifier in Figure 11 (dotted lines) follow a similar pattern to the estimated measure *CKL* index (Figure 11 (dashed lines)) in the sense that their extreme points occur at the same β values. The ordering of these points in magnitude is also preserved to a large extent, meaning that the proposed measurement is a reliable indicator of the classification performance at almost all temperatures within the range.

Figure 11. Observed discrimination performance of a linear SVM classifier of each sensor on the 6-class identification problem (dotted lines). Profiles for each sensor as estimated by the CKL index (dashed lines) with respect to β. Based on the proposed criterion, the optimal operating condition that best discriminates between the set of classes can be determined for each sensor individually by obtaining the maximum value of the curve shown. Figure reprinted from Vergara et al. (2010), Copyright (2010), with permission Elsevier Science.

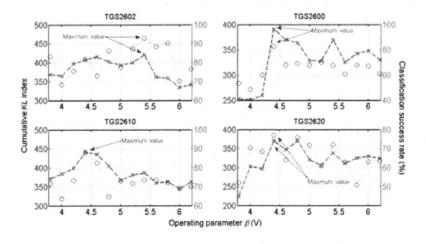

Furthermore, the authors validated the whole optimization process with the second dataset four months later. To validate the results, they re-calculated the proposed cost function *CKL* of the second dataset by applying the same procedure described above. Based on this re-evaluation, the best operating condition to distinguish between the new set of classes was determined, and compared to the performance yielded by the linear-SVM classifier. As can be seen in Table 3, the results obtained in the validation stage perfectly match with the information given by the classifier, showing the consistency of the method. These results indicate that the proposed *CKL* measure-index is optimum for any complexity of probability distribution models; hence, for any type and number of odorants as well as any type of sensor technology with a conditioning parameter, provided that these models are accurate in identifying the response distribution. Nevertheless, the method could be extended to an arbitrary classification instance as needed, including complex odors at different concentrations or mixtures of gases, provided that a sufficiently representative database of relevant measurements is available. It is also important to emphasize that the solution β^* does not impose a particular classification method. Therefore, the parameter value resulting from the maximization of Equation (18) simplifies the task of an arbitrary unbiased classifier.

It is important to comment on one last issue here. An operating condition is optimal for a well-defined task. If this task changes then the best condition should be re-calculated. This applies to any optimization method, not just this one. For example, consider a generic classifier training approach: If the training data changes (e.g., some data turns out to be invalid or relabeled), then the device needs to be re-trained in order to determine the optimal performance. In this optimization case, a re-calculation of β^* with the updated dataset is therefore needed, too.

Table 3. Optimal operating parameter values β selected versus the observed classification performances for each metal-oxide gas sensor given by the linear-SVM classifier during the validation stage. The performance of the linear-SVM classifier was quantified for each sensor on each optimized parameter value. Adapted from Vergara et al. (2010), with permission.

Sensor Type →	TGS2602	TGS2600	TGS2610	TGS2620
Optimal parameter value β using the *CKL*-distance (V)	5.4	4.4	4.4	4.4
Validation discrimination performance rate in (%) (*CKL*-distance)	90.50	84.55	87.68	94.23

Active Sensing Optimization

The idea of applying sophisticated signal processing procedures and optimization strategies to ameliorate the performance of metal oxide gas sensors has been around for more than two decades. Researchers have used a wide array of dynamic features obtained from transient responses, but most of these studies have been empirical. To the best of our knowledge, very few studies have proposed systematic approaches to optimizing the sensor performance as a single device (Kunt et al. 1998, Cavicchi et al. 1996, Vergara et al. 2005a, 2005b, 2007, 2008, 2009, 2010). These methods, though, require that the optimization be performed off-line; therefore they cannot adapt to changes in the environment. In view of this, a novel active-sensing approach that can optimize the temperature profile online, (i.e., as the sensor collects data from its environment), has recently emerged in literature. The most relevant works on this thematic issue are reviewed in this section.

Active-sensing strategies are inspired by the fact that perception is not a passive process (Gibson 1979), but an active one, in which an organism controls its sensory organs in order to extract behaviorally relevant information from the environment (see Figure 12 (a)). Active sensing has been traditionally used in robotics and computer vision, in which the localization and navigation tasks, on the one hand, and the recognition of three-dimensional (3-D) objects from 2-D image, on the other hand, respectively is a recurrent theme (Paletta & Pinz 2000, Floreano et al. 2004, Denzler & Brown 2002). In chemical sensing, however, it has received only minimal attention. In one of the earliest studies, Nakamoto, Okazaki, and Matsushita (1995) developed a method for active odor blending, where the goal was to reproduce an odor blend by creating a mixture from its individual components. The authors developed a control algorithm that adjusted the mixture ratio, so the response of a gas-sensor array to the mixture could matched the response to the odor blend.

It was not until 2010, when Gosangi and Gutierrez-Osuna (2009, 2010) proposed an active-sensing approach to optimize the temperature profile of metal oxide sensors in real time, as the sensor reacts to its environment. To see how their approach works let us consider the problem of classifying an unknown gas sample into one of M known categories $\{\omega^{(1)}, \omega^{(2)}, ..., \omega^{(M)}\}$ using a metal oxide (MOX) sensor with D different operating temperatures $\{\rho^1, \rho^2, ..., \rho^D\}$. To solve this sensing problem, one typically measures the sensor's response at each of the D temperatures, then analyze the complete feature vector $x = [\chi^1, \chi^2, ..., \chi^D]^T$ with a pattern-recognition algorithm. Although straightforward, this passive sensing approach is unlikely to be cost effective because only a fraction of the measurements are generally necessary to classify the chemical sample. Instead, the authors seek to determine an optimal sequence of actions $a = [a_1, a_2, ..., a_T]$, where each action corresponds to setting the sensor to one of the D possible temperatures or terminating the process

Figure 12. (a) In active sensing, the system adapts its sensing parameters based on its belief about the world (e.g., class membership of a stimulus). (b) Illustration of active-classification with an array of four metal-oxide gas sensors, ten temperatures per sensor, and a discrimination problem with six chemicals. At time zero, no information is available except that classes are a priori equiprobable: p(ω(i)*=1/6). Based on this information, the active classifier decides to measure the response of sensor S2 at temperature T4, which leads to observation o*1* and an updated posterior p(ω*(i)*|o*1*,a*1*). After four sensing actions, evidence accumulated in the posterior p(ω*(i)*|o*1*... o*1*, a*1*... a*1*) and the cost of additional measurements are sufficient for the algorithm to assign the unknown sample to class ω*(3)*. In this toy example, accurate classification is reached using only 10% of all sensor configurations. (c) Classification performance and average sequence length as a function of feature acquisition costs. Figure adapted from Gosangi et al. (2009) © IEEE.*

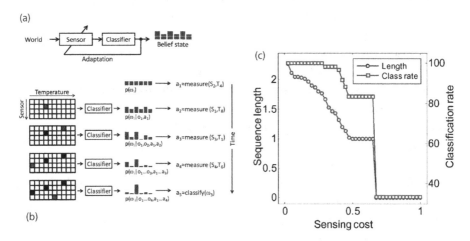

by assigning the sample to one of the M chemical classes. More importantly, they seek to select this sequence of actions dynamically on the basis of accumulating evidence. This process is illustrated in Figure 12 (b).

In demonstrating their approach, the authors first model the sensor's steady-state response at temperature ρ_i to chemical $\omega^{(c)}$ with a Gaussian mixture:

$$p\left(x_i \omega^{(c)}\right) = \sum_{m_i=1}^{M_i} \alpha_{i,m_i}^{(c)} N\left(x_i \mid \mu_{i,m_i}^{(c)}, \Sigma_{i,m_i}^{(c)}\right) \tag{19}$$

where M_i is the number of Gaussians, and $\alpha_{i,m_i}^{(c)}$, $\mu_{i,m_i}^{(c)}$, $\Sigma_{i,m_i}^{(c)}$ are the mixing coefficient, mean vector, and covariance matrix of each Gaussian for class $\omega^{(c)}$, respectively. Given a sequence of actions $[a_1, a_2, ..., a_T]$, the authors assumed that the sensor progresses through a series of states $s=[s_1, s_2, ..., s_T]$ to produce an observation sequence $o=[o_1, o_2, ..., o_T]$. Each state s_i represents a Gaussian in (19) and is therefore hidden. Following this, they modeled the dynamic response of a sensor to a sequence of temperature pulses by means of an input-output hidden Markov model. This is a machine learning technique that can be used to learn a dynamic mapping between two data streams: (*a*) an input (temperature in this case) and (*b*) an output (sensor conductance). Once a dynamic sensor model has been learned, they then approach the temperature-optimization process as one of sequential decision-making steps under uncertainty, where the goal is to balance the cost of applying additional temperature pulses against the risk of classifying the chemical analyte on the basis of the available information. As a result, the problem is solved through a partially observable Markov decision process (Papadimitriou & Tsitsiklis 1987).

Simulation results from this study are shown in Figure 12 (c); these results indicate that the method can balance sensing costs and classification accuracy: higher classification rates can be achieved by decreasing sensing costs, which in turns increases the length of the temperature sequence and the amount of information available to the classifier. One last think to comment on here is that the active sensing approach proposed here has great potential in pioneering new strategies to be implemented in energy-aware chemical sensing networks using low-cost commercial sensors.

CONCLUSION AND OUTLOOK

It can be concluded from the contents of this chapter, that the use of various chemical transducer arrays together with variable selection techniques is, indeed, beneficial with regard to the performance of such sensor arrays. Variable selection has become the subject of a considerable amount of research in areas of application for which datasets with thousands of variables are available. This is particularly true in the field of machine olfaction, where the use of multiple variables together, besides coming at the expense of an increased computational demand, could compromise the online applicability and the adaptability of the formulation to different sensor arrays and/or classifiers. The objective of feature or sensor selection (i.e. array optimization) in machine olfaction is three-fold: improving the prediction performance of the classifiers, providing faster and more cost-effective predictors, and providing a better understanding of the underlying process that generated the data.

Recent developments in feature and sensor selection for machine olfaction have addressed the problem from the pragmatic point of view to improve the performance of classifiers. Sophisticated wrappers (some making use of an initial filter step) or embedded methods (e.g. feature/sensor selection employing a support vector machine) improve classifier performance compared to simpler variable ranking methods like correlation methods, but the improvements are not always significant: domains with large numbers of input variables suffer from the curse of dimensionality and multivariate methods may overfit the data.

On the technological side, the progress in micro/nano-technology, micro-electronics, and in data-processing speed and capability have dramatically influenced the design and development of chemical sensors and thus sensory systems with capabilities that only a decade ago were confined to the lab bench of research laboratories. However, we believe that the sensor-based detection of chemical analytes in a dynamic real-world environment is a complex task, in which the interest of the final-user is to have reliable, user-friendly, and affordable sensory systems, irrespective of the internal system complexity. Therefore, the concept of an adaptive optimal sensory system can be most successful. Adaptive sensory systems may be devices that include various chemical transducer types, sensor operation modes, the use of auxiliary sensors, and separation and pre-concentration units, which can respond or adapt their optimal operation to the occurring analysis situations or events. Then, in the instance where a certain odorant compound or a major interfering chemical is present, the sensor selection, sensor operation mode, feature extraction, and data treatment should be able to adapt to this event so that their protocols should execute in such a way that the best-possible target-analyte detection is achieved or that the influence of the interfering analyte can be recognized and minimized, if not suppressed at all. In dealing with the just described issues, it may be very effective to purposefully select or deselect sensors, to find the optimal sensor's operation mode, or to use signal ratios or differential values instead of merely increasing the array size or the transducer diversity.

Finally, when facing a general problem of sensor array optimization or feature selection it would be worth considering the following steps (Guyon et al. 2003):

1. When there is domain knowledge (e.g. underlying physicochemical phenomena is known or a sensor response model is available), then consider building a better set of 'ad hoc' features.
2. Are features commensurate? If a hybrid multi-sensor system is employed, which combines different odor sensing technologies it is likely that feature normalization will be of help.
3. If there is a need to prune the number of sensors or input features (e.g. for simplicity, data understanding, etc.) then start by assessing features individually. This will help in understanding their relative influence on the system. Additionally, if their number is too large use a variable ranking method to implement a first step of filtering.

4. In cases where some response patterns within the optimization database are suspected to be meaningless or have the wrong class labels, outliers should be detected by employing the top ranking features/sensors obtained in step 3.
5. When there is not an evident option for the classifier model to be used, start by trying first a linear model. Following the ranking of step 3, construct a sequence of classifiers of similar nature using increasing (or decreasing) subsets of features (e.g. by implementing a forward or backward selection strategy). In case performance is matched or improved with a smaller subset, then try a non-linear classifier model with this subset. As a rule of thumb, it is better to try simple strategies first.
6. If the database available has a large number of samples and there is time enough and computational resources, then it is worth comparing several sensor/feature selection methods coupled to linear or non-linear classifier models. Consider combining filters either with wrapper or embedded approaches. Do not refrain from trying your own ideas.
7. In order to achieve a stable solution to the optimization problem and effectively improve performance, employ data re-sampling methods (e.g. by constructing bootstrap sets) and redo the sensor/feature selection analysis for different sets.

ACKNOWLEDGMENT

A.V. was supported by U.S. Office of Naval Research (ONR) under contract N00014-07-1-0741 and by Jet Propulsion Laboratory-NASA contract 2010–1396686. This work was funded in part by NATO under the Science for Peace Program grant no. CBP.MD.CLG 983914.

REFERENCES

Alkasab, T. K., White, J., & Kauer, J. S. (2002). A computational system for simulating and analyzing arrays of biological and artificial chemical sensors. *Chemical Senses, 27,* 261–275. doi:10.1093/chemse/27.3.261

Artursson, T., & Holmberg, M. (2002). Wavelet transform of electronic tongue data. *Sensors and Actuators. B, Chemical, 87,* 379–391. doi:10.1016/S0925-4005(02)00270-8

Bărsan, N., Schweizer-Berberich, M., & Göpel, W. (1999). Fundamental and practical aspects in the design of nanoscaled SnO_2 gas sensors: A status report. *Fresenius' Journal of Analytical Chemistry, 365,* 287–304. doi:10.1007/s002160051490

Bellman, R. (1961). *Adaptive control processes: A guided tour*. Princeton, NJ: Princeton University Press.

Bhattacharyya, A. (1943). On a measure of divergence between two statistical populations defined by their probability distributions. *Bulletin of the Calcutta Mathematics Society, 35*, 99–109.

Bishop, C. M. (1995). *Neural networks for pattern recognition*. Oxford, UK: Oxford University Press.

Blum, A. L., & Langely, P. (1997). Selection of relevant features and examples in machine learning. *Artificial Intelligence, 97*, 245–271. doi:10.1016/S0004-3702(97)00063-5

Brereton, R. G. (1992). *Multivariate pattern recognition in chemometrics*. Amsterdam, The Netherlands: Elsevier.

Brezmes, J., Cabré, P., Rojo, S., Llobet, E., Vilanova, X., & Correig, X. (2002). Discrimination between different samples of olive using variable selection techniques and modified fuzzy ARTMAP neural networks. *Proceedings of the 9th International Symposium on Olfaction and Electronic Nose*, ISOEN'02, Rome, Italy, (pp. 188-190).

Bro, R. (1997). PARAFAC: Tutorial and applications. *Chemometrics and Intelligent Laboratory Systems, 38*, 149–171. doi:10.1016/S0169-7439(97)00032-4

Buratti, S., Ballabio, D., Benedetti, S., & Cosio, M. S. (2007). Prediction of Italian red wine sensorial descriptors from electronic nose, electronic tongue and spectrophotometric measurements by means of genetic algorithm regression models. *Food Chemistry, 100*, 211–218. doi:10.1016/j.foodchem.2005.09.040

Burian, C., Brezmes, J., Vinaixa, M., Cañellas, N., Llobet, E., Vilanova, X., & Correig, X. (2010). MS-electronic nose performance improvement using the retention time dimension and two-way and three-way data processing methods. *Sensors and Actuators. B, Chemical, 143*, 758–768. doi:10.1016/j.snb.2009.10.015

Cavicchi, R. E., Suehle, J. S., Kreider, K. G., Gaitan, M., & Chaparala, P. (1996). Optimized temperature-pulse sequences for the enhancement of chemically specific response patterns from micro-hotplates gas sensors. *Sensors and Actuators. B, Chemical, 33*, 142–146. doi:10.1016/0925-4005(96)01821-7

Choi, N. H., Shim, C. H., Song, K. D., Lee, D. S., Huh, J. S., & Lee, D. D. (2002). Classification of workplace gases using temperature modulation and two SnO_2 sensing films on substrate. *Sensors and Actuators. B, Chemical, 86*, 251–258. doi:10.1016/S0925-4005(02)00196-X

Clifford, P. K., & Tuma, D. T. (1983). Characteristics of semiconductor gas sensor II: Transient response to temperature change. *Sensors and Actuators, 3*, 233–254. doi:10.1016/0250-6874(82)80026-7

Corcoran, P., Lowery, P., & Anglesea, J. (1998). Optimal configuration of a thermally cycled gas sensor array with neural network pattern recognition. *Sensors and Actuators. B, Chemical, 48*, 448–455. doi:10.1016/S0925-4005(98)00083-5

Cozzolino, D., Smyth, H. E., Cynkar, W., Dambergs, R. G., & Gishen, M. (2005). Usefulness of chemometrics and mass spectrometry-based electronic nose to classify Australian white wines by their varietal origin. *Talanta, 68*, 382–387. doi:10.1016/j.talanta.2005.08.057

Davis, L. (1991). *The handbook of genetic algorithms*. New York, NY: Van Nostrand Reinhold.

Denzler, J., & Brown, C. M. (2002). Information theoretic sensor data selection for active object recognition and state estimation. *IEEE Transactions on Pattern Analysis and Machine Intelligence, 24*, 145–157. doi:10.1109/34.982896

Devijver, P. A., & Kittler, J. (1982). *Pattern recognition: A statistical approach*. Prentice Hall.

Dickinson, T. A., White, J., Kauer, J. S., & Walt, D. R. (1996). A chemical-detecting system based on a cross-reactive optical sensor array. *Nature, 382*, 697–700. doi:10.1038/382697a0

Dittmann, B., & Nitz, S. (2000). Strategies for the development of reliable QA/QC methods when working with mass spectrometry-based chemosensory systems. *Sensors and Actuators. B, Chemical, 69*, 253257. doi:10.1016/S0925-4005(00)00504-9

Eklöv, T., Mårtensson, P., & Lundström, I. (1999). Selection of variables for interpreting multivariable gas sensor data. *Analytica Chimica Acta, 381*, 221–232. doi:10.1016/S0003-2670(98)00739-9

El Barbri, N., Duran, C., Brezmes, J., Cañellas, N., Ramírez, J. L., Bouchikhi, B., & Llobet, E. (2008). Selectivity enhancement in multisensor systems using flow modulation techniques. *Sensors (Basel, Switzerland), 8*, 7369–7379. doi:10.3390/s8117369

Fallik, E., Alkali-Tuvia, S., Horev, B., Copel, A., Rodov, V., & Aharoni, Y. (2001). Characterisation of Galia melon aroma by GC and mass spectrometric sensor measurements after prolonged storage. *Postharvest Biology and Technology, 22*, 8591. doi:10.1016/S0925-5214(00)00185-X

Figaro Engineering Inc. *Japan*. (2010). Retrieved from http://www.figaro.co.jp

Floreano, D., Kato, T., Marocco, D., & Sauser, E. (2004). Coevolution of active vision and feature selection. *Biological Cybernetics, 90*, 218–228. doi:10.1007/s00422-004-0467-5

Fort, A., Gregorkiewitz, M., Machetti, M., Rocchi, S., Serrano, B., & Tondi, L. (2002). Selectivity enhancement of SnO_2 sensors by means of operating temperature modulation. *Thin Solid Films, 418*, 2–8. doi:10.1016/S0040-6090(02)00575-8

Fort, A., Machetti, M., Rocchi, S., Serrano, B., Tondi, L., & Ulivieri, N. (2003). Tin oxide gas sensing: Comparison among different measurement techniques for gas mixture classification. *IEEE Transactions on Instrumentation and Measurement, 52*, 921–926. doi:10.1109/TIM.2003.814362

Freund, M. S., & Lewis, N. S. (1995). A chemically diverse, conducting polymer-based electronic nose. *Proceedings of the National Academy of Sciences of the United States of America, 92*, 2652–2656. doi:10.1073/pnas.92.7.2652

Gardner, J. W., & Bartlett, P. N. (1996). Performance definition and standardization of electronic noses. *Sensors and Actuators. B, Chemical, 33*, 60–67. doi:10.1016/0925-4005(96)01819-9

Gardner, J. W., & Bartlett, P. N. (1999). *Electronic noses: Principles and applications*. Oxford, UK: Oxford University Press.

Gardner, J. W., Boilot, P., & Hines, E. L. (2005). Enhancing electronic nose performance by sensor selection using a new integer-based genetic algorithm approach. *Sensors and Actuators. B, Chemical, 106*, 114–121. doi:10.1016/j.snb.2004.05.043

Geladi, P. (1989). Analysis of multi-way (multi-mode) data. *Chemometrics and Intelligent Laboratory Systems, 7*, 11–30. doi:10.1016/0169-7439(89)80108-X

Gibson, J. J. (1979). *The ecological approach to visual perception*. Boston, MA: Houghton Mifflin.

Godfrey, K. (1993). *Perturbation signals for system identification*. (pp. 39-49, 181-187, 321-347). Prentice Hall.

Göpel, W. (1985). Chemisorption and charge transfer at ionic semiconductor surfaces: Implications in designing gas sensors. *Progress in Surface Science, 20*, 1, 9–103. doi:10.1016/0079-6816(85)90004-8

Göpel, W. (1988). Chemical imaging I: Concepts and visions for electronic and bioelectronic noses. *Sensors and Actuators. B, Chemical, 52*, 125–142. doi:10.1016/S0925-4005(98)00267-6

Göpel, W., Hesse, J., & Zemel, J. N. (1991). *Sensors: A comprehensive survey* (*Vol. 2*). Weinheim, Germany: VCH.

Gosangi, R., & Gutierrez-Osuna, R. (2009). Active chemical sensing with partially observable Markov decision processes. *Proceedings of the International Symposium on Olfaction and Electronic Noses* (ISOEN 2009), Brescia, Italy, April 15-17.

Gosangi, R., & Gutierrez-Osuna, R. (2010). Active temperature programming for metal-oxide chemoresistors. *IEEE Sensors Journal, 10*, 1075–1082. doi:10.1109/JSEN.2010.2042165

Gualdrón, O., Brezmes, J., Llobet, E., Amari, A., Vilanova, X., Bouchikhi, B., & Correig, X. (2007). Variable selection for support vector machine based multisensor systems. *Sensors and Actuators. B, Chemical, 122*, 259–268. doi:10.1016/j.snb.2006.05.029

Gualdrón, O., Llobet, E., Brezmes, J., Vilanova, X., & Correig, X. (2006). Coupling fast variable selection methods to neural network based classifiers: Application to multisensor systems. *Sensors and Actuators. B, Chemical, 114*, 522–529. doi:10.1016/j.snb.2005.04.046

Guyon, I., & Elisseeff, A. (2003). An introduction to variable and feature selection. *Journal of Machine Learning Research, 3*, 1157–1182. doi:10.1162/153244303322753616

Guyon, I., Gunn, S., Nikravesh, M., & Zadeh, L. (2006). *Feature extraction: Foundations and applications, studies in fuzziness and soft computing. Physica-Verlag.* Springer.

Hierlemann, A., & Gutierrez-Osuna, R. (2008). Higher-order chemical sensing. *Chemical Reviews, 108*, 563–613. doi:10.1021/cr068116m

Huang, X., Liu, J., Shao, D., Pi, Z., & Yu, Z. (2003). Rectangular mode of operation for detecting pesticide residue by using a single SnO_2 based gas sensor. *Sensors and Actuators. B, Chemical, 96*, 630–635. doi:10.1016/j.snb.2003.07.006

Jain, A. K., Duin, R. P. W., & Mao, J. C. (2000). Statistical pattern recognition: A review. *IEEE Pattern Analysis and Machine Intelligence, 22*, 4–37. doi:10.1109/34.824819

Jouan-Rimbaud, D., Massart, D. L., & Noord, O. E. (1996). Random correlation in variable selection for multivariate calibration with a genetic algorithm. *Chemometrics and Intelligent Laboratory Systems, 35*, 213–220. doi:10.1016/S0169-7439(96)00062-7

Kirkpatrick, S., Gelatt, C. D., & Vecchi, M. P. (1983). Optimization by simulated annealing. *Science, 220*, 671–680. doi:10.1126/science.220.4598.671

Kullback, S., & Leibler, R. A. (1951). On information and sufficiency. *Annals of Mathematical Statistics, 22*(1), 79–86. doi:10.1214/aoms/1177729694

Kunt, T. A., McAvoy, T. J., Cavicchi, R. E., & Semancik, S. (1998). Optimization of temperature programmed sensing for gas identification using micro-hotplate sensors. *Sensors and Actuators. B, Chemical, 53*, 24–43. doi:10.1016/S0925-4005(98)00244-5

Llobet, E. (2006). Temperature modulated gas sensors. In Grimes, C. A. (Ed.), *Encyclopaedia of sensors* (pp. 131–152). American Scientific Publishers.

Llobet, E., Brezmes, J., Gualdrón, O., Vilanova, X., & Correig, X. (2004). Building parsimonious fuzzy ARTMAP models by variable selection with a cascaded genetic algorithm: application to multisensor systems for gas analysis. *Sensors and Actuators. B, Chemical, 99*, 267–272. doi:10.1016/j.snb.2003.11.019

Llobet, E., Gualdrón, O., Vinaixa, M., El-Barbri, N., Brezmes, J., & Vilanova, X. (2007). Efficient feature selection for mass-spectrometry based electronic nose applications. *Chemometrics and Intelligent Laboratory Systems, 85*, 253–261. doi:10.1016/j.chemolab.2006.07.002

Lorber, A., & Kowalski, B. R. (1988). Estimation of prediction error for multivariate calibration. *Journal of Chemometrics, 2*, 93–109. doi:10.1002/cem.1180020203

Maldonado-Bascon, S., Khalifa, S. A., & Lopez-Ferreras, F. (2003). *Feature reduction using support vector machines for binary gas detection.* (LNCS 2687), (pp. 798–805).

Marín, S., Vinaixa, M., Brezmes, J., Llobet, E., Vilanova, X., & Correig, X. (2007). Use of a MS-electronic nose for prediction of early fungal spoilage of bakery products. *International Journal of Microbiology, 114*, 10–16. doi:10.1016/j.ijfoodmicro.2006.11.003

Marsili, R. (1999). SPME-MS-MVA as an electronic nose for the study of off-flavors in milk. *Journal of Agricultural and Food Chemistry, 47*, 648–654. doi:10.1021/jf9807925

Martí, M. P., Boqué, R., Riu, M., Busto, O., & Guasch, J. (2003). Fast screening method for determining 2,4,6-trichloroanisole in wines using a headspace–mass spectrometry (HS–MS) system and multivariate calibration. *Analytical and Bioanalytical Chemistry, 376*, 497–501. doi:10.1007/s00216-003-1940-z

Martí, M. P., Pino, J., Boqué, R., Busto, O., & Guasch, J. (2005). Determination of ageing time of spirits in oak barrels using a headspace–mass spectrometry (HS-MS) electronic nose system and multivariate calibration. *Analytical and Bioanalytical Chemistry, 382*, 440–443. doi:10.1007/s00216-004-2969-3

Maziarz, W., & Pisarkiewicz, T. (2008). Gas sensors in a dynamic operation mode. *Measurement Science & Technology, 19*.

Meyer, D., Leisch, F., & Hornik, K. (2003). The support vector machine under test. *Neurocomputing, 55*, 169–186. doi:10.1016/S0925-2312(03)00431-4

Moseley, P. T., & Tofield, B. C. (Eds.). (1987). *Solid-state gas sensors*. Bristol, UK: The Adam Hilger series on sensors.

Muezzinoglu, M., Vergara, A., Huerta, R., & Rabinovich, M. (2010). A sensor conditioning principle for odor identification. *Sensors and Actuators. B, Chemical, 146*, 472–476. doi:10.1016/j.snb.2009.11.036

Naes, T., & Martens, H. (1998). Principal component regression in NIR analysis: Viewpoints, background details and selection of components. *Journal of Chemometrics, 2*, 155–167. doi:10.1002/cem.1180020207

Nakamoto, T., Okazaki, N., & Matsushita, H. (1995). Improvement of optimization algorithm in active gas/odor sensing system. *Sensors and Actuators. A, Physical, 50*, 191–196. doi:10.1016/0924-4247(95)01039-4

Nakata, S., Akakabe, S., Nakasuji, M., & Yoshikawa, K. (1996). Gas sensing based on a nonlinear response: Discrimination between hydrocarbons and quantification of individual components in a gas mixture. *Analytical Chemistry, 68*, 2067–2072. doi:10.1021/ac9510954

Nakata, S., Kaneda, Y., Nakamura, H., & Yoshikawa, K. (1991). Detection and quantification of CO gas based on the dynamic response of a ceramic sensor. *Chemistry Letters*, 1505–1508. doi:10.1246/cl.1991.1505

Nakata, S., Kaneda, Y., & Yoshikawa, K. (1992). Novel strategy to develop chemical sensors based on nonlinear dynamics-intelligent gas sensor. *Senses and Materials, 4*, 101–110.

Nakata, S., Ozaki, E., & Ojima, N. (1998). Gas sensing based on the dynamic nonlinear responses of a semiconductor gas sensor: Dependence on the range and frequency of a cyclic temperature change. *Analytica Chimica Acta, 361*, 93–100. doi:10.1016/S0003-2670(98)00013-0

Nanto, H., & Stetter, J. R. (2003). Introduction to chemosensors. In Pearce, T. C., Schiffman, S., Nagle, H. T., & Gardner, J. (Eds.), *Handbook of artificial olfaction machines*. Weinheim, Germany: Wiley–VCH.

Narendra, P. M., & Fukunaga, K. (1977). A branch and bound algorithm for feature subset selection. *IEEE Transactions on Computers, C-26*, 917–922. doi:10.1109/TC.1977.1674939

Niebling, G., & Müller, R. (1995). Design of sensor arrays by use of an inverse feature space. *Sensors and Actuators. B, Chemical, 25*, 781–784. doi:10.1016/0925-4005(95)85173-9

Paletta, L., & Pinz, A. (2000). Active object recognition by view integration and reinforcement learning. *Robotics and Autonomous Systems, 31*, 71–86. doi:10.1016/S0921-8890(99)00079-2

Papadimitriou, C. H., & Tsitsiklis, J. N. (1987). The complexity of Markov decision processes. *Mathematics of Operations Research, 12*, 441–450. doi:10.1287/moor.12.3.441

Pardo, M., & Sberveglieri, G. (2007). Comparing the performance of different features in sensor arrays. *Sensors and Actuators. B, Chemical, 116*, 437–443. doi:10.1016/j.snb.2006.09.041

Paulsson, N., Larson, E., & Winquist, F. (2000). Extraction and selection of parameters for evaluation of breath alcohol measurement with an electronic nose. *Sensors and Actuators. A, Physical, 84*, 187–197. doi:10.1016/S0924-4247(00)00419-2

Pearce, T. C., & Sanchez-Montañes, M. (2003). Chemical sensor array optimization: Geometric and information theoretic approaches. In Pearce, T. C., Schiffman, S., Nagle, H. T., & Gardner, J. (Eds.), *Handbook of artificial olfaction machines.* Weinheim, Germany: Wiley–VCH.

Perera, A., Yamanaka, T., Gutierrez-Galvez, A., Raman, B., & Gutierrez-Osuna, R. (2006). A dimensionality-reduction technique inspired by receptor convergence in the olfactory system. *Sensors and Actuators. B, Chemical, 116*, 17–22. doi:10.1016/j.snb.2005.11.082

Peres, C., Begnaud, F., Eveleigh, L., & Berdagué, J. L. (2003). Fast characterization of foodstuff by headspace mass spectrometry (HS-MS). *Trends in Analytical Chemistry, 22*, 858–866. doi:10.1016/S0165-9936(03)01206-8

Persaud, K., & Dodd, G. (1982). Analysis of discrimination mechanisms in the mammalian olfactory system using a model nose. *Nature, 299*, 352–355. doi:10.1038/299352a0

Persaud, K. C., & Travers, P. J. (1997). In Kress-Rogers, E. (Ed.), *Handbook of biosensors and electronic noses* (pp. 563–592). CRC Press.

Raman, B., Meier, D. C., Evju, J. K., & Semancik, S. (2009). Designing and optimizing microsensor arrays for recognizing chemical hazards in complex environments. *Sensors and Actuators. B, Chemical, 137*, 617–629. doi:10.1016/j.snb.2008.11.053

Ruhland, B., Becker, T., & Müller, G. (1998). Gas-kinetic interactions of nitrous oxides with SnO_2 surfaces. *Sensors and Actuators. B, Chemical, 50*, 85–94. doi:10.1016/S0925-4005(98)00160-9

Saeys, Y., Inza, I., & Larrañaga, P. (2007). A review of feature selection techniques in bioinformatics. *Bioinformatics (Oxford, England), 23*, 2507–2517. doi:10.1093/bioinformatics/btm344

Sears, W. M., Colbow, K., & Consadori, F. (1989a). General characteristics of thermally cycled tin oxide gas sensors. *Semiconductor Science and Technology, 4*, 351–359. doi:10.1088/0268-1242/4/5/004

Sears, W. M., Colbow, K., & Consadori, F. (1989b). Algorithms to improve the selectivity of thermally cycled tin oxide gas sensors. *Sensors and Actuators, 19*, 333–349. doi:10.1016/0250-6874(89)87084-2

Sears, W. M., Colbow, K., Slamka, R., & Consadori, F. (1990). Selective thermally cycled gas sensing using fast Fourier-transform techniques. *Sensors and Actuators. B, Chemical, 2*, 283–289. doi:10.1016/0925-4005(90)80155-S

Semancik, S., & Cavicchi, R. E. (1999). Kinetically controlled chemical sensing using micromachined structures. *Accounts of Chemical Research, 31*(5), 279–287. doi:10.1021/ar970071b

Sun, J. (1995). A correlation principal component regression analysis of NIR data. *Journal of Chemometrics, 9*, 21–29. doi:10.1002/cem.1180090104

Vergara, A., Llobet, E., Brezmes, J., Ivanov, P., Cané, C., & Gràcia, I. (2007). Quantitative gas mixture analysis using temperature-modulated micro-hotplate gas sensors: Selection and validation of the optimal modulating frequencies. *Sensors and Actuators. B, Chemical, 123*, 1002–1016. doi:10.1016/j.snb.2006.11.010

Vergara, A., Llobet, E., Brezmes, J., Ivanov, P., Vilanova, X., & Gràcia, I. (2005a). Optimised temperature modulation of metal oxide micro-hotplate gas sensors through multilevel pseudo random sequences. *Sensors and Actuators. B, Chemical, 111-112*, 271–280. doi:10.1016/j.snb.2005.06.039

Vergara, A., Llobet, E., Brezmes, J., Vilanova, X., Ivanov, P., & Gràcia, I. (2005b). Optimized temperature modulation of micro-hotplate gas sensors through pseudo random binary sequences. *IEEE Sensors Journal, 5*, 1369–1378. doi:10.1109/JSEN.2005.855605

Vergara, A., Muezzinoglu, M. K., Rulkov, N., & Huerta, R. (2009). *Kullback-Leibler distance optimization for artificial chemo-sensors*. IEEE Sensors Conference, Christchurch, New Zealand, Oct. 25-28.

Vergara, A., Muezzinoglu, M. K., Rulkov, N., & Huerta, R. (2010). Information theory of chemical sensors. *Sensors and Actuators. B, Chemical, 148*, 298–306. doi:10.1016/j.snb.2010.04.040

Vergara, A., Ramirez, J. L., & Llobet, E. (2008). Reducing power consumption via a discontinuous operation of temperature-modulated micro-hotplate gas sensors: Application to the logistics chain of fruit. *Sensors and Actuators. B, Chemical, 129*, 311–318. doi:10.1016/j.snb.2007.08.029

Vinaixa, M., Llobet, E., Brezmes, J., Vilanova, X., & Correig, X. (2005b). A fuzzy ARTMAP- and PLS-based MS e-nose for the qualitative and quantitative assessment of rancidity in crisps. *Sensors and Actuators. B, Chemical, 106*, 677–686. doi:10.1016/j.snb.2004.09.015

Vinaixa, M., Marín, S., Brezmes, J., Llobet, E., Vilanova, X., & Correig, X. (2004). Early detection of fungal growth in bakery products using an e-nose based on mass spectrometry. *Journal of Agricultural and Food Chemistry, 52*, 6068–6074. doi:10.1021/jf049399r

Vinaixa, M., Vergara, A., Duran, C., Llobet, E., Badia, C., & Brezmes, J. (2005). Fast detection of rancidity in potato crisps using e-noses based on mass spectrometry or gas sensors. *Sensors and Actuators. B, Chemical, 106*, 67–75. doi:10.1016/j.snb.2004.05.038

White, J., Kauer, J. S., Dickinson, T. A., & Walt, D. R. (1996). Rapid analyte recognition in a device based on optical sensors and the olfactory system. *Analytical Chemistry, 68*, 2191–2202. doi:10.1021/ac9511197

Wlodek, S., Colbow, K., & Consadori, F. (1991). Kinetic model of thermally cycled tin oxide gas sensor. *Sensors and Actuators. B, Chemical, 3*, 123–127. doi:10.1016/0925-4005(91)80204-W

Zaromb, S., & Stetter, J. R. (1984). Theoretical basis for identification and measurement of air contaminants using an array of sensors having partly overlapping selectivities. *Sensors and Actuators. B, Chemical, 6*, 225–243. doi:10.1016/0250-6874(84)85019-2

Zierler, N. (1959). Linear recurring sequences. *Journal of the Society for Industrial and Applied Mathematics, 7*, 31–48. doi:10.1137/0107003

APPENDIX

Metal Oxide Gas Sensors and Temperature-Dependence

It is well-known that, due to the basic operating principles of metal-oxide chemo-sensors, there is a strict and highly deterministic dependence of the sensor response on its operating temperature. In order to understand better how the optimization processes above described are occurring at the sensor level, we believe that it is worthwhile to provide a brief review of the basic operating principle of metal oxide gas sensors. This issue is reviewed in this appendix.

The basic operating principle of metal-oxide chemo-sensors can be summarized as follows. The sensitive layer, in this case the metal oxide layer, made of particles that range from nanometers up to microns, possesses two operating mechanisms. The former is associated with an ideally specific interaction of the surface with the target analyte, whilst the latter refers to an effective transduction of the bulk conductance. If this interaction takes place exclusively at the surface of the selective layer, then the bulk conductivity does not contribute and represents only a shunt which decreases the signal-to-noise ratio. On the other hand, for materials in which interaction originates in the bulk of the selective layer, the response time of the sensor is affected by its thickness. Accordingly, for a given type of base material, the sensor property sensitively depends on the structural features, the presence and state of catalytically active surface dopants, and the working temperature.

The central reaction mechanism responsible for most of the chemical compound responses/interactions involves changes in the concentration of surface oxygen species (Göpel 1985). The formation of such ions means that the oxygen adsorbed at the gas/solid interface abstracts electrons from the conduction band of the sensing material, which results in the development of Schottky potential barriers at the grain boundaries (see Figure 13). Depending on the temperature, oxygen is ionosorbed on the surface predominantly as O_2^- ions below 150 C, or as O^- ions between 150 and 400 C, which is the general operating temperature range. Above 400 C, the parallel formation of O^{2-} occurs, which is then directly incorporated into the lattice above 600 C (Bărsan, Schweizer-Berberich, & Göpel 1999).

In response to an analyte and under stationary conditions i.e., without humidity; constant flow; and fixed operating temperature, the sensor involves an exponential change in the conductance/resistance across its sensing layer. This resulting change can be interpreted as a shift of the state of equilibrium of the surface oxygen reaction due to the presence of the target analyte, which can be either a reducing or oxidizing specie. The response of semiconductor gas sensors to reducing species implies a change in the concentration of adsorbed oxygen species. On the other hand, oxidizing species can interact with the sensor surface in a variety of ways;

Figure 13. Structural and band model showing the role of intergranular contact regions in determining the conductance over a polycrystalline metal oxide semiconductor. Three grains with adsorbed oxygen providing surface depletion layers. The depleted layers are responsible for a high contact resistance. For conduction, electrons must cross over the surface barriers.

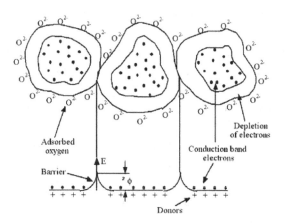

for example, interacting directly with the surface and forming negatively-charged ionosorbed species or in competition with ionosorbed oxygen or oxygen ions for the adsorption sites available (Ruhland, Becker, & Müller 1998). These changes modulate the height of the potential barriers and thus the conductance of the sensing layer. The reason these characteristic conductance-temperature profiles arise is summarized as follows:

- There are different adsorbed oxygen species such as O^-, O^{2-}, and O_2^- over the temperature range (Sears et al. 1989a, Bărsan et al 1999).
- Different gases have different optimum oxidation temperatures (Moseley et al. 1987).
- Adsorption, desorption and diffusion rates (of oxygen species, reducing and oxidizing gases, and oxidation by-products) are temperature-dependent (Clifford & Tuma 1983, Wlodek, Colbow, & Consadori 1991, Nakata, et al. 1991).

Accordingly, when the operating temperature of the sensor varies, the kinetics of adsorption, desorption and reaction occurring at the sensor surface in the presence of atmospheric oxygen and other reducing or oxidizing species is altered. This approach leads to sensor responses (e.g. transient conductance patterns) that are characteristic of the species present in the gas mixture. Having such an easy way of interacting with the sensor and its characteristics justifies the use of temperature as a control variable in a deterministic setting; thus, the optimization of the sensor device with respect to this parameter (i.e., the sensor's operating temperature).

Chapter 2
Evolutionary Algorithms for Multisensor Data Fusion

Jianhua Yang
University of Warwick, UK

Evor L. Hines
University of Warwick, UK

John E. Sloper
University of Warwick, UK

D. Daciana Iliescu
University of Warwick, UK

Mark S. Leeson
University of Warwick, UK

ABSTRACT

The aim of Multisensor Data Fusion (MDF) is to eliminate redundant, noisy or irrelevant information and thus find an optimal subset from an array of high dimensionality. An important feature of MDF is that the signals are constantly evolving instead of being static. This provides an opportunity for Evolutionary Computation (EC) algorithms to be developed to solve MDF tasks. This chapter describes the application of three EC algorithms to widely used datasets. Comparative studies were performed so that relative advantage and disadvantages of the different approaches could be investigated. From this study, authros found that ECs performed in the feature selection stage can greatly reduce the dataset dimensionality and

DOI: 10.4018/978-1-61520-915-6.ch002

hence enhance the MDF system performance; when being used in a way to represent knowledge, ECs can dramatically increase rules when input data are not clustered.

INTRODUCTION

The emergence of new sensors, coupled with advanced processing techniques and improved processing hardware has meant that Multisensor Data Fusion (MDF) technology has undergone rapid growth since the late 1980s (Huang, Lan, Hoffmann, & Lacey, 2007); nevertheless, the field is still in its infancy. In general, MDF is a technique by which data from a number of sensors are combined through a centralized data processor to provide comprehensive and accurate information. Sensors can be located in different ways (collocated, distributed, mobile) producing measurements of the same or of different type. Among these, the fusion of passive sensor data (for example from an electronic nose or EN), especially in the context of defence and security, is of particular importance.

Usually a sensor element operates by measuring a physical or (bio-) chemical property and outputting an analog signal which is amplified, filtered and then converted to a digital signal by the analog-to-digital (A/D) unit (Mitchell, 2007). As a result, sensor responses do not provide information on the nature of the physical property under investigation, but only give a 'digital fingerprint', which can be subsequently investigated by means of data processing methods. Another feature of MDF is that, due to recent advances in sensor developments, feature extraction, and data processing techniques, users are always provided with an increased amount of information using multi-sensor arrays. However, even if each sensor is linked to specific classes of compounds, not all the sensors contribute to the characterisation being analysed, as some may contain irrelevant or noisy data (Ballabio, Cosio, Mannino, & Todeschini, 2006). Furthermore, not all sensor responses are equally relevant to the particular Pattern Recognition (PR) classification task. An associated problem with the increased amount of data is known as the curse of high dimensionality (Bishop, 2006; Gardner, Boilot, & Hines, 2005; Scott, James, & Ali, 2006), meaning that increasing the dimensionality rapidly leads to the point where there may not be enough training patterns, in which case a very poor representation of the input/output mapping may be provided.

The aim of MDF is to eliminate redundant, noisy or irrelevant information and thus find an optimal subset from an array of high dimensionality. By optimising the array size, the overall system performance can potentially be increased by maximising the information content and hence increasing the predictive accuracy. Hall and Llinas (2008) have identified three basic alternatives that can be used for multisensor data: (1) direct fusion of sensor data; (2) representation of sensor data via feature vectors, with subsequent fusion of the feature vectors; or (3) processing of each sensor to achieve high-level inferences or decisions, which are subsequently combined. However, due to the fact that sensor fusion models heavily depend on the application, there is no generally accepted model of sensor fusion but rather a plethora of architectures and models for it (Elmenreich, 2007). Correspondingly, MDF techniques are drawn from, and bring together, a diverse set of more traditional disciplines, including digital signal processing, statistical estimation, control theory and computer vision.

In the current chapter, we will provide a comparative study of evolutionary algorithms applied to MDF. The dataset used in this chapter is a set of benchmarking data that have been widely studied in the literature (Gardner, Hines, & Tang, 1992; 1990). This chapter is organized as follows: in the next section, we will give a brief introduction of Evolutionary Computation (EC); this is followed by a detailed description of the techniques used in our study including Genetic Neural Mathematical Methods (GNMM), Evolving Fuzzy Neural Network (EFuNN), and Cartesian Genetic Programming (CGP); in the section that follows, we will present the MDF results and analysis; and finally in the last section, we will present our conclusions.

EVOLUTIONARY COMPUTATION

As pointed out by Hines et al. (Hines, Boilot, Gardner, Gongora, & Llobet, 2003), compared with statistical/chemometric methods, which are parametric based on the assumption that the spread of the data can be described by a probability density function (PDF), Intelligent Systems (ISs) based PR techniques, e.g. Evolutionary Computations (ECs) and Artificial Neural Networks (ANNs), offer advantages such as learning capabilities, self-organization, generalization and noise tolerance. In particular, ECs are well suited to the task of modern MDF as they have the ability to search through large numbers of combinations, where interdependencies between variables may exist (Reeves & Rowe, 2003; Rothlauf, 2006).

EC is the most widely used stochastic technique. It is based on Darwinian evolutionary systems and includes for example, Genetic Algorithms (GAs), Genetic Programming (GP) and other hybrid evolutionary algorithms. In general, EC systems will incorporate (Figure 1): one or more populations of individuals competing for limited resources; the notion of dynamically changing populations due to the birth and death of individuals; a concept of fitness which reflects the ability of an individual to survive and reproduce; and a concept of variational inheritance: offspring closely resemble their parents but are not identical (De Jong, 2006). Compared to other stochastic methods ECs have the advantage that they can be parallelized with little effort (Rojas, 1996). Since the calculations of the fitness function for each chromosome of a population are independent from each other, they can be carried

Figure 1. Evolutionary computation components

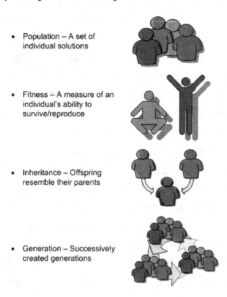

- Population – A set of individual solutions

- Fitness – A measure of an individual's ability to survive/reproduce

- Inheritance – Offspring resemble their parents

- Generation – Successively created generations

out using several processors. Thus ECs are inherently parallel. ECs can be particularly effective in finding solutions where the individual pieces of the solution are important in combination, or where a sequence is important.

A stochastic optimization method similar to EC is called simulated annealing (SA). Although SA is not biologically based, EC and SA share very similar theoretical roots (Davis, 1987). However, ECs are population-based approaches, where there is the concept of competition (i.e. selection) between candidate solutions to a given problem. Furthermore, SAs generate new candidate points in the neighbourhood of the current point, while ECs allow the examination of points in the neighbourhood of two (or more) candidate solutions via the use of genetic operators such as crossover (De Castro, 2006). Therefore, EC tends to improve the solution consistently when given more time.

EC has been reported in the literature that determines an optimal subset of sensors for machine olfaction. For example, Gardner et al. (2005) introduced a modified genetic algorithm (GA) called V-integer GA. In this V-integer GA, each chromosome was used with integer values from one to a pre-defined number of features/sensors representing the selected subset of features, and evaluated using probabilistic neural network (PNN) classifiers within the population. They also compared this V-integer GA with other search methods such as sequential forward or backward searches (SFS or SBS) and normal (binary) GAs. For the data-set used in their work, SFS achieved over 89% correct classification by selecting just three features, whereas SBS needed at least five features to reach the same level. With binary gene GAs, the dimensionality is reduced by 50–60% and the classification rates are on average 91%. Considering eight, six or four features, the optimal subsets returned by the V-integer genes GA selections have dimensionality reduced by over 80% and on average achieve around 90% correct classification. These results showed that the V-integer genes GA approach is an accurate search method when compared to some other feature selection techniques such as SFS or SBS. However, in the V-integer GA, the number of sensors to be selected has to be defined in advance – in other words, there is potentially a lack of flexibility in some application scenarios.

ECs have many variations and hybridizations apart from its standard form such as GAs and GPs. In fact, the integration of different learning and adaptation techniques, to overcome individual limitations and achieve synergetic effects through hybridization or fusion of these techniques, has in recent years contributed to a large number of new intelligent system designs (Abraham, Corchado, & Corchado, 2009). The resulting evolutionary algorithms are often a more intelligent and robust system providing a human-interpretable, low-cost, approximate solution, as compared to where only a single technique is employed (Mitra & Acharya, 2003).

THEORETICAL FOUNDATIONS

The evolutionary approaches studied in this chapter include Genetic Neural Mathematical Methods (GNMM), Evolving Fuzzy Neural Network (EFuNN), and Cartesian Genetic Programming (CGP). These are now considered in turn:

The Genetic Neural Mathematical Method

The Genetic Neural Mathematical Method (GNMM) is a pattern classifier and analyzer based on GAs, Multi-Layer Perceptron (MLP) neural networks, and Mathematical Programming (MP) (Yang et al., 2008; Yang, Hines, Iliescu, & Leeson, 2008). It utilizes GAs to optimize input variables for MLPs and extract regression rules using MP upon successful training. GNMM consists of three steps: 1) GA-based feature selection, 2) MLP-based pattern classification and finally 3) MP-based knowledge extraction.

First, in the GA-based feature selection stage, an initial population of chromosomes is randomly generated. A chromosome consists of as many genes as input attributes. The encoding of a gene is binary, meaning that a particular attribute is considered as an input or not. The assessment of the fitness of a chromosome is the Mean Squared Error (MSE) when a three-layer MLP is being trained with the input attribute subset and output target for a limited number of epochs using the

Levenberg–Marquardt (LM) algorithm. The input selection is then realised through the evolutionary process of the GA.

In the second pattern classification step, an MLP is used to perform the pattern classification task using selected attributes and classification targets as inputs and outputs respectively. The aim of the current step is to minimize the classification error, and hence the epochs (iterations) number is large.

Upon successful training, in the third step, GNMM extract regression rules from trained MLPs. Let the activation function for all hidden layers be the *hyperbolic tangent* (tanh)

$$f(x) = \tanh(x) = \frac{1 - e^{-2x}}{1 + e^{-2x}} = \frac{2}{1 + e^{-2x}} - 1 \tag{1}$$

and a linear function be used in the output layer. The following equation can be used to approximate tanh:

$$g(x) = \begin{cases} 1 & x \geq \kappa \\ \beta_1 x + \beta_2 x^2 & 0 \leq x \leq \kappa \\ \beta_1 x - \beta_2 x^2 & -\kappa \leq x \leq 0 \\ -1 & x \leq -\kappa \end{cases} \tag{2}$$

in which $\beta_1 = 1.002, \beta_2 = -0.2510, \kappa = 1.9961$. Equation (2) divides the input domain into four sub-domains. Therefore, once the training is complete, rules associated with the trained MLP can be derived.

Evolving Fuzzy Neural Network

The Evolving Fuzzy Neural Network (EFuNN) proposed by Kasabov (1998, 2008; 2007) implements a strategy of dynamically growing and pruning the connectionist (i.e. ANN) architecture and parameter values. It consists of five layers: the input layer only represents the input variables; the second layer of nodes (fuzzy input neurons or fuzzy inputs) represents the fuzzification of each variable of the input space. These nodes can use Gaussian, triangular or other Membership Functions (MFs); here we have used triangular ones in order to reduce the computational complexity. The third layer is made up of rule nodes, evolving through time in a supervised way. The fourth layer represents the rule weights. Finally, the last layer implements the output variable, providing the system output (del-Hoyo, Martín-del-Brío, Medrano, & Fernández-Navajas, 2009; N. Kasabov, 1998).

EFuNN learns by associating (learning) new data points (vectors) to a rule node r_j: the centres of this node's hyperspheres (i.e. $W1(r_j)$ and $W2(r_j)$) adjust in the fuzzy input space depending on the distance between the new input vector and the rule node through a learning rate l_j, and in the fuzzy output space depending on the output error through the Widrow-Hoff least mean square delta algorithm:

$$\text{W1}\left(r_j^{(t+1)}\right) = \text{W1}\left(r_j^{(t)}\right) + l_j.(x_f - \text{W1}(r_j^{(t)})) \tag{3}$$

$$\text{W2}\left(r_j^{(t+1)}\right) = \text{W2}\left(r_j^{(t)}\right) + l_j.(y_f - \text{A2}).\text{A1}\left(r_j^{(t)}\right) \tag{4}$$

where x_f and y_f are fuzzy input and output vectors respectively; $\text{A2}=f_2(\text{W2}.\text{A1})$ is the activation vector of the fuzzy output neurons in the EFuNN structure when x is presented; $\text{A1}\left(r_j^{(t)}\right) = f_2(D(\text{W1}\left(r_j^{(t)}\right), x_f)$ is the activation of the rule node $r_j^{(t)}$. In other words, both weight vectors are iteratively adjusted – $W1$ through unsupervised training based on a similarity measure and $W2$ through supervised learning based on output error.

Furthermore, EFuNN allows for the construction of fuzzy rules from the network weights, and hence knowledge extraction – there is a rule layer in EFuNN to represent fuzzy rules. Thus, once the training is finished, fuzzy rules can be extracted from the system.

Cartesian Genetic Programming

Cartesian Genetic Programming (CGP) was originally developed by Miller and Thomson (2000) for the purpose of evolving digital circuits. CGP represents a program using a directed indexed graph as opposed to the tree representation normally used in conventional GP. The genotype is a fixed length representation consisting of a list of integers which encode the function and connections of each node in the directed graph. However, CGP uses a genotype-phenotype mapping that does not require all of the nodes to be connected to each other. As a result, the phenotype is bounded but has variable length. This allows areas of the genotype to be inactive and have no influence on the phenotype, leading to a neutral effect on genotype fitness called neutrality. An example of a CGP genotype and the corresponding phenotype that arose in the evolution of a 2-bit parallel multiplier is shown in Figure 2.

A benefit of CGP is that it allows the implicit reuse of nodes, as a node can be connected to the output of any previous node in the graph, thereby allowing the repeated reuse of sub-graphs. This is an advantage over tree-based GP representa-

Figure 2. A possible CGP genotype and corresponding phenotype for a 2-bit parallel multiplier circuit (adapted from Walker & Miller, 2008)

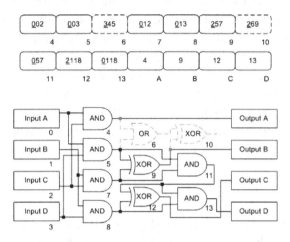

tions where identical sub-trees have to be constructed independently (Walker & Miller, 2008). The CGP technique has some similarities with Parallel Distributed Genetic Programming (PDGP) (Poli, 1997). PDGP directly represents the graphs using a two-dimensional grid topology, in which each row of the grid is executed in parallel in the direction of data flow, with the program output being taken from the final row of the grid. This allows the formation of efficient programs by reusing partial results. Originally, CGP also used a program topology defined by a rectangular grid of nodes with a user defined number of rows and columns. However, later work on CGP showed that it was more effective when the number of rows is chosen to be one (Harding, 2008; Wilson & Banzhaf, 2008). This one-dimensional topology is used in this chapter.

Due to its GP nature, rule extraction in CGP is straightforward – as the whole program is evolving arithmetic operators, the set of operators minimizing the training error can thus be used to present arithmetic rules. The CGP used here was implemented using the package developed by Sloper, Miotto et al. (2008).

RESULTS AND ANALYSIS

The Dataset

The dataset (denoted by ALC) were collected by sensing five different alcohols using 12 commercial tin oxide gas sensors. Briefly, the measurands were allowed to stand for 12 hours in air, then test liquids (0.4 μl) were injected into the test chamber, a small fan ensured rapid mixing, and the response of the sensors was recorded over a period of 3 min. In this manner a series of eight consecutive tests were carried out on methanol, 1-butanol, 2-propanol, 2-methyl-1-butanol, and ethanol. The data collected were normalized in terms of the average change in conductance after 3 min, in order to reduce the response values to the range [0, 1] and reduce the concentration dependence. As a result, ALC contains 40 patterns belonging to the five different odour classes described with eight patterns each. The patterns have 12 input features coming from 12 different commercial tin oxide gas sensors comprising the EN array. For a detailed description of experiment settings, please refer to Gardner, Hines et al. (1992; 1990).

GNMM Results

First of all, an MLP was trained using ALC with all available sensors using the LM algorithm. As a result, it achieved an RMSE of 0.0054 within 6 epochs. Applying GNMM to ALC, the two most significant sensors were found – sensor 6 and 9 have the same appearance percentage of 98.89%. Training the subset formed by these two sensors (denoted by $ALC_{(6,9)}$) and the classification target, with two hidden neurons MLP achieved the classification accuracy of 99.11% for R^2 and 0.3133 for RMSE, which implies that the model was successfully trained to achieve the PR tasks.

Rules extracted from ALC are shown in Table 1, in which ALC_t stands for the training subset, and ALC_s denotes the validation subset. Rule number denotes the hidden neuron and its subspaces (i.e. conditions in Equation (2)) that the data sample falls into. From Table 1 it is evident that the validation set is representative – while the most significant rule for ALC_t is rule No.23 (counts for ~33% of total training set), the same is true for ALC_t (counts for 75% of total validation set). Furthermore, it is clear that only six sub-spaces out of possible 16 are actually active (i.e. containing data samples). The most significant sub-space is the intersection of sub-space 2 and sub-space 3 of input neuron 1 and 2. This means that in general most data

Table 1. Rules fired for ALC

No.	ALC_t	ALC_s
13	5	
22	4	
23	12	3
32	8	
41	7	1
13	5	

sample reside within this intersection and the number gradually decrease as data sample moves further away from it. In this way, GNMM not only gives the number of rules associated with each data sample, but also provides the importance of the sub-spaces and the distribution of data sample.

Rather than a simplified representation of the distribution of ALC as in Table 1, Figure 3 depicts the rule space formed by GNMM. Note that in Figure 3 the separating line between the first and second sub-spaces for the second neuron is not shown since few data samples fall into that range. From Figure 3 it is clear that the rule space is not continuous (i.e. there are jumps) at intersections between the third sub-spaces of the two input neurons, which implies that there are less data samples within this area. This is clearly the case as no data samples were found under rule No. 33 in Table 1. Furthermore, as we already found that the most significant rule in ALC is rule No. 23. However, from Figure 3 it is evident that data residing in this area do not belong to a certain class. This means that although the input spaces of each neuron is divided into subspaces to extract regression rules, the classification of the data cannot be solely rely on them – instead, calculations have to done to mimic the behaviour of the output neuron(s).

EFuNN Results

Applying EFuNN to ALC, after the first epoch EFuNN achieved an RMSE of 0.51. Within 20 epochs, RMSE was reduced to 0.13. However, as the system iterates there is also a dramatic increase in the number of rule nodes (14 at the 1st epoch vs 50 at the 20th epoch). Consequently, too many rules affect the interpretability the system,

Figure 3. Rule space formed by GNMM for ALC

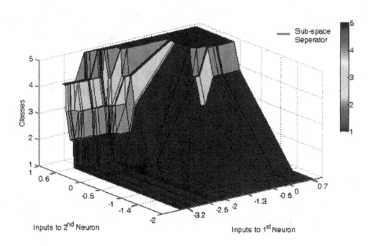

Figure 4. EFuNN rule space for ALC

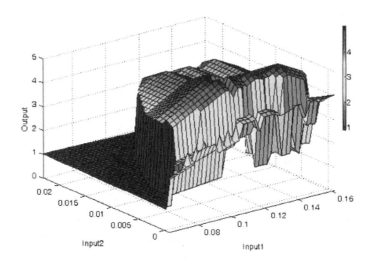

and also make applying new inputs problematic. Thus it was decided that sensors selected by GNMM are used instead of the whole dataset.

Applying EFuNN to the subset formed by variables found by GNMM (i.e. $ALC_{(6,9)}$), within 20 epochs, we achieved an RMSE of 0.187. Comparing with GNMM results (0.31), this result is much better. However, the trade-off is that the system generated 67 rules, which makes the system even more complex than with all available sensors. This is because in EFuNN the aim of training is to find connection nodes that associate fuzzy inputs and outputs. Thus, EFuNN rules are given in the format of membership degrees that each input/output belongs to. Let us take a rule found by EFuNN for an example. Basically it states that if input1 belongs to the 1st MF to a degree of 0.013, to the 2nd and 3rd to a degree of 0.957 and 0.030 respectively, and input2 has a degree of 0.388, 0.612 and 0 to its MFs, then the fuzzy output is [0 0.082 0.819]. Based on these fuzzy output values, aggregations can be performed to produce predicted class values.

As a result of 67 rules, the rule space formed by EFuNN is discrete comparing to GNMM (Figure 3), as shown in Figure 4. This discreteness leads to a situation where small changes in inputs result in significant changes in the outputs (i.e. consequents). However, both present similar overall shapes. Comparing GNMM rule space with its counterpart of EFuNN, it is obvious that there is a truncation when the predicted class values are above/below the allowed range.

MFs used for the two inputs are triangular-shaped. Another popular choice for input MFs are Gaussian functions. As these MFs do not change over iterations, choices have to be made before training starts. However, this implies another important disadvantage of EFuNN, i.e. the determination of the network parameters. There are many parameters in EFuNN such as number and type of MF for each input variable, sensitivity threshold, error threshold and the learning rates etc. Even though a trial and error approach is practical, when the problem becomes complicated (large number of input variables) determining the optimal parameters will be a tedious task (Abraham & Nath, 2001).

CGP Results

Applying CGP to the ALC using 3-fold cross validation, the system achieved a classification accuracy of 92.8% (RMSE 0.032). Since 8 nodes were used with the level of connections being 4, it results in 8 arithmetic expressions. However, not all nodes were used to calculate the final results. Furthermore, not all input attributes were used to calculate the final results – only attributes6 and 8 were used.

Compared with GNMM and EFuNN, CGP achieved an automatic input variable deduction without an explicit input selection step. This was realized by evolving different input variables combined with various arithmetic operators. Furthermore, due to its GP nature, rule extraction from the CGP system is straight forward. However, functions that can be constructed by the algorithm need to be selected carefully – on the one hand, the number of possible functions is immense; on the other hand, fewer functions will increase the efficiency of the algorithm (Schmutter, 2002).

CONCLUSION

To summarize the above analysis, it can be found that an important feature of GNMM is that it produces continuous outputs which results in a smaller RMSE. Furthermore, GNMM's MLP nature ensures that it achieves higher classification accuracy than GP methods and first-order Fuzzy Inference Systems (FISs). On the other hand, fuzzy-space-mapping approaches such as EFuNN can dramatically increase the number of fuzzy rules by implementing both supervised and unsupervised learning. This is particularly useful when input patterns are less clustered. The advantage of CGP is that it produces an automatic input feature selection; and the rule extraction after successful training is straightforward. A feature comparison of these techniques is shown in Table 2. A common feature shared by these approaches is that they all, to some extent, fall into the EC category – as later iterations rely heavily on previous ones to continuously improve computation results. This also highlights the merits of EC in the context of MDF. In MDF, the task is to fuse continuously evolving signals instead of static patterns. Hence, the MDF algorithm has to have some aspects of EC included so that it will perform in an adaptive manner. However, one of the main

Table 2. Comparisons of EC features

	Core technique	Input	Output	Training	Rule
GNMM	MLP	GA optimization needed	No limits	ICA weights initialization and LM	By dividing input space
EFuNN	Mamdani-style FIS	Can evolve over iterations	Can evolve over iterations	Hybrid unsupervised and supervised learning	Fuzzy rules
CGP	GP	Fix	No limits	Darwinian evolution theory	Arithmetic rules

disadvantages of EC based techniques is that they can be very computer intensive, often requiring extensive computing power (Hughes & Ruprai, 1999). This can be solved by carefully selecting features that are fed into the algorithms.

Regarding future research trends, in the scientific literature there is a growing interest in the exchange of information between natural systems and computational systems (Potvin, 2008). Bio-inspired algorithms such as ECs are representative of this trend. However, our current understanding of biological processes such as natural evolution is yet very limited. Thus, more thorough understanding of natural processes will result in a better design of evolutionary algorithms that will in turn benefit the scientific world.

REFERENCES

Abraham, A., Corchado, E., & Corchado, J. M. (2009). Hybrid learning machines. *Neurocomputing, 72*(13-15), 2729-2730. doi: DOI: 10.1016/j.neucom.2009.02.017

Abraham, A., & Nath, B. (2001). A neuro-fuzzy approach for modelling electricity demand in Victoria. *Applied Soft Computing, 1*(2), 127–138. doi:10.1016/S1568-4946(01)00013-8

Ballabio, D., Cosio, M. S., Mannino, S., & Todeschini, R. (2006). A chemometric approach based on a novel similarity/diversity measure for the characterisation and selection of electronic nose sensors. *Analytica Chimica Acta, 578*(2), 170–177. doi:10.1016/j.aca.2006.06.067

Bishop, C. M. (2006). *Pattern recognition and machine learning.* New York, NY: Springer.

Davis, L. (1987). *Genetic algorithms and simulated annealing.* London, UK/ Los Altos, CA: Pitman/ Morgan Kaufmann Publishers.

De Castro, L. N. (2006). *Fundamentals of natural computing basic concepts, algorithms, and applications*. Boca Raton, FL: Chapman & Hall/CRC.

De Jong, K. A. (2006). *Evolutionary computation: A unified approach*. Cambridge, MA: MIT Press.

del-Hoyo, R., Martín-del-Brío, B., Medrano, N., & Fernández-Navajas, J. (2009). Computational intelligence tools for next generation quality of service management. *Neurocomputing*.

Elmenreich, W. (2007). *A review on system architectures for sensor fusion applications*. Paper presented at the Software Technologies for Embedded and Ubiquitous Systems. 5th IFIP WG 10.2 International Workshop, SEUS 2007. Revised Papers. (LNCS 4761), Santorini Island, Greece.

Gardner, J. W., Boilot, P., & Hines, E. L. (2005). Enhancing electronic nose performance by sensor selection using a new integer-based genetic algorithm approach. *Sensors and Actuators. B, Chemical, 106*(1), 114–121. doi:10.1016/j.snb.2004.05.043

Gardner, J. W., Hines, E. L., & Tang, H. C. (1992). Detection of vapours and odours from a multisensor array using pattern-recognition techniques. Part 2: Artificial neural networks. *Sensors and Actuators. B, Chemical, B9*(1), 9–15. doi:10.1016/0925-4005(92)80187-3

Gardner, J. W., Hines, E. L., & Wilkinson, M. (1990). Application of artificial neural networks to an electronic olfactory system. *Measurement Science & Technology, 1*(5), 446–451. doi:10.1088/0957-0233/1/5/012

Hall, D. L., & Llinas, J. (2008). Multisensor data fusion. In Liggins, M. E., Hall, D. L., & Llinas, J. (Eds.), *Handbook of multisensor data fusion: Theory and practice* (2nd ed., pp. 1–14). Boca Raton, FL: CRC Press.

Harding, S. (2008). *Evolution of image filters on graphics processor units using cartesian genetic programming*. Hong Kong, China.

Hines, E. L., Boilot, P., Gardner, J. W., Gongora, M. A., & Llobet, E. (2003). Pattern analysis for electronic noses. In Pearce, T. C., Schiffman, S. S., Nagle, H. T., & Gardner, J. W. (Eds.), *Handbook of machine olfaction: Electronic nose technology* (pp. 133–160). Weinheim, Germany: Wiley-VCH.

Huang, Y.-B., Lan, Y.-B., Hoffmann, W. C., & Lacey, R. E. (2007). Multisensor data fusion for high quality data analysis and processing in measurement and instrumentation. *Journal of Bionics Engineering, 4*(1), 53–62. doi:10.1016/S1672-6529(07)60013-4

Hughes, J., & Ruprai, B. (1999). *Distributed genetic programming: Google Patents.*

Kasabov, N. (1998). Evolving fuzzy neural networks-algorithms, applications and biological motivation: Methodologies for the conception, design and application of soft computing. *World Scientific,* 271-274.

Kasabov, N. (2008). Evolving intelligence in humans and machines: Integrative evolving connectionist systems approach. *IEEE Computational Intelligence Magazine, 3*(3), 23–37. doi:10.1109/MCI.2008.926584

Kasabov, N. K. (2007). *Evolving connectionist systems: The knowledge engineering approach* (2nd ed.). London, UK: Springer.

Miller, J. F., & Thomson, P. (2000). *Cartesian genetic programming.* (LNCS 1802), (pp. 121-132).

Mitchell, H. B. (2007). *Multi-sensor data fusion: An introduction.* Berlin, Germany: Springer Verlag.

Mitra, S., & Acharya, T. (2003). *Data mining: Multimedia, soft computing, and bioinformatics.* Hoboken, NJ: John Wiley.

Poli, R. (1997). *Parallel distributed genetic programming applied to the evolution of natural language recognisers.* Berlin, Germany.

Potvin, J.-Y. (2008). A review of bio-inspired algorithms for vehicle routing. In Pereira, F. B., & Tavares, J. (Eds.), *Bio-inspired algorithms for the vehicle routing problem* (1st ed., pp. 1–34). New York, NY: Springer.

Reeves, C. R., & Rowe, J. E. (2003). *Genetic algorithms: Principles and perspectives: A guide to GA theory.* Boston, MA: Kluwer Academic Publishers.

Rojas, R. (1996). *Neural networks: A systematic introduction.* Berlin, Germany/ New York, NY: Springer-Verlag.

Rothlauf, F. (2006). *Representations for genetic and evolutionary algorithms* (2nd ed.). Heidelberg, Germany: Springer.

Schmutter, P. (2002). *Object oriented ontogenetic programming: Breeding computer programms that work like multicellular creatures.* Dortmund, Germany: University Systems Analysis Research Group.

Scott, S. M., James, D., & Ali, Z. (2006). Data analysis for electronic nose systems. *Mikrochimica Acta, 156,* 3–4. doi:10.1007/s00604-006-0623-9

Sloper, J. E., Miotto, G. L., & Hines, E. (2008). Dynamic error recovery in the ATLAS TDAQ system. *IEEE Transactions on Nuclear Science, 55*(1), 405–410. doi:10.1109/TNS.2007.913472

Walker, J. A., & Miller, J. F. (2008). The automatic acquisition, evolution and reuse of modules in Cartesian genetic programming. *IEEE Transactions on Evolutionary Computation, 12*(4), 397–417. doi:10.1109/TEVC.2007.903549

Wilson, G., & Banzhaf, W. (2008). *A comparison of cartesian genetic programming and linear genetic programming.* Italy: Naples.

Yang, J., Hines, E. L., Guymer, I., Iliescu, D. D., Leeson, M. S., & King, G. P. (2008). A genetic algorithm-artificial neural network method for the prediction of longitudinal dispersion coefficient in rivers. In Porto, A., Pazos, A., & Buño, W. (Eds.), *Advancing artificial intelligence through biological process applications* (pp. 358–374). Hershey, PA: Idea Group Inc.

Yang, J., Hines, E. L., Iliescu, D. D., & Leeson, M. S. (2008). Multi-input optimisation of river flow parameters and rule extraction using genetic-neural technique. In Hines, E. L., Leeson, M. S., Martínez-Ramón, M., Pardo, M., Llobet, E., Iliescu, D. D., & Yang, J. (Eds.), *Intelligent systems: Techniques and applications* (pp. 173–198). Shaker Publishing.

Chapter 3
Making an Electronic Nose Versatile:
The Role of Incremental Learning Algorithms

Nabarun Bhattacharyya
Centre for the Development of Advanced Computing (C-DAC), India

Bipan Tudu
Jadavpur University, India

Rajib Bandyopadhyay
Jadavpur University, India

ABSTRACT

Development of a pattern recognition system in the area of machine olfaction is a complex and challenging task due to the following reasons: (1) It is practically very difficult to get adequate data required to train the computation model, compared to the other applications of pattern recognition like image processing; (2) In many applications, the samples arrive in batches or are available over multiple seasons or even over multiple years; (3) The user industry, in general, shows reluctance when approached for samples and wants immediate result; (4) Data availability in batches makes the training process difficult, and requires storage of data for all the samples.

Because of these factors, it is necessary to make the system flexible in such a way that the system is able to update an existing classifier without affecting the classification performance on old data, and such classifiers should have the property

DOI: 10.4018/978-1-61520-915-6.ch003

as being both stable and plastic. Conventional pattern classification algorithms require the entire dataset during training, and thereby fail to meet the criteria of being plastic and stable at the same time. The incremental learning algorithms possess these features, and thus, the electronic nose systems become extremely versatile when equipped with these classifiers. In this chapter, the authors describe different incremental learning algorithms for machine olfaction.

INTRODUCTION TO INCREMENTAL LEARNING

In conventional supervised classifiers, the entire dataset is required during training and thus their role is severely limited in some applications of machine olfaction systems. In such applications, it may not be possible to collect the entire dataset within a short time and assembling of data may spread over multiple seasons or even years. Hence, the pattern classifier should have the following two important features:

1. Plasticity: the property to incorporate new knowledge without accessing the old dataset
2. Stability: the property to retain the old and acquired knowledge.

Plasticity and stability are two contradictory requirements for machine learning algorithms and this is commonly known as the stability – plasticity dilemma (Giraud-Carrier, 2000). Conventional training algorithms fail to meet both these requirements, as the models require the entire dataset before the commencement of the training session. Augmentation of new knowledge requires the old as well as new dataset, and after training with the augmented dataset, there may be some loss of knowledge. This is indeed a severe limitation while introducing a new technology employing a machine olfaction system. The situation may change significantly if the user industry starts getting some results with a few data, even though the classification may not be accurate enough initially. In such a situation, incremental learning algorithms can play a very important role. These incremental learning procedures can learn perpetually without forgetting the learned knowledge and can start classifying with very few data as well. For example, when an electronic nose is equipped with a computational model that has the feature of incremental learning, the instrument may be sent from one field or plant to another and trained with the new samples. It will try to classify the signature when subjected to a sample and at the same time, learn the new patterns without forgetting previous knowledge. Since this instrument once trained with some samples will give a result of classification, the user industry would either be satisfied with the result or, if they desire, may retrain the instrument.

This feature makes the instrument versatile and thus an electronic nose instrument with an incremental classifier is more likely to be acceptable to the user industry.

To summarize, an incremental learning algorithm should meet the following criteria (Polikar et al., 2001):

a. It should be able to learn additional information using new data.
b. It should not require access to the original old data, used to train the existing classifier.
c. It should not forget previously acquired knowledge.
d. It should be able to accommodate new classes that may be introduced with new data.

There are many approaches for designing such types of classifiers and in this chapter; design of such classifiers is discussed employing both fuzzy logic and neural networks. For these classifiers, while the fuzzy logic based incremental learning is based on the principle of on-line rule generation, the radial basis function neural network model utilizes the facility of adding new kernels in the hidden layer. There are many incremental models with back-propagation multilayer perceptron (BP-MLP), and we discuss a simple model where the incremental feature is incorporated by merging multiple networks in parallel. In all the models, we have assumed that the electronic olfactory system has multiple sensors as inputs and only one output attribute.

FUZZY LOGIC BASED INCREMENTAL LEARNING

Fuzzy incremental learning techniques have been used in (Singh, 1999; Mouchaweh et al., 2002) for classification purposes and are found to be quite useful. For improving decision making in real environments, fuzzy techniques are reported to be better than the conventional non-fuzzy methods (Klir & Folger, 1989; Pal & Majumder, 1986). Here we describe the incremental fuzzy model using the Wang Mendel method (Wang & Mendel, 1992) for on-line rule generation.

The Fuzzy Model

The fuzzy model is a multiple-input single-output (MISO) type and is shown in Figure 1. It follows the Tagaki-Sugeno model (Takagi & Sugeno, 1985), where the antecedents are fuzzy and the consequent is a crisp variable. The responses of the sensors are first fuzzified into a fuzzy set. The inference engine generates the output using the rulebase, which are defuzzified to declare the final crisp output.

Figure 1. Fuzzy model with multiple inputs and single output

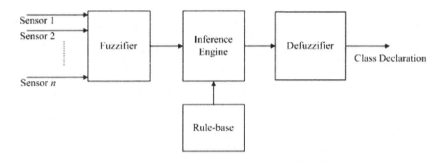

Generating Fuzzy Rules from Electronic Nose Data

The fuzzy model proposed by Wang and Mendel (WM) (Wang & Mendel, 1992; Wang, 2003) is widely used for generating rules online from input-output data and has been found to be quite successful. During the initial training phase of the incremental classifier, a preliminary rulebase is realized by means of WM method from the available input-output data. In the testing phase, the inference mechanism starts its decision making with these initial rules; at the same time the incremental learning algorithm adds new rules as data for new classes arrive in.

The set of input-output (desired) data pairs for the '*i*'th sample are:

$$\left(x_1^{(i)}, x_2^{(i)}, \ldots\ldots, x_{n-1}^{(i)}, x_n^{(i)}; g^{(i)} \right)$$

Here x_1^i to x_n^i are the normalized values of the sensor responses and g^i is the class of the sample. This is a simple *n* input single output case. Here a set of fuzzy rules from the above data are generated and these fuzzy rules are used to determine a mapping $f:(x_1 \ldots x_n) \rightarrow g$. Different steps for generating fuzzy rule base are given below:

Step 1: Divide the input and output spaces into fuzzy regions

Determine the domain intervals of x_1, x_2, ...,x_n and g and designate as $\left[x_1^-, x_1^+ \right], \left[x_2^-, x_2^+ \right], \ldots, \left[x_n^-, x_n^+ \right]$ and $[g^-, g^+]$. Divide each domain interval into $(2N+1)$ fuzzy regions. The representative membership function for these inputs and outputs are shown in Figure 2, where $N=4$ and the lengths of the regions are equal. The shape of each membership function is triangular and the membership value (μ) lies in [0,1]. The vertex for each variable lies at the center of the region and has a mem-

Figure 2. Membership functions of the sensors. (The regions are represented as $r_1 \cdots r_9$)

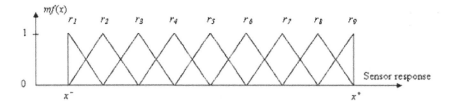

bership value of 1. This triangular shape has several advantages (Pedrycz, 1994) and has been used by many researchers primarily for its simplicity in implementation (Chang & Liao, 2006; Marseguerra et al., 2003; Ma et al., 2000), although other types of membership functions can also be considered.

Step 2: Generate fuzzy rules from given data pairs

First, obtain the membership values of $x_1^{(i)}, x_2^{(i)}, ..., x_n^{(i)}$, and $g^{(i)}$ in different regions, and then assign each variable with maximum membership value with that region (r). Then, the rules are obtained from each pair of input-output data.

$$IF\ x_1^{(i)}\ is\ r_a(\mu_{r_a}^{(i)})\ and\ x_2^{(i)}\ is\ r_b(\mu_{r_b}^{(i)}).\ ......and\ x_n^{(i)}\ is\ r_c(\mu_{r_c}^{(i)})$$
$$THEN\ g^i\ is\ r_d(\mu_{r_d}^{(i)})$$

$$(1)$$

where, r_a, r_b, r_c are the regions of the input space, r_d is the region in the output space, and $\mu^{(i)}$ s are the corresponding membership values. The rules generated in this way are "and" rules, and in each rule, there are n atomic clauses in the antecedent part corresponding to the n sensors. The maximum number of rules that can be generated is thus n^{2N+1}. This number is quite large, but in practice, the actual number of rules in the rule base would be quite less and should not pose any problem for the implementation.

Step 3: Assign a degree to each rule

It may be possible that there are a large number of samples and same rule could be generated more than once. The rules with the same antecedent but different consequent should be eliminated to keep the integrity of the rule base. This is done by assigning a degree (D) to each rule by using the following product strategy,

Table 1. Training algorithm

Step 1: Data from both the sensor array as well as the corresponding target output of the sample are given as input.

Step 2: *if* the data are for an existing class, then

if the all the atomic clauses of the antecedent

and the consequent match with an existing rule / *already in rule base*

Go to **Step 1**

Step 3: *m* readings are taken for the same sample and

average response (x_i) and average deviation $(\pm\sigma_i)$ for each sensor are recorded

A new rule is formed with the antecedent as in Equation (3) or Equation (4) and the consequent as its class.

The rules along with the product of the membership values of the atomic clauses of the antecedent are added to the rule base.

Go to **S*tep 1***

$$D\left(rule\ i\right) = \mu_{r_a}\left(x_1^{(i)}\right) * \mu_{r_b}\left(x_2^{(i)}\right) * \ldots\ldots * \mu_{r_n}\left(x_n^{(i)}\right) * \mu_{r_d}\left(g^{(i)}\right) \qquad (2)$$

when there is a conflict, i.e. for the same inputs, the target or the output is different and the rules with the highest degree *D,* are considered.

Step 4: Determine a mapping based on the fuzzy rule base

The centroid defuzzification strategy is mostly used for obtaining the crisp output and to determine the output class *g* for given input x_1 to x_n, this method may be employed. This is described in the next section.

Description of the Incremental Fuzzy Classifier

The training algorithm, shown in Table 1, describes how the classifier can incrementally acquire new data without forgetting the previous knowledge. During the initialization phase, the electronic nose is to be trained with reasonably large number of samples so that the rule base generated has substantial inference capability. But in practice, it may be difficult to get a large collection of samples initially, and the performance of the electronic nose classifier may not be reasonably good in the beginning. However, as data for more and more samples are added, the rule base would be gradually enriched and so also the inference capability.

First, the training algorithm in Table 1 is executed to frame the initial database. Each odourant sample is subjected to multiple (*m*) sniffing cycles and in each sniffing cycle, only the steady state value for each of the sensors is stored. The average response (x_i) of each sensor and the average deviation $(\pm\sigma_i)$ are noted from these *m* readings for a particular sample. The region specified by $x_i \pm \sigma_i$ is defined as the domain of that sensor output for the class of that sample. The average deviation is considered instead of the maximum deviation because the number of conflicting rules generated has been found to be significantly higher than when the average deviation of the sensors responses are considered. Here during the fuzzification method, the sensor input is represented by a fuzzy region (r_i) and two membership values (μ_{1i} and μ_{2i}) corresponding to the domain boundaries of the sensor response. It may so happen that because of the deviation ($\pm\sigma_i$), the domain boundaries will lie in two different but adjacent regions. In this case, the antecedent of the rules will have two fuzzy regions and two membership values. So, the antecedents of the rules are like:

$$IF\left(sensor\,1\,is\left(r_4,\mu_{1i}\;and\;r_4,\mu_{2i}\right)\right)AND\left(sensor\,2\cdots\right)\cdots//domain\;of\;sensor\,1\;in\;r_4\;only$$

(3)

or

$$IF\left(sensor\,1\,is\left(r_4,\mu_{1i}\;and\;r_5,\mu_{2i}\right)\right)AND\left(sensor\,2\cdots\right)\cdots//domain\;of\;sensor\,1\;in\;r_4\;and\;r_5\;only$$

(4)

Here μ_{1i} is the membership value corresponding to x_i-σ_i and μ_{2i} is the membership value corresponding to x_i+σ_i.

While data for new samples are added, there is a possibility of conflict in the rules, e.g. a new rule may be generated where all the atomic clauses of the antecedent are same, but the consequent is different. There are two methods to resolve this conflicting situation:

a. The human panel may be consulted to remove one of the conflicting rules.
b. The algorithm may assign a weight to each rule, which is the product of the membership values of each of the atomic clauses of the antecedent as in Equation 2. The rule having the product value maximum may be considered in the rule base.

Once the electronic nose is trained with some known samples, the rule base would be non-empty and the instrument would be ready for field trial. For unknown samples, the testing algorithm is to be executed and it would declare the class of the sample. It is unlikely that for any new sample, the sensor responses would match with any of the existing rules. So, in addition to declaring the class, the algorithm also declares a confidence value which is calculated based on the similarity of the

Figure 3. Augmentation of the rule base

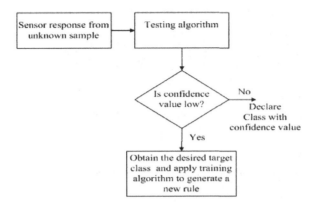

antecedent of the existing rules. If the confidence value is quite low, it indicates that the declared class is not reliable and the sensor data along with its class should be given as input to the training algorithm to augment the rule base. This is explained in Figure 3. The testing algorithm is explained in Table 2 and algorithm for matching the antecedent of a rule is presented in Table 3.

The factor b_j is used to provide more weight to the rules where more number of clauses in the antecedents matches.

Table 2. Testing algorithm

> **Step 1:** Sensor responses for a new sample are given as input.
> **Step 2:** Calculate the membership value (μ_i) and the fuzzy region (r_i) of unknown data for each sensor.
> **Step 3:** Search for the rules which are partially or fully matching.
>   *for j=1:number of rules*
> *if* one or more sensor responses in the antecedent match // *detailed in* Table 3 *and*
>   Figures 4-7.
> m_j= *the product of the membership values fo each atomic clause in the antecedent*
> b_j= 1/exp(*no. of sensors-no. of matched atomic clauses for each fuzzy rule*)
> // *confidence factor*
> g_j= *center value of output region*
>   *end if*
>   *end for*
> **Step 4:** Centroid defuzzification formula is used to calculate the class of the unknown sample.
>
> $$calculated \quad grade = \frac{\sum_{j=1}^{k} m_j * g_j * b_j}{\sum_{j=1}^{k} m_j}$$ where, k is the number of fuzzy rule in the fuzzy rule base.

Table 3. Algorithm for matching the antecedent of a rule

Initialize count = 0
for i = 1: number of sensors

if $\left(\mu_i \leq \mu_{1i}{}^j \text{ and } r_i = r_{1i}{}^j\right)$ or $\left(\mu_i \leq \mu_{2i}{}^j \text{ and } r_i = r_{2i}{}^j\right)$ // *domain boundary on two different fuzzy regions (*Figure 4*)*
      count = count + 1

  else if $\left(\mu_i \geq \mu_{1i}{}^j \text{ and } \mu_i \geq \mu_{2i}{}^j \text{ and } r_i = r_{1i}{}^j\right)$ //*domain boundaries on two different slopes of the same fuzzy region (*Figure 5*)*
    count = count + 1

  else if $\left(\mu_{1i}{}^j \leq \mu_i \leq \mu_{2i}{}^j \text{ and } r_i = r_{1i}{}^j\right)$ //*domain boundaries on the negative slope of the fuzzy region (*Figure 6*)*
count = count + 1

      else if $\left(\mu_{1i}{}^j \geq \mu_i \geq \mu_{2i}{}^j \text{ and } r_i = r_{1i}{}^j\right)$ //*domain boundaries on the positive slope of the fuzzy region (*Figure 7*)*
count = count + 1
      end if
      end if
      end if
  end if
end for

Figure 4. Membership values when domain boundaries are in two different regions

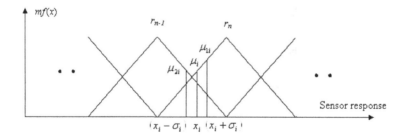

INCREMENTAL LEARNING USING THE FUZZY-C-MEANS ALGORITHM

Fuzzy-C-Means (FCM) introduced by (Bezdek, 1981) is a method of clustering and partitioning algorithm of fuzzy data. The basic idea of fuzzy clustering is to divide the data into fuzzy partitions that are overlapped with one another. The FCM employs fuzzy partitioning such that a data point can belong to all existing classes with different membership values between 0 and 1.

Figure 5. Membership values when domain boundaries are in same regions but on different slope

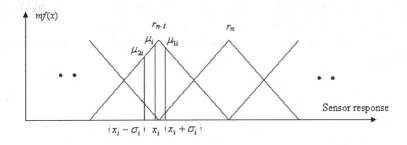

Figure 6. Membership values when domain boundaries are in same regions and on negative slope

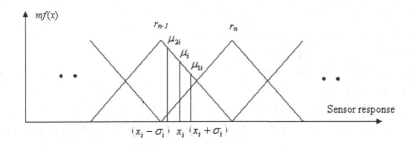

Figure 7. Membership values when domain boundaries are in same regions and on positive slope

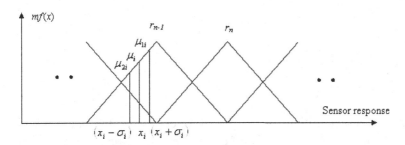

The FCM method of clustering enables a data to belong to multiple classes according to the degree of closeness of the data to those classes. A data may not strictly belong to a single class and may have certain inherit traits that pertain to one or more different classes. So the data will be a part of all these overlapping sets according to its degree of similarity to them referred as the *membership function*. It determines the extent to which a data will be a part of a certain class. A data can belong to a particular class with membership value ranging from 0 to 1 and the sum of all membership functions for a particular data of all the classes is 1.

The FCM is an iterative algorithm whose aim is to minimize the objective function given by:

$$J_m = \sum_{i=1}^{N} \sum_{j=1}^{C} \mu_{ij}^m \left\| x_i - c_j \right\|^2 \qquad 1 \leq m < \infty \tag{5}$$

where,

m is any real number greater than 1 (usually taken as 2), which is a weighing coefficient denoting the fuzziness of the cluster,

x_i is the $i^{th}d$- dimensional measured data,

c_j is the d- dimensional center of the cluster,

μ_{ij} is the degree of membership of x_i in cluster j,

N is the number of samples and

C is the number of classes.

d represents the total number of sensors present. $\|x_i\text{-}c_j\|$ denotes the Euclidean distance between x_i and c_j. Fuzzy partitioning is carried out through an iterative optimization of the objective function as given by Equation (5), with the update of membership function μ_{ij} and the cluster center c_j given by:

$$\mu_{ij} = 1 / \sum_{k=1}^{C} \left(\left\| x_i - c_j \right\| / \left\| x_i - c_k \right\| \right)^{2/(m-1)} \tag{6}$$

$$c_j = \left(\sum_{i=1}^{N} \mu_{ij}^m . x_i \right) / \left(\sum_{i=1}^{N} \mu_{ij}^m \right) \tag{7}$$

The stopping condition for the iteration depends on the minimization of the objective function. After the classification, the authenticity of the process may be verified by a rule base formed on the basis of the membership functions of the samples. The rule base is an ensemble of clauses guiding the inclusion of a sample within the existing clusters.

The Training Algorithm

The incremental FCM algorithm is an advancement that stems from the original FCM. It starts with the parameters generated from its non-incremental counterpart in the initial step. The FCM algorithm when applied to a set of initial data, calculates the three parameters, namely the objective function, the membership function values, and the cluster centers given by Equations (5)-(7), respectively. The parameters evaluated are preserved and a rule base is formed with them for subsequent classification of new samples. The incremental FCM training algorithm in its generalized form is given in Table 4.

On encountering a new set of data, testing is effected with the existing rule base for determining the number of data clusters involved. The rule base in its simplified format is a collection of clauses determining the degree of existence of a sample within a cluster. If a certain number of samples within the new dataset is unclassified by the rule base then the number of new class is increased by one. Prudent choice of threshold value for the rule base is required to avoid the involvement of misclassified data patterns from the existing class in the evaluation process and 10-15% of the latest available volume of data may be taken in practice.

The center location for the new class is taken to be the mean value of the samples presumed to be falling under this class i.e. the samples that have been rendered uncertain by the rule base.

Rule Base for Testing with Unknown Sample

The fuzzy rule base is required for testing, when the trained classifier is subjected to unknown samples. The incremental FCM procedure along with the rule base can be thought of as the training-testing algorithm pair, where the incremental FCM algorithm adapts latest available dataset to form the clusters, and the rule base authenticates the evaluation. In addition, the rule base performs another function of determining the existing cluster number within the available samples.

The rule base calculates the membership function values of a sample to each of the clusters as per Equation (6) formed by the incremental FCM classifier as a preamble to the decision making stage. Since the rule base is implemented with an incremental classifier the total number of rules generated in each incremental step is different, owing to the fact that at each increment new classes of data are available and new clusters are formed. Any given data sample, after evaluation by the rule base encompasses the possibility of belonging to one of the following categories:

1. **Pure class:** The sample highlights traits of a single class only.

Table 4. Incremental FCM training algorithm

Step 1: Perform conventional FCM with original data.
    Step 1.1: Randomly initialize the membership matrix.
    Step 1.2: At k-step: calculate the center vectors using Equation (7).
    Step 1.3: *if* the objective function is less than a predetermined small value
    then Go to **Step 3**
    Else Go to **Step 1.4**
Step 1.4: Update membership values with the help of centers calculated from **Step 1.2**
using Equation (6).
    Update centers with the help of new membership values by Equation (7).
    Go to **Step 1.2**
Step 2: The new available data from the electronic nose are given as input to the incremental FCM classifier.
Step 3: Check for the existence of new classes.
    Step 3.1. Test the new set of data with the existing centers.
    Step 3.2. *if* the total data evaluated as UNCERTAIN class > threshold percentage, *then* declare a new
class and Go to S**tep 4else** STOP.
Step 4: Calculate the center location of the assumed new class to be the mean of all uncertain samples, which
do not fall under any existing clusters.
Step 5: With the new set of data, calculate the membership function values with the existing classes using
Equation (6).
Step 6: Form the objective function using Equation (5) with the membership function values and center
matrices obtained in **Step 4** and **Step 5**.
Step 7: *if* the objective function is less than a predetermined small value
then Go to **step 9**.
Step 8: Update the cluster centers with the help of membership values calculated from **Step 5** and the new
data set using Equation (7). Update the membership values with these centers using Equation (6).
Go to **Step 6**.
Step 9: Test the dataset with the corresponding rule base (explained later) for the incremental step of the
algorithm with the total number of classes increased by 1.
Step 10: *if* the total data generated for UNCERTAIN class > the threshold percentage, *then* add a new class
and Go to **Step 5**.
Else modify the new centre locations for the class that already existed in the previous incremental steps by
Equation (7) *and* **STOP.**

2.   **Mixture of multiple classes:** The attributes of the sample demonstrates mixture of traits pertaining to two or more classes.

3.   **Uncertain class:** The sample cannot be fit into any of the present clusters with confidence.

At any given incremental step let there be n number of different classes resulting in n different clusters formed by the incremental FCM classifier. A generalized rule implemented for the determination of pure class can be defined as:

if $\mu(s_l) > \mu^{Thl}$ **then** *the score is* s_l, *where* $\mu(s_l)$ *is the degree of membership value of each cluster,* $l=1,2,...,n$, *and* μ^{Thl} *is the activation threshold of rule for pure class.*

The threshold values of the membership functions should be chosen judicially so as only a single rule is fired at a time. As there are multiple additions of new

Table 5. Rule base for testing

Step 1: Get the unknown data by the electronic nose instrument.

Step 2: Calculate the membership function ($\mu(s_i)$) for the data for each of the clusters formed where i is the cluster identifying index.

Step 3: *if* $\mu(s_l) > 0.80$ *then* declare the sample as a pure class of s_l *and* stop the search. where $l=1,2,\ldots,6$, μp being the threshold membership value for pure class. // For pure class

else if $0.6 < \mu(sl_j) < 0.80$ *and* $.15 < \mu(sp_j) < .25$ *then* declare the sample to belong to two overlapping domains formed by classes sl and sp_a *nd* stop the search.

  where $l,p=1,2,\ldots,6$ and $l \neq p$ // For mixture of two classes

else if $0.25 < \mu(sl_{p,q}) \cdot 0.60$ *then* declare the data to belong to three overlapping domains formed by classes sl sp and sq *nd* stop the search.

  where $l,p,q=1,2,\ldots,6$ and $l \neq p \neq q$ // For mixture of three classes

else if $\mu(sl_j) < 0.27$ or $\sum \left(any\ five(\mu(s_l)) \right) > 0.20$ then declare the sample as uncertain. // For uncertain class

---

samples to the existing dataset at each incremental step therefore the rule base is reconstructed for each of these incremental steps.

A sample rule base for testing is presented in Table 5, where the threshold values for the membership functions are taken judiciously and may be used in any applications.

INCREMENTAL BACK-PROPAGATION MULTILAYER PERCEPTRON MODEL

The back-propagation multilayer perceptron (BP-MLP) model is the most commonly used neural network for electronic nose applications (Pardo & Sberveglieri, 2002). The network consists of a set of sensory units (source nodes) that constitute the *input layer*, one or more *hidden layers* of computation nodes and an *output layer* of output nodes. The architecture of the BP-MLP network is shown in Figure 8.

Error back propagation learning consists of two passes through the different layers of the network - a forward pass and a backward pass. In the *forward pass* data patterns are applied to the source nodes of the network, and their effect is propagated through the network. Finally, a set of outputs is produced as the actual response of the network. During the forward pass the synaptic weights and bias weights of the network are all *fixed*. The actual response of the network is subtracted form the desired response to produce an *error signal*. This error signal is then propagated backward through the network against the direction of the synaptic connection – hence the name *error back-propagation*. The synaptic weights are adjusted to make the actual response of the network move closer to the desired response in a statistical sense.

Figure 8. Architecture of a multilayer perceptron with one hidden layer

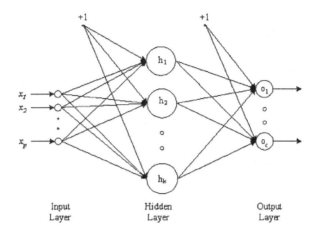

The Incremental Model

There are quite a few incremental learning algorithms reported in the literature using BP-MLP (Fu, Huang & Principe, 1996). In this section, we discuss a simple model by merging multiple MLPs proposed by (Chakraborty & Pal, 2003). In this model, the input sample set is divided into k number of subsets (S_i). Each training subset (data patterns) is trained by the network one after another. After completion of each training phase, the newly generated learning parameters are merged with old network learning parameters. This signifies that the k numbers of trained MLPs corresponding to k number of subsets are merged together. This is shown in Figure 9.

Here M_i corresponds to a trained network with data patterns of S_i.

After the training is over we get a composite network, which, given a test input $x \in R^p$ with unknown class label, will produce a k dimensional output vector. If there is no overlap among the training data patterns from various classes, then at most one of the existing trained networks produces high response and the remaining ones produce low responses. Responses from all the M_is are low when knowledge of the test data patterns is not present i.e. class is absent. If the training data patterns from classes j_1 and j_2 are overlapped, and if the test data patterns $x \in R^p$ is from the overlapped region, then output of nodes corresponding to j_1 and j_2 of the composite network will be high. In such a case, we cannot assign the class, but should make a decision that the sample can be in either of the two classes. This gives additional information about, that it probably comes from an overlapped region.

This training scheme signifies that, it has the ability to augment a trained network with a new set of training data patterns. When new data patterns arrive in to train

Figure 9. Merging of trained MLPs

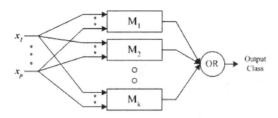

the network (classifier), the classifier automatically generates m_{new} depending on the availability of new information regarding the incoming data patterns.

The newly available data patterns represent $X_{new} = X_{new}^c \cup X_{new}^d$, where X_{new}^c represents the number of newly available data patterns which are correctly classified by the existing classifier and X_{new}^d is the set of data patterns which are not correctly classified by the existing classifier i.e. $X_{new}^d = X_{new} \cap \left(X_{new}^c \right)^C$. Here, a number X_{new}^c of data patterns are correctly classified by the classifier, and this means that the knowledge these data patterns are already present in the existing classifier. Hence the number of data patterns in X_{new}^c need not be considered for further training of the existing classifier. The knowledge of data patterns in X_{new}^d is not present in the classifier, since the classifier cannot correctly classify these data patterns. These unclassified data patterns X_{new}^d are considered as training data patterns to train the classifier and it generates new learning parameters for the classifier. The newly trained network M_{new} for data patterns X_{new}^d is merged with the old trained networks M and finally get $M_{final} = [M_i]_{i=1}^{k+1}$. In this way, new data patterns are trained and incremental learning ability of the network is achieved. The output of all $[M_i]_{i=1}^{k+1}$ are combined by an *OR* operator to get the final output.

INCREMENTAL RADIAL BASIS FUNCTION NEURAL NETWORK MODEL

The architecture of incremental RBF neural network as shown in Figure 10 comprises of three layers. As in BP-MLP network, the input layer is made up of source nodes that connect the network to the sensors. The second layer is the hidden layer; it applies a nonlinear transformation from the input space to the hidden space. The output layer is linear, supplying the response of the network to the activation pattern applied to the input layer.

Figure 10. Architecture of the incremental classifier based on RBF neural network

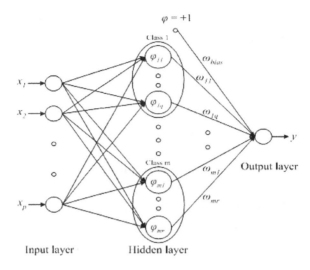

From the network architecture it is apparent that the input layer consists of p number of nodes corresponding to the p sensors of an electronic nose. For m classes in the data, there are m sets of nodes in the hidden layer and for each class, there may be one or more hidden nodes. Each hidden node uses a Gaussian kernel function and parameters of these nodes are represented by prototypes, which are explained later. The number of hidden nodes present in each class depends on the precision of the data patterns – less the precision; more is the number of hidden nodes. Before training the network, there are no classes present in the hidden layer. The network grows gradually as the classifier is trained with new data patterns. The weights of the connecting links are calculated automatically by the classifier during the training session.

The incremental classifier, based on a Gaussian RBF neural network (Evans et al., 2000; Bruzzone & Fernandez Prieto, 1999a), provides the features of fast training, ability to recognize and include an unknown pattern vector and also shows high classification accuracy on electronic nose data. Input features are propagated through the input neurons of a Gaussian RBF network to the next layer. Each neuron in the hidden layer is associated with Gaussian kernel function φ_{ij}, where i represents the class number and j represents the jth kernel in the ith class and its expression is given in Equation (8).

$$\phi_{ij}(x, \alpha_{ij}) = \frac{\exp(-\left\|x - \alpha_{ij}\right\|)^2}{2\sigma_{ij}^{2}} \tag{8}$$

where α_{ij} and σ_{ij} are the centre and width respectively. The output neuron computes a simple weighted summation over the response of the hidden neurons for a given input pattern vector x written as:

$$y = \sum_{i=1}^{m} \sum_{j=1}^{k_i} w_{ij} \phi_{ij} \left(\left\| x - \alpha_{ij} \right\| \right) + w_{bias} \tag{9}$$

where m is the number of classes in the existing classifier, k_i is the number of kernels (nodes in the hidden layer) in class i, w_{ij} represents the synaptic weight associated with the kernel ϕ_{ij} and w_{bias} is the weight bias associated with the output neuron.

Each kernel in the hidden layer of the incremental neural network classifier is associated with some knowledge of the trained pattern vector. This knowledge is the local description of the training data pattern. The long term memory of the network is described through a set of prototypes, $P = \left\{ \Omega_{11}, \Omega_{12}, ..., \Omega_{mk_m} \right\}$, where, each prototype Ω_{ij} (Bruzzone & Fernandez Prieto, 1999a; Constantinopoulos & Likas, 2006; Bruzzone & Fernandez Prieto, 1999b) is comprised of $\{\alpha_{ij}, \sigma_{ij}, \beta_{ij}, \delta_{ij}\}$. Here, β_{ij}, the mass coefficient denotes the number of training sample associated with the kernel ϕ_{ij}, and δ_{ij} is the vector containing the average deviation for each sensor associated with the kernel ϕ_{ij}. Knowledge acquired during the training phase (the status of the network) is represented as $\{P, W\}$, where P is the set of prototypes and W is the weight matrix.

Incremental Training of the Classifier

Training phase of the classifier is divided into two steps - the initial training phase, where the classifier is trained with existing data patterns and the retraining phase, where the classifier is trained with newly available data patterns. These are discussed in the next section.

Initial Training Phase of the Classifier

Initially the status of the classifier is empty, because the classifier has not been trained by any data pattern. That is, the prototype P and the weight matrices W are NULL($P \equiv W \equiv \varnothing$). The learning strategy of the classifier is divided into two parts: the calculation of prototypes P by means of statistical measure and the calculation of weight matrix (Haykin, 2001) W using the following Equations (10-13).

$$d = \left[d_1, d_2, ..., d_N\right]^T \tag{10}$$

$$G = \begin{bmatrix} \phi\left(x_1, \alpha_1\right) & \phi\left(x_1, \alpha_2\right) & \cdots & \phi\left(x_1, \alpha_n\right) \\ \phi\left(x_2, \alpha_1\right) & \phi\left(x_2, \alpha_2\right) & \cdots & \phi\left(x_2, \alpha_n\right) \\ \vdots & \vdots & \vdots & \vdots \\ \vdots & \vdots & \vdots & \vdots \\ \phi\left(x_N, \alpha_1\right) & \phi\left(x_N, \alpha_2\right) & \cdots & \phi\left(x_N, \alpha_n\right) \end{bmatrix} \tag{11}$$

$$W = G^+ d = \left(G^T G\right)^{-1} G^T d \tag{12}$$

$$W = \left[w_1, w_2, ...w_n\right]^T \tag{13}$$

where G^+ is the pseudoinverse of Green matrix, G.

G, is a matrix formed by radial basic function ϕ_{ij} centered at n number of kernels (α_{ij}) and d is a set of output vector of length N.

Retraining Phase of the Classifier

During the retraining phase of the classifier, either the prototypes plus the weight matrix are updated for the existing kernels, or a new kernel is appended for incorporating new knowledge present in the new data patterns. The procedure of updation is explained below where it is assumed that the data pattern x_{t+1} is presented at the instant $t+1$.

First the incremental classifier tries to find a match for the new data pattern among all the existing kernel functions by satisfying the condition $S(x_{y+1})=1$ (Bruzzone & Fernandez Prieto, 1999a). Condition of similarity $S(x_{y+1})$, is defined as:

$$S\left(x_{t+1}\right) = \begin{cases} 1 & if \left\|x_{t+1} - \alpha_{ij}\right\| < \gamma \sigma_{ij}, \\ 0 & otherwise, \end{cases} \tag{14}$$

where γ is the distance parameter. The value of γ is kept slightly greater than 1 so that any new data pattern, which is outside an existing kernel, but very close to it can be associated with that kernel by modifying its prototype as well as the weights. According to this condition of similarity, if $S(x_{y+1})=1$ then the knowledge of the data

Figure 11. Retraining phase of the incremental RBF classifier

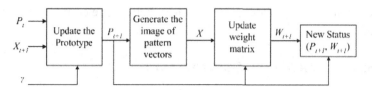

pattern is assumed to be present and the prototype for the matched kernel is updated. If the match is not found, then there are two possibilities: i) the class is not present or ii) the class is present, but the knowledge of new data pattern is not present. In the former case, the classifier appends a new kernel function in the hidden layer of the classifier architecture, calculates prototype Ω_{ij} for that new kernel and declares a new class to be associated with that kernel. Otherwise, if the class is already present, a new kernel function is appended within that class and the prototype Ω_{ij} for that kernel is computed and appended in the classifier architecture. The retraining phase of the incremental RBF neural network classifier is depicted in Figure 11.

After estimation of the set of prototypes P_{t+1}, the classifier generates an image of pattern vector X from the knowledge of the data patterns, which are previously and presently used during training to build the classifier architecture. The data-set corresponding to each kernel is represented by an image pattern which comprises of the following three points:

1. Centre point of the kernel α_{ij},
2. The point corresponding to $\alpha_{ij}-\delta_{ij}$,
3. The point corresponding to $\alpha_{ij}+\delta_{ij}$,

These three points for each kernel are used to form the Green matrix G, while updating the weights of the existing network and the original data-set are not accessed. Thus, these updated set of prototypes P_{t+1} and updated weight matrix W_{t+1} represent the present configuration of the RBF based neural network classifier.

During this updation procedure, there is a possibility of conflict. It may so happen that for a new data pattern, a match is obtained with an existing kernel and the electronic nose declares a score based on its previous training, but the user opines in a different way and wants to put the sample in a different class. This is due to the reason that the calibration procedure for an electronic nose is purely subjective and in practice, the judgment of the organoleptic panels is used in the supervised incremental training algorithm. The decision of the human expert panel should be given more importance and if required, the matched kernel is deleted from the hidden layer and a new one is created. But at the same time, the prototypes of the deleted kernels are stored so that the information can be used for overall standardization of the electronic nose at a later point of time when a huge corpus of data would be available.

Case Study: Tea Aroma Classification

Different types of tea are produced in many countries all over the globe, and the quality as well as the price of the final product varies considerably. Till date, the quality of tea is evaluated by human tea tasters, and this method is highly subjective and depends upon very much on the experience and mood of the tea taster. In order to objectively assess the quality of black tea using instrumental means, electronic nose instruments have been deployed in the tea industries in India and correlation with the tea taster marks have been established (Bhattacharyya et al., 2008).

It has been observed that the conventional pattern classifiers have severe limitations, as augmentation of the trained model is not possible in these models. In north and north-east India, the tea leaves are plucked in five sessions over a year, called as flushes and they are termed as the first flush, the second flush, the rain flush, the autumn flush and the winter flush. Out of these five flushes, the quality of tea produced in the second and the autumn flushes is usually better than the tea produced in the other three flushes from that garden. If we train the electronic nose using samples available in one garden during a particular flush, it is likely that the same model may give erroneous results when subjected to data from a different garden or in a different flush. So in order to design a versatile electronic nose pattern classifier, a suitable incremental learning algorithm is the most appropriate one. The instrument, once designed, may be sent from one region to other and trained over several flushes and seasons. It will try to classify the signature when subjected to a sample and at the same time, learn the new patterns without forgetting previous knowledge. Thus, elaborate experimentation was carried out at the tea gardens in India with electronic nose instruments equipped with the feature of incremental learning. The electronic nose instruments with five Figaro Sensors TGS-832, TGS-823, TGS-2600, TGS-2610 and TGS-2611 and equipped with all the incremental learning methods have been field trialed in different tea gardens in India. In all the cases (Tuda et al., 2009a; Tudu et al., 2009b), it has been observed that when the classifier is trained with samples from one garden, the performance with the samples of another garden is very poor. But, with incremental learning feature, the instrument can learn new patterns without forgetting the previous knowledge and this feature makes the instrument very much acceptable to the user industries. Thus, an electronic nose instrument with an incremental classifier, which can solve the plasticity-stability dilemma, may serve as a very useful instrument for standardization of black tea quality.

ACKNOWLEDGMENT

The authors wish to acknowledge the contribution of the students – Barun Das, Animesh Metla, Saptashi Ghosh and Project Engineers of CDAC, Kolkata Mr. Arun Jana and Mr. Debdulal Ghosh for their sincere and diligent efforts to carry out the experimentation with the incremental classifiers. The authors also acknowledge their indebtness to the tea industries where the incremental classifiers have been field tried.

REFERENCES

Bezdek, J. (1981). *Pattern recognition with fuzzy objective function*. New York, NY: Plenum Press.

Bhattacharyya, N., Bandyopadhyay, R., Bhuyan, M., Tudu, B., Ghosh, D., & Jana, A. (2008). Electronic nose for black tea classification and correlation of measurements with tea taster marks. *IEEE Transactions on Instrumentation and Measurement, 57*, 1313–1321. doi:10.1109/TIM.2008.917189

Bruzzone, L., & Fernandez Prieto, D. (1999a). An incremental-learning neural network for the classification of remote-sensing images. *Pattern Recognition Letters, 20*, 1241–1248. doi:10.1016/S0167-8655(99)00091-4

Bruzzone, L., & Fernandez Prieto, D. (1999b). A technique for the selection of kernel-function parameters in RBF neural networks for classification of remote–sensing images. *IEEE Transactions on Geoscience and Remote Sensing, 37*, 1179–1184. doi:10.1109/36.752239

Chakraborty, D., & Pal, N. R. (2003). A novel training scheme for multilayered perceptrons to realize proper generalization and incremental learning. *IEEE Transactions on Neural Networks, 14*, 1–14. doi:10.1109/TNN.2002.806953

Chang, P. C., & Liao, T. W. (2006). Combining SOM and fuzzy rule base for flow time prediction in semiconductor manufacturing factory. *Applied Soft Computing, 6*, 198–206. doi:10.1016/j.asoc.2004.12.004

Constantinopoulos, C., & Likas, A. (2006). An incremental training method for the probabilistic RBF Network. *IEEE Transactions on Neural Networks, 17*, 966–974. doi:10.1109/TNN.2006.875982

Evans, P., Persaud, K. C., McNeish, A. S., Sneath, R. W., Hobson, N., & Magan, N. (2000). Evaluation of a radial basis function neural network for the determination of wheat quality from electronic nose data. *Sensors and Actuators. B, Chemical, 69,* 348–358. doi:10.1016/S0925-4005(00)00485-8

Fu, L., Huang, H., & Principe, J. C. (1996). Incremental backpropagation learning networks. *IEEE Transactions on Neural Networks, 7,* 757–761. doi:10.1109/72.501732

Giraud-Carrier, C. (2000). A note on the utility of incremental learning. *AI Communications, 13,* 215–223.

Haykin, S. (2001). *Neural networks: A comprehensive foundation* (2nd ed.). Hong Kong: Pearson Education Asia.

Klir, G. J., & Folger, T. (1989). *Fuzzy sets, uncertainty and information.* Addison-Wesley.

Ma, M., Zhang, Y., Langholz, G., & Kandel, A. (2000). On direct construction of fuzzy systems. *Fuzzy Sets and Systems, 112,* 165–171. doi:10.1016/S0165-0114(97)00387-4

Marseguerra, M., Zio, E., Baraldi, P., & Oldrini, A. (2003). Fuzzy logic for signal prediction in nuclear systems. *Progress in Nuclear Energy, 43,* 373–380. doi:10.1016/S0149-1970(03)00048-9

Mouchaweh, M. S., Devillez, A., Lecolier, G. V., & Billaudel, P. (2002). Incremental learning in fuzzy pattern matching. *Fuzzy Sets and Systems, 132,* 49–62. doi:10.1016/S0165-0114(02)00060-X

Pal, S. K., & Majumder, D. D. (1986). *Fuzzy mathematical approach to pattern recognition.* New York, NY: John Wiley.

Pardo, M., & Sberveglieri, G. (2002). Coffee analysis with an electronic nose. *IEEE Transactions on Instrumentation and Measurement, 51,* 1334–1339. doi:10.1109/TIM.2002.808038

Pedrycz, W. (1994). Why triangular membership functions? *Fuzzy Sets and Systems, 64,* 21–30. doi:10.1016/0165-0114(94)90003-5

Polikar, R., Udpa, L., Udpa, S. S., & Honavar, V. (2001). Learn++: An incremental learning algorithm for supervised neural networks. *IEEE Transactions on Systems, Man, and Cybernetics C. Applications and Reviews, 31,* 497–508.

Singh, S. (1999). A single nearest neighbour fuzzy approach for pattern recognition. *International Journal of Pattern Recognition and Artificial Intelligence, 13,* 49–54. doi:10.1142/S0218001499000045

Takagi, T., & Sugeno, M. (1985). Fuzzy identification of systems and its applications to modeling and control. *IEEE Transactions on Systems, Man, and Cybernetics, 15*(1), 116–132.

Tudu, B., Jana, A., Metla, A., Ghosh, D., Bhattacharyya, N., & Bandyopadhyay, R. (2009a). Electronic nose for black tea quality evaluation by an incremental RBF network. *Sensors and Actuators. B, Chemical, 138*, 90–95. doi:10.1016/j.snb.2009.02.025

Tudu, B., Metla, A., Das, B., Bhattacharyya, N., Jana, A., Ghosh, D., & Bandyopadhyay, R. (2009b). Towards versatile electronic nose pattern classifier for black tea quality evaluation: An incremental fuzzy approach. *IEEE Transactions on Instrumentation and Measurement, 58*, 3069–3078. doi:10.1109/TIM.2009.2016874

Wang, L.-X. (2003). The WM method completed: A flexible fuzzy system approach to data mining. *IEEE Transactions on Fuzzy Systems, 11*, 768–782. doi:10.1109/TFUZZ.2003.819839

Wang, L.-X., & Mendel, J. M. (1992). Generating fuzzy rules by learning from examples. *IEEE Transactions on Systems, Man, and Cybernetics, 22*, 414–1428. doi:10.1109/21.199466

Chapter 4
Noise and Repeatability of Odorant Gas Sensors in an E-Nose

Fengchun Tian
Chongqing University, China

Simon X. Yang
University of Guelph, Canada

Xuntao Xu
Mianyang Vocational and Technical College, China

Tao Liu
Chongqing University, China

ABSTRACT

The impact of the characteristics of the sensors used for electronic nose (e-nose) systems on the repeatability of the measurements is considered. The noise performance of the different types of sensors available for e-nose utilization is first examined. Following the theoretical background, the probability density functions and power spectra of noise from real sensors are presented. The impact of sensor imperfections including noise on repeatability forms the basis of the remainder of the chapter. The impact of the sensors themselves, the effect of data pre-processing methods, and the feature extraction algorithm on the repeatability are considered.

DOI: 10.4018/978-1-61520-915-6.ch004

INTRODUCTION

An electronic nose (e-nose) is composed of a gas sensor array and corresponding signal processing and pattern recognition algorithms. It is capable of mimicking the olfaction system of humans and mammals, and recognizing odorant gases. E-noses are more and more widely used in environmental monitoring, food production, and medicine such as odor evaluation (Xu *et al.*, 2008; Pearce, 2003; Gardner & Bartlett, 1999; Schiffman, Bennett. & Raymer, 2001). The response of all sensors in an e-nose together constitutes a unique profile that gives the "fingerprint" of odor. The gas sensors of an e-nose have several salient features. The sensors in the array interfere with each other and different sensor types are used, some of which have large heating current and power dissipation. Some of the sensors require amplifiers with an extremely high input impedance (e.g. higher than 10^{11} Ω) that makes them susceptible to interference. Sensors may have large dynamic currents that produce electromagnetic disturbance to the output of other sensors in the same array. Limitations of the gas sensors include sensitivity to temperature and humidity, with shifting baselines with time and high noise levels at the sensor outputs. The accuracy and repeatability of gas sensor response is heavily affected by the above factors.

NOISE FEATURES IN THE ODORANT GAS SENSORS

The noise from the sensor array comprising of several odorant gas sensors may result in inaccurate cluster analysis of the tested material (Goodner, Dreher & Rouseff, 2001). In our experiments, it is observed that the noise of gas sensors cannot be ignored. In the worst case, the noise magnitude may be some 20% of the signal magnitude of particular sensors. This section considers the noise features of several typical gas sensors used in the e-nose developed in our research laboratory (shown in Figure 1), including their probability distribution functions (*pdfs*) and power spectrum estimation, which are essential in noise cancellation (Wang & Zhang, 2002; Biswal, DeYoe, & Hyde, 1996; Friedrichs, 1995) and odor analysis by noise power spectrum (Solis, *et al.*, 2001).

Typical Gas Sensors and Their Noise

Resistive Gas Sensors

The resistive gas sensors we studied are of MOS (Metal-Oxide Semiconductor) such as tin dioxide. Figure 2 shows a typical sensor circuit and its interface diagram. Pins 2 and 5 are connected to the heater of the sensor, and the resistance between Pins

Figure 1. A photo of the electronic nose developed in our research laboratory

1 and 6 is designated as R_s. With pure air the resistance of R_s is high but with the presence of detectable gases, its value changes with the variation of gas concentration. Since V_C is a fixed voltage, by measuring the voltage on the resistor R_L, the change on R_s as well as the gas concentration can be calculated. This type of sensor makes a large noise contribution features largely by its heater power with dissipation ranging from several hundreds of mW to 1 W. The working temperature is as high as 400°C and this will result in higher resistor thermal noise. Moreover, there are also other typical semiconductor noise contributions such as Schottky noise and flicker noise. The interface circuit uses only a voltage follower as a buffer between the sensor output and the A/D converter since the output signal of the sensor is large and this makes the system less sensitive to external interference.

Gas Sensors with Electromotive Output

Figure 3 shows the circuit of a gas sensor with electromotive output and its interface diagram. There is a heater between Pins 1 and 6. A thermometer for temperature compensation is between Pins 2 and 5. The electromotive V_{EMF} between Pins 3 and 4 reflects the concentration of detectable gas. Lower capability of payload is the main feature of this type of sensor. It requires a pre-amplifier with extremely high input impedance at a value over 10^{11} Ω. As a result, it has the disadvantage of being

Figure 2. Circuit diagram of a resistive gas sensor and its interface

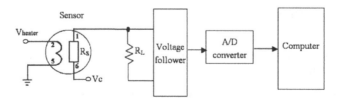

Figure 3. Circuit diagram of an electromotive gas sensor and its interface

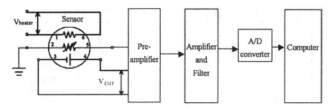

vulnerable to external electromagnetic interference in addition to the noise of the resistive gas sensor.

Sensors with Dynamic Heating

The two types of sensor above have a fixed voltage for their heaters, the current of which is constant, whereas the current of the sensor in Figure 4 is dynamic. The difference between this type of gas sensor and the one in Figure 2 lies in the voltage on the sensor heater. Here the voltage on the heater is a pulse signal that results in a large dynamic current as well as electromagnetic interference to other sensors in the sensor array of the e-nose. The timing control circuit is used to control the voltage applied to the sensor heater and the sampling epoch. Figure 5 is an oscilloscope-recorded waveform from the interference before any noise cancelling measure is taken, where the upper channel is the voltage waveform of heater in Figure 4, which also indicates the current on the heater. The lower channel in Figure 5 is the output waveform of another electromotive gas sensor in pure air that should be a straight line without the interference.

Gas Sensors with Current Output

Figure 6 shows a typical electrochemical gas sensor and its interface. The working current and voltage of the circuit are low and do not produce interference to the

Figure 4. Schematic diagram of a dynamically heated sensor and its interface

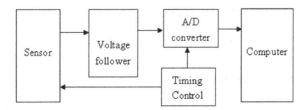

Figure 5. Interference on an odorant gas sensor with dynamic heating

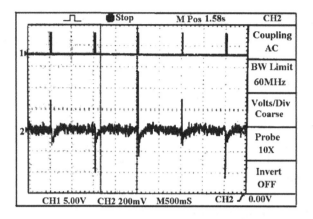

outputs of other sensors. Since the sensor's output current is extremely weak (only several μA), the gain of the amplifying circuit is required to be up to several thousand. Thus the whole circuit is more sensitive to external disturbance from other sensors than that of sensors with a lower amplifier gain. The noise is also amplified by several thousand times and it has stricter requirement on the equivalent input noise of the amplifier.

Probability Density Function (pdf) of the Noise

The histogram method, which has been proved to be an unbiased estimation for a random variable, is used to estimate the *pdf* of the noise. The estimation error decreases at a rate of $N^{-2/3}$ as a function of the total number N of the samples (Wasserman, 2004). Let X_1, X_2, ..., X_N be independent and identically distributed on [0,1] with N the total number of samples. Let m be an integer and $h = 1/m$ and define bins $B_1 = [0, h)$, $B_2 = [h, 2h)$, ... $B_m = [(m-1)h, 1]$. The estimated probability in a bin is $\hat{p}_j = v_j/N$, where v_j is the number of observations in B_j. The histogram estimation of probability distribution function $f(x)$ is then:

Figure 6. Gas sensor with current output and its interface

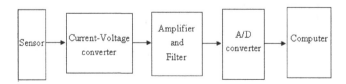

$$\hat{f}_n(x) = \hat{p}_n/h, \{n = 1, x \in B_1\}, \{n = 2, x \in B_2\}, ..., \{n = m, x \in B_m\} \tag{1}$$

Two points immediately arise when the histogram estimation method is used. Frist, how the error $\hat{f}_n(x)$ and the true probability distribution function $f(x)$ is to be measured. Second, the optimal value of h that gives the best approximation of $f(x)$ by $\hat{f}_n(x)$.

To deal with the first of these, we use the risk function or mean integrated squared error $R(f, \hat{f})$ between the two functions to measure the error between $\hat{f}_n(x)$ and the true probability distribution function $f(x)$. The function $R(f, \hat{f})$ is given by:

$$R(f, \hat{f}) = \bullet \left\{ \int (f(x) - \hat{f}(x))^2 dx \right\} \tag{2}$$

where $\mathbf{E}\{\cdot\}$ represented the expected value. For the second point, it is clear that the smaller the value of $R(f, \hat{f})$, the closer $\hat{f}_n(x)$ is to $f(x)$ (with the exception of only some point sets with zero measure). Since $f(x)$ is unknown, $R(f, \hat{f})$ cannot be calculated directly, but its minimum can be reached by considering the function $\hat{J}(h)$ (Wasserman, 2004).

$$\hat{J}(h) = \frac{2}{(n-1)h} + \frac{n+1}{n-1} \sum_j^m p_j^2 \tag{3}$$

and minimizing this. The optimal h that results in the minimum value of $\hat{J}(h)$ can be obtained by increasing the value of m from 1. Here the corresponding formula in (Wasserman, 2004) is improved by making the empirically determined changing of the minus sign between the first and the second item into a plus sign to accelerate convergence.

Power Spectrum Estimation of Noise

The periodical graph and averaged segmenting periodical graph methods were used to obtain the power spectrum estimation of noise (Mulgrew, Grant & Thompson, 1999). For a periodical graph, the power spectrum estimation is given as:

$$S(k) = \frac{1}{N} \left| \hat{X}(k) \right|^2 \quad k=0,1, ...N\text{-}1, \tag{4}$$

where $\left|\hat{X}(k)\right|$ is the modulus of the Discrete Fourier Transformation (DFT) of X_1, $X_2, ..., X_N$, and N is the total number of data sets.

To highlight the features of the noise, the mean value of the data is removed before the DFT. Otherwise the dc component (zero frequency) will be too large to show the other components. The variance of the periodical graph is bigger than that of the averaged segmenting periodical graph but it is useful in observing the baseline shifting of sensors (it corresponds to the lower frequency components near zero frequency).

The averaged segmenting periodical graph is obtained by segmenting the data X_1, $X_2, ..., X_N$ into K small non-overlapping sections. The length of each small section is M with $KM = N$. First, the power spectrum is estimated for each small section (here we also remove the mean of the small section before the DFT). Then the power spectrum estimation will be the average of the K small sections. The disadvantage of this method lies in its losing of information on sensor's baseline shifting that is much smaller during the small section than that of the whole section. The advantage is its asymptotically consistent estimation of the true power spectrum. With increasing M, the variance of the averaged segmenting periodical graph approaches zero. By this manner, the power spectrum estimation of the small section j is given as:

$$S_j(k) = \frac{1}{M}\left|\hat{X}(k)\right|^2, \ k=0, 1, ..., M\text{-}1, \tag{5}$$

where $\hat{X}(k)$ is the DFT of $X_1, X_2, ..., X_M$. The total power spectrum estimation is given as:

$$S(k) = \frac{1}{K}\sum_{j=1}^{K} S_j(k), \ k=0, 1, ..., M\text{-}1. \tag{6}$$

Experimental Noise Analysis Results

Four types of sensors were used in the test (Tian, Yang & Dong, 2005a, 2005b): (1) resistive gas sensors (such as TGS830 and TGS2600); (2) gas sensors with electromotive output (such as TGS4160); (3) gas sensors with dynamic heating (such as TGS2442); (4) gas sensors with current output (such as 3ETO). The first three types of sensors were MOS sensors produced by Figaro Ltd., while the fourth one was an electrochemical gas sensor produced by City Technology Ltd.

Figure 7 depicts the response of the above sixteen sensors, each of which was sampled by a 12-bit A/D converter at 6.4Hz sampling frequency. A charcoal filter

Figure 7. Power supply and response of the16 sensors in an e-nose

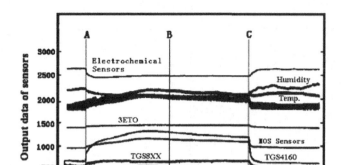

(which results in pure air input) was used from epoch A. Since no detectable gas appeared, the output of the sensors was noise only. A pump was used to intake the pure air into a chamber within which the sensor array lies. After epoch C, the chamber was open which resulted in the temperature dropping. To get the features of the noise, the stabilized data (from epoch B to C) was used to compute the power spectrum and for pdf estimation. The number of data sets for each sensor used in the calculation was 30000 representing 90 minutes. In the averaged segmenting periodical graph method, the data was segmented into six small sections ($M = 5000$, 15 minutes). In depicting the pdf curve, to highlight the non-zero part, without the loss of generality we normalized the sensor's output data into [0,1], that is for the maximum and minimum of the sensor output data be Xmax and Xmin respectively, the normalized data were given by

$$X_N = \frac{\left(X - X_{\min}\right)}{\left(X_{\max} - X_{\min}\right)} \qquad (7)$$

Our experiments showed that the sensors can be categorized into three types according to their noise power spectrum and *pdf* estimation. The noise can be white meaning that its power spectrum magnitude remains almost constant in the whole frequency range except the dc and its nearby component or colored, containing considerable low frequency components besides that of the white noise. There may also be one peak in the *pdf* or two.

For the case of colored noise with a single peak *pdf*, Figures 8(a) and 8(b) show the time-domain curve and the power-spectrum-estimation curve, respectively. It

Figure 8. The noise (a) and its power spectrum estimation (b) of the first type of sensor in Table 1

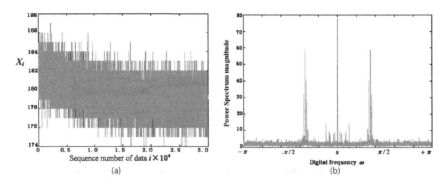

(a)   (b)

may be seen that the power spectrum of the noise consists mainly of two parts: one is the almost-constant-magnitude part filling the whole frequency band, and the other is composed of some lower frequency components that may be caused by some inherent feature of the sensor and its circuit. Some of the elements have the same frequency as the signal and cannot be filtered out by just a simple low-pass filter.

Figure 9 shows the curve of $\hat{J}(h)$ from Equation (3) with $h = 1/m$. It can be seen that when $m = 10$, i.e., $h = 0.1$, $\hat{J}(h)$ reaches its minimum that makes the risk function $R(f, \hat{f})$ minimum. The h value at $h = 0.1$ makes the estimation of *pdf* optimal. Figure 10 gives the *pdf* estimation using this h value and it is close to a Gaussian distribution.

Figure 9. $\hat{J}(h)$ as a function of m

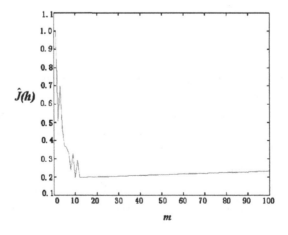

Figure 10. Histogram with the optimal value of h

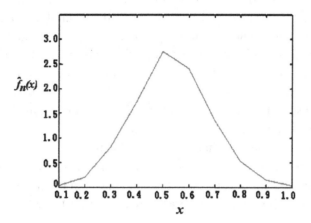

For white noise with single peak, the noise in the time domain and its power-spectrum-estimation curve are shown in Figures 11(a) and 11(b), respectively. The *pdf* estimation is shown in Figure 11(c) with the optimal value at $h = 1/75$. It is similar to a Gaussian distribution. The envelope of the noise power spectrum is almost constant in the whole band. Thus it is reasonable to consider this type of noise as normal white noise. For the sensors 3SH (current output) and TGS4160 (electromotive), their output signals are too weak and the gain of amplifier has to

Figure 11. The noise (a), its power spectrum (b) and pdf estimation (c) of the second type of sensor in Table 1

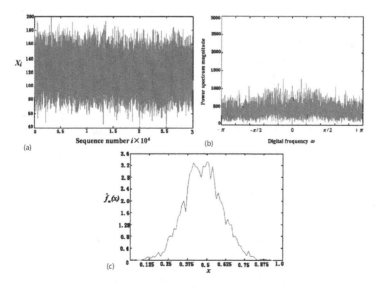

be large enough (~6000), or the input impedance is too high (more than 10^{11} Ω). The noise energy of these sensors is much bigger than that of the first type in Table 1, which implies that the noise in this type of sensor cannot be ignored.

For colored noise with a double peaked *pdf*, Figures 12(a) and 12(b) show the noise in the time domain and its power spectrum estimation respectively. Figure 12(c) is the estimation of *pdf* with the optimal value at $h = 1/29$. In comparison to the first type of sensors in Table 1, both have similar colored noise power spectrum and many of their low frequency components have the same location in the frequency domain. This implies that the inherent features of the sensors are similar, as they are produced by the same manufacturer. The only obvious difference here is the double peaked *pdf* in contrast to the single peak in the first type. The double peaks in the *pdf* imply a high appearance frequency of these two types of noise magnitude.

For some sensors such as the TGS830 and TGS2600, a remarkable difference exists in their zero frequency component of noise power spectrum between the periodical graphs and the averaged segmenting periodical graph methods. This can be observed when comparing Figure 12(b) and Figure 13. No peak appears in the nearby zero frequency of the averaged segmenting periodical graph in Figure 12(b) which is opposite to its counterpart in Figure 13. It is due to the fact that the sensor baseline shifts slowly within the whole time period (the total 30000 data sets), although in both methods the mean is removed. Whereas in each small section (the

Figure 12. The noise (a), its power spectrum (b) and pdf estimation (c) of the third type of sensors in Table 1

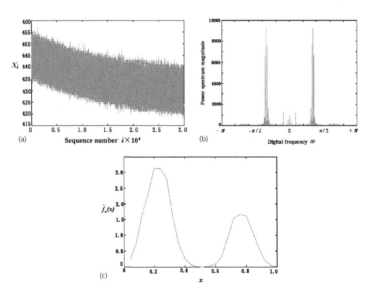

data sets of 5000) the baseline changes little and results in almost no nearby zero frequency component. This indicates that such sensors can work more stably and have much smaller baseline shift than other sensors.

REPEATABILTY OF THE ODORANT GAS SENSORS

Repeatability is a key issue of e-noses. This section gives the definition of repeatability of the e-nose and examines the main factors that influence it addition to the noise considered above, namely experimental errors, sensor drift and the environment. Also, we present box plots and the repeatability score, which represent the qualitative and quantitative indicators to evaluate the repeatability of the e-nose. Studies of the repeatability of the sensor array, the signal pre-processing method and the feature extraction method using these indicators are presented.

Definition of Repeatability

Repeatability of a sensor in an e-nose is a measure of the difference between output results of periodic measurements of the same object under the same conditions. The main factors that influence the repeatability of an e-nose include experimental errors, noise, sensor drift and environmental factors. Experimental errors include system error, accidental error and gross error. System error is mainly derived from method error caused by the analytical method itself. Instrument error is caused by the insufficient precision of instruments, sample error is caused by the instability of reagents or samples, and operation error caused by different operators. Accidental error comes from the change of unpredictable elements. Gross error is induced by

Figure 13. Power spectrum by periodical graph

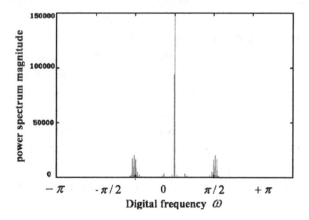

mistakes of the operator, such as errors in reading, errors in adding samples and errors in the operating process.

The response of a gas sensor to the same sample changes with time and this phenomenon is known as gas sensor drift. This may result from sensor poisoning, aging and the change of environmental factors (Holmberga *et al.*, 1996; Zuppa *et al.*, 2004, 2007). Drift is a dynamic process, caused by physical and chemical changes in the gas sensor and sensitive materials, and manifesting itself as the sensitivity of the gas sensor to the same sample changing slowly with time. Gas sensor drift can be divided into short-term drift and long-term drift. The former is reversible, whilst the latter is not.

E-noses usually recognize new patterns based on the established training patterns. Because of the change of many factors such as ambient temperature, humidity, pressure and so on, the same sample may exhibit different response modes when tested in different environments. Although temperature, humidity and pressure sensors can be added to the system to synchronously acquire environmental factor data, due to the variations of the application environment, it is very difficult to consider and simulate all effects of environmental factors on the e-nose measurements.

Methods to Discriminate the Repeatability of Sensors in an E-Nose

Box-plots and repeatability scores can be used to qualitatively and quantitatively express the repeatability of sensors in an e-nose.

Box-plots, also referred to as Box-whisker Plots, are a method of depicting data through five-number summaries: the smallest observation (sample minimum), lower quartile (Q1), median (Q2), upper quartile (Q3), and largest observation (sample maximum). They may also give an approximate indication of such information as the symmetry of the data and the degree of dispersion of the distribution, which are especially suitable for the comparison of several samples. Figure 14 gives the box-plot for comparison between repeated measurement results of two classes of samples. It can be seen that the box-plot contains the information as follows. The bottom and top of the box correspond to the 25% quantile and the 75% quantile of the sample data, respectively. The distance between the bottom and the top is the interquartile range and this can reflect the dispersion degree of the sample data. A smaller within-class sample distance indicates a smaller box-plot interquartile range. The line in the middle of the box represents the median of the sample. If the median line is not at the middle of the box, then the sample is comprised of data that deviates. The whiskers that extend to outside the box denote the sample maximum and sample minimum and the outliers that lie farther away than the whiskers

Figure 14. Box-plots demonstration

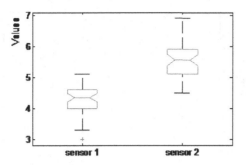

represent the singularities of the sample data, which should be treated carefully in data processing.

For two or more classes of samples, there will be a greater difference between the medians in the box-plot, with a larger between-class distance and more accurate possible classification. For the test results of the same class of samples, the smaller the interquartile range is, and the more symmetric the sample data is, the better its repeatability will be.

The **repeatability score** for test samples $(x_1, x_2, \ldots, x_N)$, with the sample mean $\bar{x}$ and sample standard deviation (SD) defined by their usual formulas (Navidi, 2007), is given by:

$$score = \frac{\bar{x}}{SD} \qquad (8)$$

Experimental Investigation of Sensor Repeatability

Based on the definitions above, tests were performed on the e-nose system using 200ppb nonane, isopropanol and hypnone gas samples. There were 30 trials for each, enabling study of the repeatability of the e-nose sensor responses, the effect of the data pre-processing method on the repeatability and comparison of various feature extraction methods in terms of repeatability.

Gas Sensor Repeatability

The e-nose system developed in-house consisted of seven gas sensors, including six metal oxide sensors and one electrochemical sensor. These were as follows (number:type): S1:4ETO; S2:TGS822; S3:TGS2620; S4:TGS2602; S5:TGS2600; S6:GSBT11; S7:QS01. The three classes of samples were measured 90 times. Taking

Figure 15. Box-plots of gas sensors in nonane gas sample

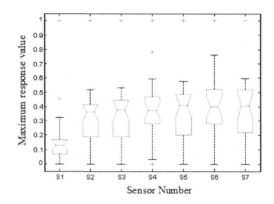

the maximum response value in the adsorption step of the gas sensor as the feature, the repeatabilities of the gas sensors are shown in Figures.15-18.

To guarantee repeatability of test results in e-nose system, its gas sensor array should clearly be composed of gas sensors with a high repeatability. However, Figures 15 to 18 show that in the measurement of the three classes of samples, all gas sensors exhibit some change in their repeatability. Therefore, we should make a concrete analysis of the repeatability of gas sensors in the array based on specific applications, and select the values measured by gas sensors with a high repeatability for the succeeding pattern classification. The mean values of the repeatability scores of the gas sensors for the three classes of samples are shown in Figure 19. For the 90 measurements of the three classes of samples, sensors S4 and S6 have the best mean repeatability.

Figure 16. Box-plots of gas sensors in isopropanol gas sample

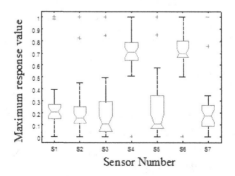

Figure 17. Box-plots of gas sensors in hypnone gas sample

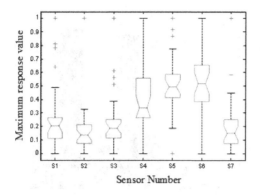

Effect Data Pre-Processing Method on Repeatability

The main purposes of data pre-processing for an e-nose include: removing noise and disturbance introduced in data acquisition (to increase the signal to noise ratio (Wasserman, 2004; Solis, *et al.*, 2001) and carrying out data compression and transformation in the measurement space (to facilitate the succeeding feature extraction and pattern classification). E-nose data pre-processing can be classified into baseline operation, data compression and data normalization. Here, the main focus is on the effect of various baseline operations on the repeatability. Baseline operations refer in particular to a series of data transformation methods employed in order to remove

Figure 18. Repeatability scores of gas sensors in samples of the three sorts

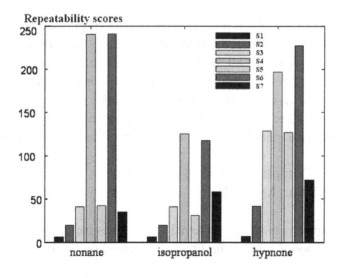

Figure 19. Average repeatability scores of gas sensors in samples of the three sorts

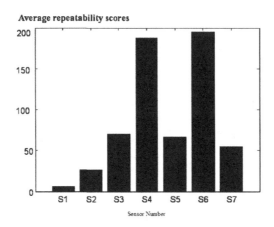

the effect of baseline drift on the sampled data (Tian *et al.*, 2009). The major data pre-processing methods of e-nose baseline operations include:

Normalization: $x_i' = (x_i - x_{i0}) / (x_{i\,\text{max}} - x_{i0})$ (9)
Difference method: $x_i' = x_i - x_{i0}$ (10)
Relative difference method: $x_i' = x_i / x_{i0}$ (11)
Fractional difference method: $x_i' = (x_i - x_{i0}) / x_{i0}$ (12)
Log-difference method: $x_i' = \lg(x_i - x_{i0})$ (13)

where x_i, x_i' are signals before and after transformation, respectively, x_{i0} is the baseline value, and $x_{i\,\text{max}}$ is the maximum value. Figures 20-22 give the repeatability scores of various pre-processing methods for test of the three classes of samples. All of them take the maximum in the absorption step as the feature.

These figures show that all the pre-processing methods for test of the three classes of samples have a certain degree of influence on the repeatability of each gas sensor. In most cases, the repeatability with relative difference method is consistent with that of fractional difference method, and the pre-processing methods of normalization and logarithmic method can ensure better repeatability.

Repeatability Comparison Using Various Feature Extraction Methods

The feature extraction methods employed with e-noses include: those based on the original curve, those based on the fitted curve and those based on the transform

Figure 20. Repeatability scores of pre-processing in the nonane gas sample

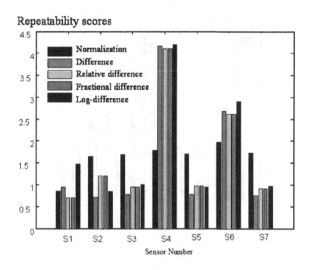

domain (Gutierrez-Osuna, 2002). Here, we report our results on repeatability comparison of various fundamental feature extraction methods based on the original curve. The methods considered were:

Maximum: the maximum response value in the absorption step.
Maximum time: the time corresponding to the maximum.
Maximum slope: the maximum slope of the ascending section in the absorption step.

Figure 21. Repeatability scores of pre-processing in the isopropanol gas sample

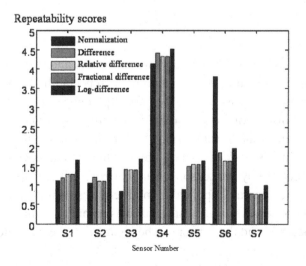

Figure 22. Repeatability scores of pre-processing in the hypnone gas sample

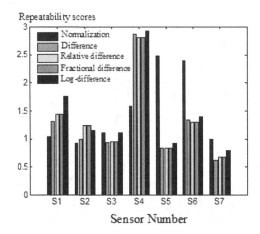

Maximum slope time: the time corresponding to the maximum slope.
Maximum area: the area under the response curve in the section from the beginning of the absorption step to the maximum time.

Figures 23-25 give the repeatability scores of various features for test of the three classes of samples. It can be found that, among the basic features based on the original curve, the features of maximum and maximum time have better repeatability. In the comparative experiment of feature repeatability, because the noise of S1 has a great influence on the obtainment of maximum slope and maximum slope time, sensor S1 was not included, and only sensors S2-S7 were compared.

CONCLUSION

We have successfully investigated odorant gas sensors and their interface circuits in an e-nose in terms of their noise features and repeatability. It should be noted that since the sensors only work with their corresponding circuits, the sensor noise means the total noise from the sensor and its amplifying circuit. The sensor noise depends on the sensor manufacturing methods plus the input impedance and gain of the amplifier. In this work, we have employed the optimal operating circuits and devices recommended by the sensor manufacturers, so it is reasonable to believe that the results are generally applicable to all e-noses using similar sensors. The noise in the e-nose sensors can be categorized as colored or white noise according to its power spectrum and the former can be regarded as the white noise plus some

Figure 23. Repeatability scores of each feature in the nonane gas sample

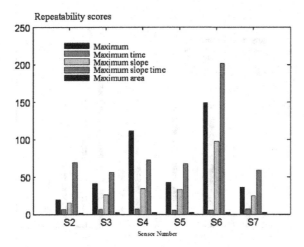

stronger low frequency components. The *pdf* of the noise exhibits either a single peak or double peaks. The noise of resistive gas sensor is colored one, whereas electromotive sensors or the sensors with current output present white noise resulting from either the weak signal or the high input impedance.

Noise *pdf* estimation was successful and showed the need to optimize the histogram bin size to deliver the closest estimation to the true *pdf* in the sense of smallest integrated mean squared error. The averaged segmenting periodical graph estimation of noise power spectrum is an asymptotic consistent estimator of the real power

Figure 24. Repeatability scores of each feature in the isopropanol gas sample

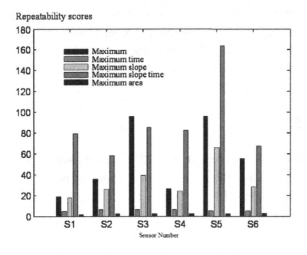

Figure 25. Repeatability scores of each feature in the hypnone gas sample

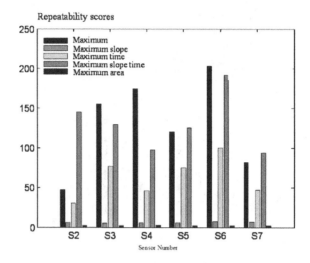

spectrum. Here, the large number of datasets has produced spectra with estimation errors that are expected to be small.

Baseline sensor shift was observed through comparing the periodical graph and the averaged segmenting periodical graph of the noise. Of all the sensors tested, the three sensors TGS830, TGS2600, TGS2602 can work more stably and have smaller baseline shift than others. Nevertheless, although they have almost no baseline shift during the 15 minute small data subsets, they still exhibit some shift during the whole 90 minute data collection period.

It is important for an e-nose system to be composed of gas sensors with high repeatability to deliver overall repeatability. The pre-processing methods tested influenced the repeatability of each gas sensor to some degree. The repeatability with the relative difference method is largely consistent with that of the fractional difference method but using normalization and the logarithmic method can ensure better repeatability. Amongst the basic feature extraction approaches based on the original curve, those employing maximum and maximum time have better repeatability.

REFERENCES

Biswal, B., DeYoe, E. A., & Hyde, J. S. (1996). Reduction of physiological fluctuations in FMRI using digital filters. *Magnetic Resonance in Medicine, 35*, 107–113. doi:10.1002/mrm.1910350114

Friedrichs, M. S. (1995). A model-free algorithm for the removal of baseline artifacts. *Journal of Biomolecular NMR, 5*, 147–153. doi:10.1007/BF00208805

Gardner, J. W., & Bartlett, P. N. (1999). *Electronic noses: Principles and applications.* New York, NY: Oxford University Press Inc.

Goodner, K. L., Dreher, J. G., & Rouseff, R. L. (2001). The dangers of creating false classifications due to noise in e-noses and similar multivariate analyses. *Sensors and Actuators. B, Chemical, 80*, 261–266. doi:10.1016/S0925-4005(01)00917-0

Gutierrez-Osuna, R. (2002). Pattern analysis for machine olfaction: A review. *IEEE Sensors Journal, 2*(3), 189–202. doi:10.1109/JSEN.2002.800688

Holmberga, M., Winquist, F., Lundstrom, I., & Davide, F. (1996). Drift counteraction for an electronic nose. *Sensors and Actuators. B, Chemical, 35-36*, 528–535. doi:10.1016/S0925-4005(97)80124-4

Mulgrew, B., Grant, P., & Thompson, J. (1999). *Digital signal processing.* New York, NY: Palgrave.

Navidi, W. (2007). *Statistics for engineers and scientists* (2nd ed.). New York, NY: McGraw-Hill.

Pearce, T. C. (2003). *Handbook of machine olfaction: Electronic nose technology.* Weinheim, Germany: Wiley-VCH.

Schiffman, S. S., Bennett, J. L., & Raymer, J. H. (2001). Quantification of odours and odorants from swine operations in North Carolina. *Agricultural and Forest Meteorology, 108*, 213–240. doi:10.1016/S0168-1923(01)00239-8

Solis, J. L., Kish, L. B., Vajtai, R., Granqvist, C. G., Olsson, J., Shnurer, J., & Lantto, V. (2001). Identifying natural and artificial odors through noise analysis with a sampling-and-hold electronic nose. *Sensors and Actators B, 77*, 312–315. doi:10.1016/S0925-4005(01)00698-0

Tian, F., Xu, X., Shen, Y., Yan, J., He, Q., Ma, J., & Liu, T. (2009). Detection of wound pathogen by an intelligent electronic nose. *Sensors and Materials, 21*, 155–166.

Tian, F., Yang, S. X., & Dong, K. (2005a). Circuit and noise analysis of odorant gas sensors in an e-nose. *Sensors (Basel, Switzerland), 5*, 85–96. doi:10.3390/s5010085

Tian, F., Yang, S. X., & Dong, K. (2005b). *Study on noise feature in sensor array of an electronic nose.* IEEE International Conference On Networking, Sensing and Control (pp. 19-22). Tucson, Arizona, U.S.A.

Wang, Y., & Zhang, C. (2002). A novel methodology to cancel the additive coloured noise for real-time communication application. *IEICE Transactions on Electronics*, *85*, 480–484.

Wasserman, L. A. (2004). *All of statistics: A concise course in statistical inference.* New York, NY: Springer.

Xu, X., Tian, F., Yang, S. X., Li, Q., Yan, J., & Ma, J. (2008). A solid trap and thermal desorption system with application to a medical electronic nose. *Sensors (Basel, Switzerland)*, *8*, 6885–6898. doi:10.3390/s8116885

Zuppa, M., Distante, C., Persaud, K. C., & Siciliano, P. (2007). Recovery of drifting sensor responses by means of DWT analysis. *Sensors and Actuators. B, Chemical*, *120*, 411–416. doi:10.1016/j.snb.2006.02.049

Zuppa, M., Distante, C., Siciliano, P., & Persaud, K. C. (2004). Drift counteraction with multiple self-organising maps for an electronic nose. *Sensors and Actuators. B, Chemical*, *98*, 305–317. doi:10.1016/j.snb.2003.10.029

Section 2
Applications

Chapter 5
Odor Reproduction with Movie and Its Application to Teleolfaction

Takamichi Nakamoto
Tokyo Institute of Technology, Japan

Takao Yamanaka
Sophia University, Japan

ABSTRACT

The authors of this chapter study the odor reproduction system synchronously with a movie. The system is made up of an odor sensing system and an olfactory display. The fruit flavors were recorded with movies using a digital video camera and the odor sensing system. The results of the sensory tests showed that the odor information recorded using the proposed method is appropriate for the smell regeneration associated with the movie. Next, the authors propose a tele-olfaction system synchronous with visual information. The olfactory display system was placed remotely from the odor sensing system, and both of them were connected via Internet. In addition to the olfactory system, a Web camera captures image around the sniffing point and that image appears at the computer display connected to the olfactory display at remote site. Moreover, the mobile stage with its sniffing point and the Web camera remotely controlled by a user was introduced so that he/she could interactively approach a smelling object. The questionnaire survey at the exhibition revealed that a user can enjoy smell synchronous with movie in real time even if he/she stays at the remote site.

DOI: 10.4018/978-1-61520-915-6.ch005

INTRODUCTION

A human perceives sensory information through senses such as vision, audition, olfaction, gustation and tactile and force impression. To enhance the quality of life, various equipment types have widely been used for recording and reproducing the visual and auditory information in daily living. Televisions, music players, digital cameras, digital video cameras and Web cameras are such common electronic devices.

Although the reproduction techniques thus far have been limited to the visual and auditory information, it would be expected to expand the reproduction techniques to other sensory information. For example, the tactile information has been used in virtual reality (Burdea and Ciffet, 2003). The olfactory information has been another target for the recording and reproduction (Barfield & Danas, 1996; Davide, Homberg, & Lundstrom, 2001; Tominaga et al., 2001). It has been reported that the olfactory information drastically enhances the sense of presence in the virtual environments (Gobbetti & Scateni, 1998; Dinh, Walker, Song, Kobayashi, & Hodges, 1999).

Electronic-nose technology (Pearce, 1997) attracts attention in respect of realizing the recording of olfactory information (Gobbetti & Scateni, 1998; Davide, Holmberg, & Lundstrom, 2001). In the electronic nose, odors are recognized based on the sensor-response pattern of an odor sensor array composed of multiple sensors with partially overlapping specificities. This technology has been utilized for recording odor compositions with signal processing based on control theory (Nakamoto,Nakahira, Hiramatsu, & Moriizumi, 2001; Yamanaka, Matsumoto, & Nakamoto, 2003). Although typical electronic-nose systems have been developed for detecting odors in a closed chamber to minimize disturbances, this odor recorder has the capability of recording odors in the atmosphere (Yamanaka, Yoshikawa, & Nakamoto, 2004). Odor recording in the atmosphere is a challenging task due to the large fluctuation in odor concentration caused by turbulent airflows (Yamanaka, Ishida, Nakamoto, & Moriizumi, 1998).

It was reported that binary odor compositions of apple flavors were recorded using this system in the atmosphere (Yamanaka, Yoshikawa, & Nakamoto, 2004). It was however difficult to achieve a high accuracy of mixture quantification for the rapid change in an odor composed of more than two components. For the practical application of olfactory reproduction to a movie production, the reproduction of a wide variety of odors would be desirable rather than the reproduction of a mixture with precise composition. Therefore, the recording of odors in the atmosphere based on pattern classification is presented in this chapter to realize the reproduction of a wide variety of odors.

In order to display the odors recorded with the electronic-nose system, an electronic device to present the olfactory stimulus is required. Recently, several studies on the olfactory display were reported. PC-controlled scent diffusers were reported by Messager (2002) and Kaye (2004). Moreover, a spot scent display (Nakaizumi, Yanagida, Noma, & Hosaka, 2006) and a wearable olfactory display (Yamada, Tanikawa, Hirota & Hirose, 2006) were proposed. Another olfactory display has also been reported to blend 32 odor components for creating a variety of smells (Nakamoto & Dinh Minh, 2007). This olfactory display was utilized in an animation with smells for providing much sensation to users (Nakamoto & Yoshikawa, 2006) and in an interactive cooking game with smells (Nakamoto, Otaguro, Kinoshita, Nagahama, Ohnishi, & Ishida, 2008). These olfactory displays enable the increase in sensation to users in the animations and games. However, it was still room for the improvement since the odors used in contents were manually created without recording the actual odors.

In this chapter, the recording and reproduction of olfactory information visually are presented using the electronic-nose and olfactory-display technologies. Our aim was to enhance the sense of presence by combining video images and olfactory stimuli. Moreover, we describe a *teleolfaction* system using the proposed system. Users can sniff smells of objects far away from the users during watching video images of the objects in real time via the Internet. Thus, users can perceive much sensation of reality of the object even at the remote site. Although there have been several reports on the fusion of vision and olfaction in virtual environments, our system so far has been the unique system which can both record and reproduce olfactory information synchronized with visual information (Yamanaka, Nitikarn, & Nakamoto, 2007; Nakamoto, Cho, Nitikarn, Wyszynski, Takushima & Kinoshita, 2008).

BACKGROUND

The visual and olfactory reproduction system can be divided into the recording part and the reproduction part. The recording part is to record the olfactory information such as odor quality and intensity, in addition to the visual information such as movie. On the other hand, the reproduction part is to regenerate the odor and to play the movie. The recording of olfactory information can be realized with odor-detection instruments including GC/MS (gas chromatography / mass spectrometry), GC/O (gas chromatography / olfactometry), and odor-sensing systems (electronic noses).

The GC/MS is an analytical instrument for a mixture of gas molecules, composed of the sample-injection part, a column coated with a polymer film, and a mass spectrometer. When the sample mixture composed of multiple compounds is injected into the inlet of the column, the compounds are separated at the output of the column because the compounds flow in the column with different speed. The mass spectrometer is connected to the outlet of the column to analyze each compound from the mass spectrum. Instead of the mass spectrometer, a human nose can be used to analyze odor of the compound at the outlet of the column. This method called GC/O is widely used in perfumery companies for analyzing the aromas.

In addition to these analytical instruments of odors, the electronic noses have been developed to analyze the odors since Persaud and Dodd presented the first prototype of the electronic nose in 1982 (Persaud & Dodd, 1982). The electronic noses have been developed mimicking the biological olfactory system, where multiple olfactory receptor neurons with partially overlapped characteristics discriminate among the odors using their response patterns. In the electronic nose, a sensor array is composed of multiple sensors, where each sensor responds to multiple odorants with different response patterns. By using the pattern recognition method, odors are classified based on their response patterns. If each sensor responds only to a specific odorant, a lot of sensors are required to cover a variety of odors. On the contrary, the electronic nose can detect a wide variety of odors with the least number of sensors using the pattern recognition method.

The pattern recognition methods commonly used in the electronic noses are multivariate analysis including both statistical analysis methods (e.g., PCA: principal component analysis, LDA: linear discriminant analysis) and biologically inspired neural network methods (e.g., MLP: multiple-layer perceptron, LVQ: learning vector quantization) (Hines, Boilot, Gardner, & Gongora, 2002).

PCA and LDA are feature extraction techniques to represent the data vectors in lower dimensions. PCA is a signal-representation technique that generates projections along the direction of maximum variance. On the other hand, LDA is a signal classification technique that directly maximizes class separation, generating projections where data distribution of each class forms a compact cluster and the different clusters are far from each other. Therefore, PCA preserves the original structure of the data, whereas LDA projections exhibit a high degree of class separation (Gutierrez-Osuna, 2002).

MLP and LVQ are artificial neural networks inspired by neural computation. In contrast to the statistical classification where only linear classification can be performed, the non-linear classification can be achieved using the neural networks. MLP is a neural network of multiple layers, typically three layers: input, hidden, output layers. Each neuron has a nonlinear input-output function such as the sigmoid function. The neurons in the input and hidden layers are connected to the neurons in the hidden and output layers, respectively. The connection weights and the threshold values of the sigmoid functions at the neurons are adjusted at the training step so that the network can represent the relationship between the inputs and the outputs of the neural network for the training data. The most popular training algorithm is the back propagation method (Bishop, 2006).

On the other hand, LVQ is a neural network that has a number of codebook vectors, called 'reference vectors,' in the input-vector space to quantize each input vector to the closest reference vector (Kohonen, 1988). Usually several reference vectors are assigned to each class, and the input vector is classified into the class where the closest reference vector belongs. Because this LVQ method is simple and easy to be implemented with relatively high performance, this method was employed in our olfactory recording system. The algorithm of LVQ is explained in detail later.

For the reproduction of the olfactory information, olfactory displays can be used. In the virtual environments, it has been reported that the olfactory cues improves the reality (Gobbetti & Scateni, 1998; Dinh, Walker, Song, Kobayashi, & Hodges, 1999). Barfield & Danas reported the summary of the important characteristics of the olfactory displays for the tasks in the virtual environments (Barfield & Danas, 1996). For example, when the participants in the virtual environments are required to locate an odor, the olfactory display should have the characteristics of expressing the field of smell, spatial resolution, intensity, and smelling volume. For the olfactory displays applied to the odor reproduction systems, the required characteristics would be both odor identification and concentration control.

Hirose proposed an olfactory display, where the smell generation part was placed on the head mount visual display (Yamada, Tanikawa, Hirota & Hirose, 2006). The smell was generated by evaporating the liquid odor sample with a heater, and was stopped by cooling the heater with a peltier device. They constructed a virtual environment using the olfactory display with a magnetic sensor to detect the place of the human nose. The olfactory display modified the smell intensity according to the distance between the odor source and the human nose in the virtual environment.

Another example of the olfactory display is the instrument developed by Yanagida (Nakaizumi, Yanagida, Noma, & Hosaka, 2006). In contrast to other typical olfactory displays where the scented air is presented under the nose through a tube, they proposed an unencumbering olfactory display by conveying a clump of scented air from a remote place to the user's nose. They implemented the olfactory display using an air cannon.

In our reproduction system, an olfactory display has been developed using solenoid values controlled by the delta-sigma modulation method (Yamanaka, Matsumoto, & Nakamoto, 2002). This olfactory display has the capability of blending multiple odor compounds and controlling each concentration. This olfactory display is explained in the 'system description' section.

MOVIE WITH SMELL

Concept of Reproduction System

The visual and olfactory reproduction system is composed of a digital video camera, an odor sensing system, a visual display and an olfactory display. In the recording, visual information and olfactory information are recorded with the digital video camera and the odor sensing system, respectively. In the reproduction, the visual information is presented as a movie on the visual display, accompanied with odors from the olfactory display. The olfactory information is recorded as odor quality and odor intensity. The odor quality is identified by a pattern classification technique, whereas odor intensity is recorded by the magnitude of the sensor response pattern. Although the recording of odor mixtures is desired, the odor-classification strategy without mixture quantification is adopted in our reproduction system as the initial step. Mixture recording will be a future challenge in this research field and will be described later.

Pattern Classification

Pattern classification for the odor identification from a sensor response pattern is a key point of the olfactory recording system. The odor identification has been a major research topic in the electronic-nose community as described in the background section. One of the pattern-classification techniques is the learning vector quantization (LVQ) proposed by Kohonen (Kohonen, 1988). In our system, this technique was employed because of its simplicity and relatively high performance.

LVQ is a vector quantization technique with supervised learning. Reference vectors are placed in the input-vector space to represent the distributions of the input-vector classes. Usually, each class takes multiple reference vectors. In the learning stage of LVQ, the reference vectors are moved to appropriately represent the classes. The learning process is as follows. For ith input vector $\mathbf{x}_i$, the closest reference vector $\mathbf{m}_{c(i)}$ is selected:

$$c\left(i\right) = \arg\min_{j} \mathbf{x}_i - \mathbf{m}_j \tag{1}$$

If $\mathbf{x}_i$ and $\mathbf{m}_{c(i)}$ belong to the same class, the selected reference vector $\mathbf{m}_{c(i)}$ is updated by the next equation:

$$\mathbf{m}'_{c(i)} = \mathbf{m}_{c(i)} + \alpha\left(\mathbf{x}_i - \mathbf{m}_{c(i)}\right) \tag{2}$$

where $\mathbf{m}'_{c(i)}$ represents the updated reference vector, and α is a learning coefficient. If $\mathbf{x}_i$ and $\mathbf{m}_{c(i)}$ belong to different classes, the selected reference vector $\mathbf{m}_{c(i)}$ is updated by the next equation:

$$\mathbf{m}'_{c(i)} = \mathbf{m}_{c(i)} - \alpha\left(\mathbf{x}_i - \mathbf{m}_{c(i)}\right) \tag{3}$$

The other reference vectors $\mathbf{m}_j$ $(j \neq c(i))$ are not moved for this input vector:

$$\mathbf{m}'_{c(i)} = \mathbf{m}_{c(i)} \tag{4}$$

Therefore, only the selected reference vector is moved toward the input vector (when $\mathbf{x}_i$ and $\mathbf{m}_{c(i)}$ belong to the same class) or to the opposite direction (when $\mathbf{x}_i$ and $\mathbf{m}_{c(i)}$ belong to different classes) for the training data $\mathbf{x}_i$. This process was applied to all the training data in sequence. Moreover, the convergence is not usually obtained in the single learning step for all the training data. Therefore, LVQ is repeatedly learned using the training data. The learning coefficient α should be set to the value between 0 and 1, and may be constant or decrease monotonically with the learning step.

The algorithm described above, called 'LVQ1,' is a basic algorithm of LVQ. The improved algorithms have been also proposed: LVQ2.1 and LVQ3. In LVQ2.1, the two reference vectors are updated simultaneously, where the reference vectors are the closest vectors belonging to the correct and wrong classes, respectively. The update was performed only when the input vector falls into a zone called 'window,' defined around the midplane of the two reference vectors. In LVQ3, the 'window' is redefined to improve the stability of the learning (Kohonen, 1988). In our reproduction system, LVQ1 was employed due to the simplicity.

SYSTEM DESCRIPTION

Recording System

The recording system is composed of a digital video camera (DVC) and an electronic-nose system. The photograph of the recording system is shown in Figure 1a. Visual information during the recording experiments are captured using the DVC (DCR-PC105K, Sony), whereas odors are recorded using the electronic-nose system. The main components of the electronic-nose system are quartz crystal microbalance

Figure 1. Experimental setup for recording and display systems. (a) Recording system, (b) Recording targets (Fruit juice cans), (c) Display system, (d) schematic of odor blender.

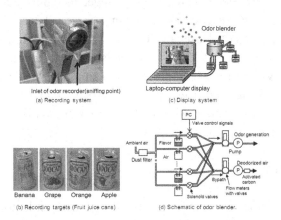

(QCM) sensors covered with different sensing films. The ambient air is sucked from the tip of Teflon tube (called the sniffing point) using an air pump. The air is provided to a sensor cell, where four QCM sensors are placed to detect odors. The sniffing point is set beneath the lens of the DVC on a homemade cart so that the DVC and sniffing point can be moved together. The length of the Teflon tube from the sniffing point to the sensor cell was 480 cm.

The QCM sensors work based upon mass loading effect where adsorbed mass of the vapor changes the resonance frequency (King, 1964; Nakamoto & Mori-izumi, 1990). In the recording system, QCM with AT cut, 20MHz coated with four different sensing films were used. These sensing films were Apiezon L (Ap-L), silicone OV-17 (OV-17), tricresyl phosphate (TCP), and polyethylene glycol 1000 (PEG1000). They are stationary phase materials for gas chromatography, and are often used as the sensing films of QCM sensors. The QCM sensor responses, namely, the oscillation frequency shifts from the baselines, were collected by a personal computer via a multichannel frequency counter. The sampling interval of the QCM sensors was 1 s. In the odor recording, response patterns of the QCM sensors are classified into odor classes using a pattern classification technique. This classification algorithm is explained in "Odor-recording algorithm" section in details.

Fruit juice cans were used as targets, as shown in Figure 1b. The height of the sniffing point was set to be the same as that of the can. Since the concentration of the juice flavor at the outlet of the actual juice can is very low, humans cannot de-tect a smell when the distance between the nose and the outlet of the can increases. Therefore, a flavor was set in the can to increase its concentration. One ml of a liquid flavor sample was placed in a petri dish (diameter, 48 mm; depth, 16mm). A small fan

(F1016AP-01WCV, Shicoh Engineering Co., Ltd.) was then set above the petri dish inside the can to enhance the concentration of the odor. The fruit juice cans used in the experiments were labeled banana, grape, orange, and apple, as shown in Figure 1b. The sample flavors corresponding to the cans, namely, banana, muscat (grape), orange, and apple flavors (T. Hasegawa Co. Ltd.), were used in the experiments.

The movie was captured at 320 x 240 pixels (QVGA: quarter video graphics array) using the DVC, and was compressed into an mpeg file. During the experiments, DVC and sniffing point were moved between 0 cm and 15 cm away from the target cans. The can in the movie became larger or smaller depending on the distance between the target cans and DVC.

Display System

The visual and olfactory information is reproduced using a laptop computer display (14 inches in diagonal, 1024 x 768 pixels) and an odor blender (Yamanaka, Matsumoto, & Nakamoto, 2002). The illustration of the display system is shown in Figure 1c. The odor blender has capabilities of blending multiple odor components and adjusting the concentration of each component. In the experiments described in this chapter, a single odor component is generated with a dynamic sequence of concentration for the odor display.

The odor blender controls the concentration using only solenoid valves, as shown in Figure 1d. Although a solenoid valve is a fluidic switching device, the concentration of each odor component can be controlled by repeatedly switching the fluidic paths from a sample bottle to an empty bottle. Odor samples are prepared in the liquid phase in bottles. The bypass is set to maintain the concentration in each bottle constant by keeping the flow rate in each bottle constant. The flow rate at each flow meter was 1500 ml/min. Each odor concentration was represented using the concentration relative to that of the full-scale concentration with the unit %RC.

Odor-Recording Algorithm and Experiment

A target odor in the atmosphere was recorded as an odor class and a concentration sequence of the odor. The odor class was identified from the sensor-response pattern of the odor using learning vector quantification (LVQ) described in the previous section. The concentration sequence was recorded from the magnitude of the sensor-response pattern.

The responses of the four QCM sensors (Ap-L, OV-17, TCP, and PEG1000) to the four fruit flavors (apple, banana, muscat, and orange) were measured in the atmosphere. During the experiments, the sniffing point was moved together with

Figure 2. Odor sensor responses to target fruit flavors in atmosphere. The sniffing point was moved from 15 cm to 0 cm away from the target together with the digital video camera. (a) Example of odor sensor response (OV-17) to apple flavor (b) PCA plots of odor sensor responses to four fruit flavors.

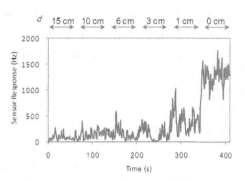

(a) Example of odor sensor response (OV-17) to apple flavor.

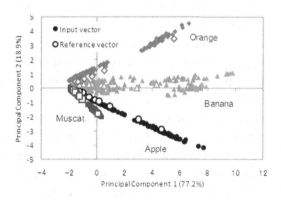

(b) PCA plots of odor sensor responses to four fruit flavors.

DVC using the cart toward the fruit juice can. The distance between the can and the sniffing point is represented by d.

An example of the sensor response is shown in Figure 2a. It shows the response of OV-17 to the apple flavor. The sniffing point was moved from $d = 15$ cm to 0cm, and stopped for 60 s at $d = 15, 10, 6, 3, 1$, and 0 cm. It can be seen from the figure that the concentration in the atmosphere rapidly fluctuated due to air turbulence (Yamanaka, Ishida, Nakamoto, & Moriizumi, 1998). Even though the long Teflon tube (480 cm) was used in the recording system of odors, the fluctuation of the odors in the atmosphere was observed in the odor sensors in spite of averaging effect on odors between the inlet and the outlet of the long tube. Since the sensor response at the distance of 15 cm was much smaller than that at 0 cm, a large dynamic range of the odor sensor was required to record odors in the atmosphere.

The responses to each fruit flavor were measured twice to obtain training and evaluation data for investigating the performance of the odor-classification algorithm. The four sensor responses were weighted to make the response levels among the sensors the same for pattern classification. Before applying the data to the odor-classification algorithm, the existence of the odors should first be judged because "no-odor" periods were observed during the odor recording due to the airflow fluctuation. This judgment was performed using the magnitude of the sensor-response pattern. The data with the magnitude below a threshold was classified into the "no-odor" class. Although this threshold was empirically determined in the experiment described below, the threshold can be set based on the noise level of the odor sensors. The data classified into the "no-odor" class was 29.9% in the training data and 33.0% in the evaluation data.

After the classification of the "no-odor" class, sensor-response patterns were classified into odor classes using LVQ. At each sampling time, the eight-dimensional input vector was composed of the responses of the four sensors at the current sampling point and those at the previous sampling point. The responses at the two sampling points were used because the transient characteristic of the sensor was taken into account. Since the classification capability was improved from that with responses at only a single sampling point in the preliminary experiment, the responses at the successive sampling points were used as the input-vector components of LVQ.

In LVQ, the parameter vectors are placed in the input-vector space, and called reference vectors (Kohonen, 1988). Each reference vector is assigned to a category, and each category usually has multiple reference vectors. The reference vectors are appropriately placed to express the distributions of the categories at the training stage of LVQ. Then the input vector is classified into the category to which the closest reference vector belongs.

In order to investigate the performance of the classification algorithm, LVQ was trained using the training data and then the classification was performed for both the training and evaluation data. The number of reference vectors was set to 20 at each flavor category. This number was determined from the results of the preliminary experiment, where classification performance saturated for more than 20 reference vectors in each category. The number of the training data was 400 x 4 = 1600 (400: every sampling point from 21 to 420 s, 4: four fruit flavors), and the data at every sampling time from 1 to 20 s were used as the initial reference vectors. The number of the evaluation data was 420 x 4 = 1680 (420: every sampling point from 1 to 420 s, 4: four fruit flavors). Because the convergence of training was not obtained in a single training step for all the training data, LVQ was trained for 40 steps.

The recognition rates for the training data and evaluation data were 98.04% and 85.96%, respectively. Since the recognition rate for the evaluation data without the "no-odor" class was 66.96%, this "no-odor" class needs to be included in the classification of the odor recording.

In order to visualize the sensor-response patterns, the PCA (principal Component Analysis) plots are shown in Figure 2b for the evaluation data. These plots are the sensor-response patterns (input vectors) and the reference vectors learned by LVQ. The PCA is used to visually show the distribution of multidimensional data. It was found that the reference vectors after training were correctly placed to cover each flavor distribution and that the location in the distribution of each flavor corresponded to the odor intensity.

Although some data of apple and orange flavors were misclassified into the muscat and banana flavors, respectively, it did not affect the impression of the smells during the regeneration because those misclassifications occurred for small sensor responses. Furthermore, when it is assumed that the type of a smell at the sniffing point does not suddenly change during the odor recording, the misclassified data can be compensated in consideration of the successive classification results. Although this algorithm was not included in the experiment described in this chapter, it would be useful when misclassified data affects smell regeneration.

For the determination of odor intensity, the calibration curve showing the relationship between sensor response magnitude and odor concentration in the odor blender (Figure 1d) is measured in advance for each flavor category. This calibration curve is obtained by measuring the steady-state responses of the sensor array using the odor blender. In the case of QCM sensors, the relationship is almost linear for all combinations of sensors and flavors. The accuracy of the odor concentration estimation based on the calibration curve increases as the slope of the calibration curve increases. Therefore, the largest sensor response among the sensors in the array is used for the estimation of odor concentration.

When the estimated concentration exceeds 100%RC, the generated concentration is set 100%RC because it is not possible to generate the odor with the concentration beyond 100%RC. When no odor is detected, the generated concentration is set 0%RC.

SMELL REPRODUCTION SYNCHRONOUS WITH MOVIE

Evaluation of Reproduction System

Based on the recording algorithm explained in the previous section, the target flavor together with the movie was recorded. The recording was performed for each fruit flavor. Example sensor responses and DVC images are shown in Figure 3. After placing them at $d = 15$ cm away from the target fruit juice can for 10 s, DVC and the sniffing point were manually moved from $d = 15$ to 0 cm for 15 s. Then they

Figure 3. Examples of odor sensor responses and images of digital video camera during recording odor with movie

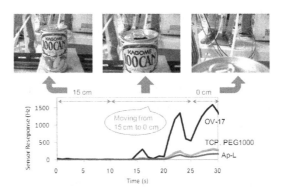

were placed for 5 s at 0 cm, as shown in Figure 3. Odor quality was estimated from the sensor responses during the recording using LVQ. The LVQ was trained in advance using the data measured under the same experimental conditions as those in the previous section. The recognition rate based on the recording algorithm was 96.72% in this experiment. Odor intensity was estimated from the calibration curve.

The recorded visual and olfactory information was evaluated by sensory tests using the display system. Two experiments were conducted: 1) the influence of a change in odor concentration on human impression, 2) the appropriateness of the reproduced odor with the movie.

In the first experiment, the influence of a change in odor concentration on human impression was investigated. The regeneration of an odor and a movie was evaluated under the following two conditions by each subject.

- **Condition 1:** Regeneration of movie and odor recorded concurrently using the proposed system in this chapter.
- **Condition 2:** Regeneration of movie with static concentration odor.

The subjects were instructed to answer if they perceived a difference between the regenerations of Conditions 1 and 2. They were further instructed to answer which odor was more appropriate for the movie, when they perceived a difference. Ten subjects (graduate students) participated in the sensory tests. The experiment was conducted for only the apple flavor to evaluate the influence of the dynamic concentration change on human impression. The order of these conditions was random during odor regeneration.

In this experiment, all the subjects perceived the difference between Conditions 1 and 2, and selected Condition 1 as more appropriate for the regeneration of the

Figure 4. Average scores of appropriateness for four fruits under three conditions

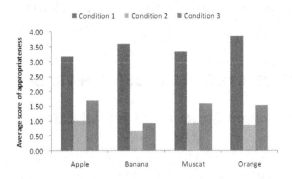

odor to the movie. This indicates that humans detect a change in odor concentration, and that this change feels more appropriate when the odor varies with the movie.

In the second experiment, the appropriateness of the reproduced odor with the movie was investigated. The appropriateness was studied using a psychophysical experiment (Zellner & Whitten, 1999). The regeneration of an odor and a movie was evaluated under the following three conditions by each subject.

- **Condition 1:** Regeneration of odor corresponding to the recorded movie (e.g., apple flavor with apple movie).
- **Condition 2:** Regeneration of the same movie as that under Condition 1 with odorless air.
- **Condition 3:** Regeneration of the same movie as that under Condition 1 with odor unrelated to the movie (e.g., orange flavor with apple movie).

After experiencing all the conditions, 15 subjects were requested to score the appropriateness (0-4) of the odor for the movie for each condition (0: least appropriate, 4: most appropriate). The movies of the four fruits (apple, banana, muscat, orange) were presented to each subject at random, where the reproduction under the three conditions was presented for each movie.

The average scores of the appropriateness of the four fruits under the three conditions are shown in Figure 4. It can be seen from the figure that the most appropriate condition was Condition 1, where the concurrently recorded odor and movie were presented. The least appropriate condition was Condition 2, where the movie was reproduced with odorless air. Furthermore, the ANOVA (analysis of variance) explained in Sato (1978) revealed significant differences among the scores under the three conditions for all of the four flavors (apple: $F(2,28) = 10.17$; $p <.001$, banana: $F(2,28) = 62.32$; $p <.001$, muscat: $F(2,28) = 40.78$; $p <.001$, orange: $F(2,28)$

= 40.78; $p <.001$). Thus, it can be concluded that the smell reproduced on the basis of the recorded information was appropriate for the smell regeneration associated with the movie.

TELEOLFACTION SYNCHRONOUS WITH VISION

Concept and System Structure of Teleolfaction

Although the smell reproduction together with movie was successfully performed in the previous section, it was not possible to reproduce it in real time at remote site. Thus, we propose a teleolfaction system using an odor sensing system and an olfactory display. Users can sniff the smell in real time even if the odor source is located far away from users. They can also smell simultaneously with watching a video, transferred from the recording system via the Internet. Thus, users can perceive much sensation of reality of the object even at the remote site. This effect is called the teleexistence of the olfaction. The proposed system was demonstrated at the exhibition and its fundamental capability was confirmed by the result of the questionnaire survey.

The concept of teleolfaction system with vision is illustrated in Figure 5 (a). An object is captured by recording system and its image and scent information is transmitted to the display system located away from the object. The display system reproduces the object in olfaction and vision. Recording system consists of odor sensing system and Web camera, whereas the display system consists of olfactory display and the screen on the computer. Scents should be displayed synchronous with movie.

Figure 5. Teleolfaction system (a) concept and (b) system structure

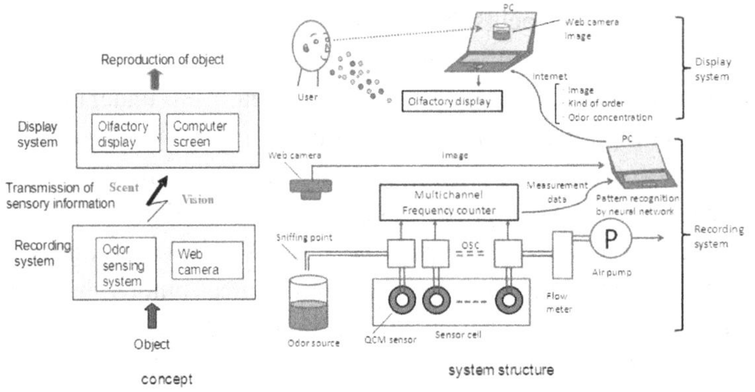

The actual diagram of teleolfaction system made up of recoding system and olfactory display system is depicted in Figure 5 (b).

Teleolfaction-System Description

The recording system records odor information and movie, and transmit them to the display system. The system consists of an odor sensing system, a Web camera and a laptop computer.

Ambient air is sucked into the sensor cell through Teflon tube using an air pump (Iwaki, APN-215NV-1) at the flow rate of 600ml/min. In the sensor cell, four QCM gas sensors (AT-CUT, 20MHz) were placed. The QCMs were coated with sensing films such as Apiezon L, polyethylene glycol 1000 (PEG1k), silicone OV-17 (OV-17) and trecresyl phosphate (TCP). Those sensing film were also used in the previous section.

The coating technique is important to obtain the reproducible sensor characteristics. The ultrasonic atomizer was used for sensing film coating (Munos, Nakamoto and Moriizumi, 2005; Wyszynski, Galvez & Nakamoto, 2007) although simple airbrush was insufficient for obtaining the stable result.

The QCM sensors are connected to oscillator circuits and the changes of oscillation frequencies are measured by a multi-channel frequency counter implemented into a FPGA (Field Programmable Gate Array). The circuit was described in VHDL. Each channel of the frequency counter is a reciprocal counter with its sampling interval of 1/8s (Segawa, Tokuhiro, Nakamoto & Moriizumi, 2002) and with the frequency resolution of approximately 1Hz. The measured data are sent to the computer via RS232C interface. In this system, the odor concentration and the classification result are used as odor information. The detail for the analysis will be described later.

To record and transfer the movie and the odor information in real time, software written in Visual Basic 6 (Microsoft Corp) was developed. This program continuously records, analyzes and transfers the data to the display system every second.

The movie taken by the Web camera (BWC-130MH03A/BK, Buffalo) is once stored in a memory and then merged with the odor information. Then, the data are transferred to the display system at remote site via the Internet by using Windows Socket API (Winsock). The image with the size of 160x120 has JPEG format. It is captured and stored into the memory every second. Thus, the image on the computer screen is updated every second. The streaming format of the movie was not used. Instead, the continuous static image was used since it is easy to synchronize odor concentration sequence with movie. In the experiment, ADSL with the rate of 50Mb/s was used for the data transfer. The smell can be generated synchronously with the movie without the influence of Internet congestion.

The display system in Figure 5 receives the transferred data and presents them in real time. The system consists of a laptop computer, an olfactory display and a headset. The developed software was also written in Visual Basic 6. The received data are separated into two parts such as movie and odor information. The odor information consists of its concentration and the kind of odor.

The movie is simply displayed on the computer screen at the rate of 1 frame/s using Web browser. The odor is generated using the olfactory display using solenoid valves in the way similar to the previous section. The current olfactory display can blend up to 32 odor components and its recipe can be updated every second, whereas the previous model dealt with 8 odor components.

The user can sniff the smell from the slit of the plastic adaptor placed at the microphone of the headset, connected to the olfactory display via Teflon tube. Although the olfactory display can blend many odor components, only two odor components were used in later experiment. Two flavors were set at two vials and the function of blending was not used here for simplicity. Instead of it, the function of adjusting odor concentration every second was used in the present study.

Although the control sequence of the solenoid valves was managed in the computer in the reference (Nakamoto and Pham, 2007), the current system includes FPGA board (Altera, EP1C2Q240C8) in the olfactory display. The CPU core with peripherals such as serial interface and the parallel I/O was implemented into FPGA. After the CPU core (NIOS, Altera) receives the recipe information from the computer via RS232C interface, it generates bit streams to control the ON/OFF sequences of each solenoid valves. The program for the CPU core was written in C language.

After the introduction of FPGA into the olfactory display, the flexibility of the olfactory display increased. When people want to use that system, it is not necessary to consider the complicated control sequence of the solenoid valves. The olfactory display works after simply specifying the concentration sequence. After this improvement, the portability of the system became much better. Then, the compact version of the olfactory display was recently developed with the collaboration of the companies for the prototype before commercialization.

Odor-Information Analysis

The odor information handled here is both the kind of odor and the odor concentration. Odor identification is performed as follows.

First it should be judged whether the odor exists. When no odor is detected, the sensor response is quite stable. Although slight noise or drift sometimes appears, the fluctuation behavior is different from them when the odor is presented. The QCM sensor response to an odor in ambient air always rapidly fluctuates due to air turbulence as is shown in Figure 2 (a) and Figure 3. The fluctuation of the sensor response is usually larger than the noise in the case of odor presence. The data for 5s were used to judge the existence of the odor. The threshold of the response variation in noise was set to 5Hz. That time span and the threshold were empirically determined. If the response variation exceeds the threshold three times during that time span, it is judged that the odor exists.

The next step is the odor classification. We used a LVQ neural network to classify the odor in the same way as that in the previous section. The odor concentration is estimated using the calibration curve also in the same manner as that in the previous section. We obtained the curve by measuring steady-state sensor response to the target odor at several concentrations. When the calibration curve is obtained, the olfactory display is used as odor generator for supplying the odor to the sensor at specified concentrations. We used the largest sensor response among four sensors to estimate the odor concentration to increase the accuracy.

Demonstration of Teleolfaction

In this system, the odor information was analyzed and transferred to the display system in real time. Thus, we had to prepare for LVQ for the odor identification. We obtained the training dataset of each category by measuring sensor responses to the sample in the ambient air for 70s. Those sensor responses were used as pattern vector. Then, we selected 10 initial reference vectors for each category from the training dataset. Therefore we had 60 pattern vectors for each category to train the neural network. The network training was repeated 20 times in this experiment.

Samples used here were orange and apple flavors. The clear pattern separation is obtained between the two categories. Since the pattern separation was clear, the classification of these two samples was 100% when the data were classified by LVQ. It was also found that the reference vectors were correctly placed after training and covered the whole distribution of each category.

We demonstrated the experiment on teleolfaction at Tokyo Big Sight (Koto-ku, Tokyo) during the Industry Academic Government Technical Exchange Fair 2007. We set the recording system at our laboratory (Meguro-ku, Tokyo) and the display system at the remote site at that exhibition. At the laboratory, the recording system was set in a wind tunnel with five sample vials. The vials were equally placed and the distance from vial to vial was 80mm.

Two of them were filled with the samples of apple and orange flavors, respectively, whereas the others were empty. It was difficult to know which vials contained the liquid when people watched only the movie. The volume of each vial was 30mL. The sniffing point was the tip of Teflon tube. The tube was connected to the sensor cell, where four sensors were placed. The tube and the Web camera were supported by the arm made of wood. The Web camera took the picture around the sniffing point. This arm was manually moved to make the sniffing point closer to the vial in this experiment. Since it was difficult to control the speed of moving sniffing point, a user could not perceive the change of odor intensity around the smelling object.

We had the booth at Tokyo Big Sight. At that booth, a user cannot grasp the situation at remote sensing site only when he/she watches the image of sniffing point and sniff the smell at the same time. Thus another Web camera was placed close to the wind tunnel to show the whole image of the objects at the remote site.

We evaluated the capability of our system by a questionnaire survey at the exhibition. Two of five vials were filled with apple and orange flavors respectively, whereas others were empty. The sniffing point was manually made close to the vial individually together with taking the movie. People at the exhibition site sniffed the smell in real time sensed at the wind tunnel in our laboratory. Simultaneously, they could watch the movie taken there. The time for sniffing smell was approximately 10s and the time from vial to vial was approximately 5s.

They were requested to identify the vials with apple and orange flavors. Figure 6 (a) shows the result of the questionnaire survey. Approximately 80% of people correctly identified the smell inside the vials.

Another question is whether movie is synchronized with smell. The result of the questionnaire survey is summarized in Figure 6(b). More than 80% people answered the synchronization worked well. Other question is whether he/she feels more real after adding the smell to the movie. The result of the questionnaire survey is shown in Figure 6 (c). More than 80% people also answered positively to this question.

Figure 6. Result of questionnaire survey for preliminary demonstration. (a) odor identification by people at remote site, (b) synchronization of movie with smell and (c) increase in reality after adding smell to movie.

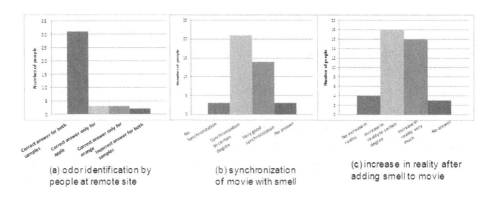

Improvement of Teleolfaction by Introduction of Mobile Stage

Although most of people answered positively at the exhibition, it is better to introduce the interactive operation to enhance the reality of teleolfaction. We further improved the teleolfaction system from that point of view. The mobile stage with sniffing point and a camera was introduced so that a user at remote site could control the location of mobile stage to approach smelling objects. Since it allows a user to do interactive operation, more reality of teleolfaction was expected.

The developed mobile stage is shown in Figure 7. That stage was driven by DC motors. It moved one-dimensionally, i.e., forward and backward when the user pushed the control button. Its direction was controlled using relays. The sensing nozzle was placed 21cm away from the center of the mobile stage. The mobile stage could be moved at the remote site via internet. The user at remote site could interactively move the mobile stage to capture each smelling object. Moreover, the user could perceive change of odor intensity when the mobile stage approached or went away from the sample, whereas it was difficult to perceive it when the sniffing nozzle was manually moved. The moving speed was too fast in case of manual operation while the mobile stage in the improved system moved slowly.

Three smelling objects such as apple, whiskey and orange were prepared for the experiment as is shown in Figure 7. The apple and orange were imitations with corresponding flavors but the whiskey was a real sample. Since only vials were

Figure 7. Improved teleolfaction system (a) mobile stage, (b) system structre and (c) smelling objects.

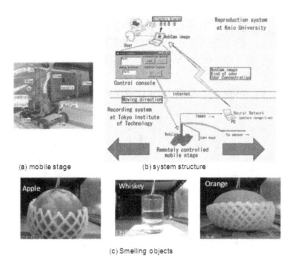

presented in the previous experiment, some people pointed out that the visual impact was poor. Thus, the fruit imitations with the flavors were used here.

The questionnaire survey was performed again at the campus festival in 2008. The campus festival was held for two days. The participants were people to visit our lab at the campus festival. The result of questionnaire survey for matching between image and smell is shown in Figure 8 (a). It was found that the smell matched image well since everyone pointed out the matching between the two (the circle indicated in the figure). The result of the questionnaire survey for synchronization of movie with smell is shown in Figure 8 (b). The synchronization worked well since no one pointed out that the smell was asynchronous with vision (the circle indicated in the figure). Since the smell comes to the nose later than the change of the image, the image was somewhat delayed in this experiment. Thus, the impression on the synchronization was improved compared with the previous demonstration. The result of questionnaire survey for increase in reality due to addition of smell to movie is shown in Figure 8 (c). It revealed that most of people answered positively about the increase in reality. The ratio of the positive answer was increased in comparison with the previous demonstration due to the interactivity and visual effect. Final

Figure 8. Result of questionnaire survey using improved teleolfaction system. (a) matching between image and smell, (b) synchronization of movie with smell, (c) increase in reality after adding smell to movie and (d) perception of odor intensity change.

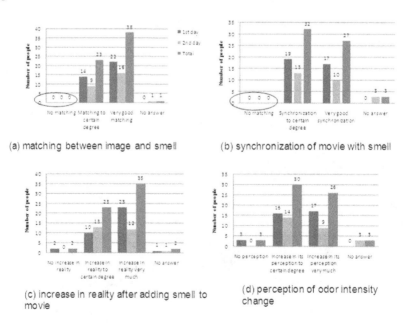

(a) matching between image and smell

(b) synchronization of movie with smell

(c) increase in reality after adding smell to movie

(d) perception of odor intensity change

question is whether a user can perceive the change of odor intensity. Most of people perceived the change of odor intensity, whereas it was not possible in the previous demonstration. The introduction of the mobile stage with the appropriate speed enabled the perception of the odor-intensity variation.

We also demonstrated the teleolfaction with movie at the international conference held at Yokohama, Japan in December, 2008 (Cho, Nimsuk, Wyszynski, Takushima, Kinoshita, & Nakamoto, 2008). The distance of the smelling object at our campus to the remote site was about 20km. Many participants of that conference enjoyed the demonstration. In 2009, the system was extended so that more samples could be reproduced. The samples were placed on the remotely-controlled turn table. Then, many samples can be presented within small space.

OUTLOOK FOR EXTENDING CURRENT SYSTEM TO MIXED-ODOR REPRODUCTION

Although the current system can reproduce the classified smell, it would be highly desirable to extend it to the quantification of a mixed odor followed by its reproduction in real time. We previously investigated that issue although the system did not have the function of smell transmission. The method called real-time reference method was developed. In that method, a sensor array is alternately exposed to either a target odor or the odor from a blender, which can generate mixed odor with its time-variant recipe. The recipe of odor from the blender is successively adjusted so that the sensor-array response pattern of the blended odor can balance that of the target odor in real time (Yamanaka & Nakamoto, 2003) using MIMO (Multi-Input Multi-Output) feedback control. Although this method has not yet been used for teleolfaction, it might be a powerful technique because it is quite robust against the environmental change.

In comparison with classification problem, more selectivity among odor components is required to obtain the accurate mixture composition. Moreover, the mixture composition always changes in the current problem and the time constant of each sensor makes the problem more difficult. One of its solutions might be a real-time mass spectrometer (Pakpum, Kinoshita, Wyszynski & Nakamoto, 2009). Although a mass spectrometer is typically used to analyze samples in the liquid phase, it can be also applied to ones in the vapor phase. A variety of m/zs in the mass spectrometry are available to enhance the selectivity. Although we succeeded in quantifying the mixture in the vapor phase using the mass spectrometry, the real-time application has not yet been tried. However, real-time mass spectrometer can be applied to teleolfaction with mixed odor. The introduction of mixed odor into teleolfaction will expand its application in the near future.

CONCLUSION

In this chapter, odor reproduction with a movie and its application to teleolfaction were presented. First, smell regeneration associated with the movie was described. A method of recording odors with large fluctuation in the atmosphere was developed using odor sensors and pattern classification such as LVQ. The experimental results showed that the four different fruit flavors were successfully recorded using the proposed method.

Then, fruit flavors were recorded with movies using a DVC and the odor sensors developed using the proposed method. The results of the sensory tests showed that the odor information recorded using the proposed method is appropriate for the smell regeneration associated with the movie. Thus, the smell attached to the movie might enhance reality.

The next step was the development of the teleolfaction system synchronous with movie. This system can record and present a movie with smell to users at remote site in real time via the Internet. In recording system, QCM gas sensors with LVQ neural network were used to classify smells and estimate odor concentration. In the display system, the olfactory display using solenoid valves was used to present smell with time-varying concentration sequence. The questionnaire survey reveals that users can perceive olfactory and visual stimuli even at the remote site. Moreover, the introduction of the mobile stage to remotely control the location of the sniffing point enabled the interactive operation. The interactivity also enhanced the reality.

In the future, more sophisticated algorithms to enhance the robustness against concentration fluctuation, humidity and temperature will be introduced (Nimsuk & Nakamoto, 2008). Since the experiments here are affected by the environmental changes, robustness in sensing technology should be increased.

Although we focused on the category classification and odor concentration change without mixing odor in the present study, the reproduction of mixed odor at remote site in real time is another future problem. Moreover, we are now seeking odor components to cover wide range of smell (Nakamoto & Murakami, 2009). Attempts to obtain the smell recipe in real time together with finding odor components to cover wide range of smell may well enhance the odor reproduction capability.

REFERENCES

Barfield, W., & Danas, E. (1996). Comments on the use of olfactory displays for virtual environments. *Presence (Cambridge, Mass.)*, 5(1), 109–121.

Bishop, C. M. (2006). *Pattern recognition and machine learning* (pp. 225–290). Springer-Verlag.

Burdea, G., & Ciffet, P. (2003). *Virtual reality technology* (pp. 92–110). Wiley-Interscience.

Cho, N., Nimsuk, N., Wyszynski, B., Takushima, H., Kinoshita, M., & Nakamoto, T. (2008). *Demonstration of interactive teleolfaction with movie*. Paper presented at the meeting of Advances in Computer Entertainment 2008, Creative showcase, Yokohama, Japan.

Davide, F., Holmberg, M., & Lundstrom, I. (2001). Virtual olfactory interfaces: Electronic noses and olfactory displays. In Riva, G., & Davide, F. (Eds.), *Communications through virtual technologies* (pp. 194–220). Amsterdam, The Netherlands: IOS Press.

Dinh, H. Q., Walker, N., Song, C., Kobayashi, A., & Hodges, L. F. (1999). *Evaluating the importance of multi-sensory input on memory and the sense of presence in virtual environments* (pp. 222–228). Houston, TX: IEEE Virtual Reality.

Gobbetti, E., & Scateni, R. (1998). Virtual reality: Past, present, and future. In Riva, G., Wiederhold, B. K., & Molinari, E. (Eds.), *Virtual environments in clinical psychology and neuroscience: Methods and techniques in advanced patient-therapist interaction* (pp. 3–20). Amsterdam, The Netherlands: IOS Press.

Gutierrez-Osuna, R. (2002). Pattern analysis for machine olfaction: A review. *IEEE Sensors Journal, 2*(3), 189–202. doi:10.1109/JSEN.2002.800688

Hines, E. L., Boilot, P., Gardner, J. W., & Gongora, M. A. (2002). Pattern analysis for electronic noses. In Pearce, T. C., Shiffman, S. S., Nagle, H. T., & Gardner, J. W. (Eds.), *Handbook of machine olfaction* (pp. 133–160). Weinheim, Germany: Wiley-VCH. doi:10.1002/3527601597.ch6

Kaye, J. J. (2004). Making scents: Aromatic output for HCI. *Interaction, 11*(1), 48–61. doi:10.1145/962342.964333

King, W. H. (1964). Piezoelectric sorption detector. *Analytical Chemistry, 36*, 1735. doi:10.1021/ac60215a012

Kohonen, T. (1988). *Self-organization and associative memory* (pp. 199–202). Springer-Verlag.

Messager, J. (2002). *The diffusion of fragrances in a multimedia environment*. Paper presented at Third Aroma Science Forum, Tokyo, Japan.

Munoz, S., Nakamoto, T., & Moriizumi, T. (2005). Study of deposition of gas sensing films on quartz crystal microbalance using an ultrasonic atomizer. *Sensors and Actuators. B, Chemical, 105*, 144–149.

Nakaizumi, F., Yanagida, Y., Noma, H., & Hosaka, K. (2006). SpotScents: A novel method of natural scent delivery using multiple scent projectors. *Proceedings of IEEE Virtual Reality Conference* (pp. 206-212). Alexandria, Virginia.

Nakamoto, T., Cho, N., Nitikarn, N., Wyszynski, B., Takushima, H., & Kinoshita, M. (2008). *Experiment on teleolfaction using odor sensing system and olfactory display synchronous with visual information*. 18th International Conference on Artificial Reality and Telexistence (pp. 85-92). Yokohama, Japan.

Nakamoto, T., & Dinh Minh, H. P. (2007). *Improvement of olfactory display using solenoid valves*. IEEE Virtual Reality Conference (pp. 179-186). Charlotte, NC.

Nakamoto, T., & Moriizumi, T. (1990). A theory of a quartz crystal microbalance based upon a Mason equivalent circuit. *Japanese Journal of Applied Physics, 29*, 963–969. doi:10.1143/JJAP.29.963

Nakamoto, T., & Murakami, K. (2009). Selection method of odor components for olfactory display using mass spectrum database. In [Lafayette, Louisiana, USA.]. *Proceedings of IEEE Virtual Reality, 2009*, 159–162.

Nakamoto, T., Nakahira, Y., Hiramatsu, H., & Moriizumi, T. (2001). Odor recorder using active odor sensing system. *Sensors and Actuators. B, Chemical, 76*, 465–469. doi:10.1016/S0925-4005(01)00587-1

Nakamoto, T., Otaguro, S., Kinoshita, M., Nagahama, M., Ohnishi, K., & Ishida, T. (2008). Cooking up an interactive olfactory display. *IEEE Computer Graphics and Applications, 28*(1), 75–78. doi:10.1109/MCG.2008.3

Nakamoto, T., & Yoshikawa, K. (2006). Movie with scents generated by olfactory display using solenoid valves. *IEICE Transactions on Fundamentals of Electronics, Communications and Computer Sciences. E (Norwalk, Conn.), 89-A*(11), 3327–3332.

Nimsuk, N., & Nakamoto, T. (2008). Study on the odor classification in dynamical concentration robust both against humidity and temperature changes. *Sensors and Actuators. B, Chemical, 234*, 252–257. doi:10.1016/j.snb.2008.04.047

Pearce, T. C. (1997). Computational parallels between the biological olfactory pathway and its analogue the electronic nose, part II: Sensor-based machine olfaction. *Bio Systems, 41*, 69–90. doi:10.1016/S0303-2647(96)01660-7

Persaud, K., & Dodd, G. (1982). Analysis of discrimination mechanisms in the mammalian olfactory system using a model nose. *Nature, 299,* 352–355. doi:10.1038/299352a0

Sato, S. (1978). *Introduction to sensory test* (pp. 78–80). JUSE Press, Ltd.

Segawa, N., Tokuhiro, T., Nakamoto, T., & Moriizumi, T. (2002). Multi-channel frequency shift measurement circuit with high sampling rate for QCM odor sensors. *IEE of Japan,* 16-22.

Somboon, P., Kinoshita, M., Wyszynski, B., & Nakamoto, T. (in press). Development of odor recorder with enhanced recording capabilities based on real-time mass spectrometry. *Sensors and Actuators. B, Chemical.*

Tominaga, K., Honda, S., Ohsawa, T., Shigeno, H., Okada, K., & Matsushita, Y. (2001). Friend Park-expression of the wind and the scent on virtual space. *Proceedings of the 7th International Conference on Virtual Systems and Multimedia* (pp. 507-515). Berkeley, CA.

Wyszynski, B., Galvez, A. G., & Nakamoto, T. (2007). Improvement of ultrasonic atomizer method for deposition of gas-sensing film on QCM. *Sensors and Actuators. B, Chemical, 127,* 253–259. doi:10.1016/j.snb.2007.07.052

Yamada, T., Tanikawa, T., Hirota, K., & Hirose, M. (2006). Wearable olfactory display: Using odor in outdoor environment. *Proceedings of IEEE Virtual Reality Conference* (pp. 199-206). Alexandria, VA.

Yamanaka, T., Ishida, H., Nakamoto, T., & Moriizumi, T. (1998). Analysis of gas sensor transient response by visualizing instantaneous gas concentration using smoke. *Sensors and Actuators. A, Physical, 69,* 77–81. doi:10.1016/S0924-4247(98)00045-4

Yamanaka, T., Matsumoto, R., & Nakamoto, T. (2002). Study of odor blender using solenoid valves controlled by delta-sigma modulation method for odor recorder. *Sensors and Actuators. B, Chemical, 87,* 457–463. doi:10.1016/S0925-4005(02)00300-3

Yamanaka, T., Matsumoto, R., & Nakamoto, T. (2003). Study of recording apple flavor using odor recorder with five components. *Sensors and Actuators. B, Chemical, 89,* 112–119. doi:10.1016/S0925-4005(02)00451-3

Yamanaka, T., & Nakamoto, T. (2003). Real-time reference method in odor blender under environmental change. *Sensors and Actuators. B, Chemical, 93,* 51–56. doi:10.1016/S0925-4005(03)00202-8

Yamanaka, T., Nitikarn, N., & Nakamoto, T. (2007). Concurrent recording and regeneration of visual and olfactory information using odor sensor. *Presence (Cambridge, Mass.)*, *16*(3), 307–317. doi:10.1162/pres.16.3.307

Yamanaka, T., Yoshikawa, K., & Nakamoto, T. (2004). Improvement of odor-recorder capability for recording dynamical change in odor. *Sensors and Actuators. B, Chemical*, *99*(2-3), 367–372. doi:10.1016/j.snb.2003.12.004

Zellner, D. A., & Whitten, L. A. (1999). The effect of color intensity and appropriateness on color-induced odor enhancement. *The American Journal of Psychology*, *112*, 585–604. doi:10.2307/1423652

Chapter 6
Statistical Gas Distribution Modeling Using Kernel Methods

Sahar Asadi
Örebro University, Sweden

Matteo Reggente
Örebro University, Sweden

Cyrill Stachniss
University of Freiburg, Germany

Christian Plagemann
Stanford University, USA

Achim J. Lilienthal
Örebro University, Sweden

ABSTRACT

Gas distribution models can provide comprehensive information about a large number of gas concentration measurements, highlighting, for example, areas of unusual gas accumulation. They can also help to locate gas sources and to plan where future measurements should be carried out. Current physical modeling methods, however, are computationally expensive and not applicable for real world scenarios with real-time and high resolution demands. This chapter reviews kernel methods that statistically model gas distribution. Gas measurements are treated as random variables, and the gas distribution is predicted at unseen locations either using a kernel density estimation or a kernel regression approach. The resulting statistical

DOI: 10.4018/978-1-61520-915-6.ch006

models do not make strong assumptions about the functional form of the gas distribution, such as the number or locations of gas sources, for example. The major focus of this chapter is on two-dimensional models that provide estimates for the means and predictive variances of the distribution. Furthermore, three extensions to the presented kernel density estimation algorithm are described, which allow to include wind information, to extend the model to three dimensions, and to reflect time-dependent changes of the random process that generates the gas distribution measurements. All methods are discussed based on experimental validation using real sensor data.

INTRODUCTION

Modeling the distribution of gas in an environment aims at deriving a truthful representation of the observed gas distribution from a set of spatially and temporally distributed measurements of relevant variables, foremost gas concentration, but also wind, pressure, and temperature (Lilienthal et al., 2009b). The task of building gas distribution models is challenging mainly because of the chaotic nature of gas dispersal. The complex interaction of gas with its surrounding is dominated by three physical effects. First, on a long time scale, diffusion mixes the gas with the surrounding atmosphere to achieve a homogeneous mixture of both in the long run. Second, turbulent air flow fragments the gas emanating from a source into intermittent patches of high concentration with steep gradients at their edges (Robert & Webster, 2002). Third, advective flow moves these patches. Due to the effects of turbulence and advective flow, it is possible to observe high concentrations in locations distant from the source location. These effects are especially important in uncontrolled environments.

Besides the physics of gas dispersal, limitations of gas sensors also make gas distribution modeling difficult. Gas sensors provide information about a small spatial region only since the measurements require direct interaction between the sensor surface and the analyte molecules. Therefore, instantaneous measurements of gas concentration over a large field would require a dense grid of sensors which is usually not a viable solution due to high cost and lack of flexibility.

Gas distribution modeling (GDM) methods can be categorized as model-based and model-free. Model-based approaches infer the parameters of an analytical gas distribution model from the measurements. In principle, Computational Fluid Dynamics (CFD) models can be applied to solve the governing set of equations numerically. Current CFD methods are computationally expensive and not suitable for realistic scenarios in which a high resolution is required and the model needs to be updated with new measurements in real time. Many other model-based approaches were developed for atmospheric dispersion (Olesen et al., 2005). Such models typically also cannot efficiently incorporate sensor information efficiently on the fly and do not provide a sufficient level of detail.

Model-free approaches do not make strong assumptions about a particular functional form of the gas distribution. They typically treat gas sensor measurements as random variables and derive a statistical model of the observed gas dispersion from the measurements.

In this chapter, we introduce and review kernel methods for statistical, model-free gas distribution modeling and present results in both indoor and outdoor environments. Section "Background" presents an overview on previous statistical gas distribution modeling methods. In section "Kernel Extrapolation Distribution Mapping", the kernel extrapolation approach (Kernel DM) will be described. Sections "Kernel DM+V" and –"Gaussian Process Mixture Model" review the Kernel DM+V algorithm and a Gaussian Processes Mixture approach as two statistical gas distribution modeling approaches to estimate both mean and variance of the distribution. A comparison of these two approaches is presented in section" Evaluation and Comparison of Gas Distribution Models". Compared to indoor environments, outdoor environments present additional challenges such as a strong and unstable wind field. Section " Kernel DM+V/W – Using Wind Information for Gas Distribution Mapping" describes a modification of the basic Kernel DM+V algorithm, which allows including wind information during model creation. Sections " Three-Dimensional Statistical Gas Distribution Mapping" and " Time-dependent Gas Distribution Modeling, TD Kernel DM+V" describe further modifications of the basic Kernel DM + V algorithm that extend the models to three dimensions and include a time-dependent component, respectively. The chapter ends with conclusions and suggestions for future work.

BACKGROUND

Several methods for statistical gas distribution modeling have been published. A straightforward solution to obtain a model of the time-averaged gas distribution is to use a dense grid of sensors. In (Ishida et al., 1998), a gas distribution model is created from measurements collected by a grid of sensors. These measurements are averaged over a prolonged period of time and discretized to a grid that represents the topology of the sensor network. A similar method is presented in (Purnamadjaja & Russell, 2005), where maximum values of the measurement interval are mapped instead of average concentrations. An alternative to a network of stationary sensors is to use a single mobile sensor. While a network of sensors has advantages in terms of coverage and sampling time, using a mobile sensor avoids calibration issues and allows for adaptive sampling of the environment. In practice, it is beneficial to combine stationary sensor networks with autonomous mobile sensors. Pyk et al. (2006) create a gas distribution map by using a single sensor, which collects measurements consecutively instead of the parallel acquisition of readings in a sensor network. This method has been applied in an experiment in a wind tunnel. At each pre-specified measurement location, the sensor was exposed to the gas distribution for two minutes. At locations other than the measurement points, the map was interpolated using bi-cubic or triangle-based cubic filtering, depending on whether the measurement locations formed an equidistant grid or not. The drawback of such interpolating methods is that there is no means of averaging out instantaneous response fluctuations at measurement locations. This leads to increasingly jagged distribution maps. In (Hayes et al., 2002), a group of mobile robots equipped with conducting polymer sensors were used to create a histogram representation of the distribution of water vapor created by a hot water pan behind a fan. The histogram bins collect the number of odor hits received by all robots in the corresponding area while they performed a random walk behavior. Odor hits were counted whenever the response level of the gas sensors exceeded a predefined threshold. A potential problem with this method is that it uses only binary information from the measurements. In this way useful information may be discarded. In addition, the proposed histogram method depends strongly on bin size and the predefined threshold. Another disadvantage of this approach is that it requires even coverage of the environment.

The Kernel extrapolation Distribution Mapping (Kernel DM) algorithm by Lilienthal and Duckett (2004), introduced in the following section, can be regarded as a refinement of a histogram-based approach that does not rely on the assumption of an even coverage of the environment. Kernel DM is inspired by non-parametric estimation of density functions using a Parzen window.

KERNEL EXTRAPOLATION DISTRIBUTION MAPPING

The Kernel DM method by Lilienthal and Duckett (2004) represents a gas distribution in the form of a grid map. This gas distribution grid map resembles occupancy grid maps in mobile robotics. However, there are important differences. Each cell in an occupancy grid map represents the belief whether the area covered by the cell is occupied or not. Cells in the Kernel DM grid map represent an estimate of the distribution mean at the location of the particular cell. Occupancy grid maps are typically built based on input from a laser scanner or sonar sensors. With each measurement, these range sensors cover a wide area and there is typically a substantial overlap between individual readings. The problem is different for grid maps based on gas sensor readings since the sensor response represents interactions at the surface of the sensors, i.e. at a very small area. A key idea of Kernel DM is therefore how to extrapolate the sensor readings beyond this small area by reasoning over the decreasing information content a single sensor reading provides about the mean estimate at locations in a certain distance from the sensor surface.

Kernel DM discretizes the available space into grid cells and computes an estimate of the distribution mean for each cell by using a symmetric Gaussian kernel, N. The Gaussian kernel models the decreasing information content of a single sensor reading depending on the distance of the measurement location from the respective cell centre. In other words: the Gaussian kernel represents a weight function, which indicates the likelihood that the measurement represents the average concentration at a given distance from the point of measurement.

Assuming that $D = \{(x_1, r_1), (x_2, r_2), ..., (x_n, r_n)\}$ is the set of measurements r_i collected at locations x_i ($1 \leq i \leq n$), the following steps are performed to predict the distribution mean at each location in the field. First, the displacement of the measurement location x_i from the centre of the grid cell k is computed as $\delta_i^{(k)} = \left| x^{(k)} - x_i \right|$. Using this distance, the value of the kernel for a given measurement is computed for each cell by

$$\omega_i^{(k)} = N(\delta_i^{(k)}, \sigma), \tag{1}$$

where σ is the kernel width. To enhance the performance in practice, the evaluation of Equation (1) is restricted to cells within a certain cut-off radius R_{co}. In the next step, two temporary maps $\Omega^{(k)}$ and $R^{(k)}$ are created that represent integrated weights (corresponding to the density of measurements) and integrated weighted readings as follows

$$\Omega^{(k)} = \sum_{i=1}^{n} \omega_i^{(k)}, \tag{2}$$

$$R^{(k)} = \sum_{i=1}^{n} \omega_i^{(k)} r_i. \tag{3}$$

Finally, the mean estimate is computed as

$$R^{(k)} = R^{(k)} / \Omega^{(k)}: \Omega^{(k)} \geq \Omega_{min}. \tag{4}$$

The threshold Ω_{min} makes sure that estimates are based on a sufficient amount of measurements collected in the vicinity of the estimate location. The Kernel DM algorithm depends on three parameters: the width σ of the Gaussian function, the

Figure 1. Discretization of the Gaussian kernel onto the grid

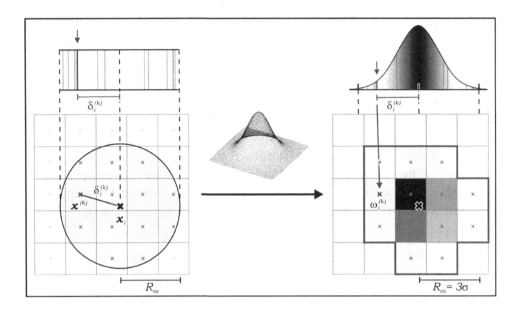

cut-off radius R_{co} and the threshold Ω_{min}. Only choosing an appropriate value of σ is critical for the performance of the method. The kernel width should be wide enough to have sufficient extrapolation. On the other hand, it should be narrow enough to preserve the fine details of the mapped structure.

Figure 1 shows how a single reading is convolved onto a 5×5 grid. On the left side, thirteen cells are found to have a distance of less than the cut-off radius (here $R_{co}=3\sigma$) from the point of measurement. These cells are indicated on the right side of Figure 1 by a surrounding strong border. The weightings for these cells are determined by evaluating the Gaussian function for the displacement values. These weights are represented in Figure 1 by shadings of grey. Darker shadings indicate higher weights, which corresponds to a stronger contribution of the measurement value r_i in the calculation of the average concentration value for a particular cell.

Lilienthal and Duckett (2004) applied the Kernel DM method to experiments in an indoor environment where data were collected with an array of sensors mounted on a mobile robot. The experimental setup includes a single target gas, but if a gas discrimination component is included gas distribution mapping can be extended to the case of multiple different gas sources, for example as described in (Loutfi et al., 2008). In the experiment presented in Lilienthal and Duckett (2004), perfect knowledge about the position of the sensors at the time of the measurement is assumed. To account also for the uncertainty about the sensor position, one can integrate gas distribution mapping into a SLAM framework as described in (Lilienthal et al., 2007).

KERNEL DM+V

Kernel DM computes an estimate of the mean gas distribution. However, also the spatial structure of the distribution *variance* can provide important information about the gas distribution by highlighting areas of high fluctuation, which are often found in close vicinity to the gas source. Kernel DM+V proposed by Lilienthal et al. (2009b) is a statistical approach which models mean and variance distribution. As it will be discussed in Sec. " Evaluation and Comparison of Gas Distribution Models", estimating the predictive variance also enables better quantitative evalua-tion of alternative statistical models and provides the base to learn meta-parameters. The predictive variance can also be beneficial for sensor planning based on the current model.

Like in Kernel DM, the distribution is represented as a grid map in Kernel DM+V and a univariate Gaussian kernel N is used to represent the importance of measure-ments r_i obtained at the location x_i for the statistical model at grid cell k. In the first step of Kernel DM+V, two temporary grid maps are computed: $\Omega^{(k)}$ by integrating spatial importance weights and $R^{(k)}$ by integrating weighted readings

$$w_i^{(k)} = \mathrm{N}\left(\left|x_i - x^{(k)}\right|, \sigma\right), \tag{5}$$

$$\Omega^{(k)} = \sum_{i=1}^{n} w_i^{(k)}, \tag{6}$$

$$R^{(k)} = \sum_{i=1}^{n} w_i^{(k)} r_i. \tag{7}$$

Here, $x^{(k)}$ denotes the centre of the cell k and the kernel width σ is a parameter of the algorithm. The integrated weights $\Omega^{(k)}$ are used to normalize the weighted readings $R^{(k)}$ and to compute a further map $\alpha^{(k)}$, which represents the confidence in the obtained estimates.

$$\alpha^{(k)} = 1 - e^{-\left(\Omega^{(k)2}/\sigma_\Omega^2\right)}, \tag{8}$$

The confidence map is used to compute the mean concentration estimate $r^{(k)}$ as

$$r^{(k)} = \alpha^{(k)} \frac{R^{(k)}}{\Omega^{(k)}} + \left\{1 - \alpha^{(k)}\right\} r_0 \qquad (9)$$

where r_0 represents the mean concentration estimate for cells for which there is not sufficient information available from nearby readings indicated by a low value of $\alpha^{(k)}$. In (Lilienthal et al, 2009b), r_0 is set to be the average over all sensor readings. Whether $\alpha^{(k)}$ is considered low or not is determined by the scaling parameter σ_Ω^2, which defines a soft margin for values of $\Omega^{(k)}$.

The variance estimate for cell k depends on the density of measurements in the vicinity of a cell and the true variance of measurements at the location of the cell, computed from variance contributions $(r_i - r^{(k(i))})^2$, where $r^{(k(i))}$ is the predicted mean for the cell $k(i)$ closest to the measurement point x_i.

The variance map $v^{(k)}$ is computed from the variance contributions integrated in a further temporary map $V^{(k)}$

$$V^{(k)} = \sum_{i=1}^{n} \mathrm{N}\left(\left|x_i - x^{(k)}\right|, \sigma\right)\left(r_i - r^{(k(i))}\right)^2, \qquad 10)$$

$$v^{(k)} = \alpha^{(k)} \frac{V^{(k)}}{\Omega^{(k)}} + \left\{1 - \alpha^{(k)}\right\} v_0, \qquad (11)$$

where v_0 is an estimate of the distribution variance in regions far from measurement points. In (Lilienthal et al, 2009b) v_0 is computed as the average over all variance contributions.

The Kernel DM+V algorithm depends on three parameters: the kernel width σ, which governs the amount of extrapolation on individual sensor measurement (and the complexity of the model); the cell size c that determines the resolution at which different predictions can be made, and the scaling parameter σ_Ω, which defines a soft threshold that decides whether it is assumed that sufficient knowledge from nearby measurements is available to make predictions. Smaller values of σ_Ω entail a lower threshold on $\Omega^{(k)}$, i.e. an increasing tendency to trust the distribution estimate obtained from extrapolation on local measurements. The exact value of σ_Ω is not critical as long as it is of the right scale. Kernel width and cell size can be learned from the collected measurements. Learning meta-parameters of Kernel DM+V is discussed in Sec. " Evaluation and Comparison of Gas Distribution Models".

Figure 2 shows an example of a weight map $\Omega^{(k)}$ (top row) and the corresponding confidence map $\alpha^{(k)}$ (bottom row). For narrow kernels and large values of σ_Ω (left column), one can see the trajectory of the gas sensor carried by the robot, indicating that the predictions from extrapolation will only be considered trustworthy at locations

Figure 2. Weight map $\Omega^{(k)}$ (top row) and the corresponding confidence map $\alpha^{(k)}$ (bottom row) obtained using parameters $\sigma=0.10m$, $\sigma_\Omega = 5.0 \cdot N$ (0, 0.10) ≈ 20.0 (left column) and $\sigma=0.5m$, $\sigma_\Omega = 1.0 \cdot N$ (0, 0.50) ≈ 0.8 (right column) on a grid with cell size c=0.05m.

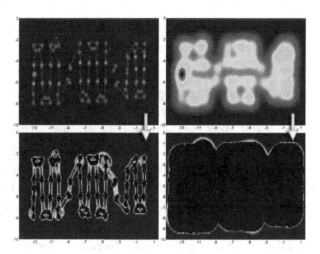

close to the actual measurement. For wider kernels or smaller values of σ_Ω (right column), the area for which predictions based on extrapolation are made is larger.

GAUSSIAN PROCESS MIXTURE MODEL

Another approach to estimate the predictive variance in gas distribution modeling is the Gaussian Process Mixture model (GPM) proposed by Stachniss et al. (2009). Gaussian Processes (GPs) are non-parametric probabilistic models for solving regression problems. One can view GPs as an infinite dimensional Gaussian distribution defined by a mean and a covariance function. A covariance matrix models the influence of neighboring data points. More formally, assuming that $\{(x_i, f_i)\}_{i=1}^n$ are samples of a Gaussian process, $f = (f_1, f_2, ..., f_n)^T$ has a Gaussian distribution

$$f_i = f(x_i) := N(\mu, K), \ \mu \in R^n, \ K \in R^{n \times n} \tag{12}$$

where μ is the mean and K corresponds to the covariance matrix which is constructed using a so-called covariance function k. For reasons of simplicity, one often assumes that $\mu = 0$. A standard choice for the covariance is the exponential function

$$[\mathbf{K}]_{ij} = k(x_i, x_j) = \sigma_f^2 \exp\left(-\frac{1}{2}\frac{|x_i - x_j|^2}{l^2}\right), \tag{13}$$

in which l is the length-scale parameter that influences the smoothness of the function f and σ_f^2 is the signal variance parameter. The parameter σ_n^2 represents the global noise. The parameters l, σ_f^2, and σ_n^2, termed the "hyper parameters" of the GP model, have to be learned. Other popular choices for the covariance function are Matern kernels or neural network kernel functions.

Let $\mathbf{X} = [x_1; \ldots; x_n]^T$ and $\mathbf{R} = [r_1; \ldots; r_n]$ be the set of locations and the corresponding measurements respectively. An arbitrary test set $\mathbf{X}_*$ is chosen from the input data set. As described in Section "Kernel Extrapolation Distribution Mapping", assuming that $D = \{(x_i, r_i)\}_{i=1}^n$ is the set of measurements r_i collected at locations x_i, the goal of gas distribution modeling is to predict accurately the value of r_* at an unseen location $x_* \in \mathbf{X}_*$.

To predict the value of the measurement at x_*, predictive mean and variance are estimated as

$$\overline{f}(\mathbf{X}_*) := \mathrm{E}[f(\mathbf{X}_*)] = k(\mathbf{X}_*, \mathbf{X})[k(\mathbf{X}, \mathbf{X}) + \sigma_n^2 \mathrm{I}]^{-1} \mathbf{r}, \tag{14}$$

and respectively,

$$V[f(\mathbf{X}_*)] = k(\mathbf{X}_*, \mathbf{X}_*) - k(\mathbf{X}_*, \mathbf{X})[k(\mathbf{X}, \mathbf{X}) + \sigma_n^2 \mathrm{I}]^{-1} k(\mathbf{X}, \mathbf{X}_*). \tag{15}$$

The main drawback of GPs is their computational complexity. To estimate the predictive mean in Equation (14) and the predictive variance in Equation (15), the inversion of $[k(\mathbf{X}, \mathbf{X}) + \sigma_n^2 \mathrm{I}]$ has to be computed. This inversion has $O(n^3)$ time complexity where n is the size of the training data set. Another limitation of using GPs in the context of gas distribution modeling is that standard GPs create a unimodal distribution for any given location while the histogram of the observations of a gas distribution over time, typically shows at least two modes corresponding to noisy measurements of concentration peaks and the background.

One solution to overcome unimodality is using Gaussian Process Mixture models. A GPM model is a locally weighted sum of GP models. Let $\{GP_i\}_{i=1}^m$ be a set of GPs as individual components of the mixture model. To predict the value of r_* at the location x_*, first, it has to be estimated that to which component this measurement belongs. Then, using the distribution model of the corresponding component the value of the measurement r_* can be predicted. A *gating function* $P(z(x_*)=i)$ is defined as the probability that x_* is associated with the component GP_i. The likelihood of observing r_* is achieved by

$$h(x_*) := p(r_* \mid x_*) = \sum_{i=1}^{m} P(z(x_*) = i) N_i(r_*; x_*), \tag{16}$$

where $N_i(r; x)$ denotes the Gaussian distribution function with mean $\overline{f}(x)$ and the corresponding variance $V[f_i(x)] + \sigma_n^2$. To create the GPM model, the predictive mean and variance are obtained by

$$\overline{h}(x_*) := E[h(x_*)] = \sum_{i=1}^{m} P(z(x_*) = i) \overline{f}_i(x_*), \tag{17}$$

$$V[h(x_*)] = \sum_{i=1}^{m} P(z(x_*) = i) \left(V[f_i(x_*)] + (\overline{f}_i(x_*) - \overline{h}(x_*))^2 \right). \tag{18}$$

The predictive model of components and the gating function are learned using the Expectation Maximization (EM) method. The following describes in detail the algorithm to build the GPM model for a given data set.

Initialization of the Mixture Components

To learn the parameters of the first component GP_1, a set of n_1 data is randomly selected from the data set D. GP_1 is used as the initial estimate of the gas distribution. This initial component usually represents areas with unusual gas accumulation poorly. To improve the accuracy of the model, an error function GP_Δ is defined. This error function is learned using data from D excluding the training set n_1. GP_Δ captures the absolute difference between a set of target values and the prediction of GP_1. The next component is initialized from the data which indicated higher error in the created model. The sub sampling procedure reduces the size of the data set and the time complexity respectively to learn the model. This method recognizes two GP components for the gas distribution modeling problem. The two components of the GPM represent a background signal and peaks.

Iterative Learning via Expectation-Maximization Method

The Expectation-Maximization (EM) algorithm is an iterative method to obtain the maximum likelihood estimate of parameters of the predictive model. The EM algorithm consists of two steps:

First, it estimates the probability that data point j ($x_j \in \mathbf{X}$) corresponds to model component i. This is done by re-estimating the gating function for each data point j as

$$P(z(x_j) = i) \leftarrow \frac{P(z(x_j) = i)N_i(r_j; x_j)}{\sum_{k=1}^{m} P(z(x_j) = k)N_k(r_j; x_j)}. \tag{19}$$

Then, in the next step, the components are updated based on the new estimate of $P(z(x_j)=i)$. To update the component i, the predictive mean and variance of the mixture model are computed. This is achieved by modifying Equation (14) to

$$\overline{f}_i(\mathbf{X}_*) = k(\mathbf{X}_*, \mathbf{X})[k(\mathbf{X}, \mathbf{X}) + \Psi^i]^{-1}\mathbf{r}, \tag{20}$$

where

$$[\Psi^i]_{jj} = \frac{\sigma_n^2}{P(z(x_j) = i)} \tag{21}$$

The mixture model has three hyper parameters $\{\sigma_f, l, \sigma_n\}$ which have to be estimated. A common way is to first initialize these values using a heuristic and then optimizing the values. A reasonable heuristic is the one proposed by (Snelson and Ghahramani, 2006), which is also used in (Stachniss et al, 2009):

$$l \leftarrow \max_{x_j} P(z(x_j) = i)\|x_j - \overline{x}\|, \tag{22}$$

$$\sigma_f^2 \leftarrow \frac{\sum_{j=1}^{n} P(z(x_j) = i)(r_j - \mathrm{E}[r])^2}{\sum_{j=1}^{n} P(z(x_j) = i)}, \tag{23}$$

$$\sigma_n^2 \leftarrow \frac{1}{4}\sigma_f^2, \tag{24}$$

where $\overline{x}$ is the weighted mean of the inputs, each x_j having a weight of $P(z(x_j)=i)$.

Learning the Gating Function for Unseen Test Points

In the EM algorithm, for each data point j from the training set, the probability of being assigned to the component GP_i is determined by maximizing the cross validation data likelihood. To generalize this to unseen locations, another GP is used to model a proper gating function. Stachniss et al. (2009) use a gating GP for each component i, that uses the x_j as input and outputs $z(x_j)$ according to the EM output. In this way, a gating function is obtained that models the assignment probability for an arbitrary location as

$$P(z(x_*) = i) = \frac{\exp(\overline{f}_i^z(x_*))}{\sum_{j=1}^{m} \exp(\overline{f}_j^z(x_*))} \,. \tag{25}$$

Here $\overline{f}_i^z(x)$ denotes the prediction of z for GP_i computed in the EM algorithm.

To illustrate this procedure, we consider the following one-dimensional toy example according to (Stachniss et al., 2009). The first part of the data points were uniformly distributed around a y value of 2, while the second part was generated with higher noise at two distinct locations. The left image of Figure 3 depicts the standard GP learned from the input data points and the right one shows the resulting error GP. Based on the error GP, the second mixture component is initialized and used together with the first component as the input to the EM algorithm. The individual images in Figure 4 illustrate the iterations of the EM algorithm (to be read from left to right and from top to bottom). They depict the two components of the mixture model. The learned gating function after the convergence of the algorithm

Figure 3. Left: The standard GP used to initialize the first mixture component. Right: The error GP used to initialize the second mixture component.

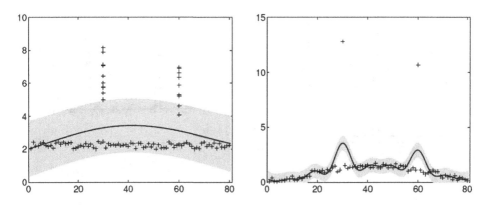

Figure 4. Components in different iterations of the learning using EM algorithm

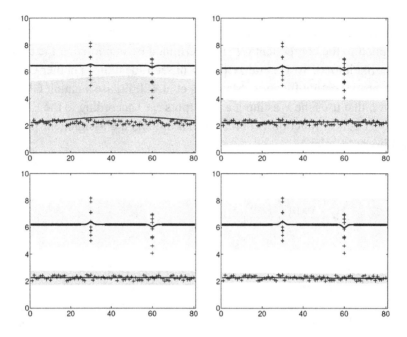

is depicted in the left image of Figure 5 and the final GP mixture model is shown in the right image. It is obvious that this model is a better representation of the input data set than the standard GP model shown in the left image of Figure 3.

Figure 5. Left: The learned gating function. Right: Resulting distribution of the GP mixture model.

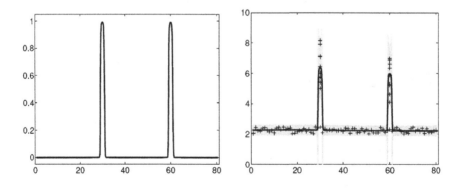

EVALUATION AND COMPARISON OF GAS DISTRIBUTION MODELS

Evaluation and Learning of Meta Parameters

After creating a model, it is important to know whether the model is "good" for a specific application or not and to compare its performance with other models. The criterion applied here for a "good" model is that it explains the training observations and accurately predicts unseen observations.

To evaluate a gas distribution model, some ground truth information is required. An indirect evaluation is to quantify the capability of the model to identify hidden parameters, for example the location of the gas source. However, local gas accumulation peaks do not necessarily correspond to the gas source location. If there is a dense grid of stationary sensors available, then one simple solution to evaluate the created model is to compare the model derived from all but one or a few sensors with the measurements of the left out sensors. However, when the sensor network is too sparse or there is only a single mobile sensor, this solution is not feasible. In (Stachniss et al., 2009) and Lilienthal et al. (2009a) a similar method is applied and model predictions are compared to unseen measurements. A gas distribution model represents the time-averaged concentration and the expected fluctuations. The mean and variance of the distribution are both considered by the average Negative Log Predictive Density (NLPD), which is a standard criterion to evaluate distribution models. Under the assumption of a Gaussian posterior $p(r_i|x_i)$, the NLPD of unseen measurements $\{r_1, r_2, \ldots, r_n\}$ acquired at locations $\{x_1, x_2, \ldots, x_n\}$ is computed as

$$NLPD = \frac{1}{2n} \sum_{\{(x_i, r_i)\} \in D} \left\{ \log \hat{v}(x_i) + \frac{(r_i - \hat{r}(x_i))^2}{\hat{v}(x_i)} \right\} + \frac{1}{2} \log(2\pi), \qquad (26)$$

where $\hat{v}(x_i)$ and $\hat{r}_i$ are estimates of the predictive variance and the mean, respectively.

Kernel methods rely mainly on the two meta-parameters kernel width σ and cell size c. Since an estimate of the variance is available, the meta parameters can be learned using the NPLD, for example by dividing the sample set $D = \{(x_i, r_i)\}_{i=1}^n$ into disjoint sets D_{train} and D_{test}, and determining optimal values of the model parameters by cross-validation on D_{train}, keeping D_{test} for evaluation.

Table 1. Comparison of GPM and Kernel DM+V

Data	NLPD (GPM)	NLPD (Kernel DM+V)
3-rooms	-1.54	-1.44
corridor	-1.60	-1.81
outdoor	-1.80	-1.75

Experimental Comparison of the Kernel DM+V and the GPM Approach

In the same way as a fixed distribution model is evaluated depending on its meta parameters, different gas distribution modeling approaches can be compared by their respective NLPD for unseen measurements. Since the goal is to maximize the likelihood of unseen data, better models minimize the NLPD. Table 1 shows an NLPD comparison of the GPM model (see Sec. "Gaussian Process Mixture Model") with the model obtained from the Kernel DM+V algorithm (Sec. "Kernel DM+V"). The comparison is based on data sets from three different environments in which a robot carried out a sweeping movement consisting of two full sweeps. The first sweep was used for training and the second sweep (in opposite direction) for testing. As a preliminary result from this investigation, GPM and Kernel DM+V exhibit a comparable performance for gas distribution modeling in the tested environments.

Discussion of Kernel DM+V and the GPM Approach

Kernel DM+V discretizes the space into grid cells and estimates a variance in addition to the mean of the gas distribution. Gas distribution modeling is treated as a density estimation problem. The predictive variance depends on the true variance of the measurements at a certain location and the distance of the measurements to this location. Kernel DM+V weighs the importance of each data point for the estimate at a certain grid cell by a kernel function that depends on the distance of the measurement location from the respective centre of the cell.

The GPM approach models gas distributions as a locally weighted sum of Gaussian Process models. Gas distribution modeling is treated as a regression problem. A kernel describes the covariance matrix, which models the influence of measurements at neighboring data points on the estimation. The approach proposed by Stachniss et al. (2009) assumes two mixture components. These components represent "peak areas" where sensors tend to respond strongly and "background", which models the signal in the absence of a distinct sensor response. At each location, these two components are mixed in different proportions. The GPM approach proposed by

Stachniss et al. (2009) learns the separate components and a gating function that determines the probability with which a location is described by the components. The basic representation of the model is the collected data set. The GPM approach also models mean and a predictive variance.

In GPM, both learning the model and making predictions require matrix inversion, which has time complexity of $O[n^3]$. The complexity of computing a distribution map with Kernel DM+V is generally $O[n \cdot (D/c)^2]$, where n is the number of training samples, D is the dimension of the environment and c is the cell size. In practice, it is not necessary to evaluate the Gaussian weighting function N for all cells. Thus, the region for which the weights are computed is limited to a circle of radius 4σ around the measurement location. Therefore, the effective computational complexity is $O[n \cdot (\sigma/c)2]$. The complexity of computing the maps $\alpha^{(k)}$, $r^{(k)}$ and $v^{(k)}$ is $O[(D/c)2]$ and computing $V^{(k)}$ requires one pass through the data ($O[n]$). The overall complexity is $O[n \cdot (\sigma/c)2]$. Making predictions requires only a look-up of the values in the map.

The performance of GPM was experimentally found to be similar to the performance of Kernel DM+V (see Sec. "Experimental Comparison of the Kernel DM+V and the GPM Approach"). The time complexity and also the fact that the learning procedure is simpler give Kernel DM+V an edge over the GPM method. On the other hand, Kernel DM+V makes stronger assumptions about the distribution at a particular grid cell than GPM, which estimates the model as mixture of distribution models.

An advantage that comes with the straightforward interpretation of the Kernel DM+V algorithm is that it lends itself to a variety of extensions. Three such extensions, inclusion of wind information for gas distribution modeling (Kernel DM+V/W), 3D modeling (3D Kernel DM+V) and modeling time-dependency are described in the following section. This is not to say that extensions of the GPM approach into these domains are not possible or would perform worse, they simply have not been developed so far.

EXTENSIONS OF KERNEL DM+V

Kernel DM+V/W: Using Wind Information for Gas Distribution Mapping

The statistical models presented in the previous sections have been used to model gas dispersion in indoor or controlled environments with relatively weak air flow. An important aspect for gas distribution modeling especially in outdoor applications is to consider wind information when building the gas distribution model. The local airflow is in general an important parameter due to the strong influence of advective transport on gas dispersal. In (Reggente & Lilienthal, 2009b), the Kernel DM+V/W algorithm is proposed. Kernel DM+V/W is an extension of Kernel DM+V. It considers wind information in order to compute the gas distribution model. Spatial integration of the point measurements is carried out using a bivariate Gaussian kernel. By selecting the shape of the kernel based on the local wind measurement, the Kernel DM+V/W algorithm models the information content depending on the direction and intensity of the wind. When reliable wind information is available, the symmetric univariate Gaussian in Equation (5) is replaced by an elliptic, bivariate Gaussian with the semi-major axis oriented along the wind direction. The 2×2 covariance matrix Σ is computed according to the current measurement of the local airflow $\vec{v}$ at the sensor location as follows.

First, the assumption is made that the total information content is the same for each measurement. This assumption results in the constraint that the area of the covariance ellipsis remains constant, that is

$$\pi\sigma^2 = \pi ab. \tag{27}$$

The semi-major axis a is then stretched according to the wind intensity assuming a linear dependency as

$$a = \sigma + \gamma \left| \vec{v} \right|. \tag{28}$$

By combining Equation (27) and Equation (28), the length of the semi-minor axis is

$$b = \frac{\sigma}{1 + \gamma \left| \vec{v} \right| / \sigma}. \tag{29}$$

Equations (28) and (29) describe the relation between the Eigenvalues of the covariance matrix and the wind intensity. The parameter γ is related to the duration over which the wind vector $\vec{v}$ is assumed to be constant. For the initial experiments described in (Reggente & Lilienthal, 2009b), γ was set heuristically to 1. γ can also be learned from the input data.

Finally, the covariance matrix is rotated so that the semi-major axis is aligned with the wind direction

$$\Sigma_R^{-1} = R^{-1} \Sigma^{-1} R, \tag{30}$$

where R is the rotation matrix and Σ_R^{-1} is the inverse of the rotated covariance matrix.

By means of the adaptive kernel described by Equations (28), (29) and (30), Kernel DM+V/W models information about the trajectory of a sensed patch of gas, given a wind measurement. The bivariate Gaussian kernel describes a distribution over the locations where the sensed patch came from and where it tends to move to (here it is important to bear in mind that the resulting model describes the time-averaged gas distribution).

Reggente & Lilienthal (2009b) showed that applying the wind extension improves the performance of the Kernel DM+V approach. As an example of the application of Kernel DM+V/W, Figure 6 shows the predictive mean (top) and variance gas distribution (middle) for an experiment in a wind tunnel with laminar flow. In the maps on the left, the Kernel DM+V method is used, i.e. without considering wind information. The maps in the right of Figure 6 are obtained by using the Kernel DM+V/W algorithm. The NLPD comparison of using these two algorithms in Figure 6 (bottom) shows that Kernel DM+V/W can predict gas distribution dramatically more accurately than Kernel DM+V, especially in the presence of strong wind.

Figure 6. Mean gas distribution map (top) and its corresponding variance gas distribution map (middle) obtained from Kernel DM+V (left) and from Kernel DM+V/W using wind information (right), units in the plots are meters. The measurements are collected in a wind tunnel with laminar flow along the x-axis. The gas source is located at (15m, 2.0m). Comparison of NLPD from using Kernel DM+V (brown line) and Kernel DM+V/W (blue line) in this experiment is illustrated in the bottom of the figure.

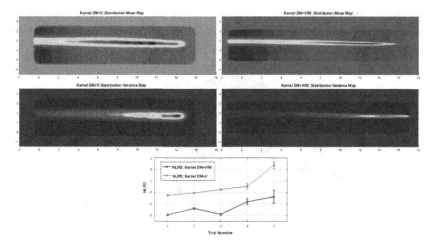

Three-Dimensional Statistical Gas Distribution Mapping

So far, all of the presented methods create two-dimensional models. Generally, however, gas dispersion has a three-dimensional structure and it can be helpful to model this 3D structure. In (Reggente & Lilienthal, 2009a), a modification of the two-dimensional Kernel DM+V algorithm to build three-dimensional gas distribution maps is introduced. The idea of 3D Kernel DM+V is similar to the basic idea of Kernel DM+V/W discussed in the previous sub-section. In both cases, only the kernel is modified compared to the original algorithm. 3D Kernel DM+V uses kernel extrapolation with a trivariate Gaussian kernel to model the decreasing likelihood that a reading represents the true concentration with respect to the distance in three dimensions. The 3D Gaussian kernel (see Figure 7) is defined by a kernel width along the three axis σ_x, σ_y, and σ_z:

$$\omega_i^k(\sigma_x, \sigma_y, \sigma_z) = N\left(\left|x_i - x^{(k)}\right|, \sigma_x, \sigma_y, \sigma_z\right). \tag{31}$$

As visualized in Figure 7, weights are evaluated at the distance between the location of the measurement x_i and the center $x^{(k)}$ of the cell k. In the same way as in the two-dimensional version, weights, weighted sensor readings, and weighted variance contributions are integrated and stored in temporary grid maps $\Omega^{(k)}$, $R^{(k)}$, and $V^{(k)}$, now using Equation (31) instead of Equation (5). Reggente and Lilienthal (2009a) used 3D Kernel DM+V to create gas distribution models in an uncontrolled indoor environment experiment. In this experiment, a mobile robot equipped with

Figure 7. Visualization of gas distribution modeling with 3D Kernel DM+V. Left side: The pollution monitoring prototype robot used to build gas distribution maps. Centre: three dimensional Gaussian kernel. Right side: the weight computed for a particular cell depends on the parameters of the 3D kernel and the distance between the centre of the cell and the measurement point.

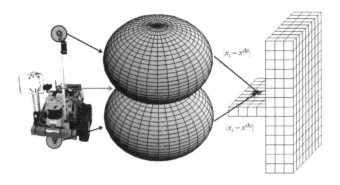

three gas sensor arrays mounted at different heights performed random walks to collect data. The 2D model created by the measurements from the sensor in the middle was used to evaluate the 3D map created from measurements taken from the lower and upper sensors as follows: First the data collected by the lower and upper sensors are used to build the 3D model of gas distribution in the environment. Then, this model is sliced into layers with different heights. To evaluate 3D Kernel DM+V, the model created for the middle layer is compared with the model created from real measurements collected by the middle sensor using 2D Kernel DM+V algorithm. The comparison between the slice of the 3D map and the 2D map at the middle sensor shows clear structural similarities. Compared to all other slices from the 3D map investigated, the slice at the height of the middle sensor was also found to have the minimum Kullback-Leibler distance. These initial results demonstrate that 3D Kernel DM+V enables creating maps in three dimensions which provide useful information at heights different from the height of the sensors.

Time-Dependent Gas Distribution Modeling, TM Kernel DM+V

So far, all the presented methods made the assumption that the gas distribution is generated by a time-invariant random process. This assumption allows to average over measurements independent of the time when they were recorded. It is reasonable, however, to assume that more recent sensor readings carry more important information in order to predict future measurements. This can be modeled by introducing a decreasing importance of measurements with increasing time between measurement and prediction.

Having a set of measurements $D = \{r_1, r_2, ..., r_N\}$ collected at locations $\{x_1, x_2, ... , x_N\}$ and times $\{t_1, t_2, ..., t_N\}$, we want to create a model to estimate a snapshot of the gas distribution at time t^* with $t^* > t_1$. The spatial kernel is the same as in the basic Kernel DM+V algorithm, except from a time-dependency term φ, which is defined as follows:

$$\varphi(t^*, t_i) = e^{(-\beta \cdot (t^* - t_i))},\tag{32}$$

where t_i is the time stamp of measurement r_i with $t_1 \leq t_i \leq t^*$ (i.e. we do not include future measurements into the prediction for t^*). β is a scaling factor for the recency of the measurements compared to time t^*. The total weight function that replaces Equation (5) then has the form

$$\omega_i^{(k)}(t^*, t_i) = \mathrm{N}\left(\left|x_i - x^{(k)}\right|, \sigma\right) \cdot \varphi(t^*, t_i).\tag{33}$$

By replacing Equation (5) with Equation (33), the predictive mean and variance can be computed as in Equation (9) and Equation (11) if the computation of the measurement average r_0 and the total variance of sensor measurements v_0 are also modified with the temporal weight function in Equation (32) so that more recent contributions have a higher influence:

$$r_0(t^*) = \frac{\sum_{t_i=t_1}^{t^*} \varphi(t^*, t_i) \cdot r_i}{\sum_{t_i=t_1}^{t^*} \varphi(t^*, t_i)}, \tag{34}$$

$$v_0(t^*) = \frac{\sum_{t_i=t_1}^{t^*} \varphi(t^*, t_i) \cdot \left(r_i - r^{(k(i))}\right)^2}{\sum_{t_i=t_1}^{t^*} \varphi(t^*, t_i)}. \tag{35}$$

Introducing time dependency in the proposed way was found to improve the modeling accuracy in initial experiments. Tab. 2 presents an NLPD comparison of time-dependent Kernel DM+V (TD Kernel DM+V) with the basic, not time-dependent version. The comparison is based on data sets from two different experiments: one experiment in a corridor, in which a single mobile sensor (carried by a robot) randomly moves and collects data; and a second experiment performed in a small room (4.9×3.4 m²) where a network of 10 stationary sensors collected the measurements. The model was created in both cases using the 80% of the data that were recorded first, and evaluated on 20% of the data that were recorded afterwards. While the meta-parameter of the temporal weight function was set heuristically to a fixed value ($\beta = 0.0072\text{s}^{-1}$ for the corridor experiment and $\beta = 0.0016\text{s}^{-1}$ for the network experiment), the width of the spatial kernel and the optimal cell size were learned by optimizing the 5-fold cross-validation NLPD over the training set.

Table 2. Comparison of models created with TD Kernel DM+V and the basic version of the Kernel DM+V algorithm. Cell and kernel size are learned in each case based on the respective data sets.

Data	NLPD (Kernel DM+V)	NLPD (TD Kernel DM+V)	Kernel size (m)	cell size (m)
Network	-1.778	-2.180	0.410	0.101
	-1.694	-1.772	0.500	0.105
Corridor	-0.793	-1.068	0.420	0.100
	-0.828	-1.092	0.600	0.105

The preliminary results presented in Tab. 2 show that TD Kernel DM+V performs better than Kernel DM+V. The TD Kernel DM+V snapshots created for the time of the last measurement in the training set indeed do improve the model accuracy by assuming an increased importance of more recent readings.

CONCLUSION

This chapter introduced several kernel methods for statistical gas distribution modeling. The resulting model-free statistical gas distribution models make no strong assumptions about the functional form of the gas distribution, such as the number of gas sources or their location, for example. The discussed methods treat gas measurements as random variables and predict the gas distribution at unseen locations.

An important recent development was the introduction of modeling approaches to estimate the distribution variance in addition to the distribution mean. The two basic approaches, Kernel DM+V and GPM, were compared in this chapter. The modeling accuracy of the two approaches was found to be similar. However, Kernel DM+V has advantages over GPM in terms of computational complexity, a more straightforward interpretation, a simpler learning approach, and its flexibility with respect to modifications of the basic algorithm. On the other hand, Kernel DM+V makes stronger assumptions about the distribution at a particular grid cell than GPM, which estimates the model as mixture of distribution models.

In addition to the basic approaches, three modifications of the Kernel DM+V algorithm were described in this chapter: Kernel DM+V/W, which adapts the kernel shape according to wind measurements; 3D Kernel DM+V, which extends the distribution model to three dimensions using a 3D kernel and TD Kernel DM+V, which introduces a temporal weight function to acknowledge that more recent measurements carry more important information to create a model for predicting future measurements. The presented evaluations using real sensor data demonstrate the potential of all three modifications. While a quantitative comparison is difficult in the case of the 3D Kernel DM+V algorithm due to calibration issues with the gas sensors, the quantitative comparisons of the two-dimensional models, Kernel DM+V/W and TD Kernel DM+V, with the basic version of the Kernel DM+V algorithm found an improved model quality for both Kernel DM+V/W and TD Kernel DM+V.

FUTURE RESEARCH DIRECTIONS

The results presented in this chapter are based on real sensor data collected in uncontrolled indoor and small-scale outdoor environments. A next step is to test

Figure 8. Kernel DM+V in a large-scale outdoor environment. Snapshot obtained using Kernel DM+V for gas distribution modeling on a sensor network deployed over the Rijmond area.

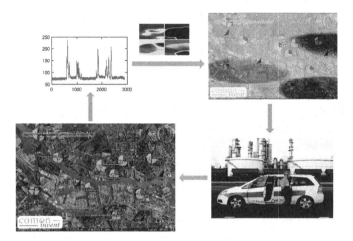

the discussed kernel methods in large scale, real world applications. This line of research is pursued in the EC project Diadem (FP7-ICT 224318, 2008). Diadem addresses Distributed Information Acquisition and Decision-making for Environmental Management, particularly in cases that involve chemical incidents that cause the emission of hazardous chemical gases. The test scenario is an area of approximately 50 km^2 at the Rotterdam port in the Netherlands, a densely inhabited industrial area. The statistical gas distribution models can provide a comprehensive view on a large number of gas measurements to the decision makers and allow identifying areas of high gas accumulation for further inspection. In Figure 8, an experiment with a network of 10 sensors over the Rijmond area of Rotterdam port is illustrated.

Since the wind measurements available in Diadem are not obtained at the same position as the gas sensor measurements, future work includes to study methods that model the wind field based on sparse measurements and estimate the local wind at each sensor position, so as to be able to apply Kernel DM+V to compute the gas distribution.

Due to the large size of the environment and the sparseness of stationary sensors, the sensor network is combined with mobile sensors carried by field operators. This raises the question where to make measurements with these mobile sensors (the problem of sensor planning). The goal is to dispatch future measurements to areas about which relatively little information is available, or which have been identified as places with potentially high gas accumulation. The statistical gas distribution model can be used for sensor planning in the considered domain. The involved cost function to evaluate will have to consider preferably areas of high gas accumulation or high predictive variance and regions in which measurements with maximum information gain are expected.

The presented gas distribution models all make Gaussian assumptions. In GPM these assumptions are not as strong as in Kernel DM+V since the GPM approach considers a mixture of distributions. Nevertheless, it is an important direction for future work to relaxing the Gaussian assumptions made.

Another possible research direction is to investigate sub-sampling strategies (as applied in the GPM approach) for the Kernel DM+V algorithm. Alternative, efficient methods to find optimal meta-parameters will also be investigated.

In this chapter, preliminary results with a time-dependent extension of Kernel DM+V are shown. There are many possibilities to improve the presented TD Kernel DM+V algorithm. One possibility is to learn the meta-parameter of the temporal weight function rather than setting it heuristically as it is done at the moment. It also needs to be studied whether the time-dependent models enable improved sensor planning compared to time-independent distribution models.

ACKNOWLEDGMENT

This work has partly been supported by the EC under contract number FP7-224318-DIADEM: Distributed Information Acquisition and Decision-Making for Environmental Management.

REFERENCES

Diadem FP7-ICT. (2008). *Diadem–distributed information acquisition decision-making for environmental management*. Retrieved from http://www.pdc.dk/diadem/

Hayes, A. T., Martinoli, A., & Goodman, R. M. (2002). Distributed odor source localization. *IEEE Sensor Journal. Special Issue on Electronic Nose Technologies, 2*(3), 260–271. doi:.doi:10.1109/JSEN.2002.800682

Ishida, H., Nakamoto, T., & Moriizumi, T. (1998). Remote sensing of gas/odor source location and concentration distribution using mobile system. *Sensors and Actuators. B, Chemical, 49*(1-2), 52–57..doi:10.1016/S0925-4005(98)00036-7

Lilienthal, A., & Duckett, T. (2004). Building gas concentration Grid maps with a mobile robot. *Robotics and Autonomous Systems, 48*(1), 3–16..doi:10.1016/j.robot.2004.05.002

Lilienthal, A. J., Asadi, S., & Reggente, M. (2009a). Estimating predictive variance for statistical gas distribution modelling. In *AIP Conference Proceedings Volume 1137: Olfaction and Electronic Nose - Proceedings of the 13th International Symposium on Olfaction and Electronic Nose* (pp. 65-68). doi:10.1063/1.3156628

Lilienthal, A. J., Loutfi, A., Blanco, J. L., Galindo, C., & Gonzalez, J. (2007). A Rao-Blackwellisation approach to GDM-SLAM–integrating SLAM and gas distribution mapping. In *Proceedings of the 3rd European Conference on Mobile Robots* (pp. 126-131).

Lilienthal, A. J., Loutfi, A., & Duckett, T. (2006). Airborne chemical sensing with mobile robots. *Sensors (Basel, Switzerland)*, 6(11), 1616–1678..doi:10.3390/s6111616

Lilienthal, A. J., Reggente, M., Trincavelli, M., Blanco, J. L., & Gonzalez, J. (2009b). A statistical approach to gas distribution modelling with mobile robots–the Kernel DM+V algorithm. In *Proceeding of the IEEE/RSJ International Conference on Intelligent Robots and Systems* (pp. 570-576). doi: 10.1109/IROS.2009.5354304

Loutfi, A., Coradeschi, S., Lilienthal, A. J., & Gonzalez, J. (2008). Gas distribution mapping of multiple odour sources using a mobile robot. *Robotica*, 27(2), 311–319.. doi:10.1017/S0263574708004694

Olesen, H. R., Løfstrøm, P., Berkowicz, R., & Ketzel, M. (2005). *Regulatory odour model development: Survey of modelling tools and datasets with focus on building effects*. (NERI Technical Report No. 541).

Purnamadjaja, A., & Russell, R. (2005). Congregation behaviour in a robot swarm using pheromone communication. In *Proceedings of the Australian Conference on Robotics and Automation*.

Pyk, P. (2006). An artificial moth: Chemical source localization using robot based neuronal model of moth optomotor anemotactic search. *Autonomous Robots*, 20(3), 197–213..doi:10.1007/s10514-006-7101-4

Reggente, M., & Lilienthal, A. J. (2009a). Three-dimensional statistical gas distribution mapping in an uncontrolled indoor environment. In *AIP Conference Proceedings Volume 1137: Olfaction and Electronic Nose - Proceedings of the 13th International Symposium on Olfaction and Electronic Nose* (pp. 109-112). doi: 10.1063/1.3156484

Reggente, M., & Lilienthal, A. J. (2009b). Using local wind information for gas distribution mapping in outdoor environments with a mobile robot. In *Proceedings of IEEE Sensors 2009 Conference* (pp. 1712-1720). doi: 10.1109/ICSENS.2009.5398498

Roberts, P. J. W., & Webster, D. R. (2002). Turbulent diffusion. In Shen, H., Cheng, A., Wang, K.-H., Teng, M. H., & Liu, C. (Eds.), *Environmental fluid mechanics-theories and application* (pp. 7–47). Reston, VA: ASCE Press.

Schölkopf & J. Platt (Ed.), *Advances in neural information processing systems* (pp. 1257–1264). Cambridge, MA: MIT Press.

Snelson, E., & Ghahramani, Z. (2006). Sparse Gaussian processes using pseudo-inputs. In Weiss, Y. (Ed.), *B*.

Stachniss, C., Plagemann, C., & Lilienthal, A. J. (2009). Learning gas distribution models using sparse Gaussian process mixtures. *Autonomous Robots, 26*(2-3), 187–202..doi:10.1007/s10514-009-9111-5

ADDITIONAL READING

Mobile Robot Olfaction

Lochmatter, T. (2010). Bio-inspired probabilistic algorithms for distributed odor source localization using mobile robots. (Doctoral dissertation, EPFL, 2010), *Dissertation Abstracts*, 4628.

Gas Sensors

Nakamoto, T., & Ishida, H. (2008). Chemical Sensing in Spatial/Temporal Domains. *Chemical Review Journal, 108*(2), 680–704. doi:10.1021/cr068117e

Environmental Monitoring

Gilbert, R. O. (1987). *Statistical Methods for Environmental Pollution Monitoring*. Wiley.

Machine Learning

Bishop, C. M. (2006). *Pattern Recognition and Machine Learning*. Springer.

Plagemann, C. (2008). Gaussian Processes for Flexible Robot Learning. PhD Thesis, University of Freiburg, Germany.

Rasmussen, C. E., & Williams, C. K. I. (2006). *Gaussian Processes for Machine Learning*. MA: The MIT Press.

Chapter 7
Characterization of Complex Patterns:
Application to Colorimetric Arrays and Vertical Structures

Yannick Caulier
Fraunhofer Institute IIS, Germany

ABSTRACT

This chapter tackles the problem of a colorimetric sensor array description method within the machine olfaction field for the visual enhancement of volatile organic components (VOC). The proposed method is based on preliminary investigations done during the elaboration of an existing machine vision system for quality control, based on the interpretation of specific structured light patterns for the visual enhancement of defective surface parts.

The primary purpose of this chapter is to demonstrate the similarity between the colorimetric and the structured pattern interpretation. The investigations are based on a linear spatial transformation between both types of patterns based on the main features characterizing the patterns, i.e. the red, green and blue for the color and the intensity, left and right deviations for the structured. Thus, such a different representation of VOC characterization patterns allows the use of other existing structured pattern description methods. Within this context, different pattern recognition processes, consisting of the combination of different feature retrieval and classification methods, but also of feature combination and selection approaches will be considered.

DOI: 10.4018/978-1-61520-915-6.ch007

The feature-based investigations are based on a reference annotated structured pattern dataset. The purpose of these investigations is to introduce an optimized feature combination, selection, and classification principle. Three top-down and one bottom-up methodologies are evaluated for retrieving, combining, and selecting the most appropriate structured feature sets. It will be demonstrated that an increase of more than 2% of the classification rates can be reached.

Hence, the same approach can be applied for the characterization of colorimetric patterns in case of particular machine olfaction tasks, as the proposed developments can be further used integrated into other quality control systems, in order to bring more "intelligence" to this technique.

INTRODUCTION

A major challenge of a typical machine inspection process is to provide rugged and cost-effective solutions for real-time problems. Such systems use different and appropriate sensors for the automatic detection and identification of various suspicious components, as production defects or VOSs and serve as a valuable process feedback and control utility. A step towards the cost reduction of such processes is, to define approaches that can be applied to a wide range of applications, provided the efforts to adapt such a solution to a specific task are minimal.

The major perspective of this chapter is to propose a general approach for real-time pattern interpretation for different quality control processes. The case of structured patterns for industrial specular surface inspection will serve as basis. The method using the interpretation of a basic *periodical and vertical* light pattern was recently proposed for the inspection and characterization purposes of cylindrical specular surfaces (Caulier et al., 2007; Caulier et al., 2009). This sensor technique permits the visual *enhancement* and *discrimination* of *various defective parts* of the specular surfaces similar to colorimetric sensors allowing the visual enhancement of organic components. Both methods use the interpretation of the visual information to discriminate between different types of components, whether these are defective metallic surfaces or organic and volatile.

In order to propose a new real-time color array description, a transformation function between color arrays and structured images is proposed. This transformation is based on a different representation of each important feature of both arrays, i.e. the hue, saturation, and value components for the former and the intensity, left and right deviation for the latter. This chapter is therefore dedicated to the generalization of *periodical and vertical* structured interpretations. The adaptation to color array description is then straightforward.

Various pattern analysis techniques have been proposed since the mid 1960s, i.e. since computers were able to solve information handling problems. According to (Raudys & Jain, 1991), the main steps defining a typical pattern recognition process are the following: data collection, pattern class's formation, characteristic features extraction, classification algorithm specification and estimation of the classification error. The results of each of these steps can be used in a feedback procedure for optimization of the final result. Then, depending on the size and the representativeness of the reference data set, various classification methodologies can be applied (Witten & Eibe, 2008).

With the interpretation of such stripe patterns, the task consists of the computation of the optimal pattern analysis methods in terms of highest classification rates. The core of our approach is dedicated to the *retrieval* and *selection* of the most appropriate feature sets for the characterization of vertical stripe structures.

For the purpose of optimizing the retrieval of the most appropriate features for stripe patterns characterization, a three-step method is proposed. Indeed, such hierarchical feature selection procedures are considered to be particularly suited to complex content-based image description tasks as we have here (Dy et al., 2003; Peng et al., 2005). Furthermore, in order to address the stripe classification task in general, and in accordance to the recommendations of (Raudys & Jain, 1991), we emphasize the fact, that several feature extraction and feature selection methods, but also various classification algorithms and classification methodologies, are taken into consideration.

The first step consists of the evaluation of 3 different top-down and 1 bottom-up methodologies. The former are defined within the field of textural analysis and consist of a general approach, the latter are specially defined for the characterization of such structures. This chapter is therefore a generalization of the bottom-up method described in (Caulier et al., 2008). The classification of specular surfaces is addressed by means of fewer stripe features as proposed in this manuscript. The second step is dedicated to the combination of the most relevant features by applying appropriate selection methods. The evaluation criterion for each of these steps is the stripe pattern classification rate. Furthermore, in order to find the most appropriate pattern analysis process and to address such a classification task within a general scope, the combination of 5 different reference image sets with 3 different classifiers is considered. The last step consists of the selection of the most appropriate features. For generalization purposes, the usage of 2 different feature selection approaches is taken into consideration.

The objectives of the chapter are:

- To propose a new colorimetric array description based on a first transform, i.e. representation of the color information into periodic structures,

- To address the characterization of colorimetric arrays within a general scope based on different image sets, classifiers, classification procedures.
- To define, i.e. to search for, the most appropriate textural features within the proposed inspection context,
- To propose a new set of adapted structured pattern, also within the proposed inspection context,

In a final step,

- To improve the detection accuracy by combining and selecting the most appropriate textural, and adapted features by means of 2 different and complementary selection methods.

This chapter is divided into 5 sections. The "Background" section describes existing open problems, the "Main Focus of the Chapter" section provides possible issues concerning the addressed problem, the "Solutions and Recommendations" section gives the proposed response to the tackled open problems, the "Future Research Directions" section proposes possible implementation issues of the developed technique and the "Conclusion" section concludes this chapter.

BACKGROUND

The main and challenging purpose of automatic systems is to mimic the human sensing systems, as e.g. the odor or vision ones, in order to replace the inspector while tedious inspection tasks but also to get objective and repeatable quality control results. Central element for every machine system, whether it is an olfactory or vision one e.g., is the sensing element capable of detecting the relevant information related to the component, i.e. gas or surface, being inspected. Sensors major requirements are their field of range and sensitivity, i.e. their resolution permitting them to detect the finest component elements, we speak of parts per million (ppm) in case of volatile components, and wavelength (λ) for visual components. These sensory all have the capability to convert the input signal into an electronic signal, whose amplitude is proportional to the intensity of the detected component.

If the description of the photo effect, i.e. the conversion of light into current, is known since the beginning of the 19th century, the capability to detect odors originated only since the late 1980s. Hence, a direct consequence is that less literature dedicated to the latter technique, whether it concerns the data acquisition or the data interpretation parts, exists. Thus, there is a real need and demand to define new and appropriate techniques for the processing of olfactory components.

As stated previously, different olfactory sensor techniques were developed during the past decades. Existing sensors mainly differ according to their type, i.e. the involved technology, as e.g. quartz resonator (Jatmiko et al., 2004), surface acoustic wave devices (Wholtjen, 1979), or conductive polymers (Harris et al., 1997). Sensor spatial arrangements, as situated at the distal end of fibers (Dickinson et al. 1996), or disposed as a pattern, in case of rectangular (Rakow & Suslick, 2000) or linear (Lonergan et al., 1997) sensor arrays. As a consequence, different data processing techniques specially developed for particular sensor types and arrangement can were defined. To cite only a few in order of appearance, (Dickinson et al. 1996) process normalized sensor array signals using PCA-based methods, (Lonergan et al., 1997) use neural-network for the time variation interpretation of line sensors, Fourier-based approaches for the discrimination of sensor arrays are involved in (Cai et al., 2002), (Suslick et al., 2004) characterize colorimetric pattern arrays by means of feature-vectors, and (Bermak et al., 2005) involved features reduction and classification approach based on the characterization of the transient signal information of gas sensors.

Among existing olfactory sensors, main advantages of colorimetric arrays, is to give a *clear* and *direct* representation of volatile component. *Clear*, as the odor information is directly linked with the sensor dyes, which react to a wide range of different VOCs and other analytes. *Direct*, as the responses of an organic component are visualized simultaneously thanks to their 2D arrangement. As, such colorimetric sensor arrays are color fingerprints serving the detection of volatile and hydrophobic organics but also hydrophilic analytes (Rakow & Suslick, 2000); their interpretation must rely on the extraction and selection on appropriate features. These may directly correspond to the RGB-values of the involved color dyes (Suslick et al., 2004), or be extracted from metadata, as color e.g. histograms (Chen et al., 2009). Common aspect of such image characterization methods is that local *and* spatial colorimetric information are taken into consideration as both are relevant characteristics of the organic component to be detected. Thus, within the context of real-time machine olfaction systems, sensitive, fast, and adapted methods have to be developed.

Thus, one possible approach could be to develop and adapt existing methods specially defined for colorimetric sensor arrays characterization. However, as to our knowledge, no method for the real-time interpretation of such patterns was proposed, a further possibility could be to adapt an existing real-time image processing method, by demonstrating that the involved images have similar characteristics like the colorimetric patterns. As it will be developed in the next section, a real-time image processing method based on the interpretation of structured patterns for machine vision applications, can serve as basis for the description of complex patterns, where the relevant information is contained in the intensity and spatial arrangement of the elementary image elements (which can be e.g. pixels or dyes). Thus this is the reason why this method can also be used for machine olfaction systems in case of colorimetric pattern interpretation.

The reference structured patterns which will serve as basis for the interpretation of colorimetric patterns were defined within the field of industrial inspection, i.e. the automatic quality control of specular cylindrical surfaces, i.e. the simultaneous discrimination of geometrical and textural defects. Industrial machine vision solutions in general, use the deflection of the light rays from the inspected surfaces to visually enhance the defective parts situated on metallic car parts (Marino et al., 1999), large steel plates (Paakkari, 1998) or steel cylindrical surfaces (Pernkopf, 2004).

As in general specular objects are more difficult to inspect than matt objects, only specific and adapted methods can be involved. 3D triangulation approaches are generally *not suited* for *specular surfaces*, as these must be covered first with a matt film before being inspected, which makes inspection in a real-time environment difficult. An alternative method to this approach is provided by deflectometric techniques (Kammel & Puente Leon, 2003, Kammel, 2004), which are based on the measurement of the reflected light rays projected onto the object of inspection. An improvement consists of the adaptation of the position and the geometry of the projected light rays to visually enhance the defective surface parts, so that no 3D reconstruction is necessary (Delcroix et al., 2001, Nayar et al., 1990). A further possibility is provided by (Reindl & O'Leary, 2007) and (Puente Leon & Beyerer, 1997) who use the light-sectioning and light-fusion techniques for the retrieval of the geometrical *and* texture information of metallic objects. However, all these techniques are *not optimal* in terms of a *real-time industrial inspection* process. Whether the methods are based on complex pre-calibration procedures, imply a complicated movement of the objects during their inspection (rotation and translation e.g.), or necessitate to record the surface to be inspected several times, which is hardly applicable in an online inspection process.

Hence, the first challenge consisted of adapting the illumination in order to depict the relevant surface information. This was achieved by elaborating an adapted lighting (Caulier et al., 2007), which delivers such structured patterns. Then, the next important aspect is to define an optimal, in terms of high detection accuracy and low processing time, image description technique, which is part of an inspection system dedicated to the real-time inline workpiece quality control. If the similarity between the structured and colorimetric pattern interpretation tasks has been demonstrated before, the developments dedicated to the real-time processing of the former patterns will serve afterwards for the characterization of the latter patterns.

ISSUES AND PROBLEMS

Concerning the automatic and robust discrimination, in terms of high detection rates, of organic components, different approaches have been introduced in the previous section. Many unsolved problems still exist, as none of these applications, including the colorimetric patterns-based ones, are dedicated to real-time applications. This section tries to bring solutions to the open problems addressed. It has been demonstrated in the introduction section, how the use of colorimetric patterns serves the detection of VOCs, as far as the molecular recognition is concerned, by using the sensor dyes as direct indicator component types. A further open similar pattern characterization task, defined within the field of visual inspection, has also been introduced. The unsolved problem is here the optimal interpretation of the considered structured patterns. In the following, we demonstrate that both image description tasks are similar, and introduce the proposed for the characterization of the structured pattern, which also serves the interpretation of the colorimetric ones.

In case of both applications, based on structured or colorimetric images, the digital signature is related to the local and spatial information, where local information consists of the color components (hue, saturation and values e.g.) for the former, and the description of the vertical structures (gray value, left and right variations) for the latter. In both cases, each local element i (sensor dye or structure element) is characterized by the variation of 3 parameters: $(^hf_i; {}^sf_i; {}^vf_i)$ for the former and $(^lf_i; {}^rf_i; {}^gf_i)$ for the latter. Hence, first issue therefore consists of defining the pattern transformation Φ permitting the representation of the colorimetric information as structured information and vice versa. Since this is achieved, the next undissolved problem is to define an appropriate image processing technique s permitting, (i) the description of the colorimetric pattern or (ii) the characterization of the depicted light structure pattern.

A real-time industrial application based on structured lighting is provided as an example (Caulier et al., 2007). In this case, 2 types of defects situated on cylindrical metallic objects of approximately 10 mm diameter and up to 2×10^3 mm length must be detected. The same inspection principle can be adapted to other geometries (planar, convex) of specular objects where different types of defective parts must be visually enhanced and discriminated. Visible means that the deformations synonymous of defective surfaces can be automatically segmented and classified with image processing methods. Quality control process then consists of the automatic characterization and classification of such visually enhanced defects. For the evaluation of the different classification procedures, the images recorded with the industrial application are used.

Figure 1 shows the previously introduced controversies, i.e. the necessity to define (i) a direct transformation between colorimetric and structured pattern representa-

Figure 1. Left: Colorimetric and structured pattern, for which both elementary components are represented by 3 parameters. The transformation Φ is the representation linking the 2 pattern types. Right: Surface inspection principle for specular objects. The illumination L projects a structured pattern, which is reflected by the inspected surface S and then projected/recorded by a camera C. The generated stripe image depicts a periodical bright and dark stripe structure of period $d_{P,px}$ whose disturbances are synonymous of defective parts.

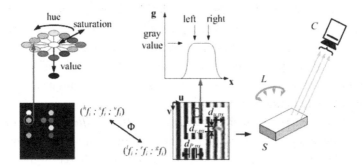

tion, and (ii) a free-form surface inspection principle based on the projection of a structured pattern (Caulier et al., 2007). The depicted structured image was recorded with the industrial application.

The colorimetric and structured representations are depicted in the figure above. The figure also shows the adapted illumination L, whose reflected light rays from the surface S are projected as a periodical stripe pattern onto the recording sensor C. The image resolution in pixel along the u- and the v-axis but also the stripe period $d_{P,px}$ must be chosen according to the minimal size of the defect to be detected. Here a depth defect synonymous of a structural change on the inspected surface of size $d_{u,px}$ and $d_{v,px}$ is depicted.

As stated in the introduction, one major purpose of this chapter is to propose a general description method for the feature-based colorimetric or structured pattern characterization. The general approach is based on considering the major image processing steps, i.e. (i) the image content description by means of appropriate features, (ii) the supervised feature classification and (iii) the feature selection methodologies. For each of these steps different existing and possible approaches are introduced in the following.

This general approach will be applied for the characterization of the structured patterns and the adaptation to color array description is then straightforward. For the rest of the chapter, the terminology stripe will be used to define the structured patterns to be characterized.

Feature Extraction

The use of textural features to characterize and classify stripe structures is particularly interesting in this case, as to our knowledge such an elaborate evaluation has never been done before. Textural features were defined to address a broad range of various pattern characterization tasks. The concept of textural analysis is based on the description of local or global image properties. This is closely related to Haralick's concept (Haralick, 1979), who defines 2 basic dimensions: the tonal primitives composing the texture and their spatial organizations. There are a tremendous number of different pattern characterization approaches which are proposed within the textural analysis community (Mihran & Anil, 1998). Thus, concerning the interpretation of stripe structures by means of such techniques, a selection of the most appropriate methods is essential.

In terms of stripe structures characterization with *specific* features, most publications are dedicated to identification for classification purposes of fringe patterns depicting bright and dark structures within the field of coherent lighting. A set of 6 principal fringe structures for characterization and synonymous of defective object structures are described in (Jüptner et al., 1994). Zhi and Johansson (Zhi & Johansson, 1992) propose a set of 14 geometrical and statistical features for the interpretation of holographic interferometric fringes for medical purposes. Some features are specifically defined for very particular types of fringe structures, as the "eyes" or the "eye chains" structures (Jüptner et al., 1994), others are defined for the characterization of structures that are similar to the stripe patterns considered in this chapter. Further methods involving wavelet (Krüger et al., 2001; Li, 2000) or Fourier (Qian et al., 2005) transformations for the characterization of faults have also been suggested. Such approaches are part of the "transform" methods within the field of textural analysis.

In the following 4 textural and 1 adapted already existing approaches are introduced.

Textural Feature: Structural Approach

Chen's (Chen et al., 1995) *structural* approach is based on statistical and geometrical features of the pattern to be characterized. The feature computation consists of a two-step procedure. First, the patterns are binarized in the grey level domain by means of several thresholds τ. Then, the connected regions of each binary image are computed. The feature vector $\mathbf{c}^C$ of the pattern is filled with the statistical characteristics of the connected regions of all binarized images. The advantage and also possibly interesting perspectives of using multiple binarizations is to consider different intensity levels of image regions and to thereby integrate the intensity information into the feature computation.

Textural Feature: Statistical Approach

The next textural method considered is based on the feature computation as stated by (Haralick et al., 1973), and is part of the *statistical* texture analysis approach. Such pattern characterization techniques are based on the co-occurrence matrices, a second-order statistical measure of the grey level variation. These matrices indicate the joint probability of the grey level occurrences of all pixel pairs in u- and v-directions in a pattern. Thus, an interesting perspective concerning the optimization of this statistical approach for our purposes could be to adapt the values of the pixel pair distances d_u and d_v according to the geometry of the stripe structure depicted in the pattern.

Textural Feature: Transform Approach

As stripe images major geometric primitive is the sinusoidal grey level variation, the use of a Fourier-based approach seams to be an evident choice. Thus, the textural transform approach proposed by (Weska, 1978) and based on the Fourier analysis was used for the characterization of the stripe structures in the spectral domain. The features are computed from amounts of values in the Fourier spectrum corresponding to different spectral regions. (Weska 1978) defines r_F as radial and d_θ as directional frequency regions. His aim is to use the particularity of the spectral domain by selecting various frequency subbands, which is equivalent to retaining certain levels of details and directions in the analyzed patterns. Thus, u_F and v_F spectral regions defined along the u- horizontal and the v- vertical image axes were used for the computation of the feature vectors based on the Fourier analysis.

Adapted Fringe and Stripe Features

In contrast to top-down methodologies, as with the three studies cited above, some bottom-up approaches dedicated to the characterization of stripe structures are also described in the literature. Specific geometry-based and intensity-based features have been considered for an adapted characterization of the bright and the dark stripe structures depicted in a stripe pattern **F**. The description of such a pattern is a two-step procedure. It first consists of the *segmentation* at sub-pixel level of the bright and dark stripes structures, and second of the characterization of these segmented structures. Each process is characterized by one parameter: the involved segmentation function f, and the image areas **a** covered by local windows w sliding over the whole described pattern. A good overview of existing sub-pixel segmentation techniques is provided by Fisher (Fisher & Naidu, 1996). Such methods are based on the estimation of the peaks to be localized. Specific mathematical functions or local grey level interpolations can be considered.

Segmenting the Stripe to be Characterized

One important step in a pattern analysis procedure involves the selection of the characterized image region. With unsupervised image segmentation techniques, segmentation errors are virtually unavoidable (Unnikrishnan et al., 2007). Moreover, even if such techniques have been extensively described in the literature, we did not yet find automatic segmentation approaches of such stripe patterns. This is in fact a rather complex task, as the depicted defective surfaces are usually not characterized by sharp contours. Extensive tests and research procedures are necessary to solve the segmentation problem of stripe structures.

Feature Classification

One major aspect concerning the selection of an appropriate classification methodology is the *size* and the *representativeness* of the reference data which are used for the evaluation of the whole classification process. The former is particularly important for the model-based classifiers as the statistical NB method is involved. The latter is directly related with the problem of data over-fitting, which occurs when the classifier is trained on a set of samples that are not representative compared to the set of test samples.

Another possible method to address such concerns is to split the reference dataset Φ into multiple training and testing subsets. This process is called the n-fold cross validation. Stratification guarantees the representativeness of each class in the training and testing sets by forcing the folds to retain the same distribution as the original data. Such a cross-validation procedure mitigates any bias due to the over-fitting of the data, as the training and testing procedures are repeated n-times. When the number of folds equals the number of elements of Φ, the procedure is called "leaving-one-out" approach. The number n of folds is an important variable here. Increasing n signifies increasing the number of training data and so reducing the bias due to over-fitting. But it is also synonymous to a larger discrepancy of correctly classified patterns across folds as the number of testing data decreases. It is also related to higher computational costs as the entire dataset has to be processed n times.

Another splitting technique originally proposed by (Efron & Tibshirani, 1993) is the Bootstrap approach. This method uses the resampling of the original dataset for the generation of b multiple training and test sets. While the Bootstrap procedure may be the best way for the classification of small datasets, its major drawback is the high computational costs as far as the classification of the *b* datasets have to be done. Moreover, it has not been demonstrated that a bootstrap-based approach outperforms "leaving-one-out" or other cross-validation procedures (Weiss, 1991).

The approach used most widely is certainly the 10-fold stratified cross-validation and according to (Witten & Eibe, 2008), a 10 times sampling is referred to as the right number of folds to get the best estimation error. Extended tests with various datasets and 2 classifiers have been conducted by (Kohavi, 1995) to compare the detection accuracy of the bootstrap technique and the *n*-fold cross-validation approach for different values of *n*. Kohavi shows that a stratified 10-fold cross-validation is the more appropriate model in terms of classification accuracy.

Feature Selection

The purpose of a feature subset selection (FSS) process is the generation of a feature subset made of the most relevant information in terms of classification accuracy. Primary research concerning FSS has been addressed for decades by the statistics community, e.g. (Lakshminarasimhan & Dasarathy, 1975) for the recognition of hand-written characters or (Mucciardi & Gose, 1971) in case of the classification of EKG data. More recently, these FSS techniques have been adapted and completed within the data mining research field, which was primary defined to address the processing of a broader range and larger amount of data.

However diverse all the FSS techniques can be, such techniques always consist of an iterative procedure, the *generation* and *evaluation* of each new subset, which terminates according to a *stopping criterion*. The performances of each FSS method are defined according to a *validation* process (Dash & Liu, 1997).

Two *generation* methods are described in the literature: the *filter* and *wrapper* techniques (Witten & Eibe, 2008; Gutierrez-Osuna, 2002; Hall, 1999; John et al., 1994). The former are independent of the classification process and consist of filtering out the irrelevant data using the feature information content. The latter uses the machine learning algorithm or classifier that is used for the learning procedure. In both cases, similar feature search strategies can be applied. We are distinguishing between a forward selection (the process starts with no selected features), a backward elimination (the process starts with the complete subset) or a bidirectional search strategy which combines both methodologies and starts with a random subset of features (Jain & Zongker, 1997).

The *evaluation* of the generated subset, i.e. its quality, is done according to certain criteria. (Dash & Liu, 1997) differentiate 2 groups: the *independent* criteria typically are used in case of filter models and the *dependent* evaluation criteria are mostly applied as far as wrapper-based FSS models are concerned. The independent criteria are based on the relations between the features eliminating highly correlated characteristics which are redundant for the prediction. Such criteria use the *distances* between the features (Niemann, 2003), such as the Bhattacharyya (Djouadi et al., 1990) or the Hausdorff distance (Huttenlocher et al., 1993). The *information gain* (Liu et al., 2003) or the *dependencies* between features (Talavera, 2000) are further independent criteria which are used by filter-based feature selection approaches. With the dependent criteria, the evaluation and the optimization of the accuracy rate is done according to the performances of the involved classifiers using the selected feature subsets. In case of small sets of reference patterns, a cross-validation procedure can often improve the evaluation determination (Kohavi, 1995).

According to the inspection task, various *stopping criteria* can be addressed. The simplest one is to finish the search of feature subsets when all computed features have been selected. The search procedure can also stop when some threshold variables are reached. These can be e.g. the minimum number of features, the maximum number of iterations or the minimum value of the error rate. More complex procedures as the restriction of the number of backtracking can also determine the stopping conditions. Feature subset search algorithms can also stop when subsequent addition or deletion of any feature does not produce a better subset.

The FSS *validation* is generally done by comparing the classification performances when the full features are considered and the performances as far as only the computed feature subsets are involved.

More information on the feature selection principle with the 4 major parts *generation, evaluation, stopping criterion* and *result validation* can be found in (Dash & Liu, 1997). It is shown that this selection principle is similar to the pattern classification task where learning and testing phases are considered. The task of selecting the most relevant features is also divided in a training step and a testing step. Once the best feature subset has been computed after a learning phase by means of a reference set of patterns, the validation is done using another set of patterns during the test phase.

SOLUTIONS AND RECCOMMENDATIONS

Concerning the solutions considered for the problems described in the preceding section, i.e. the definition of appropriate stripe features, their classification and the selection, the considered solutions are described hereafter. Each solution is related to the generally addressed task in this chapter, i.e. the definition of an optimal feature-based stripe image characterization methodology.

Colorimetric to Structured Pattern Transformation

As stated previously, one unsolved problem consists of defining the transformation Φ permitting to represent a colorimetric pattern as a structured one, and vice versa using the inverse Φ^{-1}. It has been described how each elementary element i, sensor dyes and structured pixel, depends on 3 parameters, namely the colorimetric hue, saturation and value ones $(h_i ; s_i ; v_i)$ and the left deviation, right deviation and gray value ones $(l_i ; r_i ; g_i)$ Each parameter being defined within a certain range of values.

We considered that each pattern type can be represented by an undisturbed reference pattern with an additional disturbance applied to each elementary component i. Hence, each color and structured pattern $\mathbf{F}^C$ and $\mathbf{F}^S$, can be decomposed into a reference pattern, $\mathbf{F}^C_0$ and $\mathbf{F}^S_0$, and a disturbance ϕ^C_{lm} and ϕ^S_{lm} applied to all the $[l \times m]$ elementary components i. Reference pattern $\mathbf{F}^C_0$ is a black images, and reference pattern $\mathbf{F}^S_0$ is an image depicting m undisturbed vertical lines, each represented by l pixels. Following equations with transformation Φ and its inverse Φ^{-1} holds:

$$\mathbf{F}^C = \mathbf{F}^C_0 + \phi^C_{lm} \text{ where } \phi^C_{lm} = \Sigma_{lm} (h_i ; s_i ; v_i)$$

$$\mathbf{F}^S = \mathbf{F}^S_0 + \phi^S_{lm} \text{ where } \phi^S_{lm} = \Sigma_{lm} (l_i ; r_i ; g_i)$$

$$\mathbf{F}^S = \mathbf{F}^S_0 + \Phi (\phi^C_{lm}):$$

$$\mathbf{F}^C = \mathbf{F}^C_0 + \Phi^{-1} (\phi^S_{lm}) \qquad (1)$$

These notations are used in the following Figure 2, showing the principle of transformation Φ for one colorimetric image representing the range of variation for the hue, saturation and value color components. Φ is applied to 3 color images depicting the difference maps for 3 strains of bacteria to be discriminated. The corresponding transform images show similar structures to the reference images taken by the industrial reference structured light based machine vision system.

Figure 2 shows the principle of transformation Φ, which is applied to 3 difference maps. It can clearly be seen how this transformation applied to color patterns permits to retrieve similar structured stripe patterns. Hence the colorimetric pattern discrimination problem is similar to the structured pattern discrimination. Therefore, a classification task of a colorimetric reference pattern dataset Ω^C patterns for the discrimination of organic components is equivalent to the classification task of the Φ transformed structured stripe patterns dataset Ω^S.

This is the reason why, the rest of this chapter is dedicated to the classification task of structured stripe patterns. Depicted images are parts of the reference stripe pattern dataset used for the qualification of the reference machine vision system

Figure 2. Left: Transformation Φ principle for one colorimetric image representing the variation of the h, s, v, hv, sv, hs components and the corresponding l, r, g, rg, lg, rl. for the [l x m] pattern components. Middle: Difference maps for 3 strains of bacteria with their transformed structured patterns using Φ (the difference map images were taken from http://www.chemsensing.com/technology.html). Right: Stripe image examples of relevant defects. Upper patterns: 3 examples depicting non-defective surfaces. Middle patterns: 3 defective 3D surfaces. Lower patterns: 3 defective 2D surfaces. All of the images have a size of [M_u x M_v] = [64 x 64] pixels.

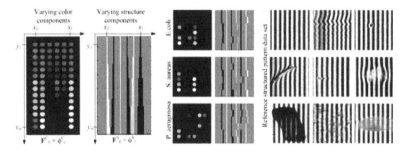

(Caulier et al., 2007). As showed at Figure 2, 3 classes were considered: the acceptable surfaces $\Omega_{A,OK}$, the rejected non-acceptable 2D surfaces $\Omega_{R,2D}$, and the rejected non-acceptable *3D* surfaces $\Omega_{R,3D}$. Figure 2.(c) shows the 3 examples of non-defective surfaces, 6 examples of defective *3D* and *2D* surfaces. The evaluation criterion for a particular classification procedure was chosen to be the classification rate of such stripe patterns.

In the following the feature extraction, classification and selection for stripe pattern characterization is presented. As stated previously, these developments also serve the interpretation of colorimetric patterns.

Feature Extraction

Textural and Adapted Feature Sets

The selection of representative textural methods for comparisons is partially based on work by (Wagner, 1999), who conducted and presented an extensive comparative study of 18 families of different texture analysis methods from literature and applied them to 7 different reference image data sets in the gray scale domain. The 3 reference methods selected in this manuscript are correlating to the methods described by Wagner with the highest recognition rates from his studies. Moreover, each of these methods is part of the main texture families as considered by (Materka & Strzelecki, 1998), namely the *structural*, the *statistical* and the *transform* ap-

Figure 3. Notations and expressions of the 20 operators

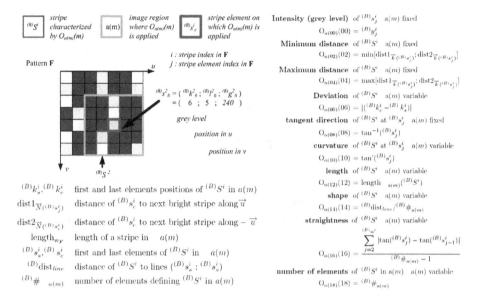

Intensity (grey level) of $^{(B)}s_j^i$ $a(m)$ fixed
$$O_{a(00)}(00) = {}^{(B)}g_j^i$$

Minimum distance of $^{(B)}S^i$ $a(m)$ fixed
$$O_{a(02)}(02) = \min[\text{dist}1_{\overline{k}({}^{(B)}s_c^i)}; \text{dist}2_{\overline{k}({}^{(B)}s_c^i)}]$$

Maximum distance of $^{(B)}S^i$ $a(m)$ fixed
$$O_{a(04)}(04) = \max[\text{dist}1_{({}^{(B)}s_c^i)}; \text{dist}2_{\overline{k}({}^{(B)}s_c^i)}]$$

Deviation of $^{(B)}S^i$ $a(m)$ variable
$$O_{a(06)}(06) = |({}^{(B)}k_c^i - {}^{(B)}k_s^i)|$$

tangent direction of $^{(B)}S^i$ at $^{(B)}s_j^i$ $a(m)$ fixed
$$O_{a(08)}(08) = \tan^{-1}({}^{(B)}s_j^i)$$

curvature of $^{(B)}S^i$ at $^{(B)}s_j^i$ $a(m)$ variable
$$O_{a(10)}(10) = \tan'({}^{(B)}s_j^i)$$

length of $^{(B)}S^i$ $a(m)$ variable
$$O_{a(12)}(12) = \text{length}_{a(m)}({}^{(B)}S^i)$$

shape of $^{(B)}S^i$ $a(m)$ variable
$$O_{a(14)}(14) = {}^{(B)}\text{dist}_{line}/{}^{(B)}\#_{a(m)}$$

straightness of $^{(B)}S^i$ $a(m)$ variable
$$O_{a(16)}(16) = \frac{\sum_{j=2}^{{}^{(B)}n^i} |\tan({}^{(B)}s_j^i) - \tan({}^{(B)}s_{j-1}^i)|}{{}^{(B)}\#_{a(m)} - 1}$$

number of elements of $^{(B)}S^i$ in $a(m)$ $a(m)$ variable
$$O_{a(18)}(18) = {}^{(B)}\#_{a(m)}$$

proaches. We are trying to optimize each textural procedure by adapting the innate parameters of each method to the depicted disturbed or non-disturbed stripe pattern, for example, its shape or its intensity.

For our purposes, *4 geometry-* and *2 statistic-based features* proposed by (Zhi & Johansson, 1992) for the characterization of bright stripe patterns are applied. The improvement consists of the completion of these features with further *4 specific features* defined within the field of stripe structure characterization. Another novel aspect concerns the use of all of these features for the characterization of the bright stripes, but also of the dark stripes in the pattern.

Textural Feature: Structural Approach

The stripe patterns present the particularity to have a bimodal grey level distribution corresponding to the distributions of the bright and dark stripe structures. Thus, the assumption is made that the consideration of various groups of binarization thresholds τ could lead to an optimization of Chen's feature extraction process. The following 4 different feature vectors were considered:

$$\mathbf{c}^C_{255}: N_c = 16, \tau \in \{0,\ldots,255\}$$

$$\mathbf{c}^C_7: N_c = 16, \tau \in \{32,64,\ldots,192,224\}$$

$\mathbf{c}^C_3: N_c = 16, \tau \in \{64,128,192\}$

$\mathbf{c}^C_1: N_c = 16, \tau \in \{128\}$ \hfill (2)

Each of these vectors integrates a different number of binarized patterns, however, their lengths all equal 16. In case of vector $\mathbf{c}^C_{255}$ all possible binarization thresholds τ are used, as only grey level images with a depth of 2^8 are considered.

Textural Feature: Statistical Approach

The values of d_u were chosen to correspond to the period of the stripe structure, which is a-priori known. The values of d_v were chosen to cover the whole range of the disturbance sizes in the v-direction. The following 4 different feature vectors were considered:

$\mathbf{c}^H_{1,1}: N_c = 14, d_u = 1 \; d_v = 1$

$\mathbf{c}^H_{8,1}: N_c = 14, d_u = 8 \; d_v = 1$

$\mathbf{c}^H_{8,10}: N_c = 14, d_u = 8 \; d_v = 10$

$\mathbf{c}^H_{8,30}: N_c = 14, d_u = 8 \; d_v = 30$ \hfill (3)

Each vector is made up of 14 features as defined by Haralick in (Haralick et al., 1973). The characterized stripe structures have a period of approximately 8 pixels, so that a value of $d_u = 8$ was repeatedly chosen.

Textural Feature: Transform Approach

The characterized stripes have a vertical and periodical structure. Thus, the directional components in the frequency domain may be strongly discriminative in terms of stripe pattern characterizations. In terms of the stripe pattern analysis, feature vectors integrating various subbands of the frequency domain were taken into consideration. The following 5 different feature vectors were used:

$\mathbf{c}^F_{r,\theta,v,u} = \{ \mathbf{c}^F_r ; \mathbf{c}^F_\theta ; \mathbf{c}^F_v ; \mathbf{c}^F_u \} \; N_c = 33$

$\mathbf{c}^F_r: N_c = 8$

$\mathbf{c}^F_\theta: N_c = 10$

$\mathbf{c}^F_v : N_c = 5$

$\mathbf{c}^F_u : N_c = 10$ \hfill (4)

The length of each feature vector depends on the frequency regions considered. The vector $\mathbf{c}^F_{r,\theta,v,u}$, considers all possible regions have a maximal length of $N_c = 33$.

Adapted Fringe and Stripes Features

Concerning the segmentation of the bright and dark stripe structures, the major requirement is the accurate determination of their spatial positions. Thus, adapted methods should be involved. Concerning existing approaches, the "Blais-and-Rioux" and the "Center-of-Mass" peak detectors were implemented (Fisher & Naidu, 1996; Asada et al., 1988) for stripe structure characterization. Both operators are used for the detection at sub-pixel level of the bright and the dark stripes along the u-axis of the pattern. In order to be comparable, the same operator's size is considered. A size of 5 elements is retained, as this value corresponds to the length of the bright and the dark peaks to be characterized. The notation for these 2 peak detectors is br5 for the "Blais-and-Rioux" and cm5 for the "Center-of-Mass". Hence, 2 types of segmentation function are considered $f \in \{br5 ; cm5\}$.

A total of 20 stripe features are used for the characterization of the extracted bright and dark regions. Eight of these features are specially developed for the present purposes, in addition, 12 features were described within the context of fringe structure characterization (Zhi & Johansson, 1992) and adapted for our purposes. Each of these 20 stripe features $c^S_{a(m)}(m)$, $m \in \{0,...,19\}$ represents the average result of an operation $O^S_{a(m)}(m)$ applied to a bright or dark stripe element. The computation of $O^S_{a(m)}(m)$ is applied on an image area $a(m)$, whose magnitude is feature dependent. Notations and detailed expressions of the 20 operators $O^S_{a(m)}(00)$ to $O^S_{a(m)}(19)$ are described in the following Figure 3.

As the minimal possible size of the reference patterns **F** of the involved image sets is about 20 pixels, the following area magnitude $a(i)$ is considered for our purposes: $[5^2] ; [7^2] ; [9^2] ; [11^2] ; [13^2] ; [15^2] ; [17^2] ; [M_u \times M_v]$. The description of the stripe feature vector is as follows:

$\mathbf{c}^S_{f,a} : N_c = 20$

$f \in \{f_{br5} ; f_{cm5}\}$

$\mathbf{a} = [a(0),...,a(m),...,a(19)],$

$$a(m) \in \{[5^2] ; [7^2] ; [9^2] ; [11^2] ; [13^2] ; [15^2] ; [17^2] ; [M_u \times M_v]\} \qquad (5)$$

As mentioned above, the computation of the stripe feature vector relies on 2 segmentation functions f. Then, each of the stripe feature vector's 20 elements can be computed by means of 8 different area sizes of $a(m)$. Hence, 2×8^{20} stripe feature vectors can be retrieved according to the definition given in Equation (5).

In order to reduce the number of possible feature stripe vectors, and thus avoid dimensionality-based problems, a preliminary optimization process to retrieve the most adequate area size of $a(m)$ for each feature $c^S_{a(m)}(m)$ is necessary.

Considering the definitions of the 20 operators depicted in Figure 3, we can distinguish between the features whose computation rely on *fixed* and *adapted* image areas $a(m)$, where m is the feature index. If we take the 2 intensity operators as an example, we note that their values computed at pixels $^B s^i_c$ or $^D s^i_c$ are independent from the area sizes of $a(00)$ or $a(01)$ centered at these pixels. The only condition is that the area sizes are large enough so that both operators can be applied. In case of the intensity operators, these areas must at least cover the central pixels. The same reasoning can be applied to the operators describing the minimum distance, the maximum distance and the tangent direction. Hence, concerning the 8 features computed with fixed image areas, maximal possible magnitudes of $[M_u \times M_v]$ are considered.

As far as the 12 remaining operators, whose computation relies on adapted image areas, are concerned, the most appropriate size of each area must be defined according to the stripe structures needing to be characterized. Extensive tests have been conducted in this area and are described previously (Caulier et al., 2008). These investigations show that an optimal set of image areas can be defined. Such an optimal set is noted $\mathbf{a}^1$. In order to validate the tests described in (Caulier et al., 2008), a further "non-optimal" set $\mathbf{a}^2$ is taken into consideration. In terms of the adapted image areas, the values of set $\mathbf{a}^2$ are defined as the complementary values of $\mathbf{a}^1$. With respect to the fixed image areas, the values of both sets are identical. These sets are provided in Table 1.

Table 1. Values of the optimal and "non-optimal" sets a^1 and a^2 for the 20 stripe features. The maximum possible area size is noted $M^2 = [M^2 \times M^2]$.

	00	01	02	03	04	05	05	07	08	09
a^1	M^2	M^2	M^2	M^2	M^2	M^2	17^2	17^2	M^2	M^2
a^2	M^2	M^2	M^2	M^2	M^2	M^2	5^2	5^2	M^2	M^2
a^1	17^2	17^2	17^2	17^2	17^2	17^2	5^2	5^2	17^2	17^2
a^2	5^2	5^2	5^2	5^2	5^2	5^2	17^2	17^2	5^2	5^2

Feature Classification

As stated in the introduction, the main purpose of our approach consists of the *definition* and the *selection* of the most appropriate feature sets for the characterization of vertical stripe structures as far as the quality control of specular surfaces is concerned.

The feature sets described in the previous section are evaluated by means of 5 different image sets and 3 different classifiers. Hence, for each of the 4 feature sets, 15 different pattern analysis procedures are considered.

Image Sets

As stated in the previous section, we did not find any approach dedicated to the automatic segmentation of stripe structures. As a consequence, hand-segmented image regions have proven to be more reliable. In order to overcome the subjective approach of manually fixing the size of each pattern so that only the disturbed stripe structure is depicted, 3 sets of inspected surfaces are considered. Segmentation of each set has been done by 3 different persons. Two other sets of reference patterns with fixed sizes of 64^2 pixels and 128^2 pixels were involved.

Thus, image sets Φ^{ad1}, Φ^{ad2}, Φ^{ad3}, Φ^{64x64}, $\Phi^{128x128}$ will be considered. The size of each set is the same, and the same defects are depicted. These 5 sets differ only in the size of the depicted images' region. The stripe patterns were all recorded with the industrial system (Caulier et al., 2007). Typical patterns are depicted in Figure 2.

Classifiers

One aim is to evaluate the proposed features *and not* a certain classifier. Hence, we "restrain" the classification methodology using 2 classifiers: the *Naive Bayes* NB and the *Nearest-Neighbour* k-NN. The two major reasons for using these classifiers are as follows:

First, both methods are based on 2 classification models. The NB method is a probabilistic learner which makes the assumption that the feature distributions of each class can be described by a normal-distribution. The k-NN is an instance-based prediction model (Witten & Eibe, 2008) (instance in the sense of pattern) which does not try to create "rules", but works directly on the patterns themselves. Second, the NB classifier is often seen as a simple, but powerful approach. Witten (Witten & Eibe, 2008) considers that this classifier often outperforms more sophisticated classifiers. Duda even considers that this classifier led to lowest classification errors from all possible classifiers. In terms of the k-NN, Cover (Cover & Hart, 1967) and Guttierez (Gutierrez-Osuna, 2002) show that this method is known to approach the results of the NB classifier in case of a large data set as we have here.

Hence, 3 classifiers were used for our classification purposes: the Naive Bayes NB, the One-Nearest-Neighbor 1-NN and the Three-Nearest-Neighbor 3-NN.

Classification Methodology

Different possible classification methodologies were described in the previous section. The n-fold cross validation and the bootstrap techniques were introduced. It has been demonstrated that 10-fold cross-validation is described in the literature as the most efficient method. Thus, the **classification methodology** that will be used for our stripe classification purposes is a stratified 10-fold method. Each pattern analysis procedure will be evaluated by means of the classification rates C_p, which yields the number of corrected classified patterns after the stratified 10-fold cross validation of the reference datasets.

C_p is the rate in percent of correctly classified defective surfaces belonging to the 3 classes $\{ \Omega_{A,OK} ; \Omega_{R,2D} ; \Omega_{R,3D} \}$, mentioned in the introduction.

Classification Results

The results of the stripe patterns' classification by means of Chen's, Haralick's, Fourier's and Stripe's features, as described by Equations (2), (3), (4) and (5), are provided in Table 2. Each table provides the rates C_p of correctly classified patterns for the 5 image sets Φ^{ad1}, Φ^{ad2}, Φ^{ad3}, Φ^{64x64}, $\Phi^{128x128}$ and the 3 classifiers NB, 1-NN and 3-NN.

The best results for each of the 5 image sets for all the 3 classifiers are highlighted with an *. The best results for each of the 5 image sets for the 1-NN classifier ad for the Fourier and the adapted features are depicted in brackets (). Then, best results for all the 3 classifiers and for all the 5 image sets are provided in bold face.

These results show that the classification rates are hardly dependent on various factors, such as the selected image region to classify or the involved classifier. Nevertheless, it is obvious that the Fourier method with a rate C_p =87.9% and the adapted bottom-up approach with a rate C_p =88.9% both outperform Chen's and Haralick's approaches. With the involved classifiers, the Nearest-Neighbor method leads to higher rates than the Bayes method. In general, the 1-NN leads to higher classification rates than the 3-NN classifier.

With the textural transform approach, lower rates are reached in case of adapted sizes of images patterns, the best results concerns the fixed size pattern of 64^2 pixels. It is the other way round as far as the classification results using the adapted features are concerned. Higher results in case of the classification with the Φ^{ad1} image set are noticeable.

Table 2. Rates of C_p of correctly classified patterns for 5 image sets with Chen's, Haralick's, Fourier textural and adapted features. For each of these 4 groups, the results with the NB, 1-NN and 3-NN classifiers are depicted, and the best rate for each image set is shown by an *. For the Fourier and the adapted features, the best rates for a 1-NN classifier are depicted in brackets.

Vector	ϕ^{all}	ϕ^{ad2}	ϕ^{ad3}	ϕ^{64x64}	$\phi^{128x128}$		ϕ^{all}	ϕ^{ad2}	ϕ^{ad3}	ϕ^{64x64}	$\phi^{128x128}$	Vector
c^C_{255}	74.9	79.5	76.4	77.5	74.8	NB	63.4	62.1	57.2	75.4	61.5	$c^F_{r\theta,vu}$
c^C_{255}	74.9	77.1	75.7	77.5	74.9		58.3	60.0	58.4	67.2	57.8	c^F_r
c^C_{255}	70.9	67.3	66.0	77.3	73.8		66.4	64.5	64.5	80.4	55.8	c^F_θ
c^C_{255}	57.5	60.4	62.3	77.1	75.9		49.2	41.0	44.1	79.3	58.8	c^F_v
							54.8	53.9	54.8	41.0	36.2	c^F_u
c^C_{255}	81.8	82.4	80.3*	82.4*	75.7*	1-NN	(79.2*)	(77.4)	(74.7)	84.9	(84.4)	$c^F_{r\theta,vu}$
c^C_{255}	82.8	80.7	80.4	65.2	72.6		72.7	69.1	65.7	69.8	65.7	c^F_r
c^C_{255}	80.1	81.2	80.1	60.8	73.5		78.2	73.2	72.5	(87.9*)	83.6*	c^F_θ
c^C_{255}	75.6	72.6	72.0	57.9	69.8		76.9	72.7	71.6	79.2	75.9	c^F_v
							65.0	63.0	63.0	75.6	61.5	c^F_u
c^C_{255}	82.3*	83.3*	80.3*	79.4	75.8	3-NN	76.2	77.9*	76.3*	85.3	81.3	$c^F_{r\theta,vu}$
c^C_{255}	80.8	80.8	80.2	78.2	76.6		68.6	67.2	66.2	70.6	65.8	c^F_r
c^C_{255}	77.6	75.1	76.2	77.0	76.3		75.8	70.4	69.5	81.2	82.5	c^F_θ
c^C_{255}	77.4	76.1	77.0	77.2	74.6		74.3	70.3	72.0	77.8	75.7	c^F_v
							63.9	60.0	61.1	75.6	64.7	c^F_u

continued on following page

Table 2. continued

Vector	ϕ^{all}	ϕ^{al2}	ϕ^{al3}	$\phi^{64 \times 64}$	$\phi^{128 \times 128}$		ϕ^{all}	ϕ^{al2}	ϕ^{al3}	$\phi^{64 \times 64}$	$\phi^{128 \times 128}$	Vector
$c^H_{1,1}$	71.2	69.8	70.2	68.4	55.9	NB	84.9	85.9	83.6	84.5	78.3	$c^S_{ar1,br5}$
$c^H_{8,1}$	69.0	68.5	67.9	58.9	58.7		83.7	86.1*	85.2	82.8	60.0	$c^S_{ar1,cm5}$
$c^H_{8,10}$	68.1	62.3	61.9	58.0	54.6		79.6	85.6	84.3	75.8	61.4	$c^S_{ar1,br5}$
$c^H_{8,30}$	63.5	59.2	59.8	57.9	52.3		77.6	85.7	85.0	73.8	57.1	$c^S_{ar1,cm5}$
$c^H_{1,1}$	77.2	76.2	77.2	71.0	66.3	1-NN	88.1	(85.6)	(85.8*)	85.3	(86.2*)	$c^S_{ar1,br5}$
$c^H_{8,1}$	80.9	80.0*	79.3*	79.4	65.1		(88.9*)	82.9	83.5	81.6	82.8	$c^S_{ar1,cm5}$
$c^H_{8,10}$	78.7	77.6	75.4	74.1	62.6		86.1	85.2	84.8	(85.9*)	83.5	$c^S_{ar1,br5}$
$c^H_{8,30}$	81.2	77.9	77.5	72.8*	65.6*		84.6	84.7	83.6	78.4	78.8	$c^S_{ar1,cm5}$
$c^H_{1,1}$	77.1	74.2	76.2	71.6	66.2	3-NN	86.5	82.7	83.0	84.3	80.5	$c^S_{ar1,br5}$
$c^H_{8,1}$	**83.6***	78.6	76.1	75.6	65.9		88.9	82.9	83.5	81.6	82.8	$c^S_{ar1,cm5}$
$c^H_{8,10}$	79.9	77.0	73.9	72.6	62.4		86.1	85.5	84.8	85.9*	83.5	$c^S_{ar1,br5}$
$c^H_{8,30}$	80.4	78.2	76.3	69.1	63.1		84.6	84.7	83.6	78.4	74.8	$c^S_{ar1,cm5}$

In a next step we strive to improve the reached classification results by combining the Fourier and the adapted stripe features. Different selection procedures are investigated to evaluate if further improvements of the classification rates can be achieved.

Feature Selection

Feature Selection Results

In order to address the FSS task within the field of stripe pattern characterization, at least one of the two main generation and evaluation families should be involved. Indeed, it is difficult to predict which of the filter or wrapper approaches are more appropriate for our purposes. The latter are often depicted to provide better classification results as the former, as wrapper-based procedures are better at finding features suited to the learning algorithm (Gutierrez-Osuna, 2002; John et al., 1994). However, this should not be considered as a general definition. Hall (Hall, 1999) demonstrated that in small cases, the filter-based CFS (Correlation-based Feature Selection) approach outperforms some wrapper-based approaches. A major drawback of the latter is that such procedures induce high computational costs, as the whole learning procedure must be invoked at each selection step.

We will therefore consider the CFS filter-based method and the 1-NN wrapper-based approach. The latter was chosen according to the reported classification results in the previous section. In order to be comparable, each involved FSS method must be based on the same search procedures and stopping criteria. For both selection processes a feature forward selection procedure with an amount of backtracking of 5 will be addressed. The iterative process starts with an empty initial feature subset. The feature selection *and* the pattern classification follow a 10-fold cross-validation procedure. The results are depicted in Table 3.

The results reported in Table 3 show the importance of the reference dataset on the classification accuracy, as far as a combined approach and a selection of the combined 2 Fourier and stripe feature sets are concerned. In case of image sets whose sizes are adapted to the characterized surface the CFS-filter-based approach outperforms the 1-NN-wrapper-based method. On the contrary, the 2 image sets with fixed size lead to best classification rates in case of a FSS by means of the wrapper-based method.

So far we have shown that the directional Fourier and the adapted stripe features are the most appropriate within the context of stripe pattern characterization. We have also seen that the classification accuracy can be increased when appropriate feature selection methods are involved. This means that only a subset of the 30 combined features are really relevant in terms of stripe pattern characterization.

Table 3. Rates C_p of correctly classified patterns for the 5 image sets Φ^{ad1}, Φ^{ad2}, Φ^{ad3}, Φ^{64x64}, $\Phi^{128x128}$ for the most appropriate Fourier and stripe feature sets as far as a 1-NN classifier is used, see the rates shown by an * in Tables x and x. Classification rates for the 5 images sets using the combined stripe and Fourier features are $\mathbf{c}^{S,F}$. Classification rates after the selection of the most relevant features by means of a filter-based CFS method are $^{CFS}\mathbf{c}^{S,F}$and a wrapper-based 1-NN method is $^{1\text{-}NN}\mathbf{c}^{S,F}$.

	Φ^{ad1}	Φ^{ad2}	Φ^{ad3}	Φ^{64x64}	$\Phi^{128x128}$
$\mathbf{c}^S$	(88.9)	(85.6)	(85.8)	(85.9)	(86.2)
$\mathbf{c}^F$	(79.2)	(77.4)	(74.7)	(87.9)	(84.4)
$\mathbf{c}^{S,F}$	84.9	84.9	83.7	88.4	84.1
$^{CFS}\mathbf{c}^{S,F}$	**88.8**	**85.7**	**83.7**	89.6	82.5
$^{1\text{-}NN}\mathbf{c}^{S,F}$	85.3	84.9	**83.7**	**91.2**	**88.4**

Table 4 shows the selected features for the 6 best classification results involving the 5 datasets and the 2 addressed feature selection methods.

The values in Table 4 correspond to the number of times each of the 30 features has been selected after a 10-fold cross-validation. The values are comprised between

Table 4. Selected stripe and Fourier features for the 6 FSS methods marked in bold face inTable 3. The features are selected using a CFS-based method, a wrapper-1-NN-based method and a 10-fold cross-validation. The 10 time, 9 time and 8 time selected features are marked with ***, ** and *.

	Φ^{ad1}	Φ^{ad2}	Φ^{ad3}	Φ^{64x64}	$\Phi^{128x128}$	$\Phi^{128x128}$
	CFS	CFS	CFS	Wrp	Wrp	Wrp
$c^S(0)$	10***	10***	10***	5	0	0
$c^S(1)$	9**	10***	10***	4	0	0
$c^S(2)$	4	0	0	7	0	1
$c^S(3)$	3	10***	10***	6	2	0
$c^S(4)$	1	9**	9**	0	0	0
$c^S(5)$	0	0	0	5	5	1
$c^S(6)$	6	8*	8*	5	8*	3
$c^S(7)$	4	6	5	8*	6	7
$c^S(8)$	0	0	0	2	5	5
$c^S(9)$	0	0	0	0	8*	7
$c^S(10)$	1	0	0	5	4	1

continued on following page

Table 4. Continued

	ϕ^{ad1}	ϕ^{ad2}	ϕ^{ad3}	ϕ^{64x64}	$\phi^{128x128}$	$\phi^{128x128}$
	CFS	**CFS**	**CFS**	**Wrp**	**Wrp**	**Wrp**
$c^S(11)$	0	0	0	0	0	0
$c^S(12)$	9**	9**	9**	6	3	4
$c^S(13)$	1	3	3	7	4	5
$c^S(14)$	6	9**	9**	3	3	1
$c^S(15)$	7	0	0	2	1	5
$c^S(16)$	0	0	0	0	1	0
$c^S(17)$	0	0	0	0	0	0
$c^S(18)$	10***	10***	10***	8*	10***	10***
$c^S(19)$	10***	10***	10***	6	8*	7
$c^F_r(0)$	0	0	0	0	-	0
$c^F_r(1)$	1	0	0	2	-	0
$c^F_r(2)$	0	0	2	0	-	0
$c^F_r(3)$	0	0	0	1	-	0
$c^F_r(4)$	0	0	0	3	-	0
$c^F_r(5)$	0	1	2	1	-	0
$c^F_r(6)$	0	0	0	0	-	0
$c^F_r(7)$	0	0	0	0	-	0
$c^F_\theta(0)$	0	0	0	2	0	0
$c^F_\theta(1)$	0	0	0	5	2	7
$c^F_\theta(2)$	0	0	0	1	4	1
$c^F_\theta(3)$	1	0	0	0	4	4
$c^F_\theta(4)$	0	0	0	1	6	8*
$c^F_\theta(5)$	10***	10***	10***	2	10***	6
$c^F_\theta(6)$	0	0	0	1	0	3
$c^F_\theta(7)$	0	0	0	0	1	7
$c^F_\theta(8)$	0	0	0	0	1	5
$c^F_\theta(9)$	0	0	4	2	2	6
$c^F_v(0)$	0	0	0	0	-	0
$c^F_v(1)$	0	0	0	1	-	3
$c^F_v(2)$	0	0	0	0	-	0
$c^F_v(3)$	0	0	0	0	-	0
$c^F_v(4)$	0	0	0	1	-	0
$c^F_u(0)$	0	0	0	0	-	0
$c^F_u(1)$	0	0	0	2	-	0

continued on following page

Table 4. Continued

	Φ^{ad1}	Φ^{ad2}	Φ^{ad3}	Φ^{64x64}	$\Phi^{128x128}$	$\Phi^{128x128}$
	CFS	**CFS**	**CFS**	**Wrp**	**Wrp**	**Wrp**
$c^F_u(2)$	5	0	0	0	-	0
$c^F_u(3)$	0	0	0	0	-	9**
$c^F_u(4)$	10***	10***	9**	1	-	5
$c^F_u(5)$	0	0	0	0	-	0
$c^F_u(6)$	7	0	0	1	-	0
$c^F_u(7)$	0	0	0	0	-	0
$c^F_v(8)$	0	0	0	1	-	0
$c^F_v(9)$	0	0	0	3	-	0

0 and 10, so that the relevance of each feature is proportional to this value. The 10 time, 9 time and 8 time selections of a feature are therefore marked with ***, ** and *. We noticed that some features have never been selected regardless of the FSS approach or the reference dataset. This is particularly the case for the Fourier directional features. In the same manner, the reported results demonstrate that some features have a high relevance in terms of stripe pattern characterization. This is particularly true for the "number of elements" $c^S(18)$ and $c^S(19)$ stripe features and the Fourier directional $c^F_\theta(5)$ and horizontal $c^F_u(4)$ features.

The quality of a feature selection process can be evaluated by means of the classification rates reached, but also in terms of the number of relevant features. This last value can also be retrieved from Table 4. The 1-NN-wrapper-based FSS method applied for the classification of image set Φ^{64^2} leads to a classification rate of 91.2%, which is the highest rate depicted in Table 3. With respect to the selected features using this FSS approach, we observed that nearly half of the 30 initial features have a poor relevance, as these have been selected only 0, 1 or 2 times after the 10-fold cross-validation process. Moreover, only a sixth part of the initial 30 features is highly relevant, as these features have been selected at least more than 8 times after the 10-fold cross-validation process.

FUTURE RESEARCH DIRECTIONS

The major purpose of the research in this chapter is the characterization of colorimetric patterns for the detection of organic components. In order to tackle the real-time discrimination, i.e. optimized in terms of detection rate and inspection speed, a reference real-time vision system with its reference dataset was considered. It has been demonstrated that the classification task of colorimetric patterns is equivalent to the structured pattern classification task of the Φ transformed colorimetric patterns.

Thus, concerning the reference structured-based machine vision system, the particular case of the real-time quality control of specular surfaces has been addressed. The results achieved show, that the general method consisting of (i) subdividing the image characterization approach into its main steps, (ii) improving each of these steps and (iii) testing each combination with the classification rate as quality criterion, permits the retrieval of the most adequate and optimal stripe pattern characterization methodology.

Preliminary research on the proposed developments in this chapter was done during the elaboration of an existing quality control system. At that time, the main purposes were to develop a robust, in terms of non optimal recording conditions, and accurate, for the detection of all defective surfaces, system. Hence, further research opportunities would be to implement, i.e. to adapt, the proposed developments in the existing quality control system, i.e. to bring more "intelligence" to the existing technique. This would define new problems to be solved, as a major consideration for inline inspection is the real-time processing of the acquired data. Under this point of view, new optimization foci will be the use of other methodologies for feature selection, or the optimization of the considered approaches for feature extraction for example.

Hence, future trends are the fusion of different approaches, so as to propose more compact but also more efficient solutions encompassing and fusing different techniques. This combination concerns all the major steps of the surface inspection procedure, i.e. the data acquisition, with fusion of at least 2 different sensor technologies, but also the data processing, as developed in this chapter. Hence, a possible opportunity could be the development of more "intelligent" system techniques for the generalization of the proposed method to more complex surfaces.

Concerning further research, it would be interesting to elaborate of a huge reference dataset of organic components represented e.g. by colorimetric patterns. Such a gold standard dataset could be used to compare different pattern discrimination approaches, thus permitting a better evaluation of feature-based approaches, as developed in this chapter, but also other algorithms proposed in the literature, as e.g. the color histograms. More generally speaking, the proposed method, using local and spatial information, which was developed in case sensor arrays, could be adapted to other geometries, as in case of cylindrical fiber sensor distal ends. Also, applications to different representations, as in case of line sensors with time variations, are also thinkable.

CONCLUSION

A general approach of the automatic classification of complex patterns has been addressed in this chapter. The case of stripe structures was taken into consideration, as it was demonstrated that classification task of such structures is equivalent to the discrimination of colorimetric patterns, provided that an appropriate transformation, linking the 2 patterns types, was previously defined.

Based on the stripe images generated by an existing illumination technique for the visual enhancement of defective specular surface parts, several pattern recognition processes have been evaluated. The general scope of the stripe image interpretation process as stated in this chapter has been addressed by means of the combination of different image segmentation, feature retrieval, pattern classification, feature combination and feature selection techniques.

It has been shown, that best classification rates can be reached in case of a combination of specific top-down and adapted bottom-up feature extraction approaches. It was further demonstrated that higher classification rates could be obtained when appropriate FSS techniques are used. A sixth part of the features was highly relevant, whereas only half of them showed to be virtually irrelevant.

Such results are very encouraging, as they demonstrate that it was possible to tackle the optimization task of stripe image content description by means of a stepwise and adapted methodology. The optimization process consisted of increasing the stripe pattern detection rates after each step of the pattern recognition process by means of the combination and selection of general and specific approaches.

To conclude, a similar methodology could be applied in case of the optimization of any processing chain where each element of the chain interacts with the surrounding elements and at least influences the output of the chain. The number of possible approaches for each element makes the testing of all the resulting combinations nearly impossible to realize. Hence, stepwise optimization approaches as addressed in this chapter are preferred.

REFERENCES

Asada, M., Ichikawa, I., & Tsuji, S. (1988). Determining surface orientation by projecting a stripe pattern. *IEEE Transactions on Pattern Analysis and Machine Intelligence, 10*(5), 749–754. doi:10.1109/34.6787

Bermak, A., Belhouari, S. B., Shi, M., & Martinez, D. (2005). Pattern recognition techniques for odor discrimination in gas sensor array. In Grimes, C. A., Dickey, E. C., & Pishko, M. V. (Eds.), *The encyclopedia of sensors*. Valencia, CA: American Scientific Publishers.

Cai, K., Maekawa, T., & Takada, T. (2002). Identification of odors using a sensor array with kinetic working temperature and Fourier spectrum analysis. *IEEE Sensors Journal, 2*(3), 230–234. doi:10.1109/JSEN.2002.800285

Caulier, Y., Goldschmidt, A., Spinnler, K., & Arnold, M. (2009). Automatic detection of surface and structural defects on reflecting workpieces. *Photonik International, 2*, 30–32.

Caulier, Y., Spinnler, K., Bourennane, S., & Wittenberg, T. (2007). New structured illumination technique for the inspection of high reflective surfaces. *EURASIP Journal on Image and Video Processing.* doi:.doi:10.1155/2008/237459

Caulier, Y., Spinnler, K., Wittenberg, T., & Bourennane, S. (2008). Specific features for the analysis of fringe images. *Optical Engineering (Redondo Beach, Calif.), 47.*

Chen, R., Xu, J.-H., & Jiang, Y.-D. (2009). Colorimetric sensor arrays system based on FPGA for image recognition. *Journal of Electronic Science and Technology of China, 7*(2), 139–145.

Chen, Y., Nixon, M., & Thomas, D. (1995). Statistical geometrical features for texture classification. *Pattern Recognition, 28*(4), 537–552. doi:10.1016/0031-3203(94)00116-4

Cover, T. M., & Hart, P. E. (1967). Nearest neighbor pattern classification. *IEEE Transactions on Information Theory, 13*(1), 21–27. doi:10.1109/TIT.1967.1053964

Dash, M., & Liu, N. (1997). Feature selection for classification. *Intelligent Data Analysis: An International Journal, 1*(3), 131–156. doi:10.1016/S1088-467X(97)00008-5

Delcroix, G., Seulin, R., Lamalle, B., Gorria, P., & Merienne, F. (2001). Study of the imaging conditions and processing for the aspect control of specular surfaces. *International Society for Electronic Imaging, 10*(1), 196–202. doi:10.1117/1.1314333

Dickinson, T. A., White, J., Kauer, J. S., & Walt, D. R. (1996). A chemical-detecting system based on a cross-reactive optical sensor array. *Nature, 382*, 697–700. doi:10.1038/382697a0

Djouadi, A., Snorrason, Ö., & Garber, F. F. (1990). The quality of training sample estimates of the Bhattacharyya coefficient. *IEEE Transactions on Pattern Analysis and Machine Intelligence, 12*(1), 92–97. doi:10.1109/34.41388

Dy, J. G., Brodley, C. E., Kak, A., Broderick, L. S., & Aisen, A. M. (2003). Unsupervised feature selection applied to content-based retrieval of lung images. *IEEE Transactions on Pattern Analysis and Machine Intelligence, 25*(3), 373–378. doi:10.1109/TPAMI.2003.1182100

Efron, B., & Tibshirani, R. J. (1993). *An introduction to the bootstrap.* New York, NY: Chapman & Hall.

Fisher, R. B., & Naidu, D. K. (1996). A comparison of algorithms for subpixel peak detection. In *Image technology, advances in image processing, multimedia and machine vision,* (pp. 385-404).

Gutierrez-Osuna, R. (2002). Pattern analysis for machine olfaction: A review. *IEEE Sensors Journal, 2*(3), 189–202. doi:10.1109/JSEN.2002.800688

Hall, M. A. (1999). *Correlation-based feature selection for machine learning.* New Zealand: University of Waikato.

Haralick, R. (1979). Statistical and structural approaches to texture. *Proceedings of the IEEE Conference on Computer Vision and Pattern Recognition (CVPR'1979), 67,* (pp. 786–804).

Haralick, R. M., Shanmugam, K., & Dinstein, I. (1973). Texture features for image classification. [SMC]. *IEEE Transactions on Systems, Man, and Cybernetics, 3*(6), 610–621. doi:10.1109/TSMC.1973.4309314

Harris, P. D., Andrews, M. K., & Partridge, A. C. (1997). *Conductive polymer sensor measurements.* International Conference on Solid State Sensors and Actuators (pp. 1063–1066). doi:10.1109/SENSOR.1997.635377

Huttenlocher, D. P., Klanderman, G. A., & Rucklidge, W. J. (1993). Comparing images using the Hausdorff distance. *IEEE Transactions on Pattern Analysis and Machine Intelligence, 15*(9), 850–863. doi:10.1109/34.232073

Jain, A., & Zongker, D. (1997). Feature selection: Evaluation, application, and small sample performance. *IEEE Transactions on Pattern Analysis and Machine Intelligence, 19*(2), 153–158. doi:10.1109/34.574797

Jatmiko, W., Fukuda, T., Arai, F., & Kusumoputro, B. (2004). Artificial odor discrimination system using multiple quartz-resonator sensor and neural network for recognizing fragrance mixtures. In *Proceedings of the 2004 International Symposium on Micro-Nanomechatronics and Human Science* (pp. 169–174). doi:10.1109/MHS.2004.1421296

John, G. N., Kohavi, R., & Pfleger, K. (1994). *Irrelevant features and the subset selection problem.* International Conference on Machine Learning, (pp. 121–129).

Jüptner, W., Kreis, T., Mieth, U., & Osten, W. (1994). Application of neural networks and knowledge-based systems for automatic identification of fault-indicating fringe patterns. *Proceedings of SPIE, Photomechanics, 2342,* 16–26.

Kammel, S. (2004). *Deflektometrische Untersuchung spiegelnd reflektierender Freiformflächen.* University of Karlsruhe (TH), Germany.

Kammel, S., & Puente Leon, F. (2003). Deflektometrie zür Qualitätsprüfung spiegelnd reflektierender Oberflächen. *Technisches Messen, 70,* 193–198. doi:10.1524/teme.70.4.193.20181

Kohavi, R. (1995). *A study of cross-validation and bootstrap for accuracy estimation and model selection* (pp. 1137–1145). International Joint Conferences on Artificial Intelligence.

Krüger, S., Wernicke, G., Osten, W., Kayser, D., Demoli, N., & Gruber, H. (2001). Fault detection and feature analysis in interferometric fringe patterns by the application of wavelet filters in convolution processors. *International Society for Electronic Imaging, 10*(1), 228–232. doi:10.1117/1.1318908

Lakshminarasimhan, A. L., & Dasarathy, B. V. (1975). A unified approach to feature selection and learning in unsupervised environments. *IEEE Transactions on Computers, C-24*(9), 948–952. doi:10.1109/T-C.1975.224346

Li, X. (2000). Wavelet transform for detection of partial fringe patterns induced by defects in nondestructive testing of holographic interferometry and electronic speckle pattern interferometry. *Journal of Optical Engineering, 39,* 2821–2827. doi:10.1117/1.1308485

Liu, X.-M., Li, K., & Huang, H.-K. (2003). Feature selection for handwritten Chinese characters based on machine learning. *Proceedings of the 2nd International Conference on Machine Learning and Cybernetics (ICMLC '03),* (pp. 2399–2402).

Lonergan, M. C., Freund, M. S., Severin, E. J., Doleman, B. J., Grubbs, R. H., & Lewis, N. S. (1997). Array-based vapor sensing using chemically sensitive, polymer composite resistors. In *Proceedings of the IEEE Aerospace Conference* (pp. 583–631). doi:10.1109/AERO.1997.574914

Marino, P., Dominguez, M. A., & Alonso, M. (1999). *Machine-vision based detection for sheet metal industries.* The 25th Annual Conference of the IEEE Industrial Electronics Society (IECON'1999), 3, (pp. 1330–1335).

Materka, A., & Strzelecki, M. (1998). Texture analysis methods-a review. Lodz, Poland: Technical University of Lodz, Institute of Electronics. *Stefanowskiego, 18,* 90–924.

Mihran, T., & Anil, J. (1998). Texture analysis. In C. N. Chen, L. F. Pau & P. S. P. (Eds.), *The handbook of pattern recognition and computer vision* (2nd ed.) (pp. 207–248).

Mucciardi, A. N., & Gose, E. E. (1971). A comparison of seven techniques for choosing subsets of pattern recognition properties. *IEEE Transactions on Computers*, *C-20*(9), 1023–1031. doi:10.1109/T-C.1971.223398

Nayar, S. K., Sanderson, A. C., Weiss, L. E., & Simon, D. A. (1990). Specular surface inspection using structured highlight and Gaussian images. *IEEE Transactions on Robotics and Automation*, *6*(2), 208–218. doi:10.1109/70.54736

Niemann, H. (2003). *Klassifikation von Mustern* (2nd ed.). Berlin, Germany: Springer.

Paakkari, J. (1998). *Online flatness measurement of large steel plates using Moire topography*. Finland: University of Oulu.

Peng, N., Long, F., & Ding, C. (2005). Feature selection based on mutual information: Criteria of max-dependency, max-relevance, and min-redundancy. *IEEE Transactions on Pattern Analysis and Machine Intelligence*, *27*(8), 1226–1238. doi:10.1109/TPAMI.2005.159

Pernkopf, F. (2004). 3D surface inspection using coupled HMMs. *Proceedings of the 17th International Conference on Pattern Recognition (ICPR '2004)*.

Puente Leon, F., & Beyerer, J. (1997). Active vision and sensor fusion for inspection of metallic surfaces. In, D. P. Casasent (Ed.), *Proceedings of SPIE Intelligent Robots and Computer Vision XVI: Algorithms, Techniques, Active Vision, and Materials Handling*, (pp. 394–405).

Qian, K., Seah, N. S., & Asundi, A. (2005). *Fringe 2005: Fault detection from temporal unusualness in fringe patterns. Stuttgart, Germany*. W.: Osten.

Rakow, N. A., & Suslick, K. S. (2000). A colorimetric sensor array for odour visualization. *Nature*, *406*, 710–713..doi:10.1038/35021028

Raudys, S. J., & Jain, A. K. (1991). Small sample size effects in statistical pattern recognition: Recommendations for practitioners. *IEEE Transactions on Pattern Analysis and Machine Intelligence*, *13*(3), 252–264. doi:10.1109/34.75512

Reindl, I., & O'Leary, P. (2007). *Instrumentation and measurement method for the inspection of peeled steel rods*. IEEE Conference on Instrumentation and Measurement (IMTC '2007).

Suslick, K. S., Rakow, N. A., & Sen, A. (2004). Colorimetric sensor arrays for molecular recognition. *Tetrahedron*, *60*, 11133–11138. doi:10.1016/j.tet.2004.09.007

Talavera, L. (2000). Dependency-based feature selection for clustering symbolic data. *Intelligent Data Analysis*, *4*, 19–28.

Unnikrishnan, R., Pantofaru, C., & Hebert, M. (2007). Toward objective evaluation of image segmentation algorithms. *IEEE Transactions on Pattern Analysis and Machine Intelligence, 29*(6), 929–944. doi:10.1109/TPAMI.2007.1046

Wagner, T. (1999). *Automatische Konfiguration von Bildverarbeitungssysteme.* Germany: University of Erlangen-Nürnberg.

Weiss, S. M. (1991). Small sample error rate estimation for k-NN classifiers. *IEEE Transactions on Pattern Analysis and Machine Intelligence, 13*(3), 285–289. doi:10.1109/34.75516

Weska, J. S. (1978). A survey of threshold selection techniques. *Computer Graphics and Image Processing, 7*, 259–265. doi:10.1016/0146-664X(78)90116-8

Wholtjen, H., & Dessy, R. (1979). Surface acoustic wave probe chemical analysis. *Analytical Chemistry, 51*(9), 1458–1464. doi:10.1021/ac50045a024

Witten, I. H., & Eibe, F. (2008). *Data mining: Practical machine learning tools and techniques*, 2nd ed. Amsterdam, The Netherlands: Morgan Kaufmann/Elsevier (The Morgan Kaufmann series in data management systems).

Zhi, H., & Johansson, R. B. (1992). *Interpretation and classification of fringe patterns*. 11th International Conference on Image, Speech and Signal Analysis (IAPR'1992), 3, (pp. 105–108).

Chapter 8
Detection of Diseases and Volatile Discrimination of Plants:
An Electronic Nose and Self–Organizing Maps Approach

Reza Ghaffari
University of Warwick, UK

Evor L. Hines
University of Warwick, UK

Fu Zhang
University of Warwick, UK

Mark S. Leeson
University of Warwick, UK

D. Daciana Iliescu
University of Warwick, UK

Richard Napier
University of Warwick, UK

ABSTRACT

The diagnosis of plant diseases is an important part of commercial greenhouse crop production and can enable continued disease and pest control. A plant subject to infection typically releases exclusive volatile organic compounds (VOCs) which may be detected by appropriate sensors. In this work, an Electronic Nose (EN) is employed as an alternative to Gas Chromatography - Mass Spectrometry (GC-MS) to sample the VOCs emitted by control and artificially infected tomato plants. A case study in which powdery mildew and spider mites may be present on tomato plants is considered. The data from the EN was analyzed and visualized using Fuzzy

DOI: 10.4018/978-1-61520-915-6.ch008

C-Mean Clustering (FCM) and Self-Organizing Maps (SOM). The VOC samples from healthy plants were successfully distinguished from the infected ones using the clustering techniques. This study suggests that the proposed methodology is promising for enhancing the automated detection of crop pests and diseases and may be an attractive tool to be deployed in horticultural settings.

INTRODUCTION

The main objectives of a rapid plant disease detection system are first to determine if the plant is unhealthy or stressed and second to find the reasons a plant is unhealthy which will lead to a proper diagnosis and treatments. Reliable disease detection is vitally important to assist disease and pest control within both large and medium scale commercial greenhouses for economic, production, and horticultural benefits. The process of plant disease diagnosis is a complex and multifaceted one but in recent years there have been diverse modifications of existing procedures for detection of plant pathogens and rapid advancement in research for new technologies and enhanced instrumentations. Visual inspections by growers as well as laboratory based methods such as Light Microscopy, Polymerase Chain Reaction (PCR), Serology, Double-Stranded RNA Analysis and Nucleic Acid probes are within the most widely used procedures of plants pest and disease diagnosis (Putnam, 1995). In spite of availability of these methods, the laboratory based techniques are often time consuming, expensive, require destructive sampling and necessitate skilled experts. Therefore, there is a demand for a fast and sensitive method for the rapid detection of plant diseases. More recent methods such as spectroscopic and imaging techniques as well as the application of analyzing the VOCs emitted by plant as possible biomarkers for disease detection have been studied by researchers (Laothawornkitkul et. al, 2008). These methods could be deployed in an agricultural setting for a rapid, reliable and real-time plant disease monitoring and management. The early detection of crop diseases prior the onset of disease symptoms and visual signs, may be a very valuable source of information for executing appropriate pest management strategies and disease control measures by growers to prevent the spread of diseases within the commercial greenhouses (Sankaran et al., 2010).

In this chapter, we investigate plants behavior when infected by pest and disease and explore the possibility of employing gas sensor arrays coupled with suitable intelligent systems technique to categories the VOCs emitted by the plants. In next section we will debate the plant systematic approach in terms of emitting VOCs when under attacked by pest and diseases.

PLANT DISEASES AND VOCS

The first studies on the emission of VOCs from plants were conducted in the Soviet Union in the 1920s and 1930s and since then VOCs from many plant speices have been investigated (Kesselmeier & Staudt, 2004). Generally, in order to effectively combat invasion by microbial pathogens, attacks by herbivorous insects or even mechanical damage, plants require a broad range of defense mechanisms (Choudhary, Johr & Prakash, 2008). Hence, they have evolved various strategies to defend themselves against herbivores and pathogens; one of which is to emit specific and exclusive VOCs to battle the potential attackers. Although some of these strategies are constitutive and present at all times, others are induced only in response to herbivore feeding or pathogen infection (Frost, et al., 2008). These defenses are often categorized in two groups: a) direct defense in which they emit toxic or repel VOCs that reduce herbivores and b) indirect defense where volatiles attract parasitoids that increase herbivore mortality (Fernandes et al., 2010; Butrym & Hartman, 1998). In view of both direct and indirect defenses, plant VOCs play significant roles in plant–herbivore and plant–pathogen exchanges and are promising targets for improved crop protection (Kant et al., 2009). The composition of VOCs emitted by plants depends on the mode of damage such as single wounding, continuous wounding, herbivore feeding, and egg deposition (Maffei, 2010). Biologically, VOCs are produced by a wide range of physiological processes in many different parts of the plant tissues and are themselves also extremely diverse and usually include *alkanes*, *alkenes*, *alcohols*, *aldehydes*, *eters*, *esters* and *carboxylic acids* (Peñuelas, 2004).

Emission of VOCs from the plant when under attack creates the opportunity for developing a rapid and non-destructive diagnosis tool which can be deployed in commercial greenhouses. One of the most well-known devices that have been employed in recent years for examining plant and non-plant species VOCs is Gas Chromatography - Mass Spectrometry also known as GC-MS.

Gas Chromatography Mass Spectrometry (GC-MS)

Previously, Gas Chromatography - Mass Spectrometry (GC-MS) has been extensively used to investigate the VOCs in both plant and non-plant species (Lytovchenko et al., 2009). Several studies were conducted using GS-MS to investigate diverse infected crops species (Corrado, Guerrieri et al., 2007; Deng et al., 2004). For example, in a study conducted by Hayase, One hundred and thirty compounds where found when VOCs obtained from two varieties of tomato fruits at various ripening stages were examined (Hayase, Chung & Kato, 1984). A separate study was performed to successfully detect and identify specific viruses that can affect tomato plants health by using GC-MS instrumentation (Blouin et al., 2010).

Preparing samples for GC-MS involves the person to follow a specific and precise procedure which may be time consuming and costly. Moreover, analyzing the data will be a complex process which needs to be carried out by a highly-skilled expert. Although GC-MS analysis, after optimization of the system, was shown to be a highly reproducible and reliable technique for VOC analysis (Tikunov et al., 2004), the instrumentation is relatively bulky, expensive and complicated which makes it an unattractive tool for rapid, cheap and portable disease detection system for day to day usage in commercial greenhouses.

Alternatively, Sensor array systems (i.e. Electronic Noses) are known to offer a more attractive means of investigating VOCs as they are relatively cheaper, portable and can facilitate automated sampling procedures.

Electronic Nose

Artificial olfaction instrumentation, also known as Electronic Noses (ENs) has been originated and widely developed in last two decades and have been extensively used in diverse applications from chemical engineering to medical diagnosis. An EN is a machine usually coupled with classification software that is designed to distinguish and discriminate among complex odors using a gas sensor array. EN is developed to mimic the human olfactory system and was evolved dramatically as different types of sensor arrays were built in to it to make it suitable for specific odors and applications. This type of EN system was introduced in 1982 by Dodd and Persaud from the Warwick Olfaction Research Group, UK and several applications of EN were investigated (Gardner & Pang, 1996). The EN technology has been used in a variety of applications, including food and fruit quality measurements (Borah et al., 2008; Peris & Escuder-Gilabert, 2009), animal disease diagnosis (Dutta et al., 2005), automotive industry (Kalman et al., 1999) and plant health monitoring (Baratto et al., 2005).

ENs are internationally well known for being able to solve a wide variety of problems with a high precision at a potentially low cost. Later in this chapter, we will investigate the response of EN sensors and consequently its capacity in classifying plants VOCs.

CASE STUDY

Tomato Plant and EN

Currently, Tomato (Solanum lycopersicum) is one of the most valuable glasshouse crops in the world (Gutiérrez-Aguirre et al., 2009). Therefore, the VOCs emitted from its crop has been in centre of interest for researchers to be investigated by EN and several studies were carried on both the plant itself and the products of its fruit (Concina et al., 2009; Linforth et al., 1994). In a study conducted using EN, researchers could determine the optimum shelf-life for tomato fruits when they were on shop floors (Bern et al., 2003). Moreover, in 2006, there has been an investigation to find different stages of ripeness in tomato fruit and EN was proven to be able to discover four phases of ripeness from *unripe* to *fully ripe* (Gómez et al., 2006).

In this case study, we used tomato plant samples to conduct an EN-enabled experiment. The healthy tomato plants were infected by Spider Mites and Powdery Mildew and the VOCs emission then analyzed by EN.

Spider Mites and Powdery Mildew

The spider mite (Tetranychus urticae Koch) is a generalist that can feed on several hundreds of host plant species. In a study conducted by Boom, VOCs emitted by spider mite infested plants of 11 species were compared. It was evident that almost all of the investigated plant species produced compounds that dominated the volatile blend (Boom et. al, 2004). Remarkably, in a distinct study, it was apparent that VOCs emitted while spider mites are feeding on a plant, attract the carnivorous mite Phytoseiulus persimilis, a specialist predator of the spider mites that exterminates entire prey populations, and thus the volatiles contribute indirectly to plant defense (Dicke et. al, 1999). These VOCs are among the ones that our work was aimed at tracing and identifying by EN which will allow us to differentiate between healthy and infected plants.

Powdery mildew is a recognized disease that has been observed frequently in last few decades both in the tomato field and in the greenhouse all over the world (Belanger & Jarvis, 1994). Mildew colonies of white color appear on the upper and occasionally on the lower surfaces of the leaves (Kiss, 1996). Severe infections can lead to reduction in fruit size and quality (Jones et. al, 2001).

Part of this study was aiming at revealing the changes in VOCs emitting by tomato plant when infected by Powdery Mildew. The next section will cover the experimental methods and samples used.

SAMPLES AND MATERIALS

In order to replicate the greenhouse environment, we used disinfected clear glass boxes to house one plant each. Three clean glass boxes (150cm × 50cm × 50cm) simulated the greenhouse environment. A control plant was kept healthy throughout the experiment.

Humidity and temperature were logged at all times with the interval set at 10 minutes between each reading. Clean air was filtered and pumped into each box to create positive pressure inside the boxes which decreased the possibility of cross contamination between the boxes as well as maintaining environmental parameters constant throughout the experiment. Prior to sampling, air inflow was switched off for 3 hours to allow the volatile concentration around the plants to build up. The EN device was switched on for one hour prior to taking any readings to warm up/ initialize the sensor arrays. Individual box tubes were connected to the EN to take readings of volatile concentrations. Sampling tubes kept separated to reduce the possibility of cross contamination. A solution of butan-2-ol (2% in distilled water) was used as a reference sample and also acted as a sensor wash to regenerate sensor surfaces. Since the production of VOCs can be variable depending on ambient light levels (Heil, 2008), the light level was carefully controlled during the experiment.

The next section of this chapter will cover the data analysis methods that has been used to process and analyze the data acquired by the EN.

DATA ANALYSIS AND METHODS

During the experiment, the EN (Bloodhound model ST214, Scensive Technologies Ltd., Normanton, UK) continuously recorded the responses from its array of 13 sensors and saved it as a matrix for later processing. The following acquisition profile of the data was used for VOC analysis by the EN: 10 s absorption, 5 s pause, 20 s desorption and 5 s flush. The data generated by the EN was pre-processed and key dataset parameters were determined and extracted from the measurements: a) Divergence b) Absorption c) Desorption and e) Area thus forming a 52 component (13×4) matrix.

The dataset is comprised of three subsets which will be referred to as tomato (containing healthy and powdery mildew and spider mite infected plants) dataset. The entire dataset was then normalized by mean to set their range to [0, 1].

Figure 1 illustrates the average response area of each sample taken from healthy, spider mite infected and powdery mildew infested tomato plants on 4 days post infection (DPI).

Initially, the graph shows that the EN was able to be more responsive to the Powdery mildew and Spider Mite infected tomato plant. As discussed in previous sections, this may be due to the specific VOCs that the plant is releasing to combat the attackers (direct defense). However, to confirm this, smarter intelligent processing techniques are required. Data processing and analysis is a fundamental part of any sensors array system, EN in particular. Previously, a number of supervised and unsupervised pattern recognition techniques have been explored by researchers for

Figure 1. EN Average Response Area – 4 Day Post Infection – Blue: Powdery Mildew Infected – Orange: Spider Mite Infected – Green: Healthy Plant

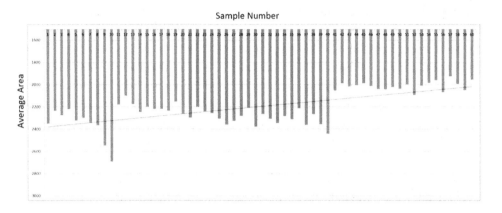

the analysis of sensors array and specially EN generated dataset, notably parametric methods (linear or quadratic), nearest neighbors, and neural networks such as multilayer perceptrons (MLP) and radial basis functions (RBF).

In the next sections we evaluate the usage of clustering and classifying tools to analyze EN dataset. The objective of most clustering methods is to provide valuable information by grouping unknown samples in clusters; within each cluster the data exhibits similarity. Similarity is defined by a distance measure, and global objective functional or regional graph-theoretic criteria are optimized to find the optimal partitions of dataset (Rezaee, 1998). The next section will discuss these methods in more details.

Fuzzy C-Mean Clustering

In order to explore the (dis)similarity within the dataset, we have used Fuzzy C-Mean Clustering (FCM) which reveals the patterns and structures hidden in the dataset. FCM generates a fuzzy partition based on the idea of partial membership expressed by the degree of membership of each pattern in a given cluster (Carvalho, 2007). Assume a set of unlabelled/unknown dataset $X = \{x_1, x_2, ..., x_n\}$ where n is the number of data points in X and $x_k \in R^p$ where p is the number of features in each vector then the output will be a c-partition of X. Therefore, multiplication of c and x will produce matrix U. A set of vectors $V = \{ v_1, v_2, ..., v_n \} \subset R^p$ represents the cluster centers also known as centroids. The objective function can be optimized by the following equation (Amiri, 2003):

$$\min(U,V)\left\{J_m\left(U,V\right)=\sum_{i=1}^{c}\sum_{k=1}^{n}u_{ik}^m D_{ik}^2\right\} \tag{1}$$

The elements of U must satisfy the following constrain:

$$\sum_{i=1}^{c}u_{ik}=1,\forall k \tag{2}$$

The distance between clusters will be calculated by:

$$D_{ik}^2=x_k-v_{iA}^2 \tag{3}$$

Optimizing the gradient of J_m with respect to V:

$$u_{ik}=\left[\sum_{j=1}^{c}\left(\frac{D_{ik}}{D_{jk}}\right)^{\frac{2}{m-1}}\right]^{-1},\forall i,k\sqcup U_t=F_\partial(V_{t-1}) \tag{4}$$

Optimizing the gradient of J_m with respect to U:

$$v_i=\left(\frac{\sum_{k=1}^{n}u_{ik}^m x_k}{\sum_{k=1}^{n}u_{ik}^m}\right),\forall i\sqcup V_t=G_\partial(U_{t-1}) \tag{5}$$

FCM requires the estimated number of clusters so it can categories samples into separate clusters. In order to determine the optimal number of cluster for each dataset, we have calculated the Classification Entropy (CE), Partition Index (SC), Separation Index (S), Xie Index (XB), Dunn Index (DI). Each of these indices when minimised indicate an optimal number of clusters. The local minima of CE, SC, S, XB, DI and ADI are 0.1, 0.18, 0.004, 2.92, 0.08 and 0.013 respectively. Figure 2 demonstrates the calculated value for each index. As shown, the optimal cluster number is 3 representing healthy, powdery mildew infected and spider mite infested plants.

We chose the optimal number of clusters to c = 3 and will use this value later in our FCM clustering tool (Amiri, 2003).

Figure 2. CE, SC, S, XB, DI and ADI values calculated so an optimal cluster value (c = 3) could be used

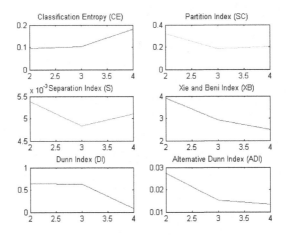

FCM was applied to 4 and 6 DPI dataset. During the optimization of clusters the FCM parameters were fixed to the following values: $m = 2$, min $c = 2$, max $c = 4$ and $p = 1$ for each cluster. As illustrated in figure 3, the clusters are not separated quite well in 4DPI, however, in 6 DPI, three separate clusters are clearly visible. The centroids of each cluster are also noticeable. This shows the spread of disease and its effect on the VOCs of the infected tomato plant and consequently the EN sensor response changes in respect to the health state of the tomato plant.

After investigating the dataset by applying FCM, we analyze the membership of each sample to each cluster. Figure 4 demonstrate the membership of each sample point to each cluster. It is evident that FCM was able to classify the datasets by a typical > 80% performance rate.

Figure 3. FCM – left: 4 DPI - right: 6 DPI

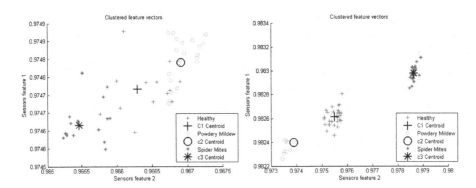

Figure 4. Left: 4DPI - FCM clusters and the membership of each sample point to each cluster, right: memebership graph for each cluster

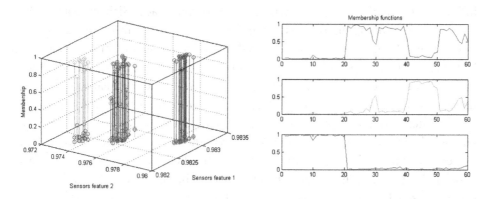

It is clear that the optimal number of clusters (c = 3) which was calculates by cluster indices was in fact the correct estimation. Using the 3 clusters allowed us to correctly classify the dataset and map each cluster to the health status of the to-mato plants.

Self-Organizing Map (SOM)

The self-organizing map (SOM) is among the most widely studied types of neural networks (Natale et. al, 1997). The principal goal of the SOM is to transform an incoming signal pattern of arbitrary dimension into a two-dimensional discrete map, and to perform this transformation adaptively in a topological ordered manner (Zuppa et. al, 2004). SOM is a popular choice for evaluating EN generated dataset and has been used by researchers in numerous EN related studies (Dutta et. al, 2003).

The input vectors are first normalized, so that they have zero mean and unity variance. In this case study, typical Principal Component Analysis (PCA) algorithm will be applied in order to balance the dimension of the input vector with the compo-nents of the vector that are highly correlated and eliminate any potential redundancy within the dataset. Effectively, this will reduce the dimension of the training dataset preparing it to be injected into SOM algorithm. This technique will eliminate those components that contribute the least to the variation in the dataset. Following that, the unsupervised SOM was applied to the pre-processed dataset in order to explore clusters and the distances between them. A two-dimensional Kohonen output layer was used to help provide a visual presentation. The SOM was overlapped and presented on top of the PCA dataset. To obtain good mapping results, it is recommended in literature that the number of output nodes in the Kohonen Neural Network should be at least 10-20% of training vectors. However, using too few output nodes may cause the congestion of input training set over an output node, which may make it difficult to distinguish the characteristics of the output space (Siripatrawan, 2008).

A 60 by 52 training matrix was constructed for each plant from the dataset. A 3 by 1 square SOM network was also created and trained using the three EN datasets. A Hexagonal layer topology function was used for the structure of the SOM network and the default Link distance function is used to find the distances between the layer's neurons given their positions. Each crop dataset (Healthy, Powdery Mildew infested and Spider Mite infected) were used to train and simulate the SOM network. The initial iteration value was set to 1000 and was increased to evaluate the performance. Once the training process had finished, each sample category was associated with one of the weights in the network. The positions of the weight were also initialized. Figure 5 demonstrates the SOM weight positions with the PCA data projection. Each cluster is indicated with a different color and the distance line is also evident which confirms the PCA classification.

The SOM exposed the three clusters in each dataset which represent the healthy and infected plants, confirming the earlier FCM results. From the figures it is evident that SOM coupled with PCA had the capacity to classify the VOCs of tomato plant EN generated dataset.

DISCUSSION AND CONCLUSION

In this chapter, an effort has been made to explore the ability of a sensor array (EN) in examining the VOCs emitted from tomato plant in both healthy and infested conditions and hence explore the possibility of replacing existing biological and laboratory

Figure 5. Self Organasing Map and Principal Component Analysis applied on Healthy, Spider Mite Infected and Powdery Mildew Dataset – 4 days Post Infection

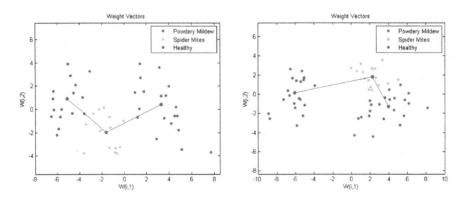

based diagnosis. Bloodhound ®ST306, EN system was employed to collect data from control and artificially infected tomato plants. FCM and SOM were independently used to analyze the data gathered to distinguish between VOCs acquired by EN. Both FCM and SOM have shown a respectable degree of classification when applied on a normalized dataset. FCM was proven to be very promising as it managed to discriminate between the plants with high performance (>80%). Although FCM as an unsupervised intelligent technique offers an eye-catching performance, it is a) highly sensitive to noise in datasets, b) requires initial estimation of cluster number and local minima and c) may take long computational time if used in real time applications. It is then necessary that the dataset is carefully normalized and preprocessed to eliminate any uncertainty in the results. Choosing the right parameters before conducting FCM plays an important role in having a successful optimization and subsequently a correct classification of the target dataset.

The pattern of infection was produced using EN during the crucial 2 weeks of post infection process. The PCA analysis coupled with SOM, employed on features extracted from pre-processed signals showed a clear improvement in the discrimination of the VOCs with an increase of the distance among the clusters in the principal components space. From this result it is evident that our tin oxide sensor based EN was fully capable of discriminating between the VOCs produced by each crop.

The investigation illustrated that that the spider mites and powdery mildew disease had a major effect on the VOCs emitted from the plant. After few days of infection there were little visual changes on the leaves both from powdery mildew or spider mite plants. However, EN was able to slightly discriminate between them from early stages.

Some of the challenges when analyzing VOCs in real greenhouses that need to be addressed are: a) the effect of background noise in the resulting VOC profile or dataset, b) optimisation of the technique for a specific plant or disease, and c) automation of the technique for continuous automated monitoring of plant diseases under real world greenhouse environment.

In a separate the study that reviewed the VOCs released by tomato plant, it was exposed that some elements such as Jasmonic Acid (JA) and Systemin (Sys) are the key molecules that mediate local and systemic signalling, leading to direct defense (Laothawornkitkul, 2008; Corrado, 2007). Identifying and quantifying the VOCs that are emitted from plants can lead us to enhance and maybe substitute the EN sensors to maximize its effectiveness. Further refinements, such as the design and optimization of EN sensor arrays for specific VOCs markers are likely to lead to a improvment in sensitivity, and other refinements will increase the robustness of the technology in the face of inconsistent commercial greenhouse environments.

In conclusion, this study showed that the Bloodhound ST214 EN has a high discrimination power and a rapid response. All of these properties, together with its compact size and ease of operation, confirm that the EN coupled with SOM/FCM is a potentially valuable and practical technology for remote sensing of pests and diseases in commercial crops to achieve superior plant disease control and management.

ACKNOWLEDGMENT

This project is co-funded by the European Commission, Directorate General for Research, within the 7th Framework Programme of RTD, Theme 2 – Biotechnology, Agriculture & Food.

REFERENCES

Acevedo, F., Maldonado, S., Domínguez, E., Narváez, A., & López, F. (2007). Probabilistic support vector machines for multi-class alcohol identification. *Sensors and Actuators. B, Chemical, 122*(1), 227–235. doi:10.1016/j.snb.2006.05.033

Ament, K., Kant, M. R., Sabelis, M. W., Haring, M. A., & Schuurink, R. C. (2004). Jasmonic acid is a key regulator of spider mite-induced volatile terpenoid and methyl salicylate emission in tomato. *Plant Physiology, 135*(4), 2025–2037. doi:10.1104/pp.104.048694

Amiri, M. (2003). *y_fcmc matlab Toolbox V1.0*. Sharif University of Technology. Retrieved from www.http://ce.sharif.edu/~m_amiri/

Baratto, C., Faglia, G., Pardo, M., Vezzoli, M., Boarino, L., & Maffei, M. (2005). Monitoring plants health in greenhouse for space missions. *Sensors and Actuators. B, Chemical, 108*(1-2), 278–284. doi:10.1016/j.snb.2004.12.108

Belanger, R., & Jarvis, W. (1994). Occurrence of powdery mildew (Erysiphe sp.) on greenhouse tomatoes in Canada. *Plant Disease, 78*(6), 640. doi:10.1094/PD-78-0640E

Bern, A. Z., Lammertyn, J., Saevels, S., Natale, C. D., & Nicolaï, B. M. (2003). Electronic nose systems to study shelf life and cultivar effect on tomato aroma profile. *Sensors and Actuators. B, Chemical, 97*(2-3), 324–333. doi:10.1016/j.snb.2003.09.020

Blouin, A. G., Greenwood, D. R., Chavan, R. R., Pearson, M. N., Clover, G. R., MacDiarmid, R. M., & Cohen, D. (2010). A generic method to identify plant viruses by high-resolution tandem mass spectrometry of their coat proteins. *Journal of Virological Methods, 163*(1), 49–56. doi:10.1016/j.jviromet.2009.08.009

Boom, C. E., Beek, T. A., Posthumus, M. A., Groot, A. D., & Dicke, M. (2004). Qualitative and quantitative variation among volatile profiles induced by tetranychus urticae feeding on plants from various families. *Journal of Chemical Ecology*, *30*(1), 69–89. doi:10.1023/B:JOEC.0000013183.72915.99

Borah, S., Hines, E., Leeson, M. S., Iliescu, D. D., Bhuyan, M., & Gardner, J. W. (2008). Neural network based electronic nose for classification of tea aroma. *Sensing and Instrumentation for Food Quality and Safety*, *2*(1), 7–14. doi:10.1007/s11694-007-9028-7

Brudzewski, K., Osowski, S., & Markiewicz, T. (2004). Classification of milk by means of an electronic nose and SVM neural network. *Sensors and Actuators. B, Chemical*, *98*(2-3), 291–298. doi:10.1016/j.snb.2003.10.028

Butrym, E. D., & Hartman, T. G. (1998). *An apparatus for sampling volatile organics from live plant material using short path thermal desorption*. Scientific Instrument Services, application note 75. Retrieved from http://www.sisweb.com

Choudhary, D. K., Johr, B. N., & Prakash, A. (2008). Volatiles as priming agents that initiate plant growth and defense responses. *Current Science*, *94*(5), 595–604.

Concina, I., Falasconi, M., Gobbi, E., Bianchi, F., Musci, M. M., & Mattarozzi, M. P. (2009). Early detection of microbial contamination in processed tomatoes by electronic nose. *Food Control*, *20*(10), 873–880. doi:10.1016/j.foodcont.2008.11.006

Corrado, G., Guerrieri, E., Pasquariello, M., Digilio, M. C., Cascone, P., & Rao, R. (2007). *Systemin regulates volatile signalling in tomato*. Plant & Animal Genomes XV Conference (pp. 669–681).

de Carvalho, A. T. (2007). Fuzzy c-means clustering methods for symbolic interval data. *Pattern Recognition Letters*, *28*(4), 423–437. doi:10.1016/j.patrec.2006.08.014

Deng, C., Zhang, X., Zhu, W., & Qian, J. (2004). Investigation of tomato plant defence response to tobacco mosaic virus by determination of methyl salicylate with SPME-capillary GC-MS. *Chromatographia*, *59*(3-4), 263–268.

Dicke, M., Gols, R., Ludeking, D., & Posthumus, M. A. (1999). Jasmonic acid and herbivory differentially induce carnivore-attracting plant volatiles in lima bean plants. *Journal of Chemical Ecology*, *25*(8), 1907–1922. doi:10.1023/A:1020942102181

Distante, C., Ancona, N., & Siciliano, P. (2003). Support vector machines for olfactory signals recognition. *Sensors and Actuators. B, Chemical*, *88*(1), 30–39. doi:10.1016/S0925-4005(02)00306-4

Du, C.-J., & Sun, D.-W. (2005). Pizza sauce spread classification using color vision and support vector machines. *Journal of Food Engineering, 66*(2), 137–145. doi:10.1016/j.jfoodeng.2004.03.011

Dutta, R., Hines, E. L., Gardner, J. W., Kashwan, K. R., & Bhuyan, M. (2003). Tea quality prediction using a tin oxide-based electronic nose: An artificial intelligence approach. *Sensors and Actuators. B, Chemical, 94*(2), 228–237. doi:10.1016/S0925-4005(03)00367-8

Dutta, R., Morgan, D., Baker, N., Gardner, J., & Hines, E. (2005). Identification of Staphylococcus aureus infections in hospital environments: Electronic nose based approach. *Sensors and Actuators. B, Chemical, 109*(2), 355–362. doi:10.1016/j.snb.2005.01.013

Fernandes, F., Pereira, D. M., Pinho, P. G., Valentão, P., Pereira, J. A., Bento, A., & Andrade, P. B. (2010). Headspace solid-phase microextraction and gas chromatography/ion trap-mass spectrometry applied to a living system: Pieris brassicae fed with kale. *Food Chemistry, 119*(4), 1681–1693. doi:10.1016/j.foodchem.2009.09.046

Frost, C. J., Mescher, M. C., Carlson, J. E., & Moraes, C. M. (2008). Plant defense priming against herbivores: Getting ready for a different battle. *Plant Physiology, 146*, 818–824. doi:10.1104/pp.107.113027

Gardner, J. W., & Pang, C. (1996). Detection of vapours and odors from a multisensor array using pattern recognition: Self-organising adaptive resonance techniques. *Measurement & Control, 29*(6), 172–178.

Gómez, A. H., Hu, G., Wang, J., & Pereira, A. G. (2006). Evaluation of tomato maturity by electronic nose. *Computers and Electronics in Agriculture, 54*(1), 44–52. doi:10.1016/j.compag.2006.07.002

Gutiérrez-Aguirre, I., Mehle, N., Delić, D., Gruden, K., Mumford, R., & Ravnikar, M. (2009). Real-time quantitative PCR based sensitive detection and genotype discrimination of Pepino mosaic virus. *Journal of Virological Methods, 162*(1-2), 46–55. doi:10.1016/j.jviromet.2009.07.008

Hayase, F., Chung, T.-Y., & Kato, H. (1984). Changes of volatile components of tomato fruits during ripening. *Food Chemistry, 14*(2), 113–124. doi:10.1016/0308-8146(84)90050-5

Jones, H., Whipps, J. M., & Gurr, S. J. (2001). The tomato powdery mildew fungus Oidium neolycopersici. *Molecular Plant Pathology, 2*(6), 303–309. doi:10.1046/j.1464-6722.2001.00084.x

Kalman, E.-L., Löfvendahl, A., Winquist, F., & Lundström, I. (1999). Classification of complex gas mixtures from automotive leather using an electronic nose. *Analytica Chimica Acta, 403*(1-2), 31–38. doi:10.1016/S0003-2670(99)00604-2

Kant, M. R., Bleeker, P. M., Wijk, M. V., Schuurink, R. C., & Haring, M. A. (2009). Plant volatiles in defence. *Advances in Botanical Research, 51*, 613–666. doi:10.1016/S0065-2296(09)51014-2

Kesselmeier, J., & Staudt, M. (2004). Biogenic Volatile Organic Compounds (VOC): An overview on emission, physiology and ecology. *Journal of Atmospheric Chemistry, 33*, 23–88. doi:10.1023/A:1006127516791

Kiss, L. (1996). Occurrence of a new powdery mildew fungus (Erysiphe sp.) on tomatoes in Hungary. *Plant Disease, 80*(2), 224. doi:10.1094/PD-80-0224E

Laothawornkitkul, J., Moore, J. P., Taylor, J. E., Possell, M., Gibson, T. D., Hewitt, C. N., & Paul, N. D. (2008). Discrimination of plant volatile signatures by an electronic nose: A potential technology for plant pest and disease. *Environmental Science & Technology, 42*(22), 8433–8439. doi:10.1021/es801738s

Linforth, R. S., Savary, I., Pattenden, B., & Taylor, A. J. (1994). Volatile compounds found in expired air during eating of fresh tomatoes and in the headspace above tomatoes. *Journal of the Science of Food and Agriculture, 65*(2), 241–247. doi:10.1002/jsfa.2740650219

Lytovchenko, A., Beleggia, R., Schauer, N., Isaacson, T., Leuendorf, J. E., & Hellmann, H. (2009). Application of GC-MS for the detection of lipophilic compounds in diverse plant tissues. *Plant Methods, 5*(4), 11.

Maffei, M. E. (2010). Sites of synthesis, biochemistry and functional role of plant volatiles. *South African Journal of Botany, 76*(4), 612–631. doi:10.1016/j.sajb.2010.03.003

Natale, C. D., Macagnano, A., D'Amico, A., & Davide, F. (1997). Electronic-nose modelling and data analysis using a self-organizing map. *Measurement Science & Technology, 8*(11), 1236–1243. doi:10.1088/0957-0233/8/11/004

Pardo, M., & Sberveglieri, G. (2005). Classification of electronic nose data with support vector machines. *Sensors and Actuators. B, Chemical, 107*(2), 730–737. doi:10.1016/j.snb.2004.12.005

Peñuelas, J., & Llusià, J. (2004). Plant VOC emissions: Making use of the unavoidable. *Trends in Ecology & Evolution, 19*(8), 402–404. doi:10.1016/j.tree.2004.06.002

Peris, M., & Escuder-Gilabert, L. (2009). A 21st century technique for food control: Electronic noses. *Analytica Chimica Acta*, *638*(1), 1–15. doi:10.1016/j.aca.2009.02.009

Putnam, M. L. (1995). Evaluation of selected methods of plant disease diagnosis. *Crop Protection (Guildford, Surrey)*, *14*(6), 517–525. doi:10.1016/0261-2194(95)00038-N

Rezaee, M. R., Lelieveldt, B. P. F., & Reiber, J. H. C. (1998). A new cluster validity index for the fuzzy c-mean. *Pattern Recognition Letters*, *19*(3-4), 237–246. doi:10.1016/S0167-8655(97)00168-2

Sankaran, S., Mishra, A., Ehsani, R., & Davis, C. (2010). A review of advanced techniques for detecting plant diseases. *Computers and Electronics in Agriculture*, *72*(1), 1–13. doi:10.1016/j.compag.2010.02.007

Siripatrawan, U. (2008). Self-organizing algorithm for classification of packaged fresh vegetable potentially contaminated with foodborne pathogens. *Sensors and Actuators. B, Chemical*, *128*(2), 435–441. doi:10.1016/j.snb.2007.06.030

Tikunov, Y., Vos, C. D., Lommen, A., Bino, R., Hall, R., & Bovy, A. (2004). Metabolomics of tomato fruit volatile compounds. *Book of abstracts of the 1st Solanaceae Genome Workshop*, (pp. 19-21).

Zuppa, M., Distante, C., Siciliano, P., & Persaud, K. C. (2004). Drift counteraction with multiple self-organising maps for an electronic nose. *Sensors and Actuators. B, Chemical*, *98*(2-3), 305–317. doi:10.1016/j.snb.2003.10.029

Chapter 9
Tomato Plant Health Monitoring:
An Electronic Nose Approach

Fu Zhang
University of Warwick, UK

D. Daciana Iliescu
University of Warwick, UK

Evor L. Hines
University of Warwick, UK

Mark S. Leeson
University of Warwick, UK

ABSTRACT

Electric noses (e-noses), taking their inspiration from the human olfactory system, have been extensively used in food quality control and human disease monitoring. This chapter presents the e-nose as a potential candidate for health monitoring and disease and pest detection on tomato plants. Two common problems in greenhouse tomatoes, namely powdery mildew and spider mites, are considered. An experimental arrangement is described based on a commercial 13-sensor e-nose where tomato plants are grown in an isolated, controlled environment inside a greenhouse. Attention is paid to the preliminary results of data post-processing using two different techniques. First, Principal Component Analysis is employed and demonstrates clear evolution of the components as the plants develop disease or infestation. Subsequently, Grey System Theory enables the identification of clear groupings in the sensor responses and thus the reduction of the model, producing stronger trend

DOI: 10.4018/978-1-61520-915-6.ch009

differences in the Principal Component between healthy and unhealthy plants. The results, although preliminary, show that the e-nose with appropriate data post-processing is a promising approach to monitoring the development of tomato plant diseases and infestations.

INTRODUCTION

Researchers have been developing Artificial Sensing (AS) systems for decades to enhance or digitize the five human senses of sight, hearing, smell, taste and touch. Amongst these, machine olfaction is one of the most well developed aspects in AS.

Machine olfaction systems, commonly known as e-noses or chemical sensor arrays, were inspired by the human olfactory system and generally consist of two key components, namely the detection unit and processing unit. There is an increasing interest in research, development and application in various fields, including the food industry, medical diagnosis and environmental monitoring. Here we concentrate on the first of these using tomatoes as a specific example since reliable supplies of high quality fruit in agreed quantities are needed by both supermarkets and tomato growers. The resilience of the food supply chain is a critical aspect of food security (Adger, 2006) and thus detailed insights are timely and necessary. Greenhouses are used to increase fruit quality and yields in many parts of the world as they facilitate control of the growing and environmental conditions. Nevertheless, in addition to weekly yield can fluctuations (Zhang et al., 2010) the plants are still prey to diseases and pests that must be rapidly detected and eliminated to prevent catastrophic losses.

This chapter reveals the potential applications of e-noses in monitoring and detecting tomato plant diseases. A continuous experiment was performed within a greenhouse, during which daily measurements were collected on three tomato plants using a commercial e-nose system. One of the tomato plants was used as the health control and the others were infected with powdery mildew (*Oidium neolycopersici*) and two spotted spider mites manually at the early stage of the experiment respectively. The post-processing on the collected data sets indicates that e-nose can be used as a tool to monitoring tomato plant disease.

BACKGROUND

The prediction of crop yields and the detection of plant damage or infestation need methods to collect data regarding plant health in addition to diagnosis and analysis tools. The detection and recognition of chemical substances produced by plants thus form suitable approaches for greenhouse use. Volatile organic compounds (VOCs) are emitted by plants when they are attacked by pests or disease and VOC emission has been investigated from many plant species (Kesselmeier & Staudt, 2004). Plants emit VOCs that are specific to the type of attack to combat the threat (Frost et al., 2008) and VOCs are major players in the interactions exchanges between plants and both herbivores and pathogens. The composition of VOCs emitted by plants depends on the mode of damage and they are produced by a wide range of physiological processes (Maffei, 2010).

There are two well known artificial technologies mimicking the human olfaction system, namely, chemical analysis and e-noses. Each of these technologies has its own advantages and disadvantages. Chemical analysis is able to identify and determine the accurate quantitative information of various chemical compounds. Gas chromatography – mass spectrometry (GC-MS) is one of the most important chemical analysis tools in odor analysis. GC-MS can separate many chemical components from a complex mixture of volatiles. The major problems of GC-MS are time and costs. GC-MS devices are expensive and the analysis process of a sample may take up to several hours. Thus, GC-MS cannot be used in real-time applications. E-noses, also known as gas sensors arrays, overcome the processing shortage of GC-MS, they are rapid, simple and inexpensive compared to GC-MS (Zhang et al., 2007). This chapter presents work on the development of powdery mildew infection and spider mite infestation on tomato plants, monitored using an e-nose. It is shown that an e-nose can be used to examine disease progression in tomatoes and detect the occurrence of diseases at an early stage.

Electronic Noses

As mentioned before, e-noses are the artificial digital olfactory systems mimicking the human sense of smell. These devices are designated to detect and discriminate complex odors and are comprised of two main units, which are the compound detection unit and processing unit, corresponding to olfactory nerves and brain of a human respectively (Peris & Escuder-Gilabert, 2009). The compound detection unit is typically an array of non-specific chemical sensors that react with various chemical compounds in gaseous phase, such as atoms, molecules, ions and so forth. Changes on the sensors are converted into electronic signals and the strengths of the signals are generally related to the concentration of the specific particles. The major categories of chemical sensors are piezoelectric sensors (also known as acoustic wave sensors), electrochemical sensors, optical sensors and thermal sensors (Nylander, 1985). There are many factors that may influence the signals, including humidity, quality of the sensors and inconsistent concentration of samples.

The processing unit is responsible for recording and analyzing the electronic signals transmitted from the chemical sensors. Depending on the design of e-noses, the processing unit could be embedded in the e-nose device or programmed as a function module of the control program on a remote computer. The major processing technique of the processing unit is pattern recognition, including principal component analysis (PCA), linear discriminant analysis (LDA) and artificial neural networks (ANNs) (Bishop, 2006). The pattern recognition techniques could be divided into two categories, which are supervised and unsupervised methods. In supervised methods, the classification information is predefined and the algorithms aim to make the groups more distinct. The best known supervised method is ANN. The major unsupervised technique is PCA, a feature extraction technique that reduces the dimensionality of the original data without significant loss of information. These techniques are used to classify the series of measurement patterns of the electronic signals from the chemical sensors. The combinational pattern of the responses to a species of odor is the characteristic pattern or signature of that odor. By matching the signature of an unknown compound against the signatures of known compounds, the unknown compound may be indentified (Pearce, Schiffman, Nagle & Gardner, 2003; Peris & Escuder-Gilabert, 2009).

E-noses have found application in many fields after a substantial research and development effort spanning some decades of research and development. For example, in medical applications it has been shown that e-noses can be used to assist medical diagnosis by analyzing the breath of patients (Gardner, Shin & Hines, 2000). Subsequently, the utility of e-noses in diagnosing urinary tract cancer was also demonstrated (Bernabei, et al., 2008). Moreover, the practical applications of e-noses have penetrated daily life, mainly in the food industry (as shown in Table 1) where the testing is less onerous than the medical trials process enabling rapid adoption.

Apart from the applications mentioned above, research work carried in China and Europe has shown that the e-nose is a simple and reliable technology for quality control and classification of cooking ingredients such as vinegar. (Gerbi et al., 1997; Zhang, et al., 2007) According to the work of Laothawomkitkul et al. (2008), e-noses can be used to discriminate among different volatiles from various plants,

Table 1. Applications of e-noses in food industry

Food	Test	Reference
Fish	Freshness	(Schweizer-Berberich, Vaihinger, & Gopel, 1994)
Pear	Effect of aging	(Zhang, Wang, & Ye, 2007)
Milk	Effect of aging	(Labreche et al., 2005)
Poultry meat	Freshness	(Boothe & Arnold, 2002)
Mandarin	Effect of aging	(Gomez et al., 2005)
Plants (tomato, cucumber, pepper)	Discrimination	(Laothawornkitkul, et al., 2008)

such as cucumber, pepper, and tomato plants under different conditions (healthy, mechanical damaged, pest infected and diseased).

Powdery Mildew

Powdery mildew is one of the most common diseases of tomato (both in greenhouses and fields) around the world and although several species exist, it is *Oidium neolycopersici* that has a substantial impact on tomato production in Europe, especially in greenhouse tomatoes (Jones, Whipps & Gurr, 2001). The symptoms of powdery mildew are the powdery white or gray lesions on the tomato leaf surface and petioles. Symptoms appear as small pale green or yellow spots on upper surface of the leaf and eventually turn brown when the leaf dies. Powdery lesions start appearing on the leaves a few days after infection, developing and infecting other leaves and plants in the field. Severe infections can lead to leaf chlorosis, premature senescence and significant reduction in fruit size, quality, and yield. (Jacob, et al., 2008; Jones, Whipps & Gurr, 2001)

Researchers have been studying powdery mildew on tomato plants for decades. In 1998, it was shown that the response of tomato species to powdery mildew is mainly associated with hypersensitive response (Huang et al., 1998). The resistance mechanism is still unknown. Whipps and Budge (2000) studied the effect of humidity on tomato powdery mildew in an experimental greenhouse and showed that high humidity may decrease its severity. They studied the influence of humidity at four levels, namely 80% relative humidity (RH) values of 80%, 87%, 90% and 95%; the temperature was controlled to be 19°C. Symptoms usually became visible five to seven days after inoculation and low humidity enhanced disease development.

Spider Mites

There are about 1600 species of spider mite around the world causing damages to hundreds of species of plants. They feed on plant cells and the symptoms are the typical small, yellowish, speckled feeding marks. Spider mites are tiny, usually less than 1mm. The most well known species of spider mite is *Tetranychus urticae*, also called glasshouse red spider mite or two-spotted spider mite. Spider mites are serious pests in tomato crops due to their great reproduction rate. Under optimal conditions, they have a life cycle of only 8-12 days, becoming sexually mature in within five days. A female spider mite can lay in excess of 100 eggs so populations grow rapidly (Cross et al., 2001). Spider mites can significantly damage tomato plants and reduce the yields and given their rapid life cycle they can destroy a plant within a few weeks if left uncontrolled.

The work of Margolies and Wrensch (1996) showed that temperature influences the reproduction rate of spider mites. Increasing the environmental temperature accelerates the development of spider mites from eggs to mature adults. Kant et al. (2004) studied the responses of tomato plants to invasion by spider mites and reported that tomato plants respond rapidly, less than one day, by increasing the emission of signaling compounds such as jasmonate, ethylene and salicylate.

DEVICE AND EXPERIMENT

Bloodhound ST214 (e-Nose)

The e-nose unit used in the experiment was a Bloodhound ST214, provided by Scensive Technology, Leeds, U.K. The unit contained 13 gas sensors with a sampling process consisting of the five that are explained as follows:

- **Baseline:** In this state, clean air was pumped into the sampling chamber for five seconds to initiate sampling and the instrument records the baseline resistance of the sensors.
- **Absorption:** In this state, the clean air inlet was shut and the gaseous sample was pumped into the chamber through sample inlet. During the exposure to the gaseous sample, the resistances of the sensors changed due to the interaction of volatile compounds with the active surface of each sensor. The responses of the sensors were usually different as the sensors were made of different materials.
- **Pause:** optional step. During this phase, both sample inlet and clean air inlet were shut. The resistances of the sensors should remained the same as in the absorption step.
- **Desorption:** in this step, the clean air inlet was opened again while the sample inlet was kept shut. The resistances ideally returned to the baseline as the volatiles left the sensor surface.
- **Flush:** this was the extension of the desorption phase.

During the experiment, the e-nose was configured with the following settings: baseline, 5 seconds; absorption, 20 seconds; pause, 1 second; desorption, 30 seconds; flush, 5 seconds. Thus, it took 61 seconds to collect one measurement. As the e-nose operated at 4Hz, 244 data points were collected for measurement on each sensor.

Figure 1. Systematic structure of experiment

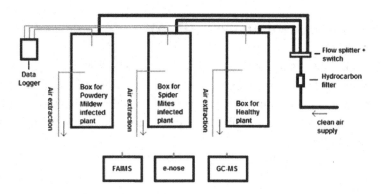

Experimental Setup

The experiment was carried out with three Espresso tomato plants provided by Warwick's School of Life Sciences. The plants were grown in a controlled chamber for six weeks from seedling and then moved into three glass boxes (150cm H, 50cm W, 50cm D) in a greenhouse. The glass boxes were made of glass panels and alloy frames only, and were specially designed for this experiment to minimize the gas exchange with the external environmental and the possibility of contamination. The glass boxes had dedicated irrigation ventilation systems. The latter blew filtered clean air into the glass box at 10L per minute continuously to generate positive pressure inside the glass box and minimize the contamination from outside. The irrigation system was operated manually and the plants were watered when necessary. Once the tomato plants were moved in, the glass boxes were locked and only opened for several minutes to perform inoculation at the early stage of the experiment. Each box was fitted with a humidity and temperature logging device and a dedicated sampling tube for the e-nose. Figure 1 illustrates the systematic structure of the experiment.

One hour before taking measurements, the ventilation system was shut down to allow the volatiles from the tomato plants to accumulate within the glass boxes. The ventilation system was switched on again once the daily measurements had been collected. During the accumulations of volatiles, the e-nose was initialized and trained with 2% butanol solution for half an hour to make the chemical sensors stabilise. Twenty measurements were taken on each plant every day. The plants were moved into the glass boxes on the 3rd July, 2009 and the powdery mildew and spider mites were inoculated into the boxes on the 7th July, 2009. Powdery mildew was inoculated by shaking leaves of powdery mildew source over the plant for a couple of minutes. Inoculation of spider mites was performed by hand picking 30 spider mites and placing them on the plant.

PROCESSING METHODS

Principal Component Analysis (PCA)

PCA (Bishop, 2006) is a mathematical technique which is used for vector space transformation. It transforms a dataset into a new system of coordinates with the possibility of reducing the number of dimensions while retaining the variation present in the dataset as much as possible. The principal components are determined by the following four steps:

Step 1: Mean value subtraction

$$X' = X - \overline{X} \tag{1}$$

where $\overline{X}$ is the mean of a data set X, and X' is the new data set.

Step 2: Covariance matrix calculation

$$\text{cov}(X) = \frac{XX^T}{N-1} \tag{2}$$

where X is the matrix consisting of data sets, X^T is the transpose of matrix X and N is the size of each data set.

Step 3: Eigenvector and eigenvalue calculation

$$Ax = \lambda Ix \tag{3}$$

$$(A - \lambda I)x = 0 \tag{4}$$

$$\det(A - \lambda I) = 0 \tag{5}$$

where A is the square covariance matrix derived in step 2, I is the identity matrix, λ is an eigenvalue and x is the eigenvector.

Step 4: Eigenvector reordering based on their associated eigenvalues, highest to lowest, which represent the explained variance of the eigenvectors.

The matrix of ordered eigenvectors represents the original data transformed into the new dimensions and the eigenvector with largest eigenvalue is called the first principal component of the dataset as it accounts for the most information (explained variance) of the dataset;. The eigenvector with the second largest eigenvalue is called the second principal component and so on. As the first few principal components usually account for the most information (variances) of the original dataset, they can be used to represent the original dataset in with fewer dimensions. For visualization purposes, two or three sets of principal components with most significance are normally selected to express the original dataset graphically.

Grey System Theory (GST)

GST is a series of techniques that initially appeared in the 1980s (Deng, 1989). The theory states that the information available is always uncertain and limited due to noise. By generating and developing the incomplete information, GST aims to describe the systemic operational behavior properly. After over two decades of development, GST had been applied successfully in various scientific areas, including industry, agriculture, economics, energy, geography and hydraulic power. The main GST approaches include, Grey Equations, Grey Matrices, Grey Systems Modeling, Grey Prediction, Grey Decisions and Grey Control. In addition, many researchers are seeking ways to combine GST with other techniques such as ANNs, Genetic Algorithms (GAs), Markov Models and so on (Liu & Lin, 2005).

In this work, we concentrate on a Grey Incidence analysis to reveal the possible relationships between the sensors signals collected in the e-nose. The basic idea of Grey Incidence analysis is that the closeness of two data series is determined by the similarity level of the patterns of the two data series. Higher similarity levels would generate higher Grey Incidences, and vice versa. By testing the Grey Incidences between the sensor signals, those with higher Grey Incidences will indicate similar signal patterns. There are four types of Grey Incidences: Standard Grey Incidence, Absolute Grey Incidence, Relative Grey Incidence and Synthetic Grey Incidence (Liu & Lin, 2005). In this work, we only use the Standard Grey Incidence.

Standard Grey Incidence

The Standard Grey Incidence can be calculated by the follow steps. Assume that there exist three sequences, each of n elements.

$$Y_0 = (y_0(1), y_0(2), ..., y_0(n))$$

$$X_0 = (x_0(1), x_0(2), ..., x_0(n))$$

$$X_1 = (x_1(1), x_1(2), ..., x_1(n))$$

where Y_0 is the target sequence, X_0 and X_1 are the influencing factors. In this case, Y_0 is the weekly tomato yields, X_0 and X_1 are two potential variables.

Step 1

The first step is to find the initial image of each sequence using

$$Y_0' = Y_0/y_0(1) = (y_0'(1), y_0'(2), ..., y_0'(n)) = (y_0(1)/y_0(1), y_0(2)/y_0(1), ..., y_0(n)/y_0(1))$$

$$X_0' = X_0/x_0(1) = (x_0'(1), x_0'(2), ..., x_0'(n)) = (x_0(1)/x_0(1), x_0(2)/x_0(1), ..., x_0(n)/x_0(1))$$

$$X_1' = X_1/x_1(1) = (x_1'(1), x_1'(2), ..., x_1'(n)) = (x_1(1)/x_1(1), x_1(2)/x_1(1), ..., x_1(n)/x_1(1))$$

where Y_0', X_0' and X_1' are the image sequences or the initial sequences of the original sequences, Y_0, X_0 and X_1 respectively.

Step 2
Find the difference sequences between the target sequence and the influencing factors using:

$$\Delta_0 = X_0' - Y_0' = (\Delta_0(1), \Delta_0(2), ..., \Delta_0(n)) = (x_0'(1) - y_0'(1), x_0'(2) - y_0'(2), ..., x_0'(n) - y_0'(n))$$

$$\Delta_1 = X_1' - Y_0' = (\Delta_1(1), \Delta_1(2), ..., \Delta_1(n)) = (x_1'(1) - y_0'(1), x_1'(2) - y_0'(2), ..., x_1'(n) - y_0'(n))$$

Step 3
Compute the global maximum and minimum differences via:

$$M = \max_i(\max_j(\Delta_i(j))$$

$$m = \min_i(\min_j(\Delta_i(j))$$

Step 4
Calculate the incidence coefficients using Equation (6)

$$\gamma_i(k) = \frac{m + \zeta M}{\Delta_i(i) + \zeta M} \tag{6}$$

where $\gamma_i(k)$ represents the incidence coefficients of the kth element in the ith influencing sequence and ζ is a user defined factor in the range [0, 1] and generally taken to be 0.5.

Step 5
Find the Standard Grey Incidence using Equation (7)

$$\gamma_i = \frac{1}{n} \sum_{k=1}^{n} \gamma_i(k)$$ (7)

RESULTS AND DISCUSSION

The e-nose device used in this experiment consisted of 13 chemical sensors. However, two of the sensors ceased normal functioning during the latter stages of the experiment meaning that only the data collected from the 11 fully effective sensors were used in data processing.

During the experiment, powdery mildew spots became visible about five days after infection. This observation was similar that in the experiment carried out by Whipps and Budge (2000) in which they detected powdery mildew spots on leaves five to seven days after infection. After transferring 30 spider mites onto the tomato plant, they were not subsequently detected in the experiment nor were the signs of their survival and reproduction obvious. The healthy control plant displayed no signs of any infections or damage throughout the experiment.

Figure 2 illustrates the typical signal pattern collected using the e-nose. The eleven traces representing the readings from the eleven fully functioning sensors may be seen and, as mentioned previously, four points were collected per second over the 61-second sampling period. All sensors generated distinct responses.

PCA was used to compress the 244 sample values of each sensor into a single characteristic value. By computing the component variance of the principal components, the results showed that, on average, the first principal components carried over 90% of the variability. The second components carried only just over 7% of the variability, leaving less than 2% for the remaining principal components. It was thus efficient to use only the first principal components as representative of the sensor signals and the amount of data volume was significantly reduced. Each sampling record then consisted of 11 data points, one from each sensor.

By processing the 'compressed' data set using PCA and extracting the first principal component again, the general patterns of the conditions of the plants were expressed graphically. Figure 3 illustrates the changing patterns of the first principal

Figure 2. Typical e-nose signals

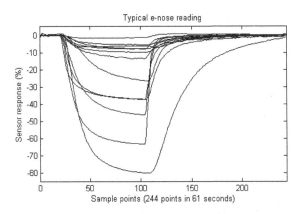

components of measurements taken in the three glass boxes. Five data points were picked a day randomly from the collected data sets and the general patterns of the data points were expressed using solid best fit trend lines.

As illustrated in Figure 3, both the powdery mildew infected plant and the spider mite infected plant gave increasing patterns and the data points in graphs are of high variability. The data from the healthy control plant were of even higher variability and the general pattern is a weak decrement. As the healthy control plant was kept

Figure 3. Changing patterns of the 1st PCs in three glass boxes. Top: powdery mildew, middle: spider mites, bottom: health control. Solid lines are the best fit trend lines. DoI: day of infection.

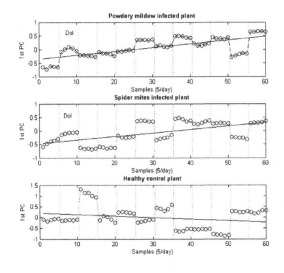

healthy throughout the experiment, it was expected to give a flat pattern. The decrement in the graph is probably due to the fact that leaves on the bottom branches were turning yellow and eventually died. The change of those leaves may generate different chemical compounds. Although the e-nose is not able to tell what chemical compounds were emitted by tomato plants under various conditions in this experiment, it clearly shows that things are changing inside the boxes.

Grey incidence is a technique that studies the closeness or similarity between two data sequence. The grey incidences between the sensors are listed in the table below:

Each value in the upper trangular matrax in Table 2 is the Grey incidence between the sensors expressed by the corresponding column and row headers. Higher values represent higher similarity. By selecting an appropriate threshold value, the sensors could be classified into groups depending on their similarities. Figure 4 illustrates the Grey incidences between all the sensors with the threshold value 0.925. All the Grey incidences greater or equal to 0.925 are replaced by black cells, representing significant similarity or closeness, and the rest are marked with white cells and are ignored.

The first row in the Grey incidence matrix (Figure 4) suggests that sensor 1 and sensors 3, 4 and 6 are closely related; the third row shows sensor 3 is significantly close to sensors 4, 6 and 9; and so on. After utilizing the Grey incidences matrix, the sensors could be divided into four groups. One of the groups consists of sensors 1, 3, 4, 5, 6, 9, 10 and 11. The remaining sensors 2, 7 and 8 each comprised a group of one sensor only. As the sensors in the same group are believed to have similar patterns of performance, sensor 1 could be considered as the representative of the group.

Table 2. Grey incidences between the e-nose sensors

	S1	S2	S3	S4	S5	S6	S7	S8	S9	S10	S11
S1	1.000	0.555	0.993	0.984	0.876	0.985	0.832	0.821	0.925	0.843	0.854
S2		1.000	0.612	0.610	0.583	0.616	0.584	0.671	0.596	0.582	0.579
S3			1.000	0.988	0.880	0.982	0.838	0.820	0.930	0.847	0.859
S4				1.000	0.889	0.971	0.841	0.813	0.936	0.848	0.862
S5					1.000	0.878	0.888	0.763	0.933	0.923	0.928
S6						1.000	0.831	0.829	0.918	0.839	0.849
S7							1.000	0.776	0.905	0.877	0.909
S8								1.000	0.712	0.659	0.663
S9									1.000	0.881	0.906
S10										1.000	0.933
S11											1.000

Figure 4. Grey incidences between sensors with threshold value 0.925

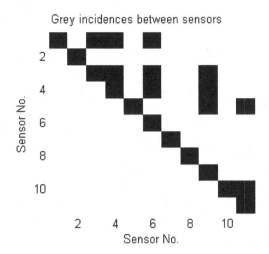

By reprocessing the available data sets using the selected sensors, (1, 2, 7 and 8), the information patterns extracted from the data sets are illustrated in Figure 5. Compared to the information patterns illustrated in Figure 3, which were generated using all the sensors, the data patterns on the same plant were very similar. This indicated that the sensors 1, 2, 7 and 8 carried a significant amount of information among all the 11 sensors and these 4 sensors could be used as the representative of the entire sensor array.

Figure 6 illustrates the daily differences between the data sets collected on three plants during the experiment. It is not hard to see that the data sets are always separable by PCA. This suggests that by studying the differences between sampling data collected from different plants, the plants with different conditions (disease, pests, growing conditions and so forth) can be spotted. In conjunction with comprehensive analysis of the changing patterns, the development of such abnormal conditions can be monitored and alerted if an appropriate threshold value is selected in the changing pattern.

CONCLUSION

This chapter has presented the potential application of e-noses in the field of tomato plant health monitoring and early disease detection. An e-nose device was used to sniff the volatiles emitted by three isolated tomato plants on a daily basis over a period of time. Two of the tomato plants were infected manually by powdery mildew and spider mites respectively at an early stage of the experiment.

Figure 5. Changing patterns of the 1st PCs generated using sensors 1, 2, 7 and 8 in three glass boxes. Top: powdery mildew, middle: spider mites, bottom: health control.

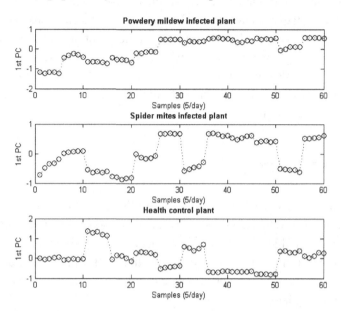

Figure 6. Comparison between the three plants during the experiment using sensors 1, 2, 7 and 8. Circles: powdery mildew infected plant; cross: spider mite infected plant; hexagon: healthy plant.

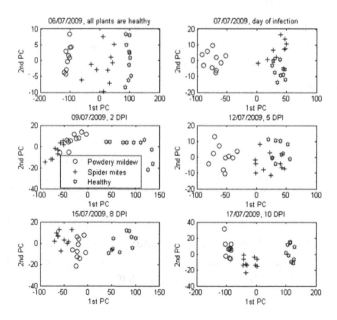

The experimental results showed that the e-nose unit could detect the changes occurring on the tomato plants. However, the e-nose device could neither identify the volatiles nor tell exactly what was changing inside the glass boxes. The data sets collected on the powdery mildew infected tomato plant and spider mites infected tomato plant gave gradually increasing patterns, representing the accumulation of response chemicals emitted by the tomato plants. By identifying the changing pattern together with the classification of volatiles inside the glass, it is possible to determine if the tomato plant is healthy or not.

FUTURE DIRECTIONS

As e-noses are sensitive to factors such as humidity and temperature, the influences of such conditions on the chemical sensors need to be studied thoroughly to make the e-nose more reliable. This chapter presents the results of a preliminary study on the application of e-noses in tomato plant health monitoring and disease detection. To take this work further, the performance of e-noses in actual greenhouses needs to be studied using larger field trials.

REFERENCES

Adger, W. N. (2006). Vulnerability. *Global Environmental Change*, *16*, 268–281. doi:10.1016/j.gloenvcha.2006.02.006

Bernabei, M., Pennazza, G., Santonico, M., Corsi, C., Roscioni, C., & Paolesse, R. (2008). A preliminary study on the possibility to diagnose urinary tract cancers by an electronic nose. *Sensors and Actuators. B, Chemical*, *131*, 1–4. doi:10.1016/j.snb.2007.12.030

Bishop, C. M. (2006). *Pattern recognition and machine learning*. New York, NY: Springer.

Boothe, D. D. H., & Arnold, J. W. (2002). Electronic nose analysis of volatile compounds from poultry meat samples, fresh and after refrigerated storage. *Journal of the Science of Food and Agriculture*, *82*(3), 315–322. doi:10.1002/jsfa.1036

Cross, J. V., Eastebrook, M. A., Crook, A. M., Crook, D., Fitzgerald, J. D., Innocenzi, P. J., & Solomon, M. G. (2001). Review: Natural enemies and biocontrol of pests of strawberry in Northern and Central Europe. *Biocontrol Science and Technology*, *11*(2), 165–216. doi:10.1080/09583150120035639

Deng, J. (1989). Introduction to Grey system theory. *Journal of Grey System, 1*(1), 1–24.

Frost, C. J., Mescher, M. C., Carlson, J. E., & Moraes, C. M. (2008). Plant defense priming against herbivores: Getting ready for a different battle. *Plant Physiology, 146*, 818–824. doi:10.1104/pp.107.113027

Gardner, J. W., Shin, H. W., & Hines, E. L. (2000). An electronic nose system to diagnose illness. *Sensors and Actuators. B, Chemical, 70*, 19–24. doi:10.1016/S0925-4005(00)00548-7

Gerbi, V., Zeppa, G., Antonelli, A., & Carnacini, A. (1997). Sensory characterisation of wine vinegars. *Food Quality and Preference, 8*(1), 27–34. doi:10.1016/S0950-3293(96)00003-1

Gomez, A. H., Wang, J., Hu, G., & Pereira, A. G. (2005). Electronic nose technique potential monitoring mandarin maturity. *Sensors and Actuators. B, Chemical, 113*, 347–353. doi:10.1016/j.snb.2005.03.090

Huang, C., Groot, T., Meijer-Dekens, F., Niks, R. E., & Lindhout, P. (1998). The resistance to powdery mildew (Oidium lycopersicum) in lycopersicon species is mainly associated with hypersensitive response. *European Journal of Plant Pathology, 104*, 399–407. doi:10.1023/A:1008092701883

Jacob, D., David, D. R., Sztjenberg, A., & Elad, Y. (2008). Conditions for development of powdery mildew of tomato caused by Oidium neolycopersici. *Ecology and Epidemiology, 98*, 270–281.

Jones, H., Whipps, J. M., & Gurr, S. J. (2001). The tomato powdery mildew fungus Oidium neolycopersici. *Molecular Plant Pathology, 2*(6), 303–309. doi:10.1046/j.1464-6722.2001.00084.x

Kesselmeier, J., & Staudt, M. (2004). Biogenic Volatile Organic Compounds (VOC): An overview on emission, physiology and ecology. *Journal of Atmospheric Chemistry, 33*, 23–88. doi:10.1023/A:1006127516791

Labreche, S., Bazzo, S., Cade, S., & Chanie, E. (2005). Shelf life determination by electronic nose: Application to milk. *Sensors and Actuators. B, Chemical, 106*, 199–206. doi:10.1016/j.snb.2004.06.027

Laothawornkitkul, J., Moore, J. P., Taylor, J. E., Possell, M., Gibson, T. D., Hewitt, C. N., & Paul, N. D. (2008). Discrimination of plant volatile signatures by an electronic nose: A potential technology for plant pest and disease monitoring. *Environmental Science & Technology, 42*(22), 8433–8439. doi:10.1021/es801738s

Liu, S., & Lin, Y. (2005). *Grey information: Theory and practical applications.* Berlin, Germany: Springer.

Maffei, M. E. (2010). Sites of synthesis, biochemistry and functional role of plant volatiles. *South African Journal of Botany, 76*(4), 612–631. doi:10.1016/j.sajb.2010.03.003

Margolies, D. C., & Wrensch, D. L. (1996). Temperature-induced changes in spider mite fitness: Offsetting effects of development time, fecundity, and sex ratio. *Entomologia Experimentalis et Applicata, 78*, 111–118.

Nylander, C. (1985). Chemical and biological sensors. *Journal of Physics. E, Scientific Instruments, 18*(9), 736–750. doi:10.1088/0022-3735/18/9/003

Pearce, T. C., Schiffman, S. S., Nagle, H. T., & Gardner, J. W. (2003). *Handbook of machine olfaction: Electronic nose technology.* Frankfurt, Germany: Wiley-VCH.

Peris, M., & Escuder-Gilabert, L. (2009). A 21st century technique for food control: Electronic noses. *Analytica Chimica Acta, 638*, 1–15. doi:10.1016/j.aca.2009.02.009

Schweizer-Berberich, M., Vaihinger, S., & Gopel, W. (1994). Characterisation of food freshness with sensor arrays. *Sensors and Actuators. B, Chemical, 18-19*, 282–290. doi:10.1016/0925-4005(94)87095-0

Whipps, J. M., & Budge, S. P. (2000). Effect of humidity on development of tomato powdery mildew (Oidium lycopersici) in the glasshouse. *European Journal of Plant Pathology, 106*, 395–397. doi:10.1023/A:1008745630393

Zhang, F., Iliescu, D. D., Hines, E. L., Leeson, M. S., & Adams, S. R. (2010). Prediction of greenhouse tomato yield: A genetic algorithm optimized neural network based approach. In Manos, B., Paparrizos, K., Matsatsinis, N., & Papathanasiou, J. (Eds.), *Decision support systems in agriculture, food and the environment: Trends, applications and advances* (pp. 155–172). Hershey, PA: IGI Global.

Zhang, H., Wang, J., & Ye, S. (2007). Predictions of acidity, soluble solids and firmness of pear using electronic nose technique. *Journal of Food Engineering, 86*, 370–378. doi:10.1016/j.jfoodeng.2007.08.026

Zhang, Q., Zhang, S., Xie, C., Fan, C., & Bai, Z. (2007). Sensory analysis of Chinese vinegars using an electronic nose. *Sensors and Actuators. B, Chemical, 128*, 586–593. doi:10.1016/j.snb.2007.07.058

Chapter 10

Improved Gas Source Localization with a Mobile Robot by Learning Analytical Gas Dispersal Models from Statistical Gas Distribution Maps Using Evolutionary Algorithms

Achim J. Lilienthal
Örebro University, Sweden

ABSTRACT

The method presented in this chapter computes an estimate of the location of a single gas source from a set of localized gas sensor measurements. The estimation process consists of three steps. First, a statistical model of the time-averaged gas distribution is estimated in the form of a two-dimensional grid map. In order to compute the gas distribution grid map the Kernel DM algorithm is applied, which carries out spatial integration by convolving localized sensor readings and modeling the information content of the point measurements with a Gaussian kernel. The statistical gas distribution grid map averages out the transitory effects of turbulence and converges to a representation of the time-averaged spatial distribution of a target gas. The second step is to learn the parameters of an analytical model of average gas distribution. Learning is achieved by nonlinear least squares fitting of the

DOI: 10.4018/978-1-61520-915-6.ch010

analytical model to the statistical gas distribution map using Evolution Strategies (ES), which are a special type of Evolutionary Algorithm (EA). This step provides an analysis of the statistical gas distribution map regarding the airflow conditions and an alternative estimate of the gas source location, i.e. the location predicted by the analytical model in addition to the location of the maximum in the statistical gas distribution map. In the third step, an improved estimate of the gas source position can then be derived by considering the maximum in the statistical gas distribution map, the best fit, as well as the corresponding fitness value. Different methods to select the most truthful estimate are introduced, and a comparison regarding their accuracy is presented, based on a total of 34 hours of gas distribution mapping experiments with a mobile robot. This chapter is an extended version of the conference paper (Lilienthal et al., 2005).

INTRODUCTION

A major problem for gas source localization in a natural environment is the strong influence of turbulence on the dispersal of gas. Typically, turbulent transport is considerably faster compared to molecular diffusion (Nakamoto et al., 1999; Roberts and Webster, 2002). Apart from very small distances where turbulence is not effective, molecular diffusion can thus be neglected concerning the spread of gas. A second important transport mechanism for gases is advective transport due to prevailing fluid flow. Relatively constant air currents are typically found even in an indoor environment without ventilation (Wandel et al., 2003) as a result of pressure (draught) and temperature inhomogeneities (convection flow).

Turbulent flow comprises at any instant a high degree of vortical motion, which creates packets of gas that follow chaotic trajectories (Shraiman and Siggia, 2000). This results in a concentration field, which consists of fluctuating, intermittent patches of high concentration. The instantaneous concentration field does not exhibit smooth concentration gradients that indicate the direction toward the centre of a gas source (Lilienthal and Duckett, 2004b; Russell, 1999). Figure 1 illustrates actual gas concentration measurements recorded with a mobile robot along a corridor containing a single gas source. It is important to note that the noise is dominated by the large fluctuations of the instantaneous gas distribution and not by the electronic noise of the gas sensors. Turbulence is chaotic in the sense that the instantaneous flow velocity at some instant of time is insufficient to predict the velocity a short time later. Consequently, a snapshot of the distribution of a target gas at a given instant contains little information about the distribution at another time. However, under certain assumptions (e.g. that the air flow is uniform and steady) the *time-averaged* concentration field varies smoothly in space with moderate concentration gradients (Roberts and Webster, 2002).

Figure 1. Normalized raw response readings from an example trial

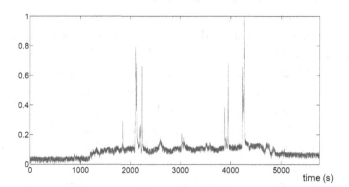

It is often desirable to know the spatial structure of the time-averaged gas distribution. The Kernel Distribution Mapping (Kernel DM) algorithm was introduced by Lilienthal and Duckett (Lilienthal and Duckett, 2003b) to compute a grid map representation of the structure of the time-averaged gas distribution. The input to the Kernel DM algorithm is a set of localized gas sensor readings. In this chapter we consider the case that the readings were collected by a mobile robot. The algorithm is summarized in Section "The Kernel DM Algorithm". In itself, gas distribution mapping is useful for any application that requires estimating the average distribution of a certain gas in a particular area of the environment. For example, mobile robots that are able to build such a map can be used for pollution monitoring (DustBot Consortium, 2006), they could indicate contaminated areas in a rescue mission, or could be used in Precision Farming (Blackmore & Griepentrog, 2002) to provide a non-intrusive way of assessing certain soil parameters or the status of plant growth to enable a more efficient usage of fertilizer.

In this chapter, which is an extended version of a paper by the authors (Lilienthal et al., 2005), we describe a method to use statistical gas distribution grid maps in order to locate a gas source. An obvious clue for the gas source position is the maximum in the map. Experiments in an indoor environment indeed demonstrated that the concentration maximum estimate (CME)[1] provides a satisfying approximation of the source location in many cases (Lilienthal & Duckett, 2004a). Under certain assumptions discussed in Sec. "Analytic Gas Distribution Model", the spread of a gas that evaporates from a stationary source can be approximated as a Fickian diffusion process. Instead of the small diffusion constant that describes molecular diffusion the turbulent diffusion is ruled by a substantially larger turbulent diffusion constant K (eddy diffusivity). In the event of negligible advective transport due to a weak air current, the resulting average gas distribution takes a circular shape. In such cases, it was observed that the distance between the CME and the true source location was small. By contrast, the localization capability of the CME was found to be considerably degraded when the concentration map showed a stretched out distribution due to a dominant wind direction. According to the equations, which describe the time-averaged stationary gas distribution analytically (see Sec. "Analytic Gas Distribution Model"), the concentration decreases slowly *along* the direction of a constant air current. Thus, even small distortions due to rudiments of turbulent concentration peaks can cause a large displacement of the point of maximum concentration. Also the localization error introduced by the fact that gas sensor measurements are acquired not exactly level with the gas source is more pronounced in the case of stronger air current.

A method that formalizes this qualitative argument is presented in Sec. "Step 3 – Selection of Source Location Estimate". The method allows distinguishing situations, where the CME is a reliable approximation of the source location from situations where the CME is unlikely to indicate the gas source position accurately. This is accomplished by comparing how well the statistical gas distribution map can be approximated by the analytical model (detailed in Sec. "Analytic Gas Distribution Model"), which describes the time-averaged gas distribution under certain idealized assumptions.

Apart from providing a measure of the reliability of the CME, the introduced method allows to derive an alternative estimate of the gas source position, which can be used in situations where the CME fails. To determine the analytical model, which approximates the given statistical gas distribution map most closely, the parameter set is optimized by means of nonlinear least squares fitting. Since the model parameters include the position of the gas source, the best fit naturally corresponds to an estimate of the source position. In contrast to the CME, the best fit estimate (BFE) is derived from the whole distribution represented in the statistical gas distribution grid map.

The rest of this chapter is structured as follows. First, the Kernel DM algorithm to compute statistical gas distribution grid maps is described in Sec. "Step 1 - Computation of a Statistical Gas Distribution Model". Second, the adapted physical model that was used to approximate the time-averaged gas concentration is introduced in Sec. "Analytic Gas Distribution Model". Then, the evolutionary strategy method to learn the optimal model parameters is detailed in Sec. "Step 2 – Learning Parameters of the Analytical Model". Next, reasons that cause deviations between the physical model and the statistical gas distribution grid map are discussed in Sec. "Sources of Inaccuracy" and two strategies to select the best estimate of the gas source location are presented in Sec. "Step 3 – Selection of Source Location Estimate". Finally details of the experimental setup are given in Sec. "Experimental Setup" and results are presented in Sec. "Results", followed by conclusions and suggestions for future work in the final Section "Conclusions and Outlook".

STEP 1: COMPUTATION OF A STATISTICAL GAS DISTRIBUTION MODEL

Creating Gas Distribution Grid Maps

By contrast to metric grid maps extracted from sonar or laser range scans, a single measurement from a gas sensor represents the measured quantity (in the case of metal oxide sensors: the rate of redox reactions) only at the comparatively small area of the sensor's surface, typically around 1 cm^2. Nevertheless, the gas sensor readings contain information about the time-averaged gas distribution of a larger area. First, this is due to the smoothness of the time-averaged gas distribution, which allows extrapolating on the averaged gas sensor measurements because the average concentration field does not change drastically in the vicinity of the point of measurement. Second, the metal-oxide gas sensors perform temporal integration of successive readings implicitly due to their slow response and long recovery time. Modeled as a first-order sensor, the time constants of rise and decay for the complete gas sensitive system used here were estimated as $\tau_r \approx 1.8$s and $\tau_d \approx 11.1$s, respectively (Lilienthal & Duckett, 2003a). Thus the measurements contain information that is spatially integrated along the path driven by the robot.

The Kernel DM Algorithm

Based on the observations mentioned in Sec. "Creating Gas Distribution Grid Maps", the Kernel DM algorithm introduced in (Lilienthal & Duckett, 2004a) uses a Gaussian kernel function to model the decreasing likelihood that a particular reading represents the true quantity (here: the time-averaged relative concentration) with respect to the distance from the point of measurement. For each measurement, two quantities are calculated for grid cells k: an importance weight and a weighted reading. In practice, only those cells in the vicinity of the point of measurement need to be considered, i.e. the cells for which the corresponding centre $x^{(k)}$ lies within a certain radius around the point x_t where the measurement was taken at time t. Cells that are further away from the measurement can be ignored since the effect of the update is negligible. The importance weight is calculated by evaluating the two-dimensional, uni-variate Gaussian function

$$N(\Delta \mathbf{x}_t^{(k)}) = \frac{1}{2\pi\sigma^2} e^{-\frac{(\Delta \mathbf{x}_t^{(k)})^2}{2\sigma^2}} \qquad (1)$$

at the displacement $\Delta x_t^{(k)} = x^{(k)} - x_t$ between the centre of grid cell k and the point of measurement x_t. This weight models the information content of a particular measurement r_t at the location $x^{(k)}$ of grid cell k. From these weights, two temporary grid maps are computed: $\Omega^{(k)}_t$ by integrating importance weights and $R^{(k)}_t$ by integrating weighted readings up to time t as

$$
\Omega_t^{(k)} = \sum_{i=1}^{t} N(|\mathbf{x}_i - \mathbf{x}^{(k)}|, \sigma),
$$
$$
R_t^{(k)} = \sum_{i=1}^{t} N(|\mathbf{x}_i - \mathbf{x}^{(k)}|, \sigma) \cdot r_i
$$

(2)

The kernel width σ is a parameter of the algorithm. Please note that the gas sensor readings r_i we consider here are first normalized by linear scaling of each sensor to the range of $[0, 1]$. Please note further that we assume perfect knowledge about the position x_i of a sensor at the time of the measurement. To account for the uncertainty about the sensor position in connection with any gas distribution modeling algorithm, the method in (Lilienthal et al., 2007) can be used.

The integrated weights $\Omega^{(k)}_t$ provide a confidence measure for the estimate at cell k. A high value means that the estimate is based on a large number of readings recorded close to the centre of the respective grid cell. A low value, on the other hand, means that few readings nearby the cell centre are available and that therefore a prediction has to be made using sensor readings taken at a rather large distance. Consequently, if the sum of the weights $\Omega^{(k)}_t$ exceeds a certain threshold value Ω_{min}, the grid cell is set to

$$
r_t^{(k)} = R_t^{(k)} / \Omega_t^{(k)} \quad : \quad \Omega_t^{(k)} \geq \Omega_{min}
$$

(3)

representing an estimate of the value of the distribution in that particular area of the environment. If the sum of weights is below Ω_{min}, the cell is considered unexplored. Since integrated weights $\Omega^{(k)}_t$ are used for normalization of the weighted readings $R^{(k)}_t$ even coverage is not necessary.

$\Omega^{(k)}_t$ models the information content of a series of gas sensor measurements in a way that reflects the sensor characteristics and the trajectory of the robot. An example is shown in Figure 2. First, the certainty about the average gas distribution is modeled as being higher if the gas sensor is moved at a slower speed. A higher information content is assumed by the Kernel DM algorithm especially in cases where a number of successive measurements were performed on the spot. In this case, the estimated value (calculated by averaging over multiple readings) represents

Figure 2. Integrated importance weightΩ_t for an example sensor trajectory. The contributions from each measurement position are shown (in black) together with the integrated value (in red). The trajectory results from a constant velocity movement along a straight path and an immediate stop after the fifth time step (i.e., measurements x_5, x_6 and x_7 were all taken at the same physical location). The Kernel DM algorithm considers a finite discretization of Ω_t to a grid map, which is not shown in this figure for the sake of a better illustration. The course of Ω_t shown here corresponds to a grid map discretization with infinite resolution.

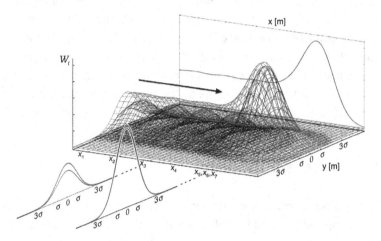

a temporally integrated quantity that naturally contains more information about the gas distribution at this particular location. This value also contains more information about adjacent places because of the higher certainty about the average gas distribution, and because the temporal mean also carries out spatial integration due to the spatial fluctuation of the gas.

Second, the information content is modeled to be particularly high *along* the sensor trajectory, i.e. at places to which the sensors have actually been exposed to. This is particularly important for gas sensors used in this study where, due to the memory effect of the metal oxide sensors, the sensor readings present a low-pass filtered response value integrated along the path driven. Correspondingly the continuously collected measurements contain information about the locations *between* the places where the sensor data were actually logged. By contrast, the importance model decreases quickly orthogonal to the sensor trajectory, corresponding to the fact that the distribution value can only be approximated by extrapolating on the actual measurements assuming smooth transitions in the time-constant gas distribution structure.

Finally, the certainty about the average concentration is modeled as being approximately constant along the path if the robot was driven at a constant, not too high speed. As long as the time constant of decay is much longer than the time between individual measurements, the information content of the sensor readings about locations along the integration path is in fact approximately independent of the actual points of measurements.

Parameters of the Kernel DM Algorithm

While the actual value of the threshold Ω_{min} was found to have a minor influence on the resulting gas distribution map (Lilienthal & Duckett, 2004a), the width σ of the Gaussian kernel function is a critical parameter. Referring to the exploration path of the robot, σ has to be chosen high enough to satisfy the requirement for sufficient extrapolation on the gas concentration measurements, but low enough to preserve the fine details of the mapped structures. In this work, fixed parameter values of $\sigma = 15$ cm, and $\Omega_{min} = 10.0 \times$ (number of sensors) were chosen based on the considerations in (Lilienthal & Duckett, 2004a).

Impact of the Sensor Dynamics

Due to the response characteristics of metal oxide sensors, a single gas sensor reading represents a temporally and, if the robot is driven at non-zero speed, also a spatially integrated concentration value. The averaging effect is considered implicitly by the model of the information content applied in the Kernel DM algorithm. The function in Equation (1) to compute importance weights contains, on the other hand, no term to model the asymmetry, which is induced by the much longer recovery time compared to the response time of the sensors. It would indeed not be possible to unambiguously determine the actual concentration distribution along the path that caused a given series of gas sensor readings. Therefore, an asymmetric term is not incorporated. Consequently, a certain level of distortion in the mapped gas distribution has to be tolerated. The magnitude of this distortion is estimated below.

As a consequence of the delayed response and the prolonged decay time of the gas sensors, the mapped values show asymmetrically blurred edges and a slightly shifted centre of the area of maximum concentration compared to the real distribution. This effect can be seen in Figure 3, which shows how a rectangular step pulse would be mapped by the Kernel DM algorithm introduced above. In the upper left part (a) the real distribution can be seen, which is a step pulse with an assumed duration of $\Delta t = 10$s. In addition, the response of the gas-sensitive system is shown in part (b). This curve was calculated using a first order sensor model with the parameters τ_r and τ_d of the Örebro Mark III mobile nose. In Figure 3 (c), the Gaussian kernel functions multiplied by the corresponding sensor readings are also shown. The samples were assumed to be recorded at a rate of 2 Hz and a width of $\sigma = 1$s

Figure 3. Mapping of a rectangular step pulse. The figure shows the step-like concentration course the gas-sensitive system is exposed to (a), the sensor response as calculated for the "Orebro Mark III mobile nose (b), the Gaussian weighting functions multiplied by the corresponding sensor readings (c), and the resulting curve of the mapped values (d).

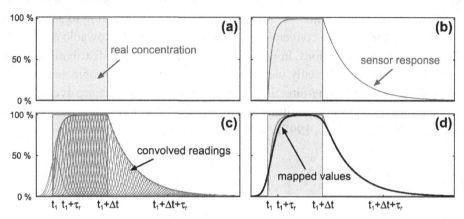

was used for the Gaussian kernel functions in Equation (1). This corresponds to a distance of $\sigma = 5$ cm, if a situation is considered where a robot drives with a constant velocity of 5 cm/s through a 50 cm wide area of constant concentration. Note that the Gaussians vanish in the front part of the graph due to the zero response of the sensor. Finally, the normalized curve of the mapped values is depicted in Figure 3 (d). This curve is calculated according to Equation (3), meaning that the sum of the Gaussians shown in Figure 3 (c) is divided by the sum of the weights.

Comparing the assumed distribution with the course of the mapped values, the asymmetrical shift as well as the blurring effect can be seen in Figure 3 (d). This distortion is, however, not critical. Due to the low speed of the robot, which never exceeded 5 cm/s during the experiments presented here, the expected shift would be in the order of 10 cm at most. This effect is even smaller for smoother distributions, which the metal-oxide sensors can follow more closely than a step-like one. Further on, the directional component of both effects gets averaged out if the robot passed the same point from different directions. For the experiments considered here, this condition is fulfilled because either a predefined exploration path was used, where the path is passed equally often from opposite directions, or the robot was controlled as a gas-sensitive Braitenberg vehicle (Braitenberg, 1984), and particular points were passed equally often from multiple directions on average. Thus, the mapping process results in a representation, which is broadened but not severely shifted compared to the true distribution.

ANALYTIC GAS DISTRIBUTION MODEL

It is currently not feasible to model all aspects of turbulent wind and gas distribution in a realistic environment. A general problem is that many boundary conditions are unknown. Even if sufficiently accurate knowledge about the state of the environment would be available, it would be very time-consuming to achieve the required resolution with a conventional finite element model (Kowadlo & Russell, 2003). For specific situations, however, the time-averaged gas distribution can be described in a computationally inexpensive way. Assuming isotropic and homogenous turbulence and a one-directional, constant wind field, the time-averaged gas distribution of a constantly emitting point source on the floor can be described as (Hinze, 1975; Ishida et al., 1998):

$$C(x,y) = \frac{q}{2\pi K} \frac{1}{r} e^{-\frac{V}{2K}(r-\mathbf{x_w})}, \tag{4}$$

$$r = \sqrt{(x_S - x)^2 + (y_S - y)^2}, \tag{5}$$

$$\mathbf{x_w} = \frac{\Delta \mathbf{x} \cdot \mathbf{w}}{|\mathbf{w}|} = (x_S - x)cos\theta + (y_S - y)sin\theta. \tag{6}$$

The concentration C at a point *(x, y)* level with the gas source is determined by the turbulent diffusion coefficient K, the location of the gas source (x_S, y_S), its release rate q, the wind speed V, and the upwind direction θ. Equation (4) comprises a term for symmetric $1/r$ decay and a second term that models asymmetric decay with respect to the wind direction. The variable $\mathbf{x_w}$ is the projection of the displacement with respect to the source to the upwind direction. Accordingly, the exponential term in Equation (4) is constant along the upwind direction and the asymmetric decay is steepest in downwind direction.

The model introduced in Equation (4) describes a system in the state of equilibrium where the gas source evaporates infinitely long into an infinite space. As a consequence, the model diverges at the source location, which is obviously an unrealistic description of the observed gas concentration. For this reason, the symmetric term is replaced here by the spatial profile of the Green's function of the diffusion equation. For a fixed time (> 0) this function declines with *exp(-const×* $r^2)$ and does not diverge at the source location. Consequently, the time-averaged gas distribution was modeled in this work as

$$\tilde{C}(x, y) = C_{00}e^{-C_S r^2} e^{-C_A (r - [(x_S - x)\cos\theta + (y_S - y)\sin\theta])} + C_B \qquad (7)$$

This model depends on seven parameters. C_{00} is the maximum concentration at the source location while C_S and C_A describe the magnitude of the symmetric and asymmetric decay, respectively. (x_S, y_S) are the coordinates of the point source and θ is the upwind direction, i.e. the angle between the upwind vector **w** and the x-axis. The parameter C_B is added in order to account for a non-zero base-level.

A comparison of the models specified in Equation (4) and Equation (7) is given in Figure 4. The model of the time-averaged gas distribution as defined in Equation (3.1) is shown in Figure 4 (a). In order to relate the models to each other, the parameters of the adapted model were chosen such that the symmetric terms are equal at a distance of 15cm in case of Figure 4 (b,c), and at a distance of 10cm in case of Figure 4 (d), respectively. The same asymmetric term was used for all four plots. Finally, the parameter C_S was chosen to represent a highly asymmetric distribution with $C_A/C_S = 5$ in Figure 4 (b) and more symmetric distributions with $C_A/C_S = 0.5$ in Figure 4 (c) and Figure 4 (d).

Figure 4. Comparison of models of the time-averaged gas distribution. A plot of the model given by Equation(3.1) (a) is compared with plots of the model given by Equation (3.4) for three different parameter sets: CA/CS = 5, symmetric term equal to the model in Equation (3.1) at a distance of 15 cm from the point source (b); CA/CS = 0.5, symmetric term equal to the model in Equation (3.1) at a distance of 15 cm (c); CA/CS = 0.5, symmetric term equal to the model in Equation (3.1) at a distance of 10 cm (d). The same asymmetric term was used for all four plots.

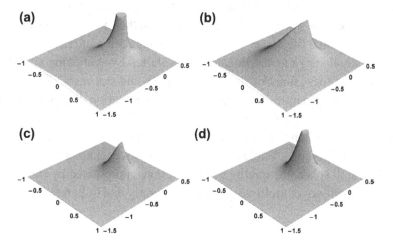

STEP 2: LEARNING PARAMETERS OF THE ANALYTICAL MODEL

The problem is now to find the set of parameters of the analytical model given in Equation (7), which approximates the statistical gas distribution grid map most closely.

In order to calculate the model quality for a given parameter set p, the gas distribution predicted by the analytical model C_p is discretized to the grid map and the deviation of $C_p^{(k)}$ from the value $r^{(k)}$ predicted by the statistical gas distribution grid map is determined for all corresponding grid cells $k \in \{1,..., N\}$. The prediction errors are then summed up and normalized over all explored cells, resulting in the average prediction error

$$\Delta_p = \sqrt{\frac{\sum_k (C_p^{(k)} - c^{(k)})^2}{N}} \tag{8}$$

with N being the total number of grid cells.

Optimization Using Evolution Strategies

Searching for the best set of parameters p in terms of minimizing the average prediction error is a typical optimization problem. Preliminary experiments showed that the particular optimization problem considered here is multi-modal, i.e. the function defined in Equation (8) comprises multiple possibly deceptive local optima apart from the global optimum.

Therefore, it was decided to use Evolutionary Algorithms (EA), which are known for their capability to perform well in multi-modal search spaces. EA are probabilistic, generational, population based optimization strategies that mimic the natural evolution based on Darwin's principle of the "survival of the fittest" by repeated simulation of a generational life cycle. Starting from a population of randomly initialized solutions (individuals) a generational cycle is started by evaluating all individuals with a target or fitness function, e.g. Equation (8), and stochastically selecting the best individuals to generate offspring for the next generation. Offspring is typically generated by making copies of the selected individuals (parents), which can then be altered through mutation (i.e. random changes) or crossover (i.e. mixing partial copies from multiple parents). While mutation and crossover enables the EA to explore the whole search space, the quality of the solutions represented by the individuals increases gradually over multiple generations simply due to iterated selection.

In this work, a special type of EA called Evolution Strategies (ES) is applied to the optimization problem. ES were developed by Rechenberg and Schwefel to solve practical application problems in mechanical engineering (Rechenberg, 1973; Schwefel, 1981). In contrast to Genetic Algorithms (GA) developed by Holland (Holland [1975]), ES abstract the key elements of EA to perform an efficient search especially on real-valued search spaces and typically use specialized mutation operators.

For example, instead of a stochastic selection scheme, ES use typically a *(μ+λ)*- or *(μ,λ)*-strategy, selecting only the *μ* best individuals as parents to generate *λ* offspring. In case of a *(μ,λ)*-strategy these offspring set up the next generation to be evaluated. A *(μ+λ)*-strategy, on the other hand, combines the *μ* parents and the *λ* offspring in the next generation. While a *(μ+λ)*-strategy is guaranteed to improve monotonically due to elitism, the *(μ,λ)*-strategy is usually better suited for multi-modal search spaces because it enables the ES to escape from local optima.

Self-Adapting Mutation Operators and Crossover

ES often use so called self-adapting mutation operators. A mutation operator that adds random values with a fixed variance to the decision parameters does not perform well in all cases. A fixed mutation step size can be too small in case an individual is in a local optimum or still far from the optimum. In this case the optimization algorithm would either converge prematurely or convergence would be achieved too slowly. On the other hand, a fixed mutation step size can also be too large if the individual is already close to the global optimum. Because oversized perturbations lead the offspring away from the global optimum this might prevent the algorithm to converge to an optimum at all.

Therefore, Rechenberg and Schwefel introduced so called strategy parameters σ^2 that define the mutation step size. Strategy parameters are used either one for all decision parameters (global mutation) or using a vector of strategy parameters one for each decision parameter (local mutation). Local mutation enables independent adaptation of the strategy parameters for each dimension of the problem space. Each individual has a unique set of decision and strategy parameters which are altered with a probability of p_{mut} by calculating the new strategy parameters σ'_j and the new model parameters p'_j as

$$\sigma'_j = \sigma_j \cdot e^{\tau \cdot N(0,1) + \tau' \cdot N_j(0,1)},$$
$$p'_j = p_j + \delta p_j \cdot \sigma'_j \cdot N_j(0,1). \tag{9}$$

$N(0, 1)$ and $N_j(0, 1)$ are random numbers independently drawn from a normal Gaussian distribution, τ is an overall learning rate and τ' is a coordinate wise learning rate. The parameters δp_j have to be assigned to each strategy parameter in advance. They specify the range for each decision variable and thus normalize the mutation step size to the size of the search space.

Ultimately, each individual can be altered by crossover of two parents $<p'_1, \sigma'_1>$ and $<p'_2, \sigma'_2>$ with a probability of p_{cross} as

$$\sigma''_j = \frac{\sigma'^1_j + \sigma'^2_j}{2},$$

$$\mathbf{p}'' = \left\langle p_1^{'R_1(1,2)}, p_2^{'R_2(1,2)}, \ldots, p_n^{'R_n(1,2)} \right\rangle.$$

(10)

Here, n gives the number of parameters, and $R_j(1, 2)$ is a random variable that is used to select for each decision parameter p_j with equal probability whether p_j is chosen from parent 1 or parent 2.

A non elitist generation strategy like the (μ, λ)-strategy will in the long run favor individuals with suitable strategy parameters, since their offspring will perform better than offspring from individuals with poorer strategy parameters. This way the ES is able to self-adapt the strategy parameters to the local properties of the search space.

Optimization Strategy Used in this Work

In order to determine suitable parameters for the ES, several test runs were performed where the model function was used with set parameters as the ground truth. These test runs showed that the performance of the ES with local mutation does not depend heavily on the actual value of the parameters used. As a parameter set that produced very good fitting results in the preliminary tests, enables self-adaption, and reduces the chance of premature convergence, the following parameters were used here: $\mu = 10$, $\lambda = 50$, $p_{mut} = 1.0$, $p_{cross} = 0.01$. The initial step width was set to $\sigma_j = \sigma_{init} = 0.1$. According to (Eiben & Smith, 2003), the overall learning rate and the coordinate wise learning rate were chosen to be $\tau = \{\sqrt{(2 \cdot \sqrt{n})}\}^{-1} \approx 0.435$ and $\tau' = \{\sqrt{(2n)}\}^{-1} \approx 0.267$, respectively. The parameter ranges p_j were chosen to be $[0,5]$ for C_{00}, $[0,20]$ for C_S and C_A, $[-4,4]$ for x_0 and y_0, $[-180°,180°]$ for θ, and $[-1,1]$ for C_B.

To reduce the chance to get stuck in a local optimum further, four independent ES optimization runs with 25000 fitness calls in each run were performed. Finally, the best individual found was selected and considered to be the best possible fit for the given gas distribution map.

SOURCES OF INACCURACY

A perfect agreement between the statistical gas distribution map and the analytical model given by Equation (7) cannot be expected in general for several reasons. First of all, the assumptions the analytical gas distribution model is based on might not be fulfilled. This mainly applies to the assumption of constant, unidirectional wind. Although no artificial air current was produced to create a dominant constant flow, the gas distribution was strikingly stable in the experiments presented in this paper, most likely due to stable temperature gradients in the room (Wandel et al., 2003). For that reason, the observed gas distribution can often be approximated reasonably well with the analytical model. Assuming only minor variations of the dominant air stream, the model will indicate the average wind direction while poorer fitness values are expected in case of stronger variations.

A further assumption, which is not completely fulfilled, is that the statistical gas distribution map represents the true time-averaged gas distribution as it would appear over infinitely long time. Due to the local character of gas sensor measurements, it takes some time to build the statistical grid map model. In addition to spatial coverage, a certain amount of temporal averaging is also necessary to represent the time-constant profile of the gas distribution. The basic structures in the map were found to stabilize within the first hour of the mapping experiments (Lilienthal & Duckett, 2004a). During this time, transient concentration peaks caused by turbulence might not be sufficiently averaged out and thus can be preserved in the statistical gas distribution map as minor deviations from the smooth course of the distribution. While this is generally more of a problem in regions of low concentration (because the peak to time-average ratio is higher there (Roberts & Webster, 2002), it is especially problematic concerning the experiments where the robot was reactively controlled to avoid low concentrations, causing a low density of measurements in regions where the average concentration is low. The distortions due to rudiments of turbulent peaks tend to influence the fit result because the region of low concentration was typically much larger than the area of high concentration in the experiments considered in this work. In order to compensate for this effect, a modified fitness function was used that compares the square of the prediction of the analytical model $C^{(k)}$ with the square of the corresponding grid cell value $r^{(k)}$.

$$\Delta_{\mathrm{p}} = \sqrt{\frac{\sum_k ((C^{(k)})^2 - (r^{(k)})^2)^2}{N}}, \qquad (11)$$

Hence, the influence of deviations in regions of low average concentration on the fitness function Δp is reduced compared to deviations in regions of high average concentration.

It is important to note that an important result of the fitting procedure, in addition to the obtained value of the fit parameters, is the fitness value itself, i.e. the average prediction error given in Equation (8) and Equation (11). A poor fitness indicates that the applied analytical model cannot describe the observed gas distribution (in terms of the statistical model) faithfully. If so, the source position estimate obtained from the best fit cannot be considered reliable and the best information at hand is the CME. On the other hand, if a good fitness can be achieved, the corresponding parameter set comprises a reasonable estimate of the source location as will be seen in Sec. "Results".

Please note that because of the difficulty to measure absolute concentrations with metal oxide gas sensors in an uncontrolled environment (Lilienthal & Duckett, 2004b), the gas distribution map directly models the sensor readings. Although the calibration function of the gas sensors is nearly linear if a small range of concentrations is considered as in the experiments presented here, it is therefore not possible to determine the absolute value of C_{00} and C_B. The remaining parameters, however, have a meaningful interpretation because they refer to the geometric dimension of the distribution profile. Therefore the fitting process described in Sec. "Step 2 – Learning Parameters of the Analytical Model" can be seen as model-based shape analysis of the statistical gas distribution grid map.

STEP 3: SELECTION OF SOURCE LOCATION ESTIMATE

The results of the second step are the parameters of the best fitting analytical model and the respective fitness value. The parameters of the analytical model include the coordinates of the source position. In the third step, the asymmetry ratio C_A/C_S and the optimal fitness value are used to determine whether the source estimate corresponding to the best analytical model or the estimate given by the maximum in the statistical gas distribution map is more reliable. This step corresponds to an analysis of the observed conditions, particularly the airflow conditions.

SABEC1: SHAPE ANALYSIS-BASED ESTIMATION CHOICE STRATEGY

Based on the observations above we propose the following strategies for determining an improved estimate of the gas source location. The first strategy is referred

Figure 5. Flowchart of the SABEC1 and SABEC2 strategy to select the most truthful estimate of the source location. Based on the fitness and the asymmetry of the best fit model obtained from optimizing the average prediction error with the ES, either the CME or the BFE is chosen, or no prediction is made at all.

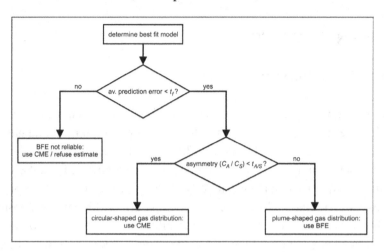

to in the following as SABEC1 strategy (Shape Analysis-Based Estimation Choice strategy). It is sketched in Figure 5, together with the SABEC2 strategy previously discussed. When applying the SABEC1 strategy, the best fitting analytical model is determined with the ES and the average prediction error (fitness) and the asymmetry ratio C_A/C_S are compared with corresponding threshold values t_f and $t_{A/S}$. If the average prediction error is above t_f, the BFE is considered not reliable and the CME is used to estimate the source location. The CME is also chosen in case of a prediction error below t_f and a low value of C_A/C_S, indicating a relatively weak stationary air current. Finally, the BFE is used in case of a small prediction error and a C_A/C_S value above $t_{A/S}$.

SABEC2: EVENTUALLY REFUSING TO PREDICT THE GAS SOURCE LOCATION

A further improvement of the accuracy can be obtained if it is acceptable to refuse a prediction of the source location in case both the BFE and the CME were found to be unreliable. The important observation in this context is that a poor fitness value, corresponding to an unstable wind field, for example, typically indicates an expanded region of high values in the statistical gas distribution map where the maximum can easily vary due to rudiments of turbulent fluctuations. This entails the

SABEC2 strategy also indicated in Figure 5, which selects the BFE or the CME in case of a reliable best fit model (depending on the asymmetry of the model) while it does not make a prediction in case of an unreliable model with a poor fitness.

EXPERIMENTAL SETUP

Robot and Gas Sensors

The experiments were performed with a Koala mobile robot equipped with the Mark III mobile nose (Lilienthal & Duckett, 2003a), comprising 6 tin oxide gas sensors manufactured by Figaro (see Figure 6). This type of chemical sensor shows a decreasing resistance in the presence of reducing volatile chemicals in the surrounding air. In consequence of the measurement principle, metal oxide sensors exhibit some drawbacks, including low selectivity, comparatively high power consumption (caused by the heating device) and weak durability. In addition, metal oxide sensors are subject to a long response time and an even longer recovery time (Lilienthal & Duckett, 2003a). However, this type of gas sensor is most often used on mobile robots because it is inexpensive, highly sensitive and relatively unaffected by changing environmental conditions such as room temperature and humidity. The gas sensors were placed in sets of three (of type TGS 2600, TGS 2610 and TGS 2620) inside two separate tubes containing a suction fan each. Papst Fans (Papst 405F) were used to generate an airflow of $8m^3/h$. Multiple, redundant sensor types were used only to increase the robustness of the system (there was no attempt to discriminate different odors). The distance between the two sets of sensors was 40 cm.

Figure 6. Koala robot with the Örebro Mark III mobile nose and the gas source used in the experiments. The small image in the top left corner shows a Figaro gas sensor used in the Mark III mobile nose.

Environment, Gas Source and Absolute Positioning System

All experiments were carried out in a rectangular laboratory room at ¨Orebro University (size 10.6×4.5 m²). The robot's movement was restricted so that its centre was always located inside the central region where precise and reliable position information is available from the external absolute positioning system WCAPS (Lilienthal & Duckett, 2003c), which was used to track the colored cardboard "hat" on top of the robot (the "hat" can be seen in Figure 6).

To emulate a typical task for an inspection robot, a gas source was chosen to imitate a leaking tank. This was realized by placing a paper cup filled with ethanol on a support in a bowl with a perimeter of 12cm (see Figure 6). The ethanol dripped through a hole in the cup into the bowl at a rate of approximately 50ml/h. Ethanol was used because it is non-toxic and easily detectable by the tin oxide sensors. The air conditioning system in the room was deactivated.

Results

An illustration of the optimization process described in Sec. "Step 2 – Learning Parameters of the Analytical Model" is given in Figure 7 and Figure 8. At the bottom right of each figure, the statistical gas distribution grid map, which is to be approxi-

Figure 7. Example of the model selection process. The statistical gas distribution grid map that is to be approximated can be seen at the bottom of the figure to the right of a fitness plot, which shows the average prediction error according to Equation (5.1). Four individual solutions corresponding to best model obtained after 500, 2500, 10000 and 25000 fitness calls are depicted in the top row.

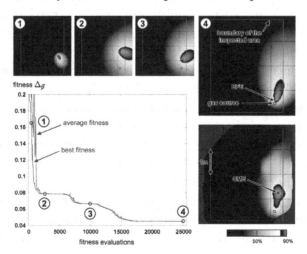

Figure 8. Example of the model selection process. In the same way as in Figure 7, a statistical gas distribution grid map, the fitness plot and best fit models obtained after 500, 2500, 7500 and 25000 fitness calls are shown.

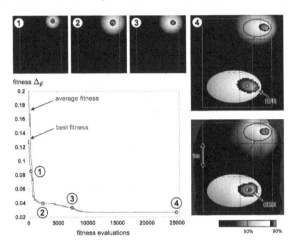

mated, is shown. The gas distribution maps in both figures were created from data collected in 90 minutes of exploration in two different experiments where the robot was reactively controlled as a Braitenberg vehicle which follows the local gradient sensed with a pair of gas sensor arrays (Lilienthal & Duckett, 2004a). To the left of the gas distribution map, the evolution of the average and the best fitness in the population is plotted depending on the number of fitness evaluations. In addition, four individual solutions are depicted in the top row. As indicated in the fitness plot, these solutions correspond to the best model obtained after a certain number of fitness evaluations. Different shadings are used to indicate relative concentration values in the gas distribution grid maps and the visualization of the model output (dark → low, light → high). Values higher than 90% of the maximum are displayed with a second range of dark-to-light shadings (of red), and unexplored cells are shown with a different color (dark green).

A good agreement between the statistical gas distribution map and the best fit model after 25000 fitness evaluations was obtained in both the cases considered in Figure 7 and Figure 8, indicated by a low fitness value. The fitting results, however, suggest that the experiments were carried out under different conditions. While the long stretched out shape of the fitted analytical model displayed in Figure 7 points to a relatively strong air current, a weaker air stream is indicated by the more circular shape of the best fit model shown in Figure 8. Such a difference is expressed by the ratio of the parameters C_A/C_B, which was 15.5 in case of the distribution in Figure 7 but only 2.8 for the distribution in Figure 8. In case of a strong asymmetry, i.e. a high C_A/C_B value, the CME is typically a poor approximation of the true source location. Due to the small variation of the gas distribution in upwind direction, small inhomogeneities of the wind field can cause a large displacement of the maximum along the direction of the air current. As in the example shown in Figure 7, the BFE is a more reliable estimate of the gas source position in case of a high ratio C_A/C_B.

On the other hand, the distance of the BFE to the gas source was often higher compared to the CME in case of a more symmetric distribution (see the example in Figure 8). A potential reason is that a circular distribution (with a corresponding source estimate in the centre of the region of increased concentration) can easily be interpreted as a plume-like structure (with a source estimate at the boundary of the same region), for example if the distribution was not explored properly around the gas source. Another reason might be due to the distortion and broadening effect due to the slow decay of the gas sensors mentioned when considering the impact of the sensor dynamics above. Regions of high concentration appear expanded in the map and consequently the fit results tend to be displaced with respect to the true gas source location by a certain amount. Here, the CME is typically a more accurate approximation of the gas source that is less sensitive to small deviations from the ideal distribution profile.

SABEC1 Results

The accuracy of different gas source location estimates was compared based on 97 snapshots of concentration maps obtained in 11 mapping experiments, including a total of 34 hours of exploration. In four runs the robot moved along a predefined path (inwards and outwards a rectangular spiral) while it was reactively controlled as a gas-sensitive Braitenberg vehicle in the remaining seven trials. The explored area was approximately $2.4 \times 2.4 \text{m}^2$ in the experiments with a predefined exploration path, and it was approximately $3.7 \times 3.7 \text{m}^2$ in the Braitenberg vehicle experiments. Snapshots of the gas distribution map were taken in intervals of 15 minutes starting after one hour of exploration to assure that the maps would represent mainly the stationary properties of the gas distribution (see Sec. "Sources of Inaccuracy").

A comparison of the results can be seen in Table 1. The first column specifies in which cases the BFE was chosen as the source position estimate instead of the

Table 1. Gas source localisation error obtained with the SABEC1 strategy

strategy (when to choose BFE)	*tf*, *tA/S*	[cm]
never	-, -	26.2 ± 20.9
if av. prediction error < *tf*	0.0470, -	22.2 ± 15.5
if av. prediction error < *tf* and *CA/CS* > *tA/S* (SABEC1)	0.0575, 8.0	17.8 ± 10.4

CME and the second column shows the optimal threshold parameters found. Finally, the average distance between the estimate and the true source location is given in the third column. The obtained accuracy was 15% better compared to using only the CME if the BFE was always selected in case a good fitness, and it was 32% lower if the BFE was selected with the SABEC1 strategy that additionally considers the asymmetry of the fit result. Note that only a weak dependency of the obtained accuracy on the values of the threshold parameters was observed. Thus, the exact choice of these values was found to be not critical.

SABEC2 Results

The accuracy obtained with the SABEC2 strategy and the percentage r_{np} of gas distribution maps, for which no prediction of the gas source location was made, are shown in Figure 9 depending on the chosen fitness threshold t_f and using a constant value of $t_{A/S} = 8.0$. As an example, a fitness threshold of $t_f = 0.055$ corresponded to an average error of (14.8 ± 7.3) cm while a prediction of the gas source location was refused for 31% of gas distribution map snapshots. The graph also shows the level of accuracy that was obtained using the CME only.

The monotonic evolution of the average error shown in Figure 9 demonstrates that the obtained fitness value is a suitable measure for the confidence about the gas source location estimate obtained from either the CME or the BFE. Thus, it

Figure 9. Dependency of the average error of gas source prediction on the fitness threshold t_f when the SABEC2 strategy is applied to determine whether the CME or the BFE is chosen as the final source location estimate, or a prediction is refused (crosses). The rate of gas distribution maps for which no prediction was made is also indicated (filled circles). The value of $t_{A/S}$ was set to 8.0.

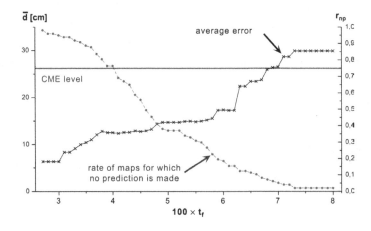

seems possible to compute from the fitness value a radius of an area around the estimate position where the source is expected with high certainty, or to choose a fitness threshold depending on the required accuracy.

CONCLUSION

The method presented in this chapter is visually summarized in Figure 10. It computes an estimate of the location of a single gas source from a set of localized gas sensor measurements and consists of three steps.

In the first step, a statistical model of the gas distribution is computed from a sequence of localized gas sensor measurements using the Kernel DM algorithm. This model represents the spatial structure of the time-averaged gas distribution in a two-dimensional grid map and averages out the transitory effects of turbulent gas dispersal. In this work, gas sensor readings and the corresponding position data were collected with a mobile robot while it was driven according to a particular exploration strategy.

In the second step, the parameters of an analytical model of the time-averaged gas distribution are learned by nonlinear least squares fitting of the analytical model to the statistical gas distribution map using Evolution Strategies. The analytical model

Figure 10. Summary of the proposed method to estimate the location of a single gas source

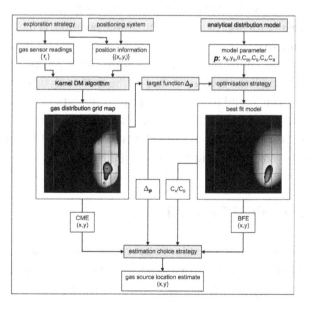

is based on a physical model that describes the time-averaged gas distribution under the assumptions of isotropic and homogenous turbulence, a constant, uniform wind field, and a constantly emitting point source on the floor. Accordingly, the fitting procedure includes an analysis of the statistical gas distribution map, which allows interpreting the shape of the statistically modeled gas distribution by quantitative means. This enables us to distinguish gas distribution maps according to different airflow conditions.

As a result of the second step we obtain the parameters of the best analytical model and the respective fitness value. The parameters of the best fitting analytical model include the coordinates of the source position (best fit estimate, BFE), and the asymmetry ratio C_A/C_S. These values are used in the third step, to determine whether the BFE or the CME is deemed more reliable. The SABEC1 strategy that always selects either the CME or the BFE is described and the SABEC2 strategy that might also refuse to output a source location estimate is also detailed. The third step formalizes the analysis of the observed conditions, particularly the airflow conditions.

The proposed method was evaluated based on a total of 34 hours of mapping experiments. Using the SABEC1 strategy, the obtained estimate of the gas source location was found to be 32% more accurate than the CME. Moreover, it was demonstrated that an even better accuracy can be obtained by using the SABEC2 strategy at the cost of an increasing rate of gas distribution maps for which no prediction about the gas source location is made. The BFE was found to be more reliable than the CME if the mapping experiment was performed under conditions of a relatively strong constant air current, indicated by a high asymmetry ratio C_A/C_S of the best fitting analytical model. Finally, it was found that the quality of the best fitting analytical model (in terms of the achieved fitness value) can be used as a confidence measure for approximating the source position. If the observed airflow is heavily deviating from the assumption of a uniform, constant flow, the best fitness is expected to be still comparatively poor and this indicates that the source location estimate obtained from the parameters of the best analytical model is not very reliable. In fact, it was found that if the best fitting analytical model approximated the gas distribution map rather poorly, both BFE *and* CME were found to be less accurate than in cases where the average deviation between the best fit model and the statistical gas distribution grid map was small.

FUTURE RESEARCH DIRECTIONS

The proposed method can be extended in several ways. First, a more sophisticated algorithm than Kernel DM can be used to build the statistical gas distribution model from a sequence of localized gas sensor measurements. In particular, algorithms that estimate both the mean field and a predictive variance are of interest, such as Kernel DM+V (Lilienthal et al., 2009) or the method using Gaussian Process mixtures proposed by (Stachniss et al., 2009). The maximum of the predictive variance provides an additional estimate of the gas source location. Another interesting extension is to use wind information collected together with the gas sensor readings for building the statistical gas distribution model as in (Reggente & Lilienthal, 2009a).

Wind information could also be used in the second step of the approach introduced in this chapter, for example as initial guess for the corresponding parameters of the analytical model or as an alternative means to determine the best estimate of the gas source location by distinguishing different airflow conditions. Based on a model of the wind field, more involved analytical models of gas dispersal could be used instead of the model described.

The proposed approach builds a two-dimensional statistical gas distribution model from the gas sensor measurements, which were collected according to a pre-defined exploration strategy. A further possibility for future research is therefore to investigate adaptive exploration, i.e. strategies that determine where to collect future measurements based on the current gas distribution model. Ultimately, a three-dimensional approach needs to be developed. An initial step is to build three-dimensional statistical gas distribution models based on gas sensor measurements such as in (Reggente & Lilienthal, 2009b). On the long run, building the gas distribution model should consider all available relevant information, including, for example, the temperature distribution and the spatial outline of the environment.

ACKNOWLEDGMENT

This work has partly been supported by the EC under contract number FP7-224318-DIADEM: Distributed Information Acquisition and Decision-Making for Environmental Management.

REFERENCES

Blackmore, B. S., & Griepentrog, H. W. (2002). A future view of precision farming. In *Proceedings of PreAgro Precision Agriculture Conference* (pp. 131-145), Müncheberg, Germany, Center for Agricultural Landscape and Land Use Research (ZALF).

Braitenberg, V. (1984). *Vehicles: Experiments in synthetic psychology*. MIT Press/Bradford Books.

DustBot Consortium. (2006). *DustBot-networked and cooperating robots for urban hygiene*. Retrieved from http://www.dustbot.org

Eiben, A. E., & Smith, J. E. (2003). *Introduction to evolutionary computing*. New York, NY: Springer.

Hinze, J. O. (1975). *Turbulence*. New York, NY: McGraw-Hill.

Holland, J. H. (1975). *Adaptation in natural and artificial systems*. MIT Press.

Ishida, H., Nakamoto, T., & Moriizumi, T. (1998). Remote sensing of gas/odor source location and concentration distribution using mobile system. *Sensors and Actuators. B, Chemical, 49*, 52–57. doi:10.1016/S0925-4005(98)00036-7

Kowadlo, G., & Russell, R. A. (2003). Naive physics for effective odour localisation. In *Proceedings of the Australian Conference on Robotics and Automation*.

Lilienthal, A. J., & Duckett, T. (2003a). A stereo electronic nose for a mobile inspection robot. In *Proceedings of the IEEE International Workshop on Robotic Sensing*.

Lilienthal, A. J., & Duckett, T. (2003b). An absolute positioning system for 100 Euros. In *Proceedings of the IEEE International Workshop on Robotic Sensing*.

Lilienthal, A. J., & Duckett, T. (2003c). Creating gas concentration gridmaps with a mobile robot. In *Proceedings of the IEEE/RSJ International Conference on Intelligent Robots and Systems* (pp. 118–123).

Lilienthal, A. J., & Duckett, T. (2004a). Building gas concentration gridmaps with a mobile robot. *Robotics and Autonomous Systems, 48*(1), 3–16. doi:10.1016/j.robot.2004.05.002

Lilienthal, A. J., & Duckett, T. (2004b). Experimental analysis of gas-sensitive Braitenberg vehicles. *Advanced Robotics, 18*(8), 817–834. doi:10.1163/1568553041738103

Lilienthal, A. J., Loutfi, A., Blanco, J. L., Galindo, C., & Gonzalez, J. (2007). A Rao- Blackwellisation approach to GDM-SLAM integrating SLAM and gas distribution mapping. In *Proceedings of the European Conference on Mobile Robotics*, (pp. 126–131).

Lilienthal, A. J., Reggente, M., Trincavelli, M., Blanco, J. L., & Gonzalez, J. (2009). A statistical approach to gas distribution modelling with mobile robots–the Kernel DM+V Algorithm. In *Proceedings of the IEEE/RSJ International Conference on Intelligent Robots and Systems*, (pp. 570-576).

Lilienthal, A. J., Streichert, F., & Zell, A. (2005). Model-based shape analysis of gas concentration gridmaps for improved gas source localisation. In *Proceedings of the IEEE International Conference on Robotics and Automation*, (pp. 3575–3580).

Nakamoto, T., Ishida, H., & Moriizumi, T. (1999). A sensing system for odor plumes. *Analytical Chemistry News & Features, 1*, 531–537.

Rechenberg, I. (1973). *Evolutionsstrategie: Optimierung technischer Systeme nach Prinzipien der biologischen Evolution*. Fromman-Holzboog.

Reggente, M., & Lilienthal, A. J. (2009a). Using local wind information for gas distribution mapping in outdoor environments with a mobile robot. In *Proceedings of IEEE Sensors*, (pp. 1715-1720).

Reggente, M., & Lilienthal, A. J. (2009b). Three-dimensional statistical gas distribution mapping in an uncontrolled indoor environment. *AIP Conference Proceedings Volume 1137: Olfaction and Electronic Nose - Proceedings of the 13th International Symposium on Olfaction and Electronic Nose* (ISOEN), (pp. 109-112).

Roberts, P. J. W., & Webster, D. R. (2002). Turbulent diffusion. In Shen, H., Cheng, A., Wang, K.-H., Teng, M. H., & Liu, C. (Eds.), *Environmental fluid mechanics-theories and application*. Reston, VA: ASCE Press.

Russell, R. A. (1999). *Odour sensing for mobile robots*. World Scientific.

Schwefel, H.-P. (1981). *Numerical optimization of computer models*. New York, NY: John Wiley & Sons, Inc.

Shraiman, B., & Siggia, E. (2000). Scalar turbulence. *Nature, 405*, 639–646. doi:10.1038/35015000

Stachniss, C., Plagemann, C., & Lilienthal, A. J. (2009). Learning gas distribution models using sparse Gaussian process mixtures. *Autonomous Robots, 26*(2-3), 187–202. doi:10.1007/s10514-009-9111-5

Wandel, M. R., Lilienthal, A. J., Duckett, T., Weimar, U., & Zell, A. (2003). Gas distribution in unventilated indoor environments inspected by a mobile robot. In *Proceedings of the IEEE International Conference on Advanced Robotics*, (pp. 507–512).

ADDITIONAL READING

Mobile Robot Olfaction

Lilienthal, A. J., Loutfi, A., & Duckett, T. (2006). Airborne Chemical Sensing with Mobile Robots. *Sensors (Basel, Switzerland)*, *6*, 1616–1678. doi:10.3390/s6111616

Russell, R. A. (1999). *Odour Sensing for Mobile Robots*. World Scientific.

Environmental Monitoring

Gilbert, R. O. (1987). *Statistical Methods for Environmental Pollution Monitoring*. Wiley.

Fluid Dynamics

Ferziger, J. H., & Peric, M. (2001). *Computational Methods for Fluid Dynamics*. Springer.

Hinze, J. O. (1975). *Turbulence*. New York: McGraw-Hill.

Evolution Strategies

Schwefel, H.-P. (1995). *Evolution and Optimum Seeking*. Wiley & Sons.

ENDNOTES

[1]   Please note that because of calibration issues with gas sensors the sensor response is typically normalised but otherwise modelled directly. To emphasize this procedure we use the term "gas distribution map" while, if the input is given in absolute concentration values, we call the resulting representation a "gas concentration map". Accordingly, in the former case, the term "concentration maximum estimate" does not imply that the absolute concentration value could be precisely estimated. The *location* of the concentration maximum will be estimated correctly, however, assuming that the response of all involved sensors depend on the concentration in the same, monotonous way.

[2]   Not to confuse with the kernel width σ in Equation (2.1), for example.

Chapter 11

Enhancing the Classification of Eye Bacteria Using Bagging to Multilayer Perceptron and Decision Tree

Xu-Qin Li
University of Warwick, UK

Evor L. Hines
University of Warwick, UK

Mark S. Leeson
University of Warwick, UK

D. Daciana Iliescu
University of Warwick, UK

ABSTRACT

Eye bacteria are vital to the diagnosis of eye disease, which makes the classification of such bacteria necessary and important. This chapter aims to classify different kinds of eye bacteria after the data were collected by an Electronic Nose. First the Multi-layer perceptron (MLP) and decision tree (DT) were introduced as the algorithm and the base classifiers. After that, the bagging technique was introduced to both algorithms and showed that the accuracy of the MLP had been significantly improved. Moreover, bagging to the DT not only reduced the misclassification rate, but enabled DT to select the most important features, and thus, decreased the dimension of the data facilitating an enhanced training and testing process.

DOI: 10.4018/978-1-61520-915-6.ch011

INTRODUCTION

The eye is one of the main human organs which links to the inner body and is continuously exposed to a harsh outside environment, where it is continually in contact with pathogenic airborne organisms. Although the eyelid may help to protect the eye, the warm, moist, enclosed environment between the conjunctiva and the eyelid also enables contaminating bacteria to establish an infection. The number of organisms responsible for infection of the eye is relatively small but they can proliferate rapidly and cause serious and irreversible damage to the eyes, which makes rapid diagnosis essential. Usually this kind of diagnosis is based on the study of the symptoms, such as changes in bodily appearance, feel, functions and so on. Since different diseases produce distinctive and specific characteristic odors, smelling the bacteria becomes a significant part of diagnosis.

Fortunately, after 20 years of development, electronic noses (ENs) have been very successful in detection applications in the areas of health and safety, and the task of diagnosing medical conditions through analyzing odors. This is because an electronic nose is an instrument, which compromises an array of electro chemical sensors with partial specificity and an appropriate pattern recognition system, capable of recognizing simple or complex odors. Many of the initial applications of ENs were concerned with the detection and classification of bacteria, which suggests that ENs can be used for medical diagnosis purposes in the detection of bacteria associated with eye diseases.

In this chapter, we focus on the use of the Cyranose 320 (Cyrano Sciences Inc.) for the detection of bacteria responsible for eye infections using pure laboratory cultures. This project represents a joint collaboration between researchers from the University of Warwick and Doctors from Heartlands Hospital and Micropathology Ltd., a medical laboratory specializing in the detection of these pathogens(Boilot et al., 2002).

EXPERIMENT AND DATA COLLECTION

Instrumentation

The most common bacterial eye infection is conjunctivitis. Organisms such as Staphylococcus aureus, Haemophilus influenzae, Streptococcus pneumonia and Escherichia coli have been associated with this condition. Although the number of organisms responsible for infection of the eye is relatively small, the damage caused may be irreversible which makes rapid diagnosis essential. Techniques such as neural network based ENs, which can almost instantly detect and classify odorous volatile components enable the nature of the infection to be diagnosed as quickly as possible. The EN, which is able to mimic the human sense of smell has been the subject of much research at the University of Warwick over the past 20 years or so (Dutta, Hines, Gardner, & Boilot, 2002).

The EN used here was a Cyrano Sciences' Cyranose 320, currently it is used in diverse industries including petrochemical, chemical, medical, food, packaging and many more. For example, the diagnosis of disease often relies on invasive testing methods, subjecting patients to unpleasant procedures. A tool such as the Cyranose 320 will enable physicians and dentists to provide immediate, accurate diagnosis of chemical components and microorganisms in breath, wounds, and bodily fluid.

The Cyranose 320 is a portable system which consists of 32 individual polymer sensors blended with carbon black composite, configured as an array. It works by exposing this array of polymer composite sensors to the chemical components in a vapor or aromatic of volatile compounds they swell. When the sensors come in contact with the vapor, the polymer expands like a sponge, changing the conductivity of the carbon pathways and causing the resistance of the composites. The change in resistance is measured as the sensor signal and captured as the digital pattern representing the test smell (Gardner, Boilot, & Hines, 2005) and from that measurement the overall response to a particular sample is produced.

Experimental Materials

For the eye bacteria experiment, the tests were conducted under typical lab conditions. The most common bacteria responsible for eye infection is conjunctivitis and organisms such as Staphylococcus aureus (sar), Haemophilus influenzae (hai), Streptococcus pneumonia (stp), Escherichia coli (ecoli), Pseudomonas aeruginosa (psa) and Moraxella catarrhalis (moc). All bacteria strains were grown on blood or lyse blood agar in standard petridishes at 37° C in a humidified atmosphere of 5% CO_2 in air. After overnight culturing, the bacteria were suspended in sterile saline solution (0.15 M NaCl) to a concentration of approximately $10^8, 10^5, 10^4$ colony forming units (cfu)/ml. A ten-fold dilution series of bacteria in saline was prepared and these three dilutions were sniffed using the ENs. The numbers of viable bacteria present were confirmed by plating out a small aliquot of the diluted samples and counting the resultant colonies after overnight incubation (Dutta et al., 2002).

DATA COLLECTION AND PROCESSING

The Cyranose 320 is based on a 32-sensor array of conducting polymers which produce a unique response signature representative of the test smell. When the sensors are exposed to vapors or aromatic volatile compounds the sensors swell, changing the conductivity of the carbon pathways and causing an increase in the resistance value that is monitored as the sensor signal. The resistance changes across the array are captured as a digital pattern that is representative of the test smell. The sensor technology yields a distinct response signature for each vapor regardless of its complexity; the overall response to a particular sample produces a 'smell print' specific to a stimulus. For each solution of our eye bacteria tests, the datalogger was introduced manually into a sterile glass vial containing a fixed volume of bacteria in suspension (4 ml) to collect samples. The operation was repeated ten times for each one of the three dilutions for each one of the six bacteria species, to give a total of 180 readings. These data ware gathered throughout a whole week. After that, the key features were extracted from the raw data files saved during the data collection in terms of static change in sensor resistance. All the data was normalized using a fractional difference model: $dR=(R-R_0)/R_0$ where R is the response of the system to the sample gas and R_0 is the baseline reading with the reference gas being the ambient room air. The complete bacteria data set was then normalized by dividing each dR (values between [1.1, 18.2] $m\Omega$) by the maximum value for each sensor, in order to set the range of each sensor parameter to [0, 1].

INTRODUCTION TO THE CLASSIFICATION TECHNIQUES

The goal of designing the pattern recognition classifiers when applied to EN data is typically to generate a class predictor for an unknown odor vector from a discrete set of previously learned patterns. The techniques we used here are artificial neural networks and Decision trees.

Introduction to Multilayer Perceptron Networks

Neural Networks (NNs) were first introduced in the 1940s, and then was motivated by the attempt to simulate the human brain on computers. NNs have been used in a wide range of applications, ranging from pattern recognition, classification to optimization problems.

Typically, a Neural Network (NN) consists of a number of layers with neurons distributed over them. All neurons in a layer are connected to all neurons in adjacent layers through unidirectional branches. Figure 1 shows a typical architecture of the neural networks.

The first layer does not perform any computation but only sees the input information, which could be a series of numbers representing data, is input into its neurons. The outputs of the first layer are presented to the second layer whose

Figure 1. An architecture of a typical structure of MLP

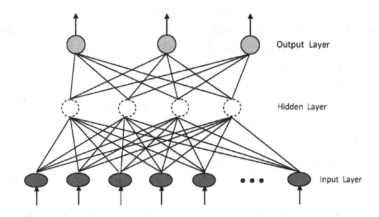

outputs are input to the third layer, which is why the term 'forward' is used. As the data travels through the network, the input is modified, and the output is updated. Subsequently, the results are generated. So it's quite natural that this kind of architecture is called Multi-layer Perceptron (MLP) Neural Networks. Figure 1 shows a typical three-layer MLP model.

Backpropagation (BP) is the most widely used learning algorithm for the MLP neural network model. BP is a supervised training algorithm where for each input pattern, the expected output is known to the network. Thus, given the input and output pair, the MLP will get its weights updated by the BP algorithm as appropriate (Ivica & Fredric, 2000).

Introduction to the Decision Tree

A decision tree partitions the input space (also known as the feature or attribute space) of a data set into mutually exclusive regions, each of which is assigned a label, a value or an action to characterize its data points. It's a tree structure consisting of nodes and branches, whose nodes being designated as an internal or terminal node. Internal nodes are ones that split into two children, while terminal nodes, also known as leaves, do not have any children and are associated with a label or value that characterizes the given data. In general, a decision tree is employed as follows. First, we present a datum (usually a vector composed of several attributes or elements) to the starting node (or root node) of the decision tree. Depending on the result of a decision function used by an internal node, the tree will branch to one of the node's children. This is repeated until a terminal node is reached and a label or value is assigned to the given input data (Wendy & Angel, 2007).

Decision trees used for classification problems are often called classification trees, and each terminal node contains a label that indicates the predicted class of a given feature vector. In the same vein, decision trees used for regression problems are often called regression trees, and the terminal node labels may be constants or equations that specify the predicted output value of a given input vector. To construct an appropriate decision tree, the Classification and Regression Tree (CART) algorithm first grows the tree extensively based on a sample (training) data set, and then prunes the tree back based on a minimum cost-complexity principle. The result is a sequence of trees of various sizes; the final tree selected is the tree that performs best when another independent (test) data set is presented. Generally, CART does this through two phases: tree growing and tree pruning (Jang, Sun, & Mizutani, 1997).

General Bootstrap Methodology and Bootstrap Aggregation

The treatment of the bootstrap methods comes from (Efron & Tibshirani, 1993). There is no generic and consistent terminology in the literature of what techniques are considered to be a bootstrap method. Here, we use bootstrap to refer to Monte Carlo simulations that treat the original sample as the pseudo-population or as an estimate of the population. Thus, we now resample from the original sample instead of sampling from the pseudo-population (Davison & Hinkley, 1997). In this section, we will discuss the general bootstrap methodology. The application of it to the MLP and decision tree will be discussed later.

The bootstrap is a method of resampling with replacement in which we generate the random samples from a population. We obtain each bootstrap replica by randomly selecting N observations out of N with replacement, where N is the dataset size. Suppose we denote the original sample as $x=(x_1,...,x_n)$. We can denote the new sample obtained from this method by $x^* = (x_1^*, \cdots, x_n^*)$. *Bagging*, the acronym for "Bootstrap Aggregation", is a method for generating an aggregate classifier by using multiple versions of a classifier. Each version of the classifier is trained by using a set of bootstrap replica training dataset, which means each version of the training set is created by randomly selecting $n<=N$ samples of a training dataset. And then each training dataset is used to train a classifier model, resulting in n classifiers. To classify a new observation, we find the class predicted by each of the bootstrap classifiers and assign the class label that is predicted most often among the bootstrap classifiers or by the average of the classifiers (Wendy & Angel, 2007).

Bagging works by reducing variance of an unbiased base classifier such as the MLP or a decision tree. The base classifier must be unstable; its configuration must vary significantly from one bootstrap replica to another.

SIMULATION RESULT

In this Chapter we first propose the use of a basic MLP and a decision tree to classify the eye bacteria data. After that we introduce the bagging technique to enhance their performance.

Using MLP as Base Classifier

An MLP is a forward network that consists of an input layer, one or more hidden layer and an output layer. The number of the input layer neurons is determined by the number of features of the input pattern. Here for the eye bacteria data, we have 32 sensors which subsequently generate a 32-dimension feature dataset. In addition to that, the number of hidden layers, the number of neurons in each hidden layer, the number of training epochs and the learning rate and the momentum are all the parameters which may influence the network's performance. These parameters have to be carefully selected to guarantee the performance through cross validation. The most frequently employed training algorithm for MLP is Back Propagation (BP). Usually, BP is executed in two phases: forward phase and backward phase. The forward phase involves feeding an input pattern to the input layer and propagating the signal to the output layer to generate the predicted class which is then compared to the target output to compute the error. In the backward phase, the error is backpropagated to adjust the weights between the hidden layer and the output layer and the weights between the hidden layer and the input layer. The standard training algorithms for feed-forward MLP are either back-propagation with gradient descent (GD) or Levenberg-Marquardt (LM). Here we choose both of these two as the back-propagation training algorithm.

For our eye bacteria experiment, the objective is to discriminate samples in terms of bacteria species. So we set the number of input layer neurons to 32 (corresponding to the number of sensors in the EN) and used one output layer neuron. The whole data was divided into three datasets: training set, validation set and testing set. However, in our testing procedure, a standard MLP cannot achieve an accuracy of more than 90 percent.

After that we introduced the bagging techniques to the MLP. This technique consists of creating new training data sets to generate a base classifier by applying a learning algorithm. The final prediction is determined by the average predictions of each created classifier. For this test, 100 replicas were produced to establish 100 ensemble classifiers. The procedure was outlined below:

1. Generate a bootstrap sample of size 72 by sampling from the original data set.
2. Construct and train a base MLP classifier with the bootstrap sample in step 1.

3.   Repeat step one and step two 100 times. This will yield 100 classifiers.
4.   Take the testing dataset to each of the classifiers. That will yield less than 100 class labels for each input pattern. Assign a appropriate class label to each of the input pattern.

For our test, we randomly select the testing dataset. After selecting 100 times from the whole data set, for an average instance, the times for it to be selected ranges between 6-15 times, which in turn generated the same number of class labels as the times it was selected for every instance. Thus we constructed a parameter called Mean Magnitude Error (MME) to evaluate the accuracy of the bagging MLP technique. The MME was defined as:

$$MME = \frac{1}{n}\sqrt{\sum_{i=1}^{n}(O_i - T)^2} \tag{1}$$

where O_i is the predicted class label for a classifier and T is the targeted output for this instance, and n is the number of times this instance was selected by the ensemble classifier. A good classifier will generate a lower value of MME (Braga, Oliveira, Ribeiro, & Meira, 2007). Figure 2 shows the MME values for all the instances generated by the ensemble.

Figure 2. MME for all the instances

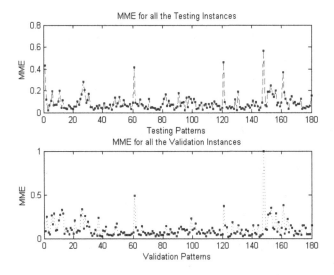

Table 1. MME vs. accuracy

MME threshold	Accuracy for LM	Accuracy for GD
0.6	100.00%	98.89%
0.5	99.44%	98.33%
0.4	97.78%	95.00%
0.3	97.22%	87.22%
0.2	95.00%	65.00%

Table 1 shows the relationship between the MME threshold and accuracy. It can be seen that the accuracy can be as high as 100% if the MME threshold was set to 0.6, which is a great improvement to the original MLP. Figure 3 shows the linear regression relationship between the network outputs and the corresponding targets. The R-values have proved that the network outputs for both testing data and validation data fit well with the targeted ones.

Using Decision Tree as the Base Classifier

The idea behind a classification tree is to split the high dimensional data into smaller and smaller partitions, such that the partitions become purer in terms of the class membership. It first grows an overly large tree using a criterion that generates optimal splits for the tree. Usually, these large trees fit the training data set very well, but they do not generalize well, so the rate at which we correctly classify new patterns is low. Figure 4 shows a cluttered-looking tree using a series of rules such as "X_{23} < 0.648033" to classify each pattern into one of 13 terminal nodes. To determine the input pattern assignment for an observation, the decision tree starts at the top node and applies the rule. If the point satisfies the rule the tree takes the left path,

Figure 3. Regression of testing and validation data

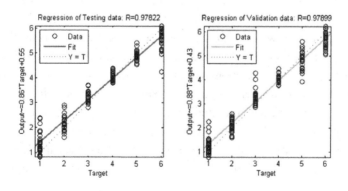

Figure 4. Classification tree structure before pruning

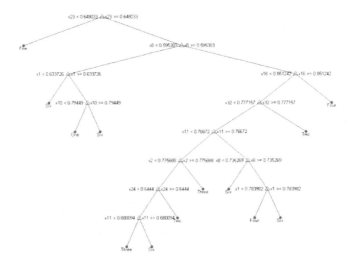

and if not it takes the right path. Ultimately it reaches a terminal node that assigns an input pattern to one of the six categories.

It is usually possible to find a simpler tree that performs as well as or even better than the more complex tree. But usually this complex tree over fits the training data and will not generalize well to new patterns. So the "true" error rate this complex classification tree would incur by using it to classify new data should be taken into account. The suggestion made by (Breiman et al., 1984) is to find a nested sequence of subtrees by successively pruning branches of the overly large tree. The best tree from this sequence is chosen based on the misclassification rate estimated by cross-validation or an independent test sample. That means a simpler subset of that tree may give a smallest error because some of the decision rules in the full tree hurt rather than help. Figure 5 shows the tree test result using a ten folder cross validation in which a subset of 10% of the data was set aside for validation and the remaining 90% of the data was used for training. First the resubstitution error or the proportion of the original observations that were misclassified by various subsets of the original tree was computed. Then cross-validation was used to estimate the true error for trees of various sizes. Figure 5 indicates that the resubstitution error is overly optimistic. It decreases as the tree size grows, but the cross-validation results show that beyond a certain point, increasing the tree size increases the error rate based on that the tree with the smallest cross-validation error was chosen. While this may be satisfactory, the preferred way is to use a simpler tree if it is roughly as good as a more complex tree. The rule used is to take the simplest tree that is within one standard error of the minimum. This was shown on Figure 5. It was

Figure 5. The estimated error for cross validation and resubstitution

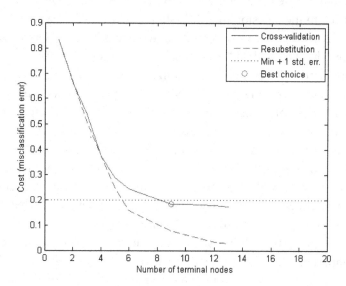

obtained by computing a cutoff value that was equal to the minimum cost plus one standard error. The best level is the smallest tree under this cutoff. Note that best-level = 0 corresponds to the unpruned tree, so one standard error was added to the minimum cost to get the cutoff value. After that, the pruned tree was obtained using the best level and the estimated misclassification cost was computed. Figure 6 displays the pruned classification tree. And for this Eye bacteria data, the misclassification error cost is 20.00%.

Figure 6. The optimal tree with nine terminal nodes after pruning

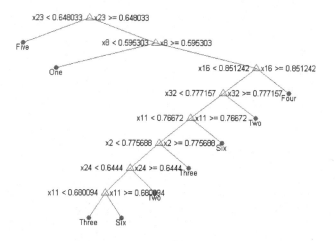

In order to decrease the misclassification error cost, the bagging technique was also introduced to the decision tree. It is statistically proved that drawing N out of N observations with replacement omits on average 37% of observations for each decision tree. These are called "out-of-bag" observations. They can be used to estimate the predictive power and feature importance. For each observation, the out-of-bag prediction was estimated by averaging over predictions from all trees in the ensemble for which this observation is out of bag. Then the computed prediction was compared against the true response for this observation. By comparing the out-of-bag predicted responses against the true responses for all observations used for training, the average out-of-bag error was achieved. This out-of-bag average is an unbiased estimator of the true ensemble error. The solid line in Figure 7 shows the out-of-bag error curve for the ensemble classifier. It can be seen that the misclassification error cost had decreased significantly to 9.44%.

Usually the prediction ability should depend more on important features and less on unimportant features. Another attractive feature of bagged decision trees is its ability to select the important features by randomly permuting out-of-bag data across one variable or column at a time and estimating the increase in the out-of-bag error due to this permutation. The larger the increase, the more important the feature is. Thus, it is not necessary to supply test data for bagged ensembles because the most important feature can be obtained through this process thus the dimension of the training data can be reduced significantly and the computation cost can be lower. Figure 8 shows the out-of-bag feature importance for all the 32 features. Using an arbitrary cutoff at 0.6, the most important 11 features were selected. The lower dimensional data (the selected features) was then used to train the ensemble

Figure 7. Misclassification error cost curve

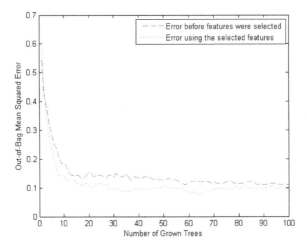

Figure 8. Feature importance histogram

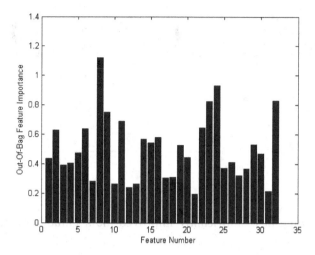

classifier following the same procedure. The dotted line in Figure 7 shows the out-of-bag error using the selected features. The performance is obviously at least as good as the one using the whole data.

After the features were selected, the dataset was also tested using Bagging MLP to test its effectiveness. Table 2 shows the relationship between the MME threshold and accuracy after using the selected features to train MLP using two different algorithms. It can be seen that the accuracy can reach 100% if the MME threshold was set to 0.5. Figure 9 shows the linear regression relationship between the network outputs and the corresponding targets using selected features. It can be seen that the output tracks the target well for both testing and validation set, both with a significantly high R-value.

To sum up, an ensemble of classifiers is a set of classifiers whose individual classifier decisions are combined in a way to classify a new instance. It performs well when the single classifier is unstable. In our example, the performance of the

Table 2. MME vs. accuracy

MME threshold	Accuracy for LM	Accuracy for GD
0.6	100.00%	99.44%
0.5	100.00%	98.33%
0.4	98.33%	94.44%
0.3	96.67%	88.89%
0.2	94.44%	66.67%

Figure 9. Regression of testing and validation data using selected features

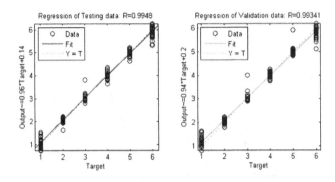

presented ensemble has significantly improved the accuracy compared with the base classifiers.

CONCLUSION

In our experiment, we want to classify six bacteria which are responsible for eye infection. First the MLP and the decision tree were employed in order to discriminate between these six bacteria species. It shows that although a single MLP can classify the data set, the accuracy is not high enough and the results are highly unstable and dependent on the network initialization. The decision tree constructed was able to discriminate different bacteria classes to some extend with a high error cost. By introducing the bagging technique to MLP, we were not only able to enhance the accuracy but also stabilize the results. By bagging the decision tree, we have successfully extracted several most important features and reduced the dimensionality of the original data. In addition to that, the error cost of the classification tree has also reduced significantly making the decision tree more reliable.

REFERENCES

Boilot, P., Hines, E. L., Gardner, J. W., Pitt, R., John, S., & Mitchell, J. (2002). Classification of bacteria responsible for ENT and eye infections using the Cyranose system. *IEEE Sensors Journal*, 2(3), 247–253. doi:10.1109/JSEN.2002.800680

Braga, P. L., Oliveira, A. L. I., Ribeiro, G. H. T., & Meira, S. R. L. (2007). *Bagging predictors for estimation of software project effort*. Paper presented at the Neural Networks, 2007. IJCNN 2007.

Breiman, L., Friedman, J. H., Olshen, R. A., & Stone, C. J. (1984). *Classification and regression trees*. Wadsworth International Group.

Davison, A. C., & Hinkley, D. V. (1997). *Bootstrap methods and their application. (Cambridge Series in Statistical and Probabilistic Mathematics, No 1)*. Cambridge University Press.

Dutta, R., Hines, E., Gardner, J., & Boilot, P. (2002). Bacteria classification using Cyranose 320 electronic nose. *Biomedical Engineering Online*, *1*(1), 4. doi:10.1186/1475-925X-1-4

Efron, B., & Tibshirani, R. J. (1993). *An introduction to the bootstrap*. London, UK: Chamman and Hall.

Gardner, J. W., Boilot, P., & Hines, E. L. (2005). Enhancing electronic nose performance by sensor selection using a new integer-based genetic algorithm approach. *Sensors and Actuators. B, Chemical*, *106*(1), 114–121. doi:10.1016/j.snb.2004.05.043

Ivica, K., & Fredric, M. H. (2000). *Principles of neurocomputing for science and engineering*. McGraw-Hill Higher Education.

Jang, J. S. R., Sun, C. T., & Mizutani, E. (1997). *Neuro-fuzzy and soft computing-a computational approach to learning and machine intelligence*. Prentice Hall.

Wendy, L. M., & Angel, R. M. (2007). *Computational statistics handbook with MATLAB* (2nd ed.). Chapman Hall/CRC.

ADDITIONAL READING

Abonyi, J., & Szeifert, F. (2003). Supervised fuzzy clustering for the identification of fuzzy classifiers. *Pattern Recognition Letters*, *24*(14), 2195–2207. doi:10.1016/S0167-8655(03)00047-3

Boilot, P. (2003). *Novel intelligent data processing techniques for electronic noses: Feature Selection and Neuro-Fuzzy Knowledge Base*, Engineering Department, PhD in Engineering dissertation at Warwick University.

Buntine, W. L., & Niblett, T. (1992). A Further Comparison of Splitting Rules for Decision-Tree Induction. *Machine Learning*, *8*(1), 75–85. doi:10.1007/BF00994006

Devroye, L., Gyorfi, L., & Lugosi, G. (1996). *A Probabilistic Theory of Pattern Recognition*. New York: Springer-Verlag.

Duda, R. O., Hart, P. E., & Stork, D. G. (2001). *Pattern Classification* (2nd ed.). New York: John Wiley & Sons.

Dutta, R., Hines, E. L., Gardner, J. W., Udrea, D. D., & Boilot, P. (2003). Non-detective egg freshness determination: an electronic nose based approach. *Measurement Science & Technology, 14*, 190–198. doi:10.1088/0957-0233/14/2/306

Efron, B. (1983). Estimating the error rate of a prediction rule: improvement on crossvalidation. *Journal of the American Statistical Association, 78*, 316–331. doi:10.2307/2288636

Efron, B. (1985). Bootstrap confidence intervals for a class of parametric problems. *Biometrika, 72*, 45–58. doi:10.1093/biomet/72.1.45

Efron, B. (1992). Jackknife-after-bootstrap standard errors and influence functions. *Journal of the Royal Statistical Society. Series B. Methodological, 54*, 83–127.

Everitt, B. S. (1993). *Cluster Analysis* (3rd ed.). New York: Edward Arnold Publishing.

Fraley, C. (1998). Algorithms for model-based Gaussian hierarchical clustering. *SIAM Journal on Scientific Computing, 20*, 270–281. doi:10.1137/S1064827596311451

Fraley, C., & Raftery, A. E. (1998). How many clusters? Which clustering method? Answers via model-based cluster analysis. *The Computer Journal, 41*, 578–588. doi:10.1093/comjnl/41.8.578

Fukunaga, K. (1990). *Introduction to Statistical Pattern Recognition* (2nd ed.). New York: Academic Press.

Gardner, J. W., & Bartlett, P. N. (1994). A brief history of the electronic nose. *Sensors and Actuators. B, Chemical, 18–19*, 211–220.

Gelfand, S. B., Ravishankar, C. S., & Delp, E. J. (1991). An Iterative Growing and Pruning Algorithm for Classification Tree Design. *IEEE Transactions on Pattern Analysis and Machine Intelligence, 13*(2), 138–150. doi:10.1109/34.67645

Gordon, A. D. (1999). *Classification*. London: Chapman and Hall.

Jain, A. K., & Dubes, R. C. (1988). *Algorithms for Clustering Data*. New York: Prentice Hall.

Kaufman, L., & Rousseeuw, P. J. (1990). *Finding Groups in Data: An Introduction to Cluster Analysis*. New York: John Wiley & Sons.

Llobet, E., Hines, E. L., Gardner, J. W., & Franco, S. (1999). Nondestructive banana ripeness determination using a neural network-based electronic nose. *Measurement Science & Technology, 10*, 538–548. doi:10.1088/0957-0233/10/6/320

Mooney, C. Z. (1997). *Monte Carlo Simulation*. London: Sage Publications.

Mooney, C. Z., & Duval, R. D. (1993). *Bootstrapping: A Nonparametric Approach to Statistical Inference*. London: Sage University Press.

Pearce, T. C., Schiffman, S. S., Nagle, H. T., & Gardner, J. W. (Eds.). (2003). *Handbook of Machine Olfaction*. Wiley–VCH.

Quinlan, J. R. (1986). Induction of Decision Trees. *Machine Learning, 1*(1), 81–106. doi:10.1007/BF00116251

Quinlan, J. R. (1987). Simplifying Decision Trees. *Int'l J. Man-Machine Studies, 27*, 221–234. doi:10.1016/S0020-7373(87)80053-6

Quinlan, J. R. (1993). *C4.5: Programs for Machine Learning*. San Mateo, Calif.: Morgan Kaufmann.

Ripley, B. D. (1996). *Pattern Recognition and Neural Networks*. Cambridge: CambridgeUniversity Press.

Safavian, S. R., & Landgrebe, D. A. (1991). A survey of decision tree classifier methodology. *IEEE Transactions on Systems, Man, and Cybernetics, 21*, 660–674. doi:10.1109/21.97458

Watkins, C. J. C. H. (1987). *Combining Cross-Validation and Search*, Progress in Machine Learning, Proc. EWSL 87, I. Bratko and N. Lavrac, eds. Wilmslow: Sigma Press, pp. 79-87

Webb, A. (1999). *Statistical Pattern Recognition*. Oxford: Oxford University Press.

Compilation of References

Abraham, A., & Nath, B. (2001). A neuro-fuzzy approach for modelling electricity demand in Victoria. *Applied Soft Computing*, *1*(2), 127–138. doi:10.1016/S1568-4946(01)00013-8

Abraham, A., Corchado, E., & Corchado, J. M. (2009). Hybrid learning machines. *Neurocomputing*, *72*(13-15), 2729-2730. doi: DOI: 10.1016/j.neucom.2009.02.017

Acevedo, F., Maldonado, S., Domínguez, E., Narváez, A., & López, F. (2007). Probabilistic support vector machines for multi-class alcohol identification. *Sensors and Actuators. B, Chemical*, *122*(1), 227–235. doi:10.1016/j.snb.2006.05.033

Adger, W. N. (2006). Vulnerability. *Global Environmental Change*, *16*, 268–281. doi:10.1016/j.gloenvcha.2006.02.006

Alkasab, T. K., White, J., & Kauer, J. S. (2002). A computational system for simulating and analyzing arrays of biological and artificial chemical sensors. *Chemical Senses*, *27*, 261–275. doi:10.1093/chemse/27.3.261

Ament, K., Kant, M. R., Sabelis, M. W., Haring, M. A., & Schuurink, R. C. (2004). Jasmonic acid is a key regulator of spider mite-induced volatile terpenoid and methyl salicylate emission in tomato. *Plant Physiology*, *135*(4), 2025–2037. doi:10.1104/pp.104.048694

Amiri, M. (2003). *y_fcmc matlab Toolbox V1.0*. Sharif University of Technology. Retrieved from www.http://ce.sharif.edu/~m_amiri/

Artursson, T., & Holmberg, M. (2002). Wavelet transform of electronic tongue data. *Sensors and Actuators. B, Chemical*, *87*, 379–391. doi:10.1016/S0925-4005(02)00270-8

Asada, M., Ichikawa, I., & Tsuji, S. (1988). Determining surface orientation by projecting a stripe pattern. *IEEE Transactions on Pattern Analysis and Machine Intelligence*, *10*(5), 749–754. doi:10.1109/34.6787

Ballabio, D., Cosio, M. S., Mannino, S., & Todeschini, R. (2006). A chemometric approach based on a novel similarity/diversity measure for the characterisation and selection of electronic nose sensors. *Analytica Chimica Acta*, *578*(2), 170–177. doi:10.1016/j.aca.2006.06.067

Compilation of References

Baratto, C., Faglia, G., Pardo, M., Vezzoli, M., Boarino, L., & Maffei, M. (2005). Monitoring plants health in greenhouse for space missions. *Sensors and Actuators. B, Chemical, 108*(1-2), 278–284. doi:10.1016/j.snb.2004.12.108

Barfield, W., & Danas, E. (1996). Comments on the use of olfactory displays for virtual environments. *Presence (Cambridge, Mass.), 5*(1), 109–121.

Bărsan, N., Schweizer-Berberich, M., & Göpel, W. (1999). Fundamental and practical aspects in the design of nanoscaled SnO$_2$ gas sensors: A status report. *Fresenius' Journal of Analytical Chemistry, 365*, 287–304. doi:10.1007/s002160051490

Belanger, R., & Jarvis, W. (1994). Occurrence of powdery mildew (Erysiphe sp.) on greenhouse tomatoes in Canada. *Plant Disease, 78*(6), 640. doi:10.1094/PD-78-0640E

Bellman, R. (1961). *Adaptive control processes: A guided tour*. Princeton, NJ: Princeton University Press.

Bermak, A., Belhouari, S. B., Shi, M., & Martinez, D. (2005). Pattern recognition techniques for odor discrimination in gas sensor array. In Grimes, C. A., Dickey, E. C., & Pishko, M. V. (Eds.), *The encyclopedia of sensors*. Valencia, CA: American Scientific Publishers.

Bern, A. Z., Lammertyn, J., Saevels, S., Natale, C. D., & Nicolaï, B. M. (2003). Electronic nose systems to study shelf life and cultivar effect on tomato aroma profile. *Sensors and Actuators. B, Chemical, 97*(2-3), 324–333. doi:10.1016/j.snb.2003.09.020

Bernabei, M., Pennazza, G., Santonico, M., Corsi, C., Roscioni, C., & Paolesse, R. (2008). A preliminary study on the possibility to diagnose urinary tract cancers by an electronic nose. *Sensors and Actuators. B, Chemical, 131*, 1–4. doi:10.1016/j.snb.2007.12.030

Bezdek, J. (1981). *Pattern recognition with fuzzy objective function*. New York, NY: Plenum Press.

Bhattacharyya, A. (1943). On a measure of divergence between two statistical populations defined by their probability distributions. *Bulletin of the Calcutta Mathematics Society, 35*, 99–109.

Bhattacharyya, N., Bandyopadhyay, R., Bhuyan, M., Tudu, B., Ghosh, D., & Jana, A. (2008). Electronic nose for black tea classification and correlation of measurements with tea taster marks. *IEEE Transactions on Instrumentation and Measurement, 57*, 1313–1321. doi:10.1109/TIM.2008.917189

Bishop, C. M. (1995). *Neural networks for pattern recognition*. Oxford, UK: Oxford University Press.

Bishop, C. M. (2006). *Pattern recognition and machine learning*. New York, NY: Springer.

Biswal, B., DeYoe, E. A., & Hyde, J. S. (1996). Reduction of physiological fluctuations in FMRI using digital filters. *Magnetic Resonance in Medicine, 35*, 107–113. doi:10.1002/mrm.1910350114

Blackmore, B. S., & Griepentrog, H. W. (2002). A future view of precision farming. In *Proceedings of PreAgro Precision Agriculture Conference* (pp. 131-145), Müncheberg, Germany, Center for Agricultural Landscape and Land Use Research (ZALF).

Blouin, A. G., Greenwood, D. R., Chavan, R. R., Pearson, M. N., Clover, G. R., MacDiarmid, R. M., & Cohen, D. (2010). A generic method to identify plant viruses by high-resolution tandem mass spectrometry of their coat proteins. *Journal of Virological Methods*, *163*(1), 49–56. doi:10.1016/j.jviromet.2009.08.009

Blum, A. L., & Langely, P. (1997). Selection of relevant features and examples in machine learning. *Artificial Intelligence*, *97*, 245–271. doi:10.1016/S0004-3702(97)00063-5

Boilot, P., Hines, E. L., Gardner, J. W., Pitt, R., John, S., & Mitchell, J. (2002). Classification of bacteria responsible for ENT and eye infections using the Cyranose system. *IEEE Sensors Journal*, *2*(3), 247–253. doi:10.1109/JSEN.2002.800680

Boom, C. E., Beek, T. A., Posthumus, M. A., Groot, A. D., & Dicke, M. (2004). Qualitative and quantitative variation among volatile profiles induced by tetranychus urticae feeding on plants from various families. *Journal of Chemical Ecology*, *30*(1), 69–89. doi:10.1023/B:JOEC.0000013183.72915.99

Boothe, D. D. H., & Arnold, J. W. (2002). Electronic nose analysis of volatile compounds from poultry meat samples, fresh and after refrigerated storage. *Journal of the Science of Food and Agriculture*, *82*(3), 315–322. doi:10.1002/jsfa.1036

Borah, S., Hines, E., Leeson, M. S., Iliescu, D. D., Bhuyan, M., & Gardner, J. W. (2008). Neural network based electronic nose for classification of tea aroma. *Sensing and Instrumentation for Food Quality and Safety*, *2*(1), 7–14. doi:10.1007/s11694-007-9028-7

Braga, P. L., Oliveira, A. L. I., Ribeiro, G. H. T., & Meira, S. R. L. (2007). *Bagging predictors for estimation of software project effort*. Paper presented at the Neural Networks, 2007. IJCNN 2007.

Braitenberg, V. (1984). *Vehicles: Experiments in synthetic psychology*. MIT Press/Bradford Books.

Breiman, L., Friedman, J. H., Olshen, R. A., & Stone, C. J. (1984). *Classification and regression trees*. Wadsworth International Group.

Brereton, R. G. (1992). *Multivariate pattern recognition in chemometrics*. Amsterdam, The Netherlands: Elsevier.

Brezmes, J., Cabré, P., Rojo, S., Llobet, E., Vilanova, X., & Correig, X. (2002). Discrimination between different samples of olive using variable selection techniques and modified fuzzy ARTMAP neural networks. *Proceedings of the 9th International Symposium on Olfaction and Electronic Nose*, ISOEN'02, Rome, Italy, (pp. 188-190).

Bro, R. (1997). PARAFAC: Tutorial and applications. *Chemometrics and Intelligent Laboratory Systems*, *38*, 149–171. doi:10.1016/S0169-7439(97)00032-4

Brudzewski, K., Osowski, S., & Markiewicz, T. (2004). Classification of milk by means of an electronic nose and SVM neural network. *Sensors and Actuators. B, Chemical*, *98*(2-3), 291–298. doi:10.1016/j.snb.2003.10.028

Compilation of References

Bruzzone, L., & Fernandez Prieto, D. (1999a). An incremental-learning neural network for the classification of remote-sensing images. *Pattern Recognition Letters, 20*, 1241–1248. doi:10.1016/S0167-8655(99)00091-4

Bruzzone, L., & Fernandez Prieto, D. (1999b). A technique for the selection of kernel-function parameters in RBF neural networks for classification of remote–sensing images. *IEEE Transactions on Geoscience and Remote Sensing, 37*, 1179–1184. doi:10.1109/36.752239

Buratti, S., Ballabio, D., Benedetti, S., & Cosio, M. S. (2007). Prediction of Italian red wine sensorial descriptors from electronic nose, electronic tongue and spectrophotometric measurements by means of genetic algorithm regression models. *Food Chemistry, 100*, 211–218. doi:10.1016/j.foodchem.2005.09.040

Burdea, G., & Ciffet, P. (2003). *Virtual reality technology* (pp. 92–110). Wiley-Interscience.

Burian, C., Brezmes, J., Vinaixa, M., Cañellas, N., Llobet, E., Vilanova, X., & Correig, X. (2010). MS-electronic nose performance improvement using the retention time dimension and two-way and three-way data processing methods. *Sensors and Actuators. B, Chemical, 143*, 758–768. doi:10.1016/j.snb.2009.10.015

Butrym, E. D., & Hartman, T. G. (1998). *An apparatus for sampling volatile organics from live plant material using short path thermal desorption.* Scientific Instrument Services, application note 75. Retrieved from http://www.sisweb.com

Cai, K., Maekawa, T., & Takada, T. (2002). Identification of odors using a sensor array with kinetic working temperature and Fourier spectrum analysis. *IEEE Sensors Journal, 2*(3), 230–234. doi:10.1109/JSEN.2002.800285

Caulier, Y., Goldschmidt, A., Spinnler, K., & Arnold, M. (2009). Automatic detection of surface and structural defects on reflecting workpieces. *Photonik International, 2*, 30–32.

Caulier, Y., Spinnler, K., Bourennane, S., & Wittenberg, T. (2007). New structured illumination technique for the inspection of high reflective surfaces. *EURASIP Journal on Image and Video Processing.* doi:.doi:10.1155/2008/237459

Caulier, Y., Spinnler, K., Wittenberg, T., & Bourennane, S. (2008). Specific features for the analysis of fringe images. *Optical Engineering (Redondo Beach, Calif.), 47.*

Cavicchi, R. E., Suehle, J. S., Kreider, K. G., Gaitan, M., & Chaparala, P. (1996). Optimized temperature-pulse sequences for the enhancement of chemically specific response patterns from micro-hotplates gas sensors. *Sensors and Actuators. B, Chemical, 33*, 142–146. doi:10.1016/0925-4005(96)01821-7

Chakraborty, D., & Pal, N. R. (2003). A novel training scheme for multilayered perceptrons to realize proper generalization and incremental learning. *IEEE Transactions on Neural Networks, 14*, 1–14. doi:10.1109/TNN.2002.806953

Chang, P. C., & Liao, T. W. (2006). Combining SOM and fuzzy rule base for flow time prediction in semiconductor manufacturing factory. *Applied Soft Computing*, 6, 198–206. doi:10.1016/j. asoc.2004.12.004

Chen, R., Xu, J.-H., & Jiang, Y.-D. (2009). Colorimetric sensor arrays system based on FPGA for image recognition. *Journal of Electronic Science and Technology of China*, 7(2), 139–145.

Chen, Y., Nixon, M., & Thomas, D. (1995). Statistical geometrical features for texture classification. *Pattern Recognition*, 28(4), 537–552. doi:10.1016/0031-3203(94)00116-4

Cho, N., Nimsuk, N., Wyszynski, B., Takushima, H., Kinoshita, M., & Nakamoto, T. (2008). *Demonstration of interactive teleolfaction with movie*. Paper presented at the meeting of Advances in Computer Entertainment 2008, Creative showcase, Yokohama, Japan.

Choi, N. H., Shim, C. H., Song, K. D., Lee, D. S., Huh, J. S., & Lee, D. D. (2002). Classification of workplace gases using temperature modulation and two SnO_2 sensing films on substrate. *Sensors and Actuators. B, Chemical*, 86, 251–258. doi:10.1016/S0925-4005(02)00196-X

Choudhary, D. K., Johr, B. N., & Prakash, A. (2008). Volatiles as priming agents that initiate plant growth and defense responses. *Current Science*, 94(5), 595–604.

Clifford, P. K., & Tuma, D. T. (1983). Characteristics of semiconductor gas sensor II: Transient response to temperature change. *Sensors and Actuators*, 3, 233–254. doi:10.1016/0250-6874(82)80026-7

Concina, I., Falasconi, M., Gobbi, E., Bianchi, F., Musci, M. M., & Mattarozzi, M. P. (2009). Early detection of microbial contamination in processed tomatoes by electronic nose. *Food Control*, 20(10), 873–880. doi:10.1016/j.foodcont.2008.11.006

Constantinopoulos, C., & Likas, A. (2006). An incremental training method for the probabilistic RBF Network. *IEEE Transactions on Neural Networks*, 17, 966–974. doi:10.1109/TNN.2006.875982

Corcoran, P., Lowery, P., & Anglesea, J. (1998). Optimal configuration of a thermally cycled gas sensor array with neural network pattern recognition. *Sensors and Actuators. B, Chemical*, 48, 448–455. doi:10.1016/S0925-4005(98)00083-5

Corrado, G., Guerrieri, E., Pasquariello, M., Digilio, M. C., Cascone, P., & Rao, R. (2007). *Systemin regulates volatile signalling in tomato*. Plant & Animal Genomes XV Conference (pp. 669–681).

Cover, T. M., & Hart, P. E. (1967). Nearest neighbor pattern classification. *IEEE Transactions on Information Theory*, 13(1), 21–27. doi:10.1109/TIT.1967.1053964

Cozzolino, D., Smyth, H. E., Cynkar, W., Dambergs, R. G., & Gishen, M. (2005). Usefulness of chemometrics and mass spectrometry-based electronic nose to classify Australian white wines by their varietal origin. *Talanta*, 68, 382–387. doi:10.1016/j.talanta.2005.08.057

Cross, J. V., Eastebrook, M. A., Crook, A. M., Crook, D., Fitzgerald, J. D., Innocenzi, P. J., & Solomon, M. G. (2001). Review: Natural enemies and biocontrol of pests of strawberry in Northern and Central Europe. *Biocontrol Science and Technology*, 11(2), 165–216. doi:10.1080/09583150120035639

Compilation of References

Dash, M., & Liu, N. (1997). Feature selection for classification. *Intelligent Data Analysis: An International Journal, 1*(3), 131–156. doi:10.1016/S1088-467X(97)00008-5

Davide, F., Holmberg, M., & Lundstrom, I. (2001). Virtual olfactory interfaces: Electronic noses and olfactory displays. In Riva, G., & Davide, F. (Eds.), *Communications through virtual technologies* (pp. 194–220). Amsterdam, The Netherlands: IOS Press.

Davis, L. (1991). *The handbook of genetic algorithms*. New York, NY: Van Nostrand Reinhold.

Davis, L. (1987). *Genetic algorithms and simulated annealing*. London, UK/ Los Altos, CA: Pitman/ Morgan Kaufmann Publishers.

Davison, A. C., & Hinkley, D. V. (1997). *Bootstrap methods and their application. (Cambridge Series in Statistical and Probabilistic Mathematics, No 1)*. Cambridge University Press.

de Carvalho, A. T. (2007). Fuzzy c-means clustering methods for symbolic interval data. *Pattern Recognition Letters, 28*(4), 423–437. doi:10.1016/j.patrec.2006.08.014

De Castro, L. N. (2006). *Fundamentals of natural computing basic concepts, algorithms, and applications*. Boca Raton, FL: Chapman & Hall/CRC.

De Jong, K. A. (2006). *Evolutionary computation: A unified approach*. Cambridge, MA: MIT Press.

Delcroix, G., Seulin, R., Lamalle, B., Gorria, P., & Merienne, F. (2001). Study of the imaging conditions and processing for the aspect control of specular surfaces. *International Society for Electronic Imaging, 10*(1), 196–202. doi:10.1117/1.1314333

del-Hoyo, R., Martín-del-Brío, B., Medrano, N., & Fernández-Navajas, J. (2009). Computational intelligence tools for next generation quality of service management. *Neurocomputing*.

Deng, C., Zhang, X., Zhu, W., & Qian, J. (2004). Investigation of tomato plant defence response to tobacco mosaic virus by determination of methyl salicylate with SPME-capillary GC-MS. *Chromatographia, 59*(3-4), 263–268.

Deng, J. (1989). Introduction to Grey system theory. *Journal of Grey System, 1*(1), 1–24.

Denzler, J., & Brown, C. M. (2002). Information theoretic sensor data selection for active object recognition and state estimation. *IEEE Transactions on Pattern Analysis and Machine Intelligence, 24*, 145–157. doi:10.1109/34.982896

Devijver, P. A., & Kittler, J. (1982). *Pattern recognition: A statistical approach*. Prentice Hall.

Diadem FP7-ICT. (2008). *Diadem–distributed information acquisition decision-making for environmental management*. Retrieved from http://www.pdc.dk/diadem/

Dicke, M., Gols, R., Ludeking, D., & Posthumus, M. A. (1999). Jasmonic acid and herbivory differentially induce carnivore-attracting plant volatiles in lima bean plants. *Journal of Chemical Ecology, 25*(8), 1907–1922. doi:10.1023/A:1020942102181

Dickinson, T. A., White, J., Kauer, J. S., & Walt, D. R. (1996). A chemical-detecting system based on a cross-reactive optical sensor array. *Nature, 382*, 697–700. doi:10.1038/382697a0

Dinh, H. Q., Walker, N., Song, C., Kobayashi, A., & Hodges, L. F. (1999). *Evaluating the importance of multi-sensory input on memory and the sense of presence in virtual environments* (pp. 222–228). Houston, TX: IEEE Virtual Reality.

Distante, C., Ancona, N., & Siciliano, P. (2003). Support vector machines for olfactory signals recognition. *Sensors and Actuators. B, Chemical, 88*(1), 30–39. doi:10.1016/S0925-4005(02)00306-4

Dittmann, B., & Nitz, S. (2000). Strategies for the development of reliable QA/QC methods when working with mass spectrometry-based chemosensory systems. *Sensors and Actuators. B, Chemical, 69*, 253257. doi:10.1016/S0925-4005(00)00504-9

Djouadi, A., Snorrason, Ö., & Garber, F. F. (1990). The quality of training sample estimates of the Bhattacharyya coefficient. *IEEE Transactions on Pattern Analysis and Machine Intelligence, 12*(1), 92–97. doi:10.1109/34.41388

Du, C.-J., & Sun, D.-W. (2005). Pizza sauce spread classification using color vision and support vector machines. *Journal of Food Engineering, 66*(2), 137–145. doi:10.1016/j.jfoodeng.2004.03.011

DustBot Consortium. (2006). *DustBot-networked and cooperating robots for urban hygiene.* Retrieved from http://www.dustbot.org

Dutta, R., Hines, E. L., Gardner, J. W., Kashwan, K. R., & Bhuyan, M. (2003). Tea quality prediction using a tin oxide-based electronic nose: An artificial intelligence approach. *Sensors and Actuators. B, Chemical, 94*(2), 228–237. doi:10.1016/S0925-4005(03)00367-8

Dutta, R., Morgan, D., Baker, N., Gardner, J., & Hines, E. (2005). Identification of Staphylococcus aureus infections in hospital environments: Electronic nose based approach. *Sensors and Actuators. B, Chemical, 109*(2), 355–362. doi:10.1016/j.snb.2005.01.013

Dutta, R., Hines, E., Gardner, J., & Boilot, P. (2002). Bacteria classification using Cyranose 320 electronic nose. *Biomedical Engineering Online, 1*(1), 4. doi:10.1186/1475-925X-1-4

Dy, J. G., Brodley, C. E., Kak, A., Broderick, L. S., & Aisen, A. M. (2003). Unsupervised feature selection applied to content-based retrieval of lung images. *IEEE Transactions on Pattern Analysis and Machine Intelligence, 25*(3), 373–378. doi:10.1109/TPAMI.2003.1182100

Efron, B., & Tibshirani, R. J. (1993). *An introduction to the bootstrap.* London, UK: Chamman and Hall.

Eiben, A. E., & Smith, J. E. (2003). *Introduction to evolutionary computing.* New York, NY: Springer.

Eklöv, T., Mårtensson, P., & Lundström, I. (1999). Selection of variables for interpreting multivariable gas sensor data. *Analytica Chimica Acta, 381*, 221–232. doi:10.1016/S0003-2670(98)00739-9

Compilation of References

El Barbri, N., Duran, C., Brezmes, J., Cañellas, N., Ramírez, J. L., Bouchikhi, B., & Llobet, E. (2008). Selectivity enhancement in multisensor systems using flow modulation techniques. *Sensors (Basel, Switzerland)*, *8*, 7369–7379. doi:10.3390/s8117369

Elmenreich, W. (2007). *A review on system architectures for sensor fusion applications.* Paper presented at the Software Technologies for Embedded and Ubiquitous Systems. 5th IFIP WG 10.2 International Workshop, SEUS 2007. Revised Papers. (LNCS 4761), Santorini Island, Greece.

Evans, P., Persaud, K. C., McNeish, A. S., Sneath, R. W., Hobson, N., & Magan, N. (2000). Evaluation of a radial basis function neural network for the determination of wheat quality from electronic nose data. *Sensors and Actuators. B, Chemical*, *69*, 348–358. doi:10.1016/S0925-4005(00)00485-8

Fallik, E., Alkali-Tuvia, S., Horev, B., Copel, A., Rodov, V., & Aharoni, Y. (2001). Characterisation of Galia melon aroma by GC and mass spectrometric sensor measurements after prolonged storage. *Postharvest Biology and Technology*, *22*, 8591. doi:10.1016/S0925-5214(00)00185-X

Fernandes, F., Pereira, D. M., Pinho, P. G., Valentão, P., Pereira, J. A., Bento, A., & Andrade, P. B. (2010). Headspace solid-phase microextraction and gas chromatography/ion trap-mass spectrometry applied to a living system: Pieris brassicae fed with kale. *Food Chemistry*, *119*(4), 1681–1693. doi:10.1016/j.foodchem.2009.09.046

Figaro Engineering Inc. *Japan.* (2010). Retrieved from http://www.figaro.co.jp

Fisher, R. B., & Naidu, D. K. (1996). A comparison of algorithms for subpixel peak detection. In *Image technology, advances in image processing, multimedia and machine vision*, (pp. 385-404).

Floreano, D., Kato, T., Marocco, D., & Sauser, E. (2004). Coevolution of active vision and feature selection. *Biological Cybernetics*, *90*, 218–228. doi:10.1007/s00422-004-0467-5

Fort, A., Gregorkiewitz, M., Machetti, M., Rocchi, S., Serrano, B., & Tondi, L. (2002). Selectivity enhancement of SnO_2 sensors by means of operating temperature modulation. *Thin Solid Films*, *418*, 2–8. doi:10.1016/S0040-6090(02)00575-8

Fort, A., Machetti, M., Rocchi, S., Serrano, B., Tondi, L., & Ulivieri, N. (2003). Tin oxide gas sensing: Comparison among different measurement techniques for gas mixture classification. *IEEE Transactions on Instrumentation and Measurement*, *52*, 921–926. doi:10.1109/TIM.2003.814362

Freund, M. S., & Lewis, N. S. (1995). A chemically diverse, conducting polymer-based electronic nose. *Proceedings of the National Academy of Sciences of the United States of America*, *92*, 2652–2656. doi:10.1073/pnas.92.7.2652

Friedrichs, M. S. (1995). A model-free algorithm for the removal of baseline artifacts. *Journal of Biomolecular NMR*, *5*, 147–153. doi:10.1007/BF00208805

Frost, C. J., Mescher, M. C., Carlson, J. E., & Moraes, C. M. (2008). Plant defense priming against herbivores: Getting ready for a different battle. *Plant Physiology*, *146*, 818–824. doi:10.1104/pp.107.113027

Fu, L., Huang, H., & Principe, J. C. (1996). Incremental backpropagation learning networks. *IEEE Transactions on Neural Networks, 7,* 757–761. doi:10.1109/72.501732

Gardner, J. W., & Bartlett, P. N. (1996). Performance definition and standardization of electronic noses. *Sensors and Actuators. B, Chemical, 33,* 60–67. doi:10.1016/0925-4005(96)01819-9

Gardner, J. W., & Bartlett, P. N. (1999). *Electronic noses: Principles and applications.* Oxford, UK: Oxford University Press.

Gardner, J. W., Boilot, P., & Hines, E. L. (2005). Enhancing electronic nose performance by sensor selection using a new integer-based genetic algorithm approach. *Sensors and Actuators. B, Chemical, 106,* 114–121. doi:10.1016/j.snb.2004.05.043

Gardner, J. W., Hines, E. L., & Tang, H. C. (1992). Detection of vapours and odours from a multisensor array using pattern-recognition techniques. Part 2: Artificial neural networks. *Sensors and Actuators. B, Chemical, B9*(1), 9–15. doi:10.1016/0925-4005(92)80187-3

Gardner, J. W., Hines, E. L., & Wilkinson, M. (1990). Application of artificial neural networks to an electronic olfactory system. *Measurement Science & Technology, 1*(5), 446–451. doi:10.1088/0957-0233/1/5/012

Gardner, J. W., & Bartlett, P. N. (1999). *Electronic noses: Principles and applications.* New York, NY: Oxford University Press Inc.

Gardner, J. W., & Pang, C. (1996). Detection of vapours and odors from a multisensor array using pattern recognition: Self-organising adaptive resonance techniques. *Measurement & Control, 29*(6), 172–178.

Gardner, J. W., Shin, H. W., & Hines, E. L. (2000). An electronic nose system to diagnose illness. *Sensors and Actuators. B, Chemical, 70,* 19–24. doi:10.1016/S0925-4005(00)00548-7

Gardner, J. W., Boilot, P., & Hines, E. L. (2005). Enhancing electronic nose performance by sensor selection using a new integer-based genetic algorithm approach. *Sensors and Actuators. B, Chemical, 106*(1), 114–121. doi:10.1016/j.snb.2004.05.043

Geladi, P. (1989). Analysis of multi-way (multi-mode) data. *Chemometrics and Intelligent Laboratory Systems, 7,* 11–30. doi:10.1016/0169-7439(89)80108-X

Gerbi, V., Zeppa, G., Antonelli, A., & Carnacini, A. (1997). Sensory characterisation of wine vinegars. *Food Quality and Preference, 8*(1), 27–34. doi:10.1016/S0950-3293(96)00003-1

Gibson, J. J. (1979). *The ecological approach to visual perception.* Boston, MA: Houghton Mifflin.

Giraud-Carrier, C. (2000). A note on the utility of incremental learning. *AI Communications, 13,* 215–223.

Gobbetti, E., & Scateni, R. (1998). Virtual reality: Past, present, and future. In Riva, G., Wiederhold, B. K., & Molinari, E. (Eds.), *Virtual environments in clinical psychology and neuroscience: Methods and techniques in advanced patient-therapist interaction* (pp. 3–20). Amsterdam, The Netherlands: IOS Press.

Compilation of References

Godfrey, K. (1993). *Perturbation signals for system identification.* (pp. 39-49, 181-187, 321-347). Prentice Hall.

Gomez, A. H., Wang, J., Hu, G., & Pereira, A. G. (2005). Electronic nose technique potential monitoring mandarin maturity. *Sensors and Actuators. B, Chemical, 113*, 347–353. doi:10.1016/j.snb.2005.03.090

Gómez, A. H., Hu, G., Wang, J., & Pereira, A. G. (2006). Evaluation of tomato maturity by electronic nose. *Computers and Electronics in Agriculture, 54*(1), 44–52. doi:10.1016/j.compag.2006.07.002

Goodner, K. L., Dreher, J. G., & Rouseff, R. L. (2001). The dangers of creating false classifications due to noise in e-noses and similar multivariate analyses. *Sensors and Actuators. B, Chemical, 80*, 261–266. doi:10.1016/S0925-4005(01)00917-0

Göpel, W. (1985). Chemisorption and charge transfer at ionic semiconductor surfaces: Implications in designing gas sensors. *Progress in Surface Science, 20*, 1, 9–103. doi:10.1016/0079-6816(85)90004-8

Göpel, W. (1988). Chemical imaging I: Concepts and visions for electronic and bioelectronic noses. *Sensors and Actuators. B, Chemical, 52*, 125–142. doi:10.1016/S0925-4005(98)00267-6

Göpel, W., Hesse, J., & Zemel, J. N. (1991). *Sensors: A comprehensive survey (Vol. 2).* Weinheim, Germany: VCH.

Gosangi, R., & Gutierrez-Osuna, R. (2010). Active temperature programming for metal-oxide chemoresistors. *IEEE Sensors Journal, 10*, 1075–1082. doi:10.1109/JSEN.2010.2042165

Gosangi, R., & Gutierrez-Osuna, R. (2009). Active chemical sensing with partially observable Markov decision processes. *Proceedings of the International Symposium on Olfaction and Electronic Noses* (ISOEN 2009), Brescia, Italy, April 15-17.

Gualdrón, O., Brezmes, J., Llobet, E., Amari, A., Vilanova, X., Bouchikhi, B., & Correig, X. (2007). Variable selection for support vector machine based multisensor systems. *Sensors and Actuators. B, Chemical, 122*, 259–268. doi:10.1016/j.snb.2006.05.029

Gualdrón, O., Llobet, E., Brezmes, J., Vilanova, X., & Correig, X. (2006). Coupling fast variable selection methods to neural network based classifiers: Application to multisensor systems. *Sensors and Actuators. B, Chemical, 114*, 522–529. doi:10.1016/j.snb.2005.04.046

Gutiérrez-Aguirre, I., Mehle, N., Delić, D., Gruden, K., Mumford, R., & Ravnikar, M. (2009). Real-time quantitative PCR based sensitive detection and genotype discrimination of Pepino mosaic virus. *Journal of Virological Methods, 162*(1-2), 46–55. doi:10.1016/j.jviromet.2009.07.008

Gutierrez-Osuna, R. (2002). Pattern analysis for machine olfaction: A review. *IEEE Sensors Journal, 2*(3), 189–202. doi:10.1109/JSEN.2002.800688

Guyon, I., & Elisseeff, A. (2003). An introduction to variable and feature selection. *Journal of Machine Learning Research, 3*, 1157–1182. doi:10.1162/153244303322753616

Guyon, I., Gunn, S., Nikravesh, M., & Zadeh, L. (2006). *Feature extraction: Foundations and applications, studies in fuzziness and soft computing. Physica-Verlag.* Springer.

Hall, M. A. (1999). *Correlation-based feature selection for machine learning.* New Zealand: University of Waikato.

Hall, D. L., & Llinas, J. (2008). Multisensor data fusion. In Liggins, M. E., Hall, D. L., & Llinas, J. (Eds.), *Handbook of multisensor data fusion: Theory and practice* (2nd ed., pp. 1–14). Boca Raton, FL: CRC Press.

Haralick, R. M., Shanmugam, K., & Dinstein, I. (1973). Texture features for image classification. [SMC]. *IEEE Transactions on Systems, Man, and Cybernetics, 3*(6), 610–621. doi:10.1109/TSMC.1973.4309314

Haralick, R. (1979). Statistical and structural approaches to texture. *Proceedings of the IEEE Conference on Computer Vision and Pattern Recognition (CVPR'1979), 67*, (pp. 786–804).

Harding, S. (2008). *Evolution of image filters on graphics processor units using cartesian genetic programming.* Hong Kong, China.

Harris, P. D., Andrews, M. K., & Partridge, A. C. (1997). *Conductive polymer sensor measurements.* International Conference on Solid State Sensors and Actuators (pp. 1063–1066). doi:10.1109/SENSOR.1997.635377

Hayase, F., Chung, T.-Y., & Kato, H. (1984). Changes of volatile components of tomato fruits during ripening. *Food Chemistry, 14*(2), 113–124. doi:10.1016/0308-8146(84)90050-5

Hayes, A. T., Martinoli, A., & Goodman, R. M. (2002). Distributed odor source localization. *IEEE Sensor Journal. Special Issue on Electronic Nose Technologies, 2*(3), 260–271. doi:. doi:10.1109/JSEN.2002.800682

Haykin, S. (2001). *Neural networks: A comprehensive foundation* (2nd ed.). Hong Kong: Pearson Education Asia.

Hierlemann, A., & Gutierrez-Osuna, R. (2008). Higher-order chemical sensing. *Chemical Reviews, 108*, 563–613. doi:10.1021/cr068116m

Hines, E. L., Boilot, P., Gardner, J. W., & Gongora, M. A. (2002). Pattern analysis for electronic noses. In Pearce, T. C., Shiffman, S. S., Nagle, H. T., & Gardner, J. W. (Eds.), *Handbook of machine olfaction* (pp. 133–160). Weinheim, Germany: Wiley-VCH. doi:10.1002/3527601597.ch6

Hinze, J. O. (1975). *Turbulence.* New York, NY: McGraw-Hill.

Holland, J. H. (1975). *Adaptation in natural and artificial systems.* MIT Press.

Holmberga, M., Winquist, F., Lundstrom, I., & Davide, F. (1996). Drift counteraction for an electronic nose. *Sensors and Actuators. B, Chemical, 35-36*, 528–535. doi:10.1016/S0925-4005(97)80124-4

Huang, X., Liu, J., Shao, D., Pi, Z., & Yu, Z. (2003). Rectangular mode of operation for detecting pesticide residue by using a single SnO_2 based gas sensor. *Sensors and Actuators. B, Chemical, 96*, 630–635. doi:10.1016/j.snb.2003.07.006

Huang, Y.-B., Lan, Y.-B., Hoffmann, W. C., & Lacey, R. E. (2007). Multisensor data fusion for high quality data analysis and processing in measurement and instrumentation. *Journal of Bionics Engineering, 4*(1), 53–62. doi:10.1016/S1672-6529(07)60013-4

Huang, C., Groot, T., Meijer-Dekens, F., Niks, R. E., & Lindhout, P. (1998). The resistance to powdery mildew (Oidium lycopersicum) in lycopersicon species is mainly associated with hypersensitive response. *European Journal of Plant Pathology, 104*, 399–407. doi:10.1023/A:1008092701883

Hughes, J., & Ruprai, B. (1999). *Distributed genetic programming: Google Patents*.

Huttenlocher, D. P., Klanderman, G. A., & Rucklidge, W. J. (1993). Comparing images using the Hausdorff distance. *IEEE Transactions on Pattern Analysis and Machine Intelligence, 15*(9), 850–863. doi:10.1109/34.232073

Ishida, H., Nakamoto, T., & Moriizumi, T. (1998). Remote sensing of gas/odor source location and concentration distribution using mobile system. *Sensors and Actuators. B, Chemical, 49*(1-2), 52–57..doi:10.1016/S0925-4005(98)00036-7

Ivica, K., & Fredric, M. H. (2000). *Principles of neurocomputing for science and engineering*. McGraw-Hill Higher Education.

Jacob, D., David, D. R., Sztjenberg, A., & Elad, Y. (2008). Conditions for development of powdery mildew of tomato caused by Oidium neolycopersici. *Ecology and Epidemiology, 98*, 270–281.

Jain, A. K., Duin, R. P. W., & Mao, J. C. (2000). Statistical pattern recognition: A review. *IEEE Pattern Analysis and Machine Intelligence, 22*, 4–37. doi:10.1109/34.824819

Jain, A., & Zongker, D. (1997). Feature selection: Evaluation, application, and small sample performance. *IEEE Transactions on Pattern Analysis and Machine Intelligence, 19*(2), 153–158. doi:10.1109/34.574797

Jang, J. S. R., Sun, C. T., & Mizutani, E. (1997). *Neuro-fuzzy and soft computing-a computational approach to learning and machine intelligence*. Prentice Hall.

Jatmiko, W., Fukuda, T., Arai, F., & Kusumoputro, B. (2004). Artificial odor discrimination system using multiple quartz-resonator sensor and neural network for recognizing fragrance mixtures. In *Proceedings of the 2004 International Symposium on Micro-Nanomechatronics and Human Science* (pp. 169–174). doi:10.1109/MHS.2004.1421296

John, G. N., Kohavi, R., & Pfleger, K. (1994). *Irrelevant features and the subset selection problem*. International Conference on Machine Learning, (pp. 121–129).

Jones, H., Whipps, J. M., & Gurr, S. J. (2001). The tomato powdery mildew fungus Oidium neolycopersici. *Molecular Plant Pathology, 2*(6), 303–309. doi:10.1046/j.1464-6722.2001.00084.x

Jouan-Rimbaud, D., Massart, D. L., & Noord, O. E. (1996). Random correlation in variable selection for multivariate calibration with a genetic algorithm. *Chemometrics and Intelligent Laboratory Systems, 35*, 213–220. doi:10.1016/S0169-7439(96)00062-7

Jüptner, W., Kreis, T., Mieth, U., & Osten, W. (1994). Application of neural networks and knowledge-based systems for automatic identification of fault-indicating fringe patterns. *Proceedings of SPIE, Photomechanics, 2342*, 16–26.

Kalman, E.-L., Löfvendahl, A., Winquist, F., & Lundström, I. (1999). Classification of complex gas mixtures from automotive leather using an electronic nose. *Analytica Chimica Acta, 403*(1-2), 31–38. doi:10.1016/S0003-2670(99)00604-2

Kammel, S., & Puente Leon, F. (2003). Deflektometrie zur Qualitätsprüfung spiegelnd reflektierender Oberflächen. *Technisches Messen, 70*, 193–198. doi:10.1524/teme.70.4.193.20181

Kammel, S. (2004). *Deflektometrische Untersuchung spiegelnd reflektierender Freiformflächen.* University of Karlsruhe (TH), Germany.

Kant, M. R., Bleeker, P. M., Wijk, M. V., Schuurink, R. C., & Haring, M. A. (2009). Plant volatiles in defence. *Advances in Botanical Research, 51*, 613–666. doi:10.1016/S0065-2296(09)51014-2

Kasabov, N. (2008). Evolving intelligence in humans and machines: Integrative evolving connectionist systems approach. *IEEE Computational Intelligence Magazine, 3*(3), 23–37. doi:10.1109/MCI.2008.926584

Kasabov, N. K. (2007). *Evolving connectionist systems: The knowledge engineering approach* (2nd ed.). London, UK: Springer.

Kasabov, N. (1998). Evolving fuzzy neural networks-algorithms, applications and biological motivation: Methodologies for the conception, design and application of soft computing. *World Scientific*, 271-274.

Kaye, J. J. (2004). Making scents: Aromatic output for HCI. *Interaction, 11*(1), 48–61. doi:10.1145/962342.964333

Kesselmeier, J., & Staudt, M. (2004). Biogenic Volatile Organic Compounds (VOC): An overview on emission, physiology and ecology. *Journal of Atmospheric Chemistry, 33*, 23–88. doi:10.1023/A:1006127516791

Kesselmeier, J., & Staudt, M. (2004). Biogenic Volatile Organic Compounds (VOC): An overview on emission, physiology and ecology. *Journal of Atmospheric Chemistry, 33*, 23–88. doi:10.1023/A:1006127516791

King, W. H. (1964). Piezoelectric sorption detector. *Analytical Chemistry, 36*, 1735. doi:10.1021/ac60215a012

Kirkpatrick, S., Gelatt, C. D., & Vecchi, M. P. (1983). Optimization by simulated annealing. *Science, 220*, 671–680. doi:10.1126/science.220.4598.671

Compilation of References

Kiss, L. (1996). Occurrence of a new powdery mildew fungus (Erysiphe sp.) on tomatoes in Hungary. *Plant Disease, 80*(2), 224. doi:10.1094/PD-80-0224E

Klir, G. J., & Folger, T. (1989). *Fuzzy sets, uncertainty and information.* Addison-Wesley.

Kohavi, R. (1995). *A study of cross-validation and bootstrap for accuracy estimation and model selection* (pp. 1137–1145). International Joint Conferences on Artificial Intelligence.

Kohonen, T. (1988). *Self-organization and associative memory* (pp. 199–202). Springer-Verlag.

Kowadlo, G., & Russell, R. A. (2003). Naive physics for effective odour localisation. In *Proceedings of the Australian Conference on Robotics and Automation.*

Krüger, S., Wernicke, G., Osten, W., Kayser, D., Demoli, N., & Gruber, H. (2001). Fault detection and feature analysis in interferometric fringe patterns by the application of wavelet filters in convolution processors. *International Society for Electronic Imaging, 10*(1), 228–232. doi:10.1117/1.1318908

Kullback, S., & Leibler, R. A. (1951). On information and sufficiency. *Annals of Mathematical Statistics, 22*(1), 79–86. doi:10.1214/aoms/1177729694

Kunt, T. A., McAvoy, T. J., Cavicchi, R. E., & Semancik, S. (1998). Optimization of temperature programmed sensing for gas identification using micro-hotplate sensors. *Sensors and Actuators. B, Chemical, 53*, 24–43. doi:10.1016/S0925-4005(98)00244-5

Labreche, S., Bazzo, S., Cade, S., & Chanie, E. (2005). Shelf life determination by electronic nose: Application to milk. *Sensors and Actuators. B, Chemical, 106*, 199–206. doi:10.1016/j.snb.2004.06.027

Lakshminarasimhan, A. L., & Dasarathy, B. V. (1975). A unified approach to feature selection and learning in unsupervised environments. *IEEE Transactions on Computers, C-24*(9), 948–952. doi:10.1109/T-C.1975.224346

Laothawornkitkul, J., Moore, J. P., Taylor, J. E., Possell, M., Gibson, T. D., Hewitt, C. N., & Paul, N. D. (2008). Discrimination of plant volatile signatures by an electronic nose: A potential technology for plant pest and disease. *Environmental Science & Technology, 42*(22), 8433–8439. doi:10.1021/es801738s

Li, X. (2000). Wavelet transform for detection of partial fringe patterns induced by defects in nondestructive testing of holographic interferometry and electronic speckle pattern interferometry. *Journal of Optical Engineering, 39*, 2821–2827. doi:10.1117/1.1308485

Lilienthal, A. J., Loutfi, A., & Duckett, T. (2006). Airborne chemical sensing with mobile robots. *Sensors (Basel, Switzerland), 6*(11), 1616–1678..doi:10.3390/s6111616

Lilienthal, A. J., & Duckett, T. (2004a). Building gas concentration gridmaps with a mobile robot. *Robotics and Autonomous Systems, 48*(1), 3–16. doi:10.1016/j.robot.2004.05.002

Lilienthal, A. J., & Duckett, T. (2004b). Experimental analysis of gas-sensitive Braitenberg vehicles. *Advanced Robotics, 18*(8), 817–834. doi:10.1163/1568553041738103

Lilienthal, A. J., & Duckett, T. (2003a). A stereo electronic nose for a mobile inspection robot. In *Proceedings of the IEEE International Workshop on Robotic Sensing.*

Lilienthal, A. J., & Duckett, T. (2003b). An absolute positioning system for 100 Euros. In *Proceedings of the IEEE International Workshop on Robotic Sensing.*

Lilienthal, A. J., & Duckett, T. (2003c). Creating gas concentration gridmaps with a mobile robot. In *Proceedings of the IEEE/RSJ International Conference on Intelligent Robots and Systems* (pp. 118–123).

Lilienthal, A. J., Asadi, S., & Reggente, M. (2009a). Estimating predictive variance for statistical gas distribution modelling. In *AIP Conference Proceedings Volume 1137: Olfaction and Electronic Nose - Proceedings of the 13th International Symposium on Olfaction and Electronic Nose* (pp. 65-68). doi:10.1063/1.3156628

Lilienthal, A. J., Loutfi, A., Blanco, J. L., Galindo, C., & Gonzalez, J. (2007). A Rao-Blackwellisation approach to GDM-SLAM–integrating SLAM and gas distribution mapping. In *Proceedings of the 3rd European Conference on Mobile Robots* (pp. 126-131).

Lilienthal, A. J., Reggente, M., Trincavelli, M., Blanco, J. L., & Gonzalez, J. (2009b). A statistical approach to gas distribution modelling with mobile robots–the Kernel DM+V algorithm. In *Proceeding of the IEEE/RSJ International Conference on Intelligent Robots and Systems* (pp. 570-576). doi: 10.1109/IROS.2009.5354304

Lilienthal, A. J., Streichert, F., & Zell, A. (2005). Model-based shape analysis of gas concentration gridmaps for improved gas source localisation. In *Proceedings of the IEEE International Conference on Robotics and Automation,* (pp. 3575–3580).

Linforth, R. S., Savary, I., Pattenden, B., & Taylor, A. J. (1994). Volatile compounds found in expired air during eating of fresh tomatoes and in the headspace above tomatoes. *Journal of the Science of Food and Agriculture, 65*(2), 241–247. doi:10.1002/jsfa.2740650219

Liu, S., & Lin, Y. (2005). *Grey information: Theory and practical applications.* Berlin, Germany: Springer.

Liu, X.-M., Li, K., & Huang, H.-K. (2003). Feature selection for handwritten Chinese characters based on machine learning. *Proceedings of the 2nd International Conference on Machine Learning and Cybernetics (ICMLC '03),* (pp. 2399–2402).

Llobet, E., Brezmes, J., Gualdrón, O., Vilanova, X., & Correig, X. (2004). Building parsimonious fuzzy ARTMAP models by variable selection with a cascaded genetic algorithm: application to multisensor systems for gas analysis. *Sensors and Actuators. B, Chemical, 99,* 267–272. doi:10.1016/j.snb.2003.11.019

Compilation of References

Llobet, E., Gualdrón, O., Vinaixa, M., El-Barbri, N., Brezmes, J., & Vilanova, X. (2007). Efficient feature selection for mass-spectrometry based electronic nose applications. *Chemometrics and Intelligent Laboratory Systems, 85*, 253–261. doi:10.1016/j.chemolab.2006.07.002

Llobet, E. (2006). Temperature modulated gas sensors. In Grimes, C. A. (Ed.), *Encyclopaedia of sensors* (pp. 131–152). American Scientific Publishers.

Lonergan, M. C., Freund, M. S., Severin, E. J., Doleman, B. J., Grubbs, R. H., & Lewis, N. S. (1997). Array-based vapor sensing using chemically sensitive, polymer composite resistors. In *Proceedings of the IEEE Aerospace Conference* (pp. 583–631). doi:10.1109/AERO.1997.574914

Lorber, A., & Kowalski, B. R. (1988). Estimation of prediction error for multivariate calibration. *Journal of Chemometrics, 2*, 93–109. doi:10.1002/cem.1180020203

Loutfi, A., Coradeschi, S., Lilienthal, A. J., & Gonzalez, J. (2008). Gas distribution mapping of multiple odour sources using a mobile robot. *Robotica, 27*(2), 311–319..doi:10.1017/S0263574708004694

Lytovchenko, A., Beleggia, R., Schauer, N., Isaacson, T., Leuendorf, J. E., & Hellmann, H. (2009). Application of GC-MS for the detection of lipophilic compounds in diverse plant tissues. *Plant Methods, 5*(4), 11.

Ma, M., Zhang, Y., Langholz, G., & Kandel, A. (2000). On direct construction of fuzzy systems. *Fuzzy Sets and Systems, 112*, 165–171. doi:10.1016/S0165-0114(97)00387-4

Maffei, M. E. (2010). Sites of synthesis, biochemistry and functional role of plant volatiles. *South African Journal of Botany, 76*(4), 612–631. doi:10.1016/j.sajb.2010.03.003

Maldonado-Bascon, S., Khalifa, S. A., & Lopez-Ferreras, F. (2003). *Feature reduction using support vector machines for binary gas detection.* (LNCS 2687), (pp. 798–805).

Margolies, D. C., & Wrensch, D. L. (1996). Temperature-induced changes in spider mite fitness: Offsetting effects of development time, fecundity, and sex ratio. *Entomologia Experimentalis et Applicata, 78*, 111–118.

Marín, S., Vinaixa, M., Brezmes, J., Llobet, E., Vilanova, X., & Correig, X. (2007). Use of a MS-electronic nose for prediction of early fungal spoilage of bakery products. *International Journal of Microbiology, 114*, 10–16. doi:10.1016/j.ijfoodmicro.2006.11.003

Marino, P., Dominguez, M. A., & Alonso, M. (1999). *Machine-vision based detection for sheet metal industries.* The 25th Annual Conference of the IEEE Industrial Electronics Society (IECON'1999), 3, (pp. 1330–1335).

Marseguerra, M., Zio, E., Baraldi, P., & Oldrini, A. (2003). Fuzzy logic for signal prediction in nuclear systems. *Progress in Nuclear Energy, 43*, 373–380. doi:10.1016/S0149-1970(03)00048-9

Marsili, R. (1999). SPME-MS-MVA as an electronic nose for the study of off-flavors in milk. *Journal of Agricultural and Food Chemistry, 47*, 648–654. doi:10.1021/jf9807925

Martí, M. P., Boqué, R., Riu, M., Busto, O., & Guasch, J. (2003). Fast screening method for determining 2,4,6-trichloroanisole in wines using a headspace–mass spectrometry (HS–MS) system and multivariate calibration. *Analytical and Bioanalytical Chemistry*, *376*, 497–501. doi:10.1007/s00216-003-1940-z

Martí, M. P., Pino, J., Boqué, R., Busto, O., & Guasch, J. (2005). Determination of ageing time of spirits in oak barrels using a headspace–mass spectrometry (HS-MS) electronic nose system and multivariate calibration. *Analytical and Bioanalytical Chemistry*, *382*, 440–443. doi:10.1007/s00216-004-2969-3

Materka, A., & Strzelecki, M. (1998). Texture analysis methods-a review. Lodz, Poland: Technical University of Lodz, Institute of Electronics. *Stefanowskiego*, *18*, 90–924.

Maziarz, W., & Pisarkiewicz, T. (2008). Gas sensors in a dynamic operation mode. *Measurement Science & Technology*, 19.

Messager, J. (2002). *The diffusion of fragrances in a multimedia environment*. Paper presented at Third Aroma Science Forum, Tokyo, Japan.

Meyer, D., Leisch, F., & Hornik, K. (2003). The support vector machine under test. *Neurocomputing*, *55*, 169–186. doi:10.1016/S0925-2312(03)00431-4

Mihran, T., & Anil, J. (1998). Texture analysis. In C. N. Chen, L. F. Pau & P. S. P. (Eds.), *The handbook of pattern recognition and computer vision* (2nd ed.) (pp. 207–248).

Miller, J. F., & Thomson, P. (2000). *Cartesian genetic programming*. (LNCS 1802), (pp. 121-132).

Mitchell, H. B. (2007). *Multi-sensor data fusion: An introduction*. Berlin, Germany: Springer Verlag.

Mitra, S., & Acharya, T. (2003). *Data mining: Multimedia, soft computing, and bioinformatics*. Hoboken, NJ: John Wiley.

Moseley, P. T., & Tofield, B. C. (Eds.). (1987). *Solid-state gas sensors*. Bristol, UK: The Adam Hilger series on sensors.

Mouchaweh, M. S., Devillez, A., Lecolier, G. V., & Billaudel, P. (2002). Incremental learning in fuzzy pattern matching. *Fuzzy Sets and Systems*, *132*, 49–62. doi:10.1016/S0165-0114(02)00060-X

Mucciardi, A. N., & Gose, E. E. (1971). A comparison of seven techniques for choosing subsets of pattern recognition properties. *IEEE Transactions on Computers*, *C-20*(9), 1023–1031. doi:10.1109/T-C.1971.223398

Muezzinoglu, M., Vergara, A., Huerta, R., & Rabinovich, M. (2010). A sensor conditioning principle for odor identification. *Sensors and Actuators. B, Chemical*, *146*, 472–476. doi:10.1016/j.snb.2009.11.036

Mulgrew, B., Grant, P., & Thompson, J. (1999). *Digital signal processing*. New York, NY: Palgrave.

Compilation of References

Munoz, S., Nakamoto, T., & Moriizumi, T. (2005). Study of deposition of gas sensing films on quartz crystal microbalance using an ultrasonic atomizer. *Sensors and Actuators. B, Chemical, 105,* 144–149.

Naes, T., & Martens, H. (1998). Principal component regression in NIR analysis: Viewpoints, background details and selection of components. *Journal of Chemometrics, 2,* 155–167. doi:10.1002/cem.1180020207

Nakaizumi, F., Yanagida, Y., Noma, H., & Hosaka, K. (2006). SpotScents: A novel method of natural scent delivery using multiple scent projectors. *Proceedings of IEEE Virtual Reality Conference* (pp. 206-212). Alexandria, Virginia.

Nakamoto, T., Okazaki, N., & Matsushita, H. (1995). Improvement of optimization algorithm in active gas/odor sensing system. *Sensors and Actuators. A, Physical, 50,* 191–196. doi:10.1016/0924-4247(95)01039-4

Nakamoto, T., & Moriizumi, T. (1990). A theory of a quartz crystal microbalance based upon a Mason equivalent circuit. *Japanese Journal of Applied Physics, 29,* 963–969. doi:10.1143/JJAP.29.963

Nakamoto, T., & Murakami, K. (2009). Selection method of odor components for olfactory display using mass spectrum database. In [Lafayette, Louisiana, USA.]. *Proceedings of IEEE Virtual Reality, 2009,* 159–162.

Nakamoto, T., Nakahira, Y., Hiramatsu, H., & Moriizumi, T. (2001). Odor recorder using active odor sensing system. *Sensors and Actuators. B, Chemical, 76,* 465–469. doi:10.1016/S0925-4005(01)00587-1

Nakamoto, T., Otaguro, S., Kinoshita, M., Nagahama, M., Ohnishi, K., & Ishida, T. (2008). Cooking up an interactive olfactory display. *IEEE Computer Graphics and Applications, 28*(1), 75–78. doi:10.1109/MCG.2008.3

Nakamoto, T., & Yoshikawa, K. (2006). Movie with scents generated by olfactory display using solenoid valves. *IEICE Transactions on Fundamentals of Electronics, Communications and Computer Sciences. E (Norwalk, Conn.), 89-A*(11), 3327–3332.

Nakamoto, T., Ishida, H., & Moriizumi, T. (1999). A sensing system for odor plumes. *Analytical Chemistry News & Features, 1,* 531–537.

Nakamoto, T., & Dinh Minh, H. P. (2007). *Improvement of olfactory display using solenoid valves.* IEEE Virtual Reality Conference (pp. 179-186). Charlotte, NC.

Nakamoto, T., Cho, N., Nitikarn, N., Wyszynski, B., Takushima, H., & Kinoshita, M. (2008). *Experiment on teleolfaction using odor sensing system and olfactory display synchronous with visual information.* 18th International Conference on Artificial Reality and Telexistence (pp. 85-92). Yokohama, Japan.

Nakata, S., Akakabe, S., Nakasuji, M., & Yoshikawa, K. (1996). Gas sensing based on a nonlinear response: Discrimination between hydrocarbons and quantification of individual components in a gas mixture. *Analytical Chemistry, 68*, 2067–2072. doi:10.1021/ac9510954

Nakata, S., Kaneda, Y., Nakamura, H., & Yoshikawa, K. (1991). Detection and quantification of CO gas based on the dynamic response of a ceramic sensor. *Chemistry Letters*, 1505–1508. doi:10.1246/cl.1991.1505

Nakata, S., Kaneda, Y., & Yoshikawa, K. (1992). Novel strategy to develop chemical sensors based on nonlinear dynamics-intelligent gas sensor. *Senses and Materials, 4*, 101–110.

Nakata, S., Ozaki, E., & Ojima, N. (1998). Gas sensing based on the dynamic nonlinear responses of a semiconductor gas sensor: Dependence on the range and frequency of a cyclic temperature change. *Analytica Chimica Acta, 361*, 93–100. doi:10.1016/S0003-2670(98)00013-0

Nanto, H., & Stetter, J. R. (2003). Introduction to chemosensors. In Pearce, T. C., Schiffman, S., Nagle, H. T., & Gardner, J. (Eds.), *Handbook of artificial olfaction machines*. Weinheim, Germany: Wiley–VCH.

Narendra, P. M., & Fukunaga, K. (1977). A branch and bound algorithm for feature subset selection. *IEEE Transactions on Computers, C-26*, 917–922. doi:10.1109/TC.1977.1674939

Natale, C. D., Macagnano, A., D'Amico, A., & Davide, F. (1997). Electronic-nose modelling and data analysis using a self-organizing map. *Measurement Science & Technology, 8*(11), 1236–1243. doi:10.1088/0957-0233/8/11/004

Navidi, W. (2007). *Statistics for engineers and scientists* (2nd ed.). New York, NY: McGraw-Hill.

Nayar, S. K., Sanderson, A. C., Weiss, L. E., & Simon, D. A. (1990). Specular surface inspection using structured highlight and Gaussian images. *IEEE Transactions on Robotics and Automation, 6*(2), 208–218. doi:10.1109/70.54736

Niebling, G., & Müller, R. (1995). Design of sensor arrays by use of an inverse feature space. *Sensors and Actuators. B, Chemical, 25*, 781–784. doi:10.1016/0925-4005(95)85173-9

Niemann, H. (2003). *Klassifikation von Mustern* (2nd ed.). Berlin, Germany: Springer.

Nimsuk, N., & Nakamoto, T. (2008). Study on the odor classification in dynamical concentration robust both against humidity and temperature changes. *Sensors and Actuators. B, Chemical, 234*, 252–257. doi:10.1016/j.snb.2008.04.047

Nylander, C. (1985). Chemical and biological sensors. *Journal of Physics. E, Scientific Instruments, 18*(9), 736–750. doi:10.1088/0022-3735/18/9/003

Olesen, H. R., Løfstrøm, P., Berkowicz, R., & Ketzel, M. (2005). *Regulatory odour model development: Survey of modelling tools and datasets with focus on building effects*. (NERI Technical Report No. 541).

Compilation of References

Paakkari, J. (1998). *Online flatness measurement of large steel plates using Moire topography.* Finland: University of Oulu.

Pal, S. K., & Majumder, D. D. (1986). *Fuzzy mathematical approach to pattern recognition.* New York, NY: John Wiley.

Paletta, L., & Pinz, A. (2000). Active object recognition by view integration and reinforcement learning. *Robotics and Autonomous Systems, 31*, 71–86. doi:10.1016/S0921-8890(99)00079-2

Papadimitriou, C. H., & Tsitsiklis, J. N. (1987). The complexity of Markov decision processes. *Mathematics of Operations Research, 12*, 441–450. doi:10.1287/moor.12.3.441

Pardo, M., & Sberveglieri, G. (2007). Comparing the performance of different features in sensor arrays. *Sensors and Actuators. B, Chemical, 116*, 437–443. doi:10.1016/j.snb.2006.09.041

Pardo, M., & Sberveglieri, G. (2002). Coffee analysis with an electronic nose. *IEEE Transactions on Instrumentation and Measurement, 51*, 1334–1339. doi:10.1109/TIM.2002.808038

Pardo, M., & Sberveglieri, G. (2005). Classification of electronic nose data with support vector machines. *Sensors and Actuators. B, Chemical, 107*(2), 730–737. doi:10.1016/j.snb.2004.12.005

Paulsson, N., Larson, E., & Winquist, F. (2000). Extraction and selection of parameters for evaluation of breath alcohol measurement with an electronic nose. *Sensors and Actuators. A, Physical, 84*, 187–197. doi:10.1016/S0924-4247(00)00419-2

Pearce, T. C. (2003). *Handbook of machine olfaction: Electronic nose technology.* Weinheim, Germany: Wiley-VCH.

Pearce, T. C. (1997). Computational parallels between the biological olfactory pathway and its analogue the electronic nose, part II: Sensor-based machine olfaction. *Bio Systems, 41*, 69–90. doi:10.1016/S0303-2647(96)01660-7

Pearce, T. C., Schiffman, S. S., Nagle, H. T., & Gardner, J. W. (2003). *Handbook of machine olfaction: Electronic nose technology.* Frankfurt, Germany: Wiley-VCH.

Pearce, T. C., & Sanchez-Montañes, M. (2003). Chemical sensor array optimization: Geometric and information theoretic approaches. In Pearce, T. C., Schiffman, S., Nagle, H. T., & Gardner, J. (Eds.), *Handbook of artificial olfaction machines.* Weinheim, Germany: Wiley–VCH.

Pedrycz, W. (1994). Why triangular membership functions? *Fuzzy Sets and Systems, 64*, 21–30. doi:10.1016/0165-0114(94)90003-5

Peng, N., Long, F., & Ding, C. (2005). Feature selection based on mutual information: Criteria of max-dependency, max-relevance, and min-redundancy. *IEEE Transactions on Pattern Analysis and Machine Intelligence, 27*(8), 1226–1238. doi:10.1109/TPAMI.2005.159

Peñuelas, J., & Llusià, J. (2004). Plant VOC emissions: Making use of the unavoidable. *Trends in Ecology & Evolution, 19*(8), 402–404. doi:10.1016/j.tree.2004.06.002

Perera, A., Yamanaka, T., Gutierrez-Galvez, A., Raman, B., & Gutierrez-Osuna, R. (2006). A dimensionality-reduction technique inspired by receptor convergence in the olfactory system. *Sensors and Actuators. B, Chemical, 116*, 17–22. doi:10.1016/j.snb.2005.11.082

Peres, C., Begnaud, F., Eveleigh, L., & Berdagué, J. L. (2003). Fast characterization of food-stuff by headspace mass spectrometry (HS-MS). *Trends in Analytical Chemistry, 22*, 858–866. doi:10.1016/S0165-9936(03)01206-8

Peris, M., & Escuder-Gilabert, L. (2009). A 21st century technique for food control: Electronic noses. *Analytica Chimica Acta, 638*(1), 1–15. doi:10.1016/j.aca.2009.02.009

Pernkopf, F. (2004). 3D surface inspection using coupled HMMs. *Proceedings of the 17th International Conference on Pattern Recognition (ICPR '2004)*.

Persaud, K., & Dodd, G. (1982). Analysis of discrimination mechanisms in the mammalian olfactory system using a model nose. *Nature, 299*, 352–355. doi:10.1038/299352a0

Persaud, K. C., & Travers, P. J. (1997). In Kress-Rogers, E. (Ed.), *Handbook of biosensors and electronic noses* (pp. 563–592). CRC Press.

Poli, R. (1997). *Parallel distributed genetic programming applied to the evolution of natural language recognisers*. Berlin, Germany.

Polikar, R., Udpa, L., Udpa, S. S., & Honavar, V. (2001). Learn++: An incremental learning algorithm for supervised neural networks. *IEEE Transactions on Systems, Man, and Cybernetics C. Applications and Reviews, 31*, 497–508.

Potvin, J.-Y. (2008). A review of bio-inspired algorithms for vehicle routing. In Pereira, F. B., & Tavares, J. (Eds.), *Bio-inspired algorithms for the vehicle routing problem* (1st ed., pp. 1–34). New York, NY: Springer.

Puente Leon, F., & Beyerer, J. (1997). Active vision and sensor fusion for inspection of metallic surfaces. In, D. P. Casasent (Ed.), *Proceedings of SPIE Intelligent Robots and Computer Vision XVI: Algorithms, Techniques, Active Vision, and Materials Handling*, (pp. 394–405).

Purnamadjaja, A., & Russell, R. (2005). Congregation behaviour in a robot swarm using phero-mone communication. In *Proceedings of the Australian Conference on Robotics and Automation*.

Putnam, M. L. (1995). Evaluation of selected methods of plant disease diagnosis. *Crop Protection (Guildford, Surrey), 14*(6), 517–525. doi:10.1016/0261-2194(95)00038-N

Pyk, P. (2006). An artificial moth: Chemical source localization using robot based neuronal model of moth optomotor anemotactic search. *Autonomous Robots, 20*(3), 197–213..doi:10.1007/s10514-006-7101-4

Qian, K., Seah, N. S., & Asundi, A. (2005). *Fringe 2005: Fault detection from temporal unusualness in fringe patterns. Stuttgart, Germany*. W.: Osten.

Compilation of References

Rakow, N. A., & Suslick, K. S. (2000). A colorimetric sensor array for odour visualization. *Nature*, *406*, 710–713..doi:10.1038/35021028

Raman, B., Meier, D. C., Evju, J. K., & Semancik, S. (2009). Designing and optimizing microsensor arrays for recognizing chemical hazards in complex environments. *Sensors and Actuators. B, Chemical*, *137*, 617–629. doi:10.1016/j.snb.2008.11.053

Raudys, S. J., & Jain, A. K. (1991). Small sample size effects in statistical pattern recognition: Recommendations for practitioners. *IEEE Transactions on Pattern Analysis and Machine Intelligence*, *13*(3), 252–264. doi:10.1109/34.75512

Rechenberg, I. (1973). *Evolutionsstrategie: Optimierung technischer Systeme nach Prinzipien der biologischen Evolution*. Fromman-Holzboog.

Reeves, C. R., & Rowe, J. E. (2003). *Genetic algorithms: Principles and perspectives: A guide to GA theory*. Boston, MA: Kluwer Academic Publishers.

Reggente, M., & Lilienthal, A. J. (2009a). Three-dimensional statistical gas distribution mapping in an uncontrolled indoor environment. In *AIP Conference Proceedings Volume 1137: Olfaction and Electronic Nose - Proceedings of the 13th International Symposium on Olfaction and Electronic Nose* (pp. 109-112). doi: 10.1063/1.3156484

Reggente, M., & Lilienthal, A. J. (2009b). Using local wind information for gas distribution mapping in outdoor environments with a mobile robot. In *Proceedings of IEEE Sensors 2009 Conference* (pp. 1712-1720). doi: 10.1109/ICSENS.2009.5398498

Reggente, M., & Lilienthal, A. J. (2009a). Using local wind information for gas distribution mapping in outdoor environments with a mobile robot. In *Proceedings of IEEE Sensors*, (pp. 1715-1720).

Reggente, M., & Lilienthal, A. J. (2009b). Three-dimensional statistical gas distribution mapping in an uncontrolled indoor environment. *AIP Conference Proceedings Volume 1137: Olfaction and Electronic Nose - Proceedings of the 13th International Symposium on Olfaction and Electronic Nose* (ISOEN), (pp. 109-112).

Reindl, I., & O'Leary, P. (2007). *Instrumentation and measurement method for the inspection of peeled steel rods*. IEEE Conference on Instrumentation and Measurement (IMTC'2007).

Rezaee, M. R., Lelieveldt, B. P. F., & Reiber, J. H. C. (1998). A new cluster validity index for the fuzzy c-mean. *Pattern Recognition Letters*, *19*(3-4), 237–246. doi:10.1016/S0167-8655(97)00168-2

Roberts, P. J. W., & Webster, D. R. (2002). Turbulent diffusion. In Shen, H., Cheng, A., Wang, K.-H., Teng, M. H., & Liu, C. (Eds.), *Environmental fluid mechanics-theories and application* (pp. 7–47). Reston, VA: ASCE Press.

Roberts, P. J. W., & Webster, D. R. (2002). Turbulent diffusion. In Shen, H., Cheng, A., Wang, K.-H., Teng, M. H., & Liu, C. (Eds.), *Environmental fluid mechanics-theories and application*. Reston, VA: ASCE Press.

Rojas, R. (1996). *Neural networks: A systematic introduction*. Berlin, Germany/ New York, NY: Springer-Verlag.

Rothlauf, F. (2006). *Representations for genetic and evolutionary algorithms* (2nd ed.). Heidelberg, Germany: Springer.

Ruhland, B., Becker, T., & Müller, G. (1998). Gas-kinetic interactions of nitrous oxides with SnO_2 surfaces. *Sensors and Actuators. B, Chemical, 50*, 85–94. doi:10.1016/S0925-4005(98)00160-9

Russell, R. A. (1999). *Odour sensing for mobile robots*. World Scientific.

Saeys, Y., Inza, I., & Larrañaga, P. (2007). A review of feature selection techniques in bioinformatics. *Bioinformatics (Oxford, England), 23*, 2507–2517. doi:10.1093/bioinformatics/btm344

Sankaran, S., Mishra, A., Ehsani, R., & Davis, C. (2010). A review of advanced techniques for detecting plant diseases. *Computers and Electronics in Agriculture, 72*(1), 1–13. doi:10.1016/j.compag.2010.02.007

Sato, S. (1978). *Introduction to sensory test* (pp. 78–80). JUSE Press, Ltd.

Schiffman, S. S., Bennett, J. L., & Raymer, J. H. (2001). Quantification of odours and odorants from swine operations in North Carolina. *Agricultural and Forest Meteorology, 108*, 213–240. doi:10.1016/S0168-1923(01)00239-8

Schmutter, P. (2002). *Object oriented ontogenetic programming: Breeding computer programms that work like multicellular creatures*. Dortmund, Germany: University Systems Analysis Research Group.

Schölkopf & J. Platt (Ed.), *Advances in neural information processing systems* (pp. 1257–1264). Cambridge, MA: MIT Press.

Schwefel, H.-P. (1981). *Numerical optimization of computer models*. New York, NY: John Wiley & Sons, Inc.

Schweizer-Berberich, M., Vaihinger, S., & Gopel, W. (1994). Characterisation of food freshness with sensor arrays. *Sensors and Actuators. B, Chemical, 18-19*, 282–290. doi:10.1016/0925-4005(94)87095-0

Scott, S. M., James, D., & Ali, Z. (2006). Data analysis for electronic nose systems. *Mikrochimica Acta, 156*, 3–4. doi:10.1007/s00604-006-0623-9

Sears, W. M., Colbow, K., & Consadori, F. (1989a). General characteristics of thermally cycled tin oxide gas sensors. *Semiconductor Science and Technology, 4*, 351–359. doi:10.1088/0268-1242/4/5/004

Sears, W. M., Colbow, K., & Consadori, F. (1989b). Algorithms to improve the selectivity of thermally cycled tin oxide gas sensors. *Sensors and Actuators, 19*, 333–349. doi:10.1016/0250-6874(89)87084-2

Compilation of References

Sears, W. M., Colbow, K., Slamka, R., & Consadori, F. (1990). Selective thermally cycled gas sensing using fast Fourier-transform techniques. *Sensors and Actuators. B, Chemical, 2*, 283–289. doi:10.1016/0925-4005(90)80155-S

Segawa, N., Tokuhiro, T., Nakamoto, T., & Moriizumi, T. (2002). Multi-channel frequency shift measurement circuit with high sampling rate for QCM odor sensors. *IEE of Japan*, 16-22.

Semancik, S., & Cavicchi, R. E. (1999). Kinetically controlled chemical sensing using micro-machined structures. *Accounts of Chemical Research, 31*(5), 279–287. doi:10.1021/ar970071b

Shraiman, B., & Siggia, E. (2000). Scalar turbulence. *Nature, 405*, 639–646. doi:10.1038/35015000

Singh, S. (1999). A single nearest neighbour fuzzy approach for pattern recognition. *International Journal of Pattern Recognition and Artificial Intelligence, 13*, 49–54. doi:10.1142/S0218001499000045

Siripatrawan, U. (2008). Self-organizing algorithm for classification of packaged fresh vegetable potentially contaminated with foodborne pathogens. *Sensors and Actuators. B, Chemical, 128*(2), 435–441. doi:10.1016/j.snb.2007.06.030

Sloper, J. E., Miotto, G. L., & Hines, E. (2008). Dynamic error recovery in the ATLAS TDAQ system. *IEEE Transactions on Nuclear Science, 55*(1), 405–410. doi:10.1109/TNS.2007.913472

Snelson, E., & Ghahramani, Z. (2006). Sparse Gaussian processes using pseudo-inputs. In Weiss, Y. (Ed.), *B*.

Solis, J. L., Kish, L. B., Vajtai, R., Granqvist, C. G., Olsson, J., Shnurer, J., & Lantto, V. (2001). Identifying natural and artificial odors through noise analysis with a sampling-and-hold electronic nose. *Sensors and Actators B, 77*, 312–315. doi:10.1016/S0925-4005(01)00698-0

Somboon, P., Kinoshita, M., Wyszynski, B., & Nakamoto, T. (in press). Development of odor recorder with enhanced recording capabilities based on real-time mass spectrometry. *Sensors and Actuators. B, Chemical*.

Stachniss, C., Plagemann, C., & Lilienthal, A. J. (2009). Learning gas distribution models using sparse Gaussian process mixtures. *Autonomous Robots, 26*(2-3), 187–202..doi:10.1007/s10514-009-9111-5

Stachniss, C., Plagemann, C., & Lilienthal, A. J. (2009). Learning gas distribution models using sparse Gaussian process mixtures. *Autonomous Robots, 26*(2-3), 187–202. doi:10.1007/s10514-009-9111-5

Sun, J. (1995). A correlation principal component regression analysis of NIR data. *Journal of Chemometrics, 9*, 21–29. doi:10.1002/cem.1180090104

Suslick, K. S., Rakow, N. A., & Sen, A. (2004). Colorimetric sensor arrays for molecular recognition. *Tetrahedron, 60*, 11133–11138. doi:10.1016/j.tet.2004.09.007

Takagi, T., & Sugeno, M. (1985). Fuzzy identification of systems and its applications to modeling and control. *IEEE Transactions on Systems, Man, and Cybernetics*, *15*(1), 116–132.

Talavera, L. (2000). Dependency-based feature selection for clustering symbolic data. *Intelligent Data Analysis*, *4*, 19–28.

Tian, F., Xu, X., Shen, Y., Yan, J., He, Q., Ma, J., & Liu, T. (2009). Detection of wound pathogen by an intelligent electronic nose. *Sensors and Materials*, *21*, 155–166.

Tian, F., Yang, S. X., & Dong, K. (2005a). Circuit and noise analysis of odorant gas sensors in an e-nose. *Sensors (Basel, Switzerland)*, *5*, 85–96. doi:10.3390/s5010085

Tian, F., Yang, S. X., & Dong, K. (2005b). *Study on noise feature in sensor array of an electronic nose*. IEEE International Conference On Networking, Sensing and Control (pp. 19-22). Tucson, Arizona, U.S.A.

Tikunov, Y., Vos, C. D., Lommen, A., Bino, R., Hall, R., & Bovy, A. (2004). Metabolomics of tomato fruit volatile compounds. *Book of abstracts of the 1st Solanaceae Genome Workshop*, (pp. 19-21).

Tominaga, K., Honda, S., Ohsawa, T., Shigeno, H., Okada, K., & Matsushita, Y. (2001). Friend Park-expression of the wind and the scent on virtual space. *Proceedings of the 7th International Conference on Virtual Systems and Multimedia* (pp. 507-515). Berkeley, CA.

Tudu, B., Jana, A., Metla, A., Ghosh, D., Bhattacharyya, N., & Bandyopadhyay, R. (2009a). Electronic nose for black tea quality evaluation by an incremental RBF network. *Sensors and Actuators. B, Chemical*, *138*, 90–95. doi:10.1016/j.snb.2009.02.025

Tudu, B., Metla, A., Das, B., Bhattacharyya, N., Jana, A., Ghosh, D., & Bandyopadhyay, R. (2009b). Towards versatile electronic nose pattern classifier for black tea quality evaluation: An incremental fuzzy approach. *IEEE Transactions on Instrumentation and Measurement*, *58*, 3069–3078. doi:10.1109/TIM.2009.2016874

Unnikrishnan, R., Pantofaru, C., & Hebert, M. (2007). Toward objective evaluation of image segmentation algorithms. *IEEE Transactions on Pattern Analysis and Machine Intelligence*, *29*(6), 929–944. doi:10.1109/TPAMI.2007.1046

Vergara, A., Llobet, E., Brezmes, J., Ivanov, P., Cané, C., & Gràcia, I. (2007). Quantitative gas mixture analysis using temperature-modulated micro-hotplate gas sensors: Selection and validation of the optimal modulating frequencies. *Sensors and Actuators. B, Chemical*, *123*, 1002–1016. doi:10.1016/j.snb.2006.11.010

Vergara, A., Llobet, E., Brezmes, J., Ivanov, P., Vilanova, X., & Gràcia, I. (2005a). Optimised temperature modulation of metal oxide micro-hotplate gas sensors through multilevel pseudo random sequences. *Sensors and Actuators. B, Chemical*, *111-112*, 271–280. doi:10.1016/j.snb.2005.06.039

Compilation of References

Vergara, A., Llobet, E., Brezmes, J., Vilanova, X., Ivanov, P., & Gràcia, I. (2005b). Optimized temperature modulation of micro-hotplate gas sensors through pseudo random binary sequences. *IEEE Sensors Journal, 5,* 1369–1378. doi:10.1109/JSEN.2005.855605

Vergara, A., Muezzinoglu, M. K., Rulkov, N., & Huerta, R. (2010). Information theory of chemical sensors. *Sensors and Actuators. B, Chemical, 148,* 298–306. doi:10.1016/j.snb.2010.04.040

Vergara, A., Ramirez, J. L., & Llobet, E. (2008). Reducing power consumption via a discontinuous operation of temperature-modulated micro-hotplate gas sensors: Application to the logistics chain of fruit. *Sensors and Actuators. B, Chemical, 129,* 311–318. doi:10.1016/j.snb.2007.08.029

Vergara, A., Muezzinoglu, M. K., Rulkov, N., & Huerta, R. (2009). *Kullback-Leibler distance optimization for artificial chemo-sensors.* IEEE Sensors Conference, Christchurch, New Zealand, Oct. 25-28.

Vinaixa, M., Llobet, E., Brezmes, J., Vilanova, X., & Correig, X. (2005b). A fuzzy ARTMAP- and PLS-based MS e-nose for the qualitative and quantitative assessment of rancidity in crisps. *Sensors and Actuators. B, Chemical, 106,* 677–686. doi:10.1016/j.snb.2004.09.015

Vinaixa, M., Marín, S., Brezmes, J., Llobet, E., Vilanova, X., & Correig, X. (2004). Early detection of fungal growth in bakery products using an e-nose based on mass spectrometry. *Journal of Agricultural and Food Chemistry, 52,* 6068–6074. doi:10.1021/jf049399r

Vinaixa, M., Vergara, A., Duran, C., Llobet, E., Badia, C., & Brezmes, J. (2005). Fast detection of rancidity in potato crisps using e-noses based on mass spectrometry or gas sensors. *Sensors and Actuators. B, Chemical, 106,* 67–75. doi:10.1016/j.snb.2004.05.038

Wagner, T. (1999). *Automatische Konfiguration von Bildverarbeitungssysteme.* Germany: University of Erlangen-Nürnberg.

Walker, J. A., & Miller, J. F. (2008). The automatic acquisition, evolution and reuse of modules in Cartesian genetic programming. *IEEE Transactions on Evolutionary Computation, 12*(4), 397–417. doi:10.1109/TEVC.2007.903549

Wandel, M. R., Lilienthal, A. J., Duckett, T., Weimar, U., & Zell, A. (2003). Gas distribution in unventilated indoor environments inspected by a mobile robot. In *Proceedings of the IEEE International Conference on Advanced Robotics,* (pp. 507–512).

Wang, L.-X. (2003). The WM method completed: A flexible fuzzy system approach to data mining. *IEEE Transactions on Fuzzy Systems, 11,* 768–782. doi:10.1109/TFUZZ.2003.819839

Wang, L.-X., & Mendel, J. M. (1992). Generating fuzzy rules by learning from examples. *IEEE Transactions on Systems, Man, and Cybernetics, 22,* 414–1428. doi:10.1109/21.199466

Wang, Y., & Zhang, C. (2002). A novel methodology to cancel the additive coloured noise for real-time communication application. *IEICE Transactions on Electronics, 85,* 480–484.

Wasserman, L. A. (2004). *All of statistics: A concise course in statistical inference.* New York, NY: Springer.

Weiss, S. M. (1991). Small sample error rate estimation for k-NN classifiers. *IEEE Transactions on Pattern Analysis and Machine Intelligence*, *13*(3), 285–289. doi:10.1109/34.75516

Wendy, L. M., & Angel, R. M. (2007). *Computational statistics handbook with MATLAB* (2nd ed.). Chapman Hall/CRC.

Weska, J. S. (1978). A survey of threshold selection techniques. *Computer Graphics and Image Processing*, *7*, 259–265. doi:10.1016/0146-664X(78)90116-8

Whipps, J. M., & Budge, S. P. (2000). Effect of humidity on development of tomato powdery mildew (Oidium lycopersici) in the glasshouse. *European Journal of Plant Pathology*, *106*, 395–397. doi:10.1023/A:1008745630393

White, J., Kauer, J. S., Dickinson, T. A., & Walt, D. R. (1996). Rapid analyte recognition in a device based on optical sensors and the olfactory system. *Analytical Chemistry*, *68*, 2191–2202. doi:10.1021/ac9511197

Wholtjen, H., & Dessy, R. (1979). Surface acoustic wave probe chemical analysis. *Analytical Chemistry*, *51*(9), 1458–1464. doi:10.1021/ac50045a024

Wilson, G., & Banzhaf, W. (2008). *A comparison of cartesian genetic programming and linear genetic programming*. Italy: Naples.

Witten, I. H., & Eibe, F. (2008). *Data mining: Practical machine learning tools and techniques*, 2nd ed. Amsterdam, The Netherlands: Morgan Kaufmann/Elsevier (The Morgan Kaufmann series in data management systems).

Wlodek, S., Colbow, K., & Consadori, F. (1991). Kinetic model of thermally cycled tin oxide gas sensor. *Sensors and Actuators. B, Chemical*, *3*, 123–127. doi:10.1016/0925-4005(91)80204-W

Wyszynski, B., Galvez, A. G., & Nakamoto, T. (2007). Improvement of ultrasonic atomizer method for deposition of gas-sensing film on QCM. *Sensors and Actuators. B, Chemical*, *127*, 253–259. doi:10.1016/j.snb.2007.07.052

Xu, X., Tian, F., Yang, S. X., Li, Q., Yan, J., & Ma, J. (2008). A solid trap and thermal desorption system with application to a medical electronic nose. *Sensors (Basel, Switzerland)*, *8*, 6885–6898. doi:10.3390/s8116885

Yamada, T., Tanikawa, T., Hirota, K., & Hirose, M. (2006). Wearable olfactory display: Using odor in outdoor environment. *Proceedings of IEEE Virtual Reality Conference* (pp. 199-206). Alexandria, VA.

Yamanaka, T., Ishida, H., Nakamoto, T., & Moriizumi, T. (1998). Analysis of gas sensor transient response by visualizing instantaneous gas concentration using smoke. *Sensors and Actuators. A, Physical*, *69*, 77–81. doi:10.1016/S0924-4247(98)00045-4

Yamanaka, T., Matsumoto, R., & Nakamoto, T. (2002). Study of odor blender using solenoid valves controlled by delta-sigma modulation method for odor recorder. *Sensors and Actuators. B, Chemical*, *87*, 457–463. doi:10.1016/S0925-4005(02)00300-3

Compilation of References

Yamanaka, T., Matsumoto, R., & Nakamoto, T. (2003). Study of recording apple flavor using odor recorder with five components. *Sensors and Actuators. B, Chemical, 89*, 112–119. doi:10.1016/S0925-4005(02)00451-3

Yamanaka, T., & Nakamoto, T. (2003). Real-time reference method in odor blender under environmental change. *Sensors and Actuators. B, Chemical, 93*, 51–56. doi:10.1016/S0925-4005(03)00202-8

Yamanaka, T., Nitikarn, N., & Nakamoto, T. (2007). Concurrent recording and regeneration of visual and olfactory information using odor sensor. *Presence (Cambridge, Mass.), 16*(3), 307–317. doi:10.1162/pres.16.3.307

Yamanaka, T., Yoshikawa, K., & Nakamoto, T. (2004). Improvement of odor-recorder capability for recording dynamical change in odor. *Sensors and Actuators. B, Chemical, 99*(2-3), 367–372. doi:10.1016/j.snb.2003.12.004

Yang, J., Hines, E. L., Iliescu, D. D., & Leeson, M. S. (2008). Multi-input optimisation of river flow parameters and rule extraction using genetic-neural technique. In Hines, E. L., Leeson, M. S., Martínez-Ramón, M., Pardo, M., Llobet, E., Iliescu, D. D., & Yang, J. (Eds.), *Intelligent systems: Techniques and applications* (pp. 173–198). Shaker Publishing.

Yang, J., Hines, E. L., Guymer, I., Iliescu, D. D., Leeson, M. S., & King, G. P. (2008). A genetic algorithm-artificial neural network method for the prediction of longitudinal dispersion coefficient in rivers. In Porto, A., Pazos, A., & Buño, W. (Eds.), *Advancing artificial intelligence through biological process applications* (pp. 358–374). Hershey, PA: Idea Group Inc.

Zaromb, S., & Stetter, J. R. (1984). Theoretical basis for identification and measurement of air contaminants using an array of sensors having partly overlapping selectivities. *Sensors and Actuators. B, Chemical, 6*, 225–243. doi:10.1016/0250-6874(84)85019-2

Zellner, D. A., & Whitten, L. A. (1999). The effect of color intensity and appropriateness on color-induced odor enhancement. *The American Journal of Psychology, 112*, 585–604. doi:10.2307/1423652

Zhang, H., Wang, J., & Ye, S. (2007). Predictions of acidity, soluble solids and firmness of pear using electronic nose technique. *Journal of Food Engineering, 86*, 370–378. doi:10.1016/j.jfoodeng.2007.08.026

Zhang, Q., Zhang, S., Xie, C., Fan, C., & Bai, Z. (2007). Sensory analysis of Chinese vinegars using an electronic nose. *Sensors and Actuators. B, Chemical, 128*, 586–593. doi:10.1016/j.snb.2007.07.058

Zhang, F., Iliescu, D. D., Hines, E. L., Leeson, M. S., & Adams, S. R. (2010). Prediction of greenhouse tomato yield: A genetic algorithm optimized neural network based approach. In Manos, B., Paparrizos, K., Matsatsinis, N., & Papathanasiou, J. (Eds.), *Decision support systems in agriculture, food and the environment: Trends, applications and advances* (pp. 155–172). Hershey, PA: IGI Global.

Zhi, H., & Johansson, R. B. (1992). *Interpretation and classification of fringe patterns*. 11th International Conference on Image, Speech and Signal Analysis (IAPR'1992), 3, (pp. 105–108).

Zierler, N. (1959). Linear recurring sequences. *Journal of the Society for Industrial and Applied Mathematics, 7,* 31–48. doi:10.1137/0107003

Zuppa, M., Distante, C., Persaud, K. C., & Siciliano, P. (2007). Recovery of drifting sensor responses by means of DWT analysis. *Sensors and Actuators. B, Chemical, 120,* 411–416. doi:10.1016/j.snb.2006.02.049

Zuppa, M., Distante, C., Siciliano, P., & Persaud, K. C. (2004). Drift counteraction with multiple self-organising maps for an electronic nose. *Sensors and Actuators. B, Chemical, 98,* 305–317. doi:10.1016/j.snb.2003.10.029

About the Contributors

Evor L. Hines joined the School of Engineering at Warwick in 1984. He was promoted to Reader in 2005 and to a personal chair in 2009. He obtained his DSc (Warwick) in 2007 and is a Fellow of both the Institute of Engineering and Technology and the Higher Education Academy, in addition to being a Chartered Engineer. His main research interest is concerned with intelligent systems and their applications. Most of the work has focused on artificial neural networks, genetic algorithms, fuzzy logic, neurofuzzy systems and genetic programming. Typical application areas include, *inter alia*, intelligent sensors such as the electronic nose, medicine, non-destructive testing, computer vision, and telecommunications. He has co-authored in excess of 230 articles and supervised over 30 research students in addition to currently leading the Information and Communication Technologies Research Group in the School of Engineering.

Mark S. Leeson received the degrees of BSc and BEng with First Class Honors in Electrical and Electronic Engineering from the University of Nottingham, UK, in 1986. He then obtained a PhD in Engineering from the University of Cambridge, UK, in 1990. From 1990 to 1992 he worked as a Network Analyst for National Westminster Bank in London. After holding academic posts in London and Manchester, in 2000 he joined the School of Engineering at Warwick, where he is now an Associate Professor. His major research interests are coding and modulation, ad hoc networking, optical communication systems and evolutionary optimization. To date, Dr. Leeson has over 180 publications and has supervised nine successful research students. He is a Senior Member of the IEEE, a Chartered Member of the UK Institute of Physics, and a Fellow of the UK Higher Education Academy.

* * *

Sahar Asadi is a PhD student at the AASS Learning Systems Lab, Örebro University (Sweden) since January 2009. Her research topic is statistical gas distribution modeling in mobile sensor networks. She received her B.Sc. in 2006 and her M.Sc. in 2008, both in Computer Science from the University of Tehran, Iran. Her current research interests are mobile robot olfaction and distributed artificial intelligence.

Rajib Bandyopadhyay is currently a Professor with the Department of Instrumentation and Electronics Engineering, Jadavpur University, Kolkata, India. He received the Ph.D. degree from Jadavpur University, India, in 2001. Before joining Jadavpur University, he served for a year in the Indian computer manufacturing company ORG. His research interests include machine olfaction, electronic tongue, chemometrics and pattern classification. He has been associated in the research team involved in the development of electronic nose and electronic tongue for tea quality assessment. He has published more than 20 papers in premier journals and presented nearly 30 papers in conferences. He has guided 4 research scholars for their PhD theses, and at present, 8 students are working for their PhD degree under his guidance. Professor Bandyopadhyay is a Fellow of the Institution of Electronics and Telecommunication Engineers, India, and a member of the International Society of Automation (ISA).

Nabarun Bhattacharyya is the Additional Director with the Centre for the Development of Advanced Computing (C-DAC), Kolkata, which is a premier R&D Institute under Department of Information Technology, Government of India. He received the Ph.D. degree from Jadavpur University, India, in 2008. Before joining C-DAC, he served in industrial posts in companies including Hindustan Aeronautics Limited, Webel Crystals, and ACC. His research areas include agri-electronics, machine olfaction, soft computing, and pattern recognition. At present, he is the Head of Agri-electronics group in C-DAC, Kolkata, and more than 15 scientists are working under him in this group. He has guided 2 research students for their Ph.D. degree, and 7 research students are working under him for their Ph.D. He has been instrumental in the development of electronic nose and electronic tongue for tea quality assessment and has taken a lead role in introducing these technologies in the tea industry. He has published more than 15 papers in premier journals and presented nearly 40 papers in national and international conferences. Dr. Bhattacharyya is a member of IEEE.

Yannick Caulier received his bi-national Ph.D. degree in Computer Vision at the Aix-Marseille University France and the Friedrich-Alexander University

Germany in 2008, and his Engineering degree and Master degree in Telecommunication Engineering from ISITV, University of Toulon France, in 1997. He has been working since 1999 as a research Engineer at the Fraunhofer-Institute for Integrated Circuits IIS, in Erlangen Germany. His research activities are in the computer vision domain with a focus in industrial image processing. His research interests include data acquisition, i.e. the optical visual enhancement techniques based on coded-light and polarized approaches, but also the data processing, i.e. the pattern recognition coupled with the feature-based classification.

Reza Ghaffari is currently a PhD student at School of Engineering, University of Warwick, United Kingdom. He graduated with a BSc in Software Engineering in 2007 from Nottingham Trent University, UK, and received his MRes degree in Electronic Systems from the same institution in 2008. He joined the School of Engineering's Intelligent Systems Engineering Laboratory at the University of Warwick in 2008. His major research interests are artificial neural networks, machine learning, genetic algorithms, and software architecture. He is currently working on a plant pest and disease diagnosis system for commercial greenhouses using electronic nose and artificial intelligence.

D. Daciana Iliescu graduated in 1991 from the Polytechnic Institute of Bucharest, Romania, where she specialized in Telecommunications and Data Networks. She received her PhD in Engineering in 1998 from the University of Warwick, UK, in the field of Optical Engineering. Currently she is Associate Professor in the School of Engineering, University of Warwick and a research member of the Systems, Measurement and Modeling Research Group and associate member of the Information and Communication Technologies Group. She is the leader of Warwick's Engineering contribution to the EU project number 211457 (EUPHOROS).

XuQin Li received his B.S degree in educational technology and M.Sc. in pattern recognition and intelligent systems from HuaZhong Normal University and Chinese Academy of Sciences in 2003 and 2006, respectively. He is now pursuing his Ph.D. degree and has served as a Postgraduate Research Fellow in the Intelligent Systems Engineering Laboratory, School of Engineering, University of Warwick, UK. His research interests include fuzzy logic, neural networks, intelligent systems, and pattern recognition. Mr. Li is also an Overseas Research Students Awards Scheme (ORSAS) awards holder.

Achim J. Lilienthal is a docent (Associate Professor) at the AASS Research Center at Örebro University, Sweden, where he is leading the Learning Systems Lab. His main research interests are mobile robot olfaction, robot vision, robotic map learning, and safe navigation systems. Achim Lilienthal obtained his Ph.D. in Computer Science from Tübingen University, Germany and his M.Sc. and B.Sc. in Physics from the University of Konstanz, Germany. His Ph.D. thesis addressed gas distribution mapping and gas source localization with a mobile robot. The M.Sc. thesis is concerned with an investigation of the structure of $(C_{60})_n\pm$ Clusters using gas phase ion chromatography.

Eduard Llobet graduated in Telecommunication Engineering from the Universitat Politècnica de Catalunya (UPC), (Barcelona, Spain) in 1991, and received his Ph.D. in 1997 from the same university. He is currently Full Professor of Electronic Technology in the Electronic Engineering Department at the Universitat Rovira i Virgili (Tarragona, Spain). His main areas of interest are in the design of nanostructured semiconductor and carbon nanotube based gas sensors and in the application of intelligent systems to complex odour analysis. Professor Llobet is the Director of the Research Centre on Engineering of Materials and micro/nanosystems (EMaS) and a Senior Member of the IEEE.

Takamichi Nakamoto received his BEng and MEng degrees from the Tokyo Institute of Technology in 1982 and 1984, respectively. In 1991, he earned his Ph.D. degree in Electrical and Electronic Engineering from the same institution. He worked for Hitachi in the area of VLSI design automation from 1984 to 1987, when he joined the Tokyo Institute of Technology as a Research Associate. He is currently an Associate Professor in the Department of Physical Electronics, Tokyo Institute of Technology. From 1996 to 1997, he was a visiting scientist at the Pacific Northwest Laboratories, Richland, WA, USA. His research interests cover chemical sensing, olfaction in virtual reality, and LSI design.

Richard Napier is a plant biologist and currently a Professor in the School of Life Sciences at the University of Warwick, UK. Graduating in 1980 from the University of Reading, UK, and obtaining a PhD at the University of Leicester, UK, in 1984, he has worked in both animal and plant biochemistry research. Most of his research career has been associated with increasing understanding about how plant hormones are perceived by their protein receptors. These receptors are natural biosensors, although their output is delayed by developmental processing. More recently, Professor Napier has been developing synthetic biosensors to report on endogenous hormone signals in real-time. An extension of these activities is an interest in applying sensor technologies to biological and crop science problems. He serves on the editorial boards of two plant biology journals.

Christian Plagemann is a postdoctoral researcher at the Artificial Intelligence Lab of Stanford University, USA. He obtained his Ph.D. in computer science from the University of Freiburg, Germany, and his M.Sc. in computer science from the University of Karlsruhe, Germany. His research interests include machine learning, robotics, and autonomous systems technology, with a special focus on nonparametric Bayesian methods and regression problems.

Matteo Reggente is a Ph.D. student at AASS Learning Systems Lab, Örebro University (Sweden). He has been a young researcher at the Budapest University of Technology and Economics Department of Electron Devices in the period 2004 - 2007. He obtained his M.Sc. in Telecommunication Engineering from University "La Sapienza" - Rome, Italy in 2002. His main research interests are currently airborne chemical sensing with mobile robots, pollution monitoring, and semiconductor gas sensors.

John E. Sloper received his first degree from Bergen University College, Norway in 2005, and then commenced a PhD in the Intelligent Systems Engineering Laboratory at the University of Warwick, UK. He is shortly to graduate after completing a thesis that applied techniques from Computational Intelligence to data from the ATLAS data acquisition system at CERN in Switzerland. His recent research interests have included artificial neural networks, support vector machines and Cartesian genetic programming.

Cyrill Stachniss studied Computer Science at the University of Freiburg and received his Ph.D. degree in 2006. After his Ph.D., he was a senior researcher at ETH Zurich. Since 2007, he has been an academic advisor at the University of Freiburg in the Laboratory for Autonomous Intelligent Systems. In 2009, he received his habilitation. His research interests lie in the areas of robot navigation, exploration, SLAM, as well as learning approaches.

Bipan Tudu is currently a Reader with the Department of Instrumentation and Electronics Engineering, Jadavpur University, Kolkata, India. He received his MTech degree in instrumentation and electronics engineering from Jadavpur University, India, in 2004 and has submitted his Ph.D. thesis. His main research interest includes pattern recognition, artificial intelligence, machine olfaction, and electronic tongue. He has published more than 10 papers in premier journals and presented nearly 25 papers in national and international conferences. He has been associated in the research team involved in the development of electronic nose and electronic tongue for tea quality assessment and has been instrumental in introducing incremental learning for electronic nose and tongue for the tea industry.

Takao Yamanaka received the Bachelor of Engineering, Master of Engineering, and Ph.D. in Engineering from Tokyo Institute of Technology in 1996, 1998 and 2004, respectively. He is currently and Associate Professor in the Department of Information and Communication Sciences, Sophia University, Japan. His research interests include sensory information processing, intelligent sensing systems, and pattern recognition.

Jianhua Yang is currently a postdoctoral researcher working on the data modeling part of the EU Framework 7 MEIOSYS project at the University of Birmingham. Following an MSc with distinction, he completed his PhD in Intelligent Systems Engineering Laboratory in the Warwick School of Engineering sponsored by the UK Overseas Research Students Awards and a Warwick Postgraduate Research Fellowship. Dr. Yang is a member of the IEEE Computational Intelligence Society. His current research focuses on applying intelligent and biostatistical techniques to model crossing-over during higher plants' meiosis.

Alexander Vergara received a B.S. degree in Electrical Engineering from the Technological Institute of Durango, Mexico in 2000 and M.S. and Ph.D. degrees in Electrical Engineering from the Universitat Rovira i Virgili, Tarragona, Spain in 2003 and 2006, respectively. He is currently a Postgraduate Researcher at the BioCircuits Institute (BCI), University of California, San Diego (UCSD). His work focuses mainly on the use of dynamic methods for the optimization of micro gas-sensory systems and on the building of autonomous vehicles that can localize odour sources through a process resembling biological olfactory processing. His areas of interest also include pattern recognition, feature extraction, chemical sensor arrays, and machine olfaction.

Fu Zhang received his first degree in Computer Science from the University of Cambridge, UK, and then an MSc in Advanced Electronic Engineering from the University of Warwick, UK. He is currently completing his PhD as a member of Warwick's Intelligent Systems Engineering Laboratory in its School of Engineering. His main research interests are in the development and applications of artificial neural networks, genetic algorithms, fuzzy logic and Grey system theory. His recent research has been concerned with utilizing these approaches to predict diseases in commercial crops and to estimate crop yields, leading to several publications.

Index

A

analog-to-digital (A/D) 63
artificial neural networks (ANN) 64,
    129, 234, 239
Artificial Sensing (AS) 232
automatic systems 183

B

Backpropagation (BP) 281, 283
back-propagation multilayer percep-
    tron (BP-MLP) 80, 91, 92, 93
bacterial eye infection 278
bagging 277, 283, 284, 288, 290
bagging technique 277, 283, 288, 290
bias voltage 3
binary odor compositions 127
bootstrap 282, 283, 291, 292
bootstrap methodology 282
box-plots 114, 115, 116, 117

C

Cartesian Genetic Programming (CGP)
    64, 66, 68, 69, 73, 74
centroids 220, 222

CFS (Correlation-based Feature Selec-
    tion) 203, 204
chemical kinetics 1
chemical sensor arrays 232
chemical sensor features 4
chemo-resistors 4, 29
Classification and Regression Tree
    (CART) 282
classification methodologies 182, 190,
    199, 200
classification tree 285, 286, 287, 290
color array description 181, 187
colorimetric 180, 181, 182, 183, 184,
    185, 186, 187, 193, 194, 206,
    207, 208, 212
colorimetric sensor array description
    method 180
commercial greenhouse 214, 225
Computational Fluid Dynamics (CFD)
    154
computation models 78
conjunctivitis 278, 279
cross-validation error 286
Cyranose 320 278, 279, 291

D

Darwinian evolutionary systems 64
data patterns 89, 91, 92, 93, 94, 95, 96, 97
data pre-processing methods 102, 118
data sets 108, 109, 112, 113, 232, 238, 239, 242, 244, 246, 280, 281, 282, 283, 284, 285, 290
days post infection (DPI) 219, 222
decision tree (DT) 277, 281, 282, 283, 285, 288, 290, 293
defective parts 181, 185, 186, 187
digital cameras 127
digital video cameras 127
direct defense 216, 219, 225
Discrete Fourier Transformation (DFT) 108
disease detection 244, 246
Distributed Information Acquisition and Decision-making for Environmental Management (Diadem) 176, 177

E

electrode configurations 4
electromagnetic interference 105
electronic noses (e-nose) 102, 103, 105, 109-124, 127, 128, 129, 131, 132, 149, 150, 214, 217, 218, 219, 220-226, 231, 232, 233, 234, 236, 237, 239, 241-244, 246, 277, 278, 279, 280, 283
error back-propagation 91
error signals 91
evolutionary computation (EC) 62, 63, 64, 65, 66, 73, 74
Evolving Fuzzy Neural Network (EFuNN) 64, 66, 67, 68, 71, 72, 73, 74

E *(continued)*

Expectation-Maximization (EM) 163, 165, 166
eye bacteria 277, 279, 280, 283
eye disease 277
eye infections 278, 290

F

feature combination 180, 181, 208
feature extraction 182, 194, 195, 207, 208
feature retrieval 180, 208
feature selection 182, 187, 192, 203, 204, 206, 207, 208, 209, 210, 211, 212
feature subset selection (FSS) 191, 192, 203, 204, 206, 208
fingerprints 103
forward pass 91
FSS validation 192
fuzzification methods 84
Fuzzy C-Mean Clustering (FCM) 214, 215, 220, 221, 222, 223, 224, 225, 226
Fuzzy-C-Means (FCM) 86, 87, 88, 89, 90, 91
Fuzzy Inference Systems (FIS) 73
fuzzy logic 80
fuzzy models 80, 81
fuzzy partition 220
fuzzy regions 81, 84, 85, 86
fuzzy rules 81, 82, 83, 85, 89, 99, 100

G

gas accumulation 153, 163, 167, 176, 177
gas chromatography / mass spectrometry (GC/MS) 128, 214, 216, 217, 227, 229, 233
gas chromatography / olfactometry (GC/O) 128, 129

gas concentration measurements 153

gas distribution 153, 154, 155, 156, 158, 159, 161, 162, 163, 167, 168, 169, 170, 171, 172, 173, 175, 176, 177, 178, 179

gas distribution modeling (GDM) 153, 154, 155, 161, 162, 163, 168, 169, 172, 175, 176, 178

gas exchange 237

gas flow 3

gas-sensitive materials 3

gas sensors 2, 3, 18, 19, 21, 22, 26, 31, 40, 41, 45, 46, 49, 50, 52, 54, 55, 57, 58, 59, 103, 104, 105, 106, 108, 114,-124, 153, 154, 156, 175, 249, 250, 253, 255, 256, 264, 266, 269, 276

gas sensors arrays 233

gas source localization 249, 250

gating function 163, 164, 165, 168, 169

Gaussian assumptions 177

Gaussian Processes (GPs) 155, 161, 162, 163, 165, 166, 168

Gaussian Process Mixture Model (GPM) 155, 161, 162, 163, 168, 169, 175, 177

genetic algorithms (GA) 64, 65, 66, 67, 74, 76, 239

Genetic Neural Mathematical Methods (GNMM) 64, 66, 67, 70, 71, 72, 73, 74

genetic programming (GP) 64, 68, 69, 73, 74

geometries 4

GP model 162, 166

gradient descent (GD) 283, 285, 289

greenhouse 231, 232, 235, 237, 248

Grey Control 239

Grey Decisions 239

Grey Equations 239

Grey Incidence 239, 241

Grey incidences matrix 243

Grey Matrices 239

Grey Prediction 239

Grey Systems Modeling 239

Grey System Theory (GST) 231, 239

H

health monitoring 231, 244, 246

hidden layers 80, 91, 93, 94, 95, 97, 98

histogram 106, 107, 121

human disease monitoring 231

human olfactory system 231, 232

human senses 232

human sensing systems 183

hybrid sensor arrays 3

hypnone gas 115, 117, 120, 122

I

image segmentation 190, 208, 213

incremental learning algorithms 79, 92

industrial inspection 185

input layers 91, 93, 94

internal node 281

isopropanol 115, 116, 119, 121

J

Jasmonic Acid (JA) 225

K

kernel density estimation 153, 154

Kernel extrapolation Distribution Mapping (Kernel DM) 155, 156, 157, 158, 159, 160, 168, 169, 170, 171, 172, 173, 174, 175, 176, 177, 178

kernel regression 153

L

learning vector quantization (LVQ) 129, 130, 131, 132, 134, 136, 137, 138, 143, 148

Levenberg-Marquardt (LM) 283, 285, 289

linear discriminant analysis (LDA) 129, 234

M

machine olfaction 232, 248

machine olfaction systems 79

machine system 183

Mahalanobis distance (MD) 26, 27, 28, 29, 49

mass-spectrometry based machine olfaction (MS-e-nose) 4

Mean Magnitude Error (MME) 284, 285, 289

mean squared error (MSE) 66

membership function 81, 88, 89, 90, 91

Membership Functions (MF) 67, 72

Metal-Oxide Semiconductor (MOS) 103, 108

microbalances 4

micro-hotplate 4, 29, 32, 36, 37, 54, 57, 58

mobile robot olfaction 249

movie production 127

multilayer perceptron (MLP) 66, 67, 70, 73, 74, 80, 91, 92, 93, 129, 220, 277, 281, 282, 283, 284, 285, 289, 290

multilayer perceptron (MLP) model 281

multiple-input single-output (MISO) 80

Multisensor Data Fusion (MDF) 62, 63, 64, 73

multi-sensor systems 1

music players 127

N

Naive Bayes (NB) 190, 199, 200, 201, 202

Negative Log Predictive Density (NLPD) 167, 168, 171, 174

neural network based ENs 278

neural networks (NN) 80, 91, 93, 94, 95, 97, 98, 99, 100, 101, 129, 220, 223, 280

O

odorant gases 103, 120, 123, 124

odorant gas sensors 103, 120, 123

odorant molecules 3

odor recording 127

odor reproduction systems 126

odor-sensing systems 128

odor sensor arrays 127

odor sensors 126, 127, 135, 151, 152

Oidium neolycopersici 232, 235, 247

olfaction 180, 181, 184, 185, 210, 249

olfaction field 180

olfactory 183, 184, 231, 232, 233

olfactory displays 128, 130, 148, 149

olfactory display systems 126, 141

operating temperature 3, 22, 23, 26, 29, 38, 39, 40, 42, 43, 52, 59, 60, 61

optical fiber 4

optimal 182, 185, 186, 192, 198, 207

organic components 180, 181, 186, 193, 206, 207

output layers 91, 93

P

Parallel Distributed Genetic Programming (PDGP) 69
pathogenic airborne organisms 278
pattern recognition (PR) 63, 78, 100, 180, 182, 208, 211, 212
pattern recognition (PR) processes 180, 208
pattern recognition (PR) systems 78
periodical graphs 107, 108, 109, 112, 113, 121, 122
pest control 214, 215
pest detection 231
plant disease 214, 215, 225, 226, 230
plant disease diagnosis 215, 230
Polymerase Chain Reaction (PCR) 215, 228
polymer film 128
powdery mildew 218, 220, 224, 231, 232, 233, 235, 237, 241, 242, 244, 245, 246, 247, 248
power-spectrum-estimation 109, 111
principal component analysis (PCA) 129, 135, 137, 184, 223, 224, 225, 231, 234, 238, 241, 244
principal component analysis (PCA)-based methods 184
principal component analysis (PCA) dataset 223
probabilistic neural network (PNN) 65
probability distribution functions (pdf) 64, 103, 106, 109, 110, 111, 112, 121, 122

Q

questionnaire surveys 126, 140, 144, 146, 148

R

radial basis functions (RBF) 220
real-time 153, 181, 184, 185, 186, 206, 207, 215
real-time industrial inspection 185
regression trees 282, 291
Relative Grey Incidence 239
relative humidity (RH) 235
repeatability score 113, 115
resistive gas sensors 103, 108
retrieval 180, 182, 185, 207, 208, 209
robust discrimination 186
root node 281

S

selection 180, 181, 182, 183, 184, 187, 188, 190, 191, 192, 194, 199, 203, 204, 206, 207, 208, 209, 210, 211, 212, 213
Self-Organizing Maps (SOM) 215, 223, 224, 225, 226
Self-Organizing Maps (SOM) network 224
sensor arrays 184, 207, 209, 212
sensor dynamics 3
SLAM framework 159
spider mites 218, 219, 221, 225, 226, 231, 232, 233, 235, 236, 237, 241, 242, 244, 245, 246, 248
standard deviation (SD) 115
Standard Grey Incidence 239, 241
starting node 281
statistical gas distribution modeling 153, 155, 175, 249
stopping criteria 191, 192, 203
surface acoustic wave devices 4
Synthetic Grey Incidence 239
Systemin (Sys) 225

T

teleolfaction systems 126, 128, 140, 141, 145, 146, 148
temperature dropping 109
terminal node 281, 282, 286
tomato plants 214, 216, 218, 219, 223, 225, 231, 232, 233, 235, 236, 237, 243, 244, 246
transducer architectures 4
tree growing 282
tree pruning 282

V

visual enhancement 180, 181, 208

volatile component 184
volatile organic compounds (VOC) 180, 184, 186, 214, 215, 216, 217, 218, 219, 222, 224, 225, 229, 232, 233, 247
volatile organic compounds (VOC) emission 233
voltage waveforms 105

W

Wang and Mendel (WM) 81, 101
Web cameras 127
white noise 109, 111, 120, 121